❧ *Baudelaire's Literary Criticism*

BAUDELAIRE'S LITERARY CRITICISM

ROSEMARY LLOYD

Fellow of New Hall and Assistant Lecturer in French
University of Cambridge

CAMBRIDGE UNIVERSITY PRESS

Cambridge
London   New York   New Rochelle
Melbourne   Sydney

Published by the Press Syndicate of the University of Cambridge
The Pitt Building, Trumpington Street, Cambridge CB2 1RP
32 East 57th Street, New York, NY 10022, USA
296 Beaconsfield Parade, Middle Park, Melbourne 3206, Australia

First published 1981

Printed in Great Britain by
Western Printing Services Ltd, Bristol

Library of Congress catalogue card number: 81–3906

British Library Cataloguing in Publication Data

Lloyd, Rosemary
Baudelaire's literary criticism.
I. Title
840'.8 PQ2191

ISBN 0 521 23552 9

'J'ai une assez vive envie de montrer ce que
j'ai su faire, en matière de critique'

For Alison and Peter

✤ *Contents*

Acknowledgements

It is a great pleasure to thank the many people who have, in various ways, helped me prepare this study. First of all, I should like to express my gratitude to the Association of Commonwealth Universities who financed my research and the British Council who administered my grant with flexibility and tolerance. I am also indebted to the staffs of the University Library, Cambridge and of the Bibliothèque nationale, Paris, and particularly those who dealt with my frequent requests for interlibrary loans. The staff of the Cambridge University Press gave much help and advice. Lloyd Austin and Garnett Rees examined my doctoral thesis and offered much valuable criticism and encouragement. Graham Chesters and Malcolm Bowie suggested alterations which greatly improved the final version. Above all, I am deeply grateful to Peter Hambly, whose advice and friendship have been invaluable, and especially to my supervisor, Alison Fairlie, whose knowledge, tact and sympathy have been an unending source of aid and inspiration.

❧ *Abbreviations used in the text*

I, II   Baudelaire, *Œuvres complètes*, 2 volumes, edited by Claude Pichois (Pléiade, 1975–6)

CI, CII   Baudelaire, *Correspondance*, 2 volumes, edited by Claude Pichois and J. Ziegler (Pléiade, 1973)

AR   *Quelques-uns de mes contemporains*, edited by J. Crépet (Louis Conard, 1925)

HB   Gautier, *Honoré de Balzac* (Poulet-Malassis et de Broise, 1859)

LAB   *Lettres à Baudelaire*, edited by Claude Pichois and Vincenette Pichois (Neuchâtel: A la Baconnière, 1973)

MO   De Quincey, *Un Mangeur d'opium*, edited by Michèle Stäuble-Lipman (Neuchâtel: A la Baconnière, 1976)

NE   Taine, *Nouveaux Essais* (Hachette, 1896)

Poe   Edgar A. Poe, *Œuvres en prose*, edited by Y.-G. Le Dantec (Pléiade, 1975)

Introduction

Baudelaire's conviction of the value of his literary criticism was well founded. This is not the work of a writer who, like Sainte-Beuve, felt that the spring of creativity had run dry, nor did he, like Proust, consider criticism above all as the first step to a work of imaginative art. Yet both these attitudes can be found in his reviews: for him, criticism can be both an aid to inspiration and an exploration of a theme or technique taken up, embellished and strengthened in his poetry. Nevertheless, his criticism is also a reflection on the act of criticism itself. His earliest articles reveal how clearly he saw that many current methods and ideals were inadequate or false, and all his articles suggest his amusement or irritation at the failure of the French public in general and contemporary critics in particular to understand basic issues and respond both emotionally and intellectually to what was best in art.

Despite this complex interaction between his criticism and, on the one hand, his poetry, and, on the other, contemporary techniques and opinions, his literary reviews have not received the same detailed and serious consideration as the art criticism. Several critics, in fact, have announced or at least implied that the literary criticism is 'souvent décevante'[1] and Claude Pichois's extremely valuable recent edition of Baudelaire's complete works opens the *notice* devoted to the articles with the remark: 'certains penseront que la critique littéraire de Baudelaire ne présente pas [. . .] l'intérêt de sa critique artistique' (II, 1069). Nonetheless, those who have examined it, in general studies of his work, in analyses of his criticism both of literature and the arts, in assessments of his relationships with other writers and above all in prefaces to annotated editions of *L'Art romantique*, indicate that an understanding of his literary criticism is essential for a fuller comprehension both of his aesthetic theory and of his creative practice.

Thus, in a sensitive introduction to his selection from the art and literary criticism, D. Parmée concludes that the most striking aspect of the reviews is the image they present of the way in which all the arts are interrelated.[2] H. Lemaitre, whose 1962 edition Pichois castigates with unnecessary pungency (II, 1143), offers a preface which, while more of

I

an imaginative essay than a serious study, suggests several avenues of exploration. He contends that, for Baudelaire, 'la connaissance critique' and 'la réflexion esthétique' are 'nullement distinctes, dans leur essence spirituelle, de la création artistique elle-même'.[3] For their part, Lois Boe Hyslop and Francis E. Hyslop, who concentrate on the judgements made rather than on the way in which Baudelaire expresses them or the way in which they are related to contemporary beliefs, preface their edition by showing how the criticism reflects the way in which Baudelaire saw the roles of the memory, the imagination and criticism itself.[4] Georges Poulet's appreciation of the literary criticism, although brief, sets it in a new perspective: Poulet, who believes that Baudelaire's power of identifying himself with those he discusses makes him 'un des fondateurs de la critique moderne',[5] stresses that his reviews also share with much modern criticism an essentially metaphorical quality. By this, Poulet means that Baudelaire's criticism offers 'un ensemble d'images où se refléteront les images appartenant à l'univers poétique que cet acte s'est donné pour fin à la fois d'évoquer et de définir'.[6] Finally, he insists that, because it finds metaphors appropriate to the work it evaluates, criticism also leads Baudelaire to an act of self-discovery and self-reflection.

The most stimulating introductions are those of L. J. Austin, whose focus is the texts themselves and the style in which they are written, and Pichois, to whom we owe both an interestingly arranged edition of Baudelaire's *Critique littéraire et musicale,* and the recent Pléiade publication. Asserting that 'Baudelaire critique n'a pas d'égal au XIXe siècle', L. J. Austin suggests that 'la critique littéraire de Baudelaire est un moyen d'exploration de son propre art, à travers l'examen approfondi de celui des autres'.[7] Most importantly, perhaps, he insists that: 'nous oublions trop combien l'avènement de Baudelaire lui-même a modifié la sensibilité moderne et bouleversé du même coup la hiérarchie des réputations. Otez Baudelaire de la poésie française du XIXe siècle, et les autres poètes brillent aussitôt d'un plus vif éclat.'[8] In both his editions, Pichois attempts to see the articles in the context both of Baudelaire's individual development and of the wider historical background. *Critique littéraire et musicale,* which dates from 1961, groups the reviews under such headings as 'L'Apprentissage du journalisme littéraire', 'De la critique sociale à la critique esthétique' and 'La Polémique des dernières années', and includes not merely conventional literary criticism, but also such pieces as 'Notes et documents pour mon avocat' and the letter written to Ancelle in February 1866. In his introduction, Pichois insists that 'il n'y a [. . .] pas en Baudelaire deux personnes: le critique et le poète sont en lui indissociables'.[9] His edition of the

Pléiade *Œuvres complètes,* a work of exemplary scholarship to which this study is deeply indebted, contains a brief but provocative study of the literary criticism, concentrating mainly on the history of the articles and on the character of Eugène Crépet. For Pichois, as for Poulet, Baudelaire's greatest gift lies in 'la critique d'identification' (II, 1070). Noting in the reviews 'des réticences aussi bien que des affirmations excessives' (II, 1069), Pichois concludes that 'à tout prendre, Baudelaire est moins libre dans la critique littéraire qu'il ne l'est dans l'appréciation des arts et de la musique' (II, 1070). Yet, in the very limited space available to him, Pichois has not been able to examine fully the reasons behind this restriction of Baudelaire's liberty, nor to discover whether Baudelaire submits to being fettered or rises to the challenges such restrictions pose.

By far the most detailed and important study is still Margaret Gilman's *Baudelaire the Critic,* first published in 1943. This work, which examines both the art and the literary criticism, concludes that in none of the anthology articles is there 'the movement of a general idea developing in connection with a particular case that is so characteristic of the great art criticism'.[10] She adds that:

> more than once the integrity of the literary criticism is vitiated by personal motives, some regrettable, some innocent enough. Unlike the art criticism, it presents no complete picture; it neglects significant figures and over-emphasizes lesser ones. Moreover, in the later literary articles, one feels that for the first time Baudelaire is making *a priori* judgements, holding his author up to a pre-established standard.[11]

Finally, she suggests that 'the question of personal experience is at the root of the matter, and ... literature never gave to Baudelaire quite the *volupté* that painting did'.[12] All these remarks call for re-examination. Firstly, certain discoveries made since the study was written cast new light on the articles: this is particularly true of the appearance of the Bandy edition of Baudelaire's first full-length study of Poe, a work which includes the American sources on which he draws. Secondly, because of the wide scope of her book, Margaret Gilman has not had the space to take into account contemporary customs and opinions. Thus, with all its qualities, its innovatory, sympathetic and intelligent analysis and its valuable paragraphs on Baudelaire's ideas about such concepts as memory, imagination, beauty and truth, *Baudelaire the Critic* still leaves considerable room for further exploration.

Most previous studies of Baudelaire's literary criticism, therefore, have tended to examine it in isolation, neither fully considering the possible influence of external factors nor suggesting in sufficient detail its relationship to Baudelaire's other works. In several instances this approach leads to interpretations and evaluations which are anachronistic. Baudelaire's critical writing, after all, dates from a period when, although journalistic criticism flourished and critics abounded, the genre was comparatively new. It was the proliferation of the press under Louis-Philippe and Napoleon III which brought with it a burgeoning crop of journalists, eager to analyse the slightest artistic event. Journals of all political, religious and aesthetic persuasions felt it necessary to offer their readers a regular *feuilleton*, in which literature, stage productions and the plastic arts were reviewed with that blend of prejudice and intensity that contemporary works alone provoke. Yet, when Henri Peyre published his *Connaissance de Baudelaire* in 1951, he noted the absence of

> une grande histoire de la critique littéraire au XIXe siècle qui ferait mieux apparaître ce que l'on entendait autour de Baudelaire par certains termes critiques dont il fait lui-même un usage original. Un tel livre marquerait aussi les limitations et les défaillances de tous ceux qui, de Nisard à Sainte-Beuve, Scherer et Weiss furent impuissants à sentir et à juger les œuvres fortes de leur époque, tandis que Baudelaire se trompait si rarement.[13]

Although such studies as those of Roger Fayolle and P. Moreau go some way to filling in the background, the lacuna still remains. Besides, it is only too often forgotten that standards and conceptions of journalistic criticism were vastly different from those reflected in learned journals of the late twentieth century.

In writing his literary criticism, Baudelaire was not attempting to convey and judge from Olympian heights the essence of another mind. It was from the centre of the fray itself that he responded to the remarks of other critics and writers and sought to influence the opinions held by the general public. Not only was he trying to encourage fellow writers while indicating areas where their experiments had not fully succeeded, but he was also attempting to turn their experience to his own creative ends. In addition, the blue pencil of the editor and the scissors of the censor were both a constant threat to free expression and a spur to create a language capable of functioning simultaneously on many levels.

An understanding of Baudelaire's literary criticism, therefore, demands a constant awareness of the background against which it was written. The writers discussed must be seen as they would have appeared to their contemporaries, not yet overshadowed by the genius of *Les Fleurs du mal*, and Baudelaire's judgements and methods must be set side by side with those of other critics of the time, always bearing in mind the possible influence of censorship, rivalry, friendship and self-interest.

Numerous questions arise. If, for example, other critics ignore some aspect of a writer's work, does Baudelaire follow suit or does he attempt to redress the balance? How does his relationship with the writer, his feelings of debt to certain literary movements, and the emotions aroused in the public by poets such as Barbier affect the way in which he discusses them? Does he write only on those he admires? Is he blind to the qualities of those he instinctively dislikes? And did he evade or bow to censorship?

These questions cannot be answered adequately without some knowledge of contemporary press laws and the way in which they were applied, and the influence exerted by a journal's editor or financial backers. The second volume of *Histoire générale de la presse française*, produced under the editorship of C. Bellanger, is a rich and fascinating source of information, suggesting answers to many such questions, and I have drawn heavily on it for the following brief summary of the most important laws concerning the press.

The law of 9 September 1835, the most vital proclamation relevant to the early criticism, increased not only the caution money demanded of all papers, but also the fines which could be imposed for such matters as incitement to revolution, attacks on the government and criticism of Louis-Philippe. It also gave the courts power to suspend, for a maximum of four months, any paper found guilty of two infringements of the law in any one year. The year 1836, as is well known, saw the introduction of the *roman-feuilleton* and of advertising, with a resultant plunge in the price of a daily paper and the flowering of both *La Presse* and its rival *Le Siècle*. Baudelaire's own introduction to Parisian journals may well have been through *La Presse*, whose art criticism he was eagerly reading as early as July 1838 (*C1*, 58). Immediately after the February Revolution of 1848 all legal restrictions on the press were lifted, an act resulting in a torrent of small, ephemeral papers, among them *Le Salut public*, which Baudelaire himself produced together with Champfleury and Toubin. On 11 July 1848, however, caution money was again demanded and fines imposed for any attack directed at Republican institutions, freedom of worship, the principle of property and the rights of the family. The following year saw an extension of the law to cover such matters as criticism of the President of the Republic and public subscription to raise fines. On 16 July 1850 the caution money was increased yet again and, most importantly of all, articles had to be signed either by the author or by the editor, a law which was strictly enforced throughout the Second Empire. The *loi Tinguy* also imposed additional stamp duty on the *roman-feuilleton*, and thus, as P. Spencer points out, 'eliminated the serialized novel and ensured its replacement by anodyne personalia and travel accounts'.[14] During the years between 1852 and 1860, according to Bellanger, 'on ne saurait trop insister [. . .] sur la sévérité de la législation',[15] and, although the government relaxed the laws slightly during the electoral campaign of 1857, Orsini's attempted assassination of Napoleon III on 14 January 1858 provoked stricter laws and increased penalties.

Censorship, moreover, was imposed not only by politicians but also by financial interests, the Rothschilds, for example, largely determining the policy of the *Journal des débats*. Indeed, when *L'Opinion nationale* appeared in 1859, it declared itself free not only of political control but also, 'ce qui est plus rare peut-être, vis-à-vis des grandes notabilités financières'.[16]

The result was, perhaps, predictable and it concerned not merely politics but literature itself. While appearing to discuss literature or the theatre, journalists subtly promoted the ideals of liberalism, a political aim which led to a literary development, since, as Louis Ulbach concluded and Nerval illustrated, 'il faut bien reconnaître que les conditions faites à la presse aident beaucoup à l'éclosion de l'ironie'.[17] Any reading of Baudelaire's criticism must, therefore, stay constantly alert to the possibility of irony or other forms of evasion.

Not only the bias and power of the contemporary papers, but also the effect both of political upheavals, such as the 1848 Revolution, the *coup d'état* and the Orsini affair, and factors affecting Baudelaire's own life, his changing relationship with his mother and stepfather, and his stormy affair with Jeanne, for example, may all have coloured the literary criticism. The very language of his articles reveals that he was far from unmoved by such events, and any study of his criticism must carefully assess the direct or indirect results that his theoretical standpoint on these issues exerted over his choice of subject, expression or even judgement. A particularly obvious case in point is his reaction to Hugo's *Les Châtiments* (*C*11, 41). Nor should opinions expressed in the carefully polished prose of articles intended for publication be considered on the same plane as comments thrown off in letters to friends. Although some critics, notably Lois Boe Hyslop, insinuate or indeed assert that Baudelaire's 'real opinion'[18] is to be found in the correspondence rather than in the reviews, the personality of the correspondent and Baudelaire's relationship with him, the desire to shock, to provoke anger or to raise a laugh greatly affect both expression and evaluation. In both his letters and his published articles, however, different levels of meaning operate, with Baudelaire making gifted and provocative use of irony, evasion, pastiche, summaries of widely-held beliefs and mockery both of the reader and of the writer under discussion.

Many more aspects of Baudelaire's literary criticism could have been examined had more space been available. I have chosen to concentrate on the completed articles and on those dealing directly with literature, leaving aside the studies of the actor Rouvière, the notes on Janin and Villemain, the 'Conseils aux jeunes littérateurs' and the *feuilletons* entitled 'Une réforme à l'Académie' and 'Anniversaire de la naissance de Shakespeare', although I have taken them into consideration when reaching my conclusions. Much has already been written about the 'Notes sur *Les Liaisons dangereuses*' and the availability of such comments, together with the fact that the brevity of the notes renders them rather cryptic, has led me to decide not to devote space to them in a book already extremely long.[19] Several of the anthology notices have also had to be omitted; since all are important for an understanding of Baudelaire's criticism, the choice was particularly difficult. I have decided, however, not to examine those on Gautier and Dupont, both of whom are discussed in earlier articles, and I have also left aside the extremely brief but beautifully constructed paragraphs devoted to Le Vavasseur.

Much of Baudelaire's critical skill, moreover, lies in the art of allusion and side-reference. Throughout his criticism – and in his letters – he devotes brief sentences or passages to writers, works and schools that interested, inspired or annoyed him. Perhaps because the need for brevity has forced his thought into so tight a mould, his references to writers such as Nerval, Barbey d'Aurevilly, Heine, Goethe, Byron, Jean-Paul and Maturin, to name only a few, burst from the confines of his reviews like short-lived but intensely illuminating fireworks. Although these are examined as they arise, I have been able to choose for detailed study one example only of this technique: the allusions to Balzac. This choice was motivated partly by the length and richness of these references, partly by the vital influence Balzac exerted over Baudelaire's thought, and partly by the publication of D. Bellos's study of Balzac criticism in the nineteenth century, some of the conclusions of which, in so far as they concern Baudelaire, called for a more thorough investigation.

Baudelaire's criticism sets up resonances not only with what he was reading, and with what he was writing in his correspondence, but also with his poetry, his translations of Poe and De Quincey, and his articles on stimulants. No doubt a full-length study could profitably be devoted to such echoes and to the way in which images first sketched in the reviews reappear, tautened or developed, in the later creative works.

Here it has been possible to indicate only a small sample of such recurring images.

Finally, in attempting to assess the way in which Baudelaire responds to the numerous challenges facing a critic of contemporary writing, I have not tried to divide his reviews into convenient thematic sections, such as his assessment of different literary genres or schools: however illuminating such an approach might have been, it would have implied clear-cut divisions where none may be present in Baudelaire's thought. Instead, I have made several chronological groupings. Thus, the reviews written before the main articles on Poe form a logical set, as do the majority of those written for the Crépet anthology. The studies of Poe, like the evaluations of Hugo, are examined together because their homogeneity reveals all the more clearly changes in attitude, facility and technique. Of the reviews written in the late 1850s, those on *Madame Bovary* and *La Double Vie* are bracketed together, since both assess an individual work of a writer relatively unknown to the general public, and since they show Baudelaire using his criticism as a means of self-justification and self-analysis. That on Gautier, together with the comments on Balzac, reveal Baudelaire considering general tendencies of well-known writers and using their discoveries to refine and develop his own aesthetic awareness. Finally, the review of *Les Martyrs ridicules* analyses a recent novel in the context of contemporary trends among the young.

In general, I have attempted to evaluate each review as a separate entity which should nevertheless not be torn from the matrix of Baudelaire's creative writing and his art criticism, nor from that of contemporary theory and practice.

1
❧ *The Early Criticism*

With the exception of that on Bathild Bouniol, Baudelaire's first articles of literary criticism are devoted to the tales and poems of close friends. The work of a young critic assessing youthful talent, they suggest particular questions. Does his approach in these reviews differ greatly from that adopted later? Are his aesthetic theories firmly fixed at this early date, as some critics of the *Salons* imply, or do they evolve? Does he allow tact to colour truth? Is he able to foresee a young writer's future development? This chapter will offer answers to some of these questions, but in general parallels and changes between the early and mature criticism will not be evaluated until the final chapters.

A Word for a Friend: Chennevières, Ménard, Champfleury

Chennevières (*Le Corsaire-Satan*, 4 November 1845)
    Baudelaire's first literary review discusses two volumes of short stories by his friend, Philippe de Chennevières, published under the pseudonym Jean de Falaise.[1] These volumes, *Les Contes normands* and *Historiettes baguenaudières*,[2] offer a mixture of moral tales, psychological studies and evocations of provincial life, told at a leisurely pace for all their brevity, with occasional sparks of irony and an atmosphere of youthful well-being.

Although entertaining, the tales neither reflect nor promise exceptional talent. They aroused no interest in the Parisian press and even Chennevières's close friend, Ernest Prarond, was sparing in his praise when discussing them some years later in *De quelques écrivains nouveaux*.[3] Barbey d'Aurevilly, in a letter not intended for publication, censured the *Contes normands* as 'une plaisanterie bien pénible; c'est de l'*humour* de parti-pris, une indigestion de Rabelais et de Nodier dans un estomac trop faible qui a le tort de trop les aimer. Puis des imitations déchiqetées à jour; çà et là pourtant quelques traits heureux.'[4] One feels very strongly that Baudelaire would not have chosen to review these two volumes had they not been written by a friend. Nevertheless, his article, for all its brevity, attempts to pinpoint certain characteristics, to balance discreet criticism with judicious praise and, no doubt under the influence of Sainte-Beuve, to place Chennevières in his literary family. Moreover, the very first lines of his article show him not only fully aware of the need to seize attention from the outset, but also picturing quite clearly the audience he seeks to interest – 'les amateurs curieux de la vraie littérature' (II, 3) – and capable of suggesting reservations with subtlety and tact.

What Baudelaire chooses to emphasize in the tales is their *naïveté* and the importance Chennevières placed on style. The claim that writers of the time, bereft of originality, borrowed wholesale from their predecessors is such a common, even obsessive, complaint among contemporary critics that Baudelaire has clearly sought to seize attention by stressing Chennevières's originality, despite its admitted eccentricity. Even at this early stage, however, he is not content merely to state a fact, but seeks out its underlying reasons. According to Baudelaire, Chennevières is able to offer 'une naïveté d'impressions toute fraîche' (II, 3) because he relies on his own *tempérament*. *Naïveté*, defined in the *Salon de 1846* as 'la science du métier combinée avec le *gnôti séauton*, mais la science modeste laissant le beau rôle au tempérament' (II, 431), is obviously an important part of Baudelaire's aesthetic beliefs at this period.

Temperament must, however, be guided and controlled by 'la science du métier', designated somewhat ambivalently as 'toutes les ruses du style'. And praise is carefully wrapped around warning when Baudelaire admits the charm of local idioms while indicating the dangers of using them too freely: they are 'une grâce nouvelle et un peu hasardée, mais dont l'auteur a usé avec une merveilleuse habileté' (II, 3).

Despite its brevity, the article offers comments on three specific tales. The criticism of the first of these, 'Lettres de Madame Scudéry', is entirely justified, since the pastiche is dull, lacking the youthful vigour of the other tales. The second work Baudelaire mentions, 'Quel souvenir de jeunesse eut un juré de Calvados', concerns a lawyer who, on returning to the house where he had lodged as a student, discovers that the girl he knew as a child is now brutally mistreating her elderly mother, thus wreaking revenge for the cruelty and neglect she suffered in childhood. As she explains to her mother: 'Vous commencez votre punition en terre, parce que l'enfer pour une mauvaise mère n'a pas d'éternité assez longue; vous mourrez désespérée et enragée.'[5] Baudelaire refrains from remarking on Chennevières's didactic intentions here: possibly his rejection of explicit moralizing in literature is a slightly later development. He compares Chennevières's analysis of contemporary *mores* to those of Balzac and, within obvious limits, the comparison both holds good and reflects the pleasure Baudelaire takes in alluding to writers not directly under discussion. The second comparison, in which 'Le Diable aux îles' is described as worthy of Hoffmann, is less apt. A mildly comic tale in the fantastic mode, it recounts the attempts of a rather ineffectual devil to win the souls of a devout, but unintelligent, fisher and his family. Not only is there an aura of piety which is absent from Hoffmann, but there is also nothing resembling Hoffmann's unique blend of terror and humour. Indeed, Barbey's reference to Nodier would seem more appropriate. Hoffmann's name has probably been chosen more because it is a commonplace of discussions concerning the fantastic than because Baudelaire perceived any real affinity between the two writers.

In these three paragraphs, then, Baudelaire indicates, concisely and with a certain sureness of touch, both the atmosphere and the limitations of the collections under discussion. Already one of the 'esprits amoureux de la rhétorique profonde' (I, 185), he conveys his reservations without didacticism, sandwiching them between expressions of praise and encouragement. He has certainly made some concessions to his friend, but not at the expense of a reader alert to suggestion and insinuation.

Ménard (*Le Corsaire-Satan*, 3 February 1846)

Baudelaire's first review praises a friend of recent date: for his second he turns to a poet he had known since his school days.[6] Yet, while the article on Chennevières is indulgent and encouraging, the *feuilleton* devoted to the more gifted Ménard plays down the young poet's achievement, accentuates his poem's flaws and fails to predict his later development.[7]

The reasons behind this attack seem partly personal, partly religious and partly aesthetic. In 1845, Baudelaire told Ménard of his attempted suicide (*C*I, 765, note 2): that Ménard doubted his friend's sincerity is obvious from his accounts of the event. As Pichois suggests (II, 1084), this could have led to an estrangement, and Baudelaire may well have sought revenge through his sarcastic review. Moreover, only a few weeks before Baudelaire's article appeared, the ardent Fourierist Alexandre Weill[8] had published a favourable account of *Prométhée délivré* in the *Démocratie pacifique*. It is possible that the editor of *Le Corsaire-Satan*, Lepoitevin Saint-Alme, asked Baudelaire to contribute, through a hostile assessment of the poem, to his journal's frequent mockery of the Fourierist press and ideals. It is also possible that it is Ménard's radical attack on all forms of religion that lies at the root of Baudelaire's irritation: as articles written a few years later reveal, he looked on religion as worthy of respect if not of credence. Principally, however, Baudelaire seems to have seized on the chance of opposing what he saw as an increasing tendency to use certain literary genres for purposes which were inappropriate to them.

Although *Prométhée délivré* belongs to a long literary tradition of poems of revolt, Ménard brings to it an ardent conviction. Indeed, if his poem lacks the bite of Byron's *Cain* and the beauty of Shelley's *Prometheus*, the reason may well lie not only in his inexperience but also in the very fervour of his belief in the vision it conveys.

Ménard had to wait a full two years for the Parisian press to respond to *Prométhée délivré*: apart from Baudelaire's, the only contemporary review I discovered was that of Alexandre Weill, which appeared in December 1845. Following the digressional tendencies of the time, Weill devoted almost half of his *feuilleton* to an evocation of the 'sainte bande' who, like 'le plus grand poète de l'humanité, Fourier', have rebelled against man's condition and the evils of society. Although Weill speaks of Ménard as 'un penseur et un poète' – without discussing the combination – and, once again using contemporary techniques, quotes extensively from his poem, he devotes little space either to the ideals it embodies or to the art with which it is created.

Baudelaire's article appeared a few months after Weill's, in February 1846. In his *Baudelaire and Nature*, Felix Leakey suggests that the review could have been written as early as 1844, an assumption based, no doubt, on the publication date of Ménard's poem, December 1843.[9] It seems to me that the article pre-dates its publication by no more than a few weeks. Firstly, it is unlikely that the chronically impecunious Baudelaire would have kept unpublished any completed article, although it is possible that he withheld it, knowing it would cause pain, and then published it because Ménard angered him in some way. Secondly, Weill's undebated assumption that poetry is an adequate vehicle for what Ménard sought to express could well have provoked both the content and the tone of Baudelaire's review. Thirdly, and most importantly, in style, theme and tone, the article is very close to others that Baudelaire published in 1845 and 1846. The direct, down-to-earth appeal to the reader, with its unmistakable echoes of Diderot, resembles the opening section of the *Salon de 1846*, while the sardonic claim in the 'Conseils aux jeunes littérateurs' (15 April 1846) that 'rien n'est vrai que la force, qui est la justice suprême' (II, 14), recalls Baudelaire's paraphrase of Ménard: 'Hercule apparaît, et la raison humaine est délivrée par la force' (II, 10).[10] Similarly, the ambivalent 'Aux bourgeois' opens with: 'Vous êtes la majorité, – nombre et intelligence; – donc vous êtes la force, – qui est la justice' (II, 415). And Baudelaire is probably thinking not just of Ménard but of all the great poets who have chosen their themes 'parmi tous les sujets *protestants*' (II, 10) when he addresses the bourgeois in the following double-edged words: 'Vous n'avez jamais en aucune noble entreprise laissé l'initiative à la minorité protestante et souffrante, qui est d'ailleurs l'ennemie naturelle de l'art' (II, 416). Again, his objection that *Prométhée délivré* attempts to combine poetry and philosophy is taken up in the *Salon de 1846*, where Baudelaire castigates 'l'empiètement d'un art sur un autre' (II, 473): 'la poésie n'est pas le but immédiat du peintre; [. . .] Chercher la poésie de parti pris dans la conception d'un tableau est le plus sûr moyen de ne pas la trouver' (II, 474).[11] Finally, just as Baudelaire accuses Ménard of over-intellectualizing his characters, of using too inflexible an allegorical form, so he asserts in the *Salon* that: 'un éclectique ignore que la première affaire d'un artiste est de substituer l'homme à la nature et de protester contre elle. Cette protestation ne se fait pas de parti pris, froidement, comme un code ou une rhétorique; elle est emportée et naïve, comme le vice, comme la passion, comme l'appétit' (II, 473). Internal evidence, then, suggests very strongly that the article was not completed until shortly before its publication.

Baudelaire's principal criticism of *Prométhée délivré* concerns less the ideology it conveys than the means of its expression. Indeed, from the outset, he launches a vigorous, amusing attack on 'la poésie philo-sophique', illustrated with a reference to Quinet, who devoted a volumi-nous poem to the subject, and with examples taken from the plastic arts. At this early stage, therefore, Baudelaire appears firmly convinced that each genre has a distinct set of purposes, which should not be misused or intermingled.

A secondary, stylistic criticism of *Prométhée délivré* follows from the first: Baudelaire asserts that Ménard's talent has been hobbled by 'les inconvénients du genre adopté' (II, 11). His condemnation is expressed with particular force at the end of the article, where *Prométhée délivré* is sneeringly denoted a *discours*, the word being italicized, no doubt to insist on how incongruous is its application to poetry. Emphasizing incongruities is only one of the means Baudelaire uses to pour scorn on stylistic and technical flaws. Thus, to underline the rather clumsy use of allegory which leads Ménard to over-intellectualize his characters, Baudelaire repeats the expression *c'est-à-dire*: 'Io, c'est-à-dire Madeleine ou Marie, c'est-à-dire l'amour, vient à son tour philosopher avec Prométhée' (II, 10). The close proximity of 'l'amour' and 'philosopher' throws into relief a further incongruity, while the obvious, mocking repetition of 'protester' also emphasizes Baudelaire's reservations. Finally, he is particularly cutting about Ménard's belief in scientific progress, wittily paraphrasing the line 'les dieux sont morts, car la foudre est à moi' by 'Franklin a détrôné Jupiter' (II, 10).

Not content merely to accuse Ménard's personifications of over-abstraction, Baudelaire seeks out the reasons behind this failure. In a passage pointing forward to the enthronement of imagination as the queen of faculties (11, 585 and 619–23), he warns against confusing 'les fantômes de la raison avec les fantômes de l'imagination; ceux-là sont des équations, et ceux-ci des êtres et des souvenirs' (11, 11). In his eyes, therefore, a poet who relies solely on reason will produce unconvincing, one-dimensional figures, serving merely to represent a precise concept and carrying none of the conviction and flexibility of figures drawn from the imagination. This sentence is one of several where Baudelaire, in concise, sometimes gnomic, formulations expresses a truth transcending the individual analysis of the writer under discussion. The rejection of allegory, with its one for one relationships and its flat explanations, in favour of symbols which leave the imagination free to explore all the suggestions they convey, is an idea which Baudelaire frequently upholds both in his literary and in his art criticism. He strengthens his assertion by referring to a work which his readers could be expected to know: he applauds the first part of Goethe's *Faust*, recently translated into French by Nerval, but, like Nerval, expresses reservations about the second part. In doing so he may well have been influenced by current opinion, and certainly the feeling that the work was completely alien in structure and conception to anything in French literature was a common reaction and one on which Baudelaire could rely to reinforce his general condemnation.

It could, however, be argued against Baudelaire's claim, that there have been great poems of revolt, Leconte de Lisle's *Qaïn* and Byron's *Cain*, for example, in which the source of oppression remains, like Ménard's Jupiter, a nebulous threat, neither 'être' nor 'souvenir'. It is not necessary for the oppressor to seem credible; what gives these poems their force is the suffering and rebellion of the oppressed. Furthermore, given the group of poems Baudelaire entitled *Révolte*, all of them belonging to his 'jeunesse littéraire' (1, 1075), one might have expected him to show Ménard more comprehension and leniency.

The final paragraph of the review makes three points clarifying Baudelaire's objections and developing his own theories. Firstly, the form of the poems is attacked as 'vague et flottante' (11, 11). The censure is unexpectedly harsh. Ménard has attempted some very experimental verse techniques and, although he has not been particularly successful, he no doubt expected greater tolerance. Baudelaire is, however, more just in criticizing Ménard's failure to appreciate the role that rich, subtle rhymes play in illuminating ideas. An evocative, carefully chosen image, which casts particular light on Baudelaire's own poetics, likens such rhymes to 'lanternes qui éclairent la route de l'idée' (II, II). Finally, Ménard, in Baudelaire's eyes, is not sufficiently sensitive to certain combinations of words. Once again, this attack is justified, for many lines in *Prométhée délivré* flounder in platitudes and clichés. Against the impressive early lines, for example, –

> Les astres d'or, roulant dans l'éternelle sphère,
> Achèvent lentement leurs cours silencieux;
> Il est nuit: des mortels l'encens et la prière
> Ont cessé de monter vers le tyran des cieux

– must be placed the infelicitous claim that

> Dans leur Olympe solitaire
> Les dieux heureux sont endormis;
> Mais ma puissante voix chez les fils de la terre
> Leur a trouvé des ennemis

and the rather flat

> Les dieux, c'est l'oubli qui les tue,
> Et Jupiter du ciel sera déshérité
> Le jour où sur la terre une voix inconnue
> Viendra crier enfin: Dieu, c'est la liberté.[12]

Other aspects of *Prométhée délivré* might have been treated with less scorn, given Baudelaire's current hopes and beliefs, among them the longing for a new Golden Age, the importance of the intellect and the possibility of turning plan into performance. In addition, although he derides a regime based on 'la science et la force' (II, II), there is a facet of Baudelaire's complex personality to which such a combination would have appealed: one thinks in particular of the prose poem 'Assommons les pauvres' and of the admission in 'Le Reniement de Saint Pierre': 'Certes, je sortirai, quant à moi, satisfait / D'un monde où l'action n'est pas la sœur du rêve' (I, 122). It seems certain that factors other than the purely literary are at work in this article.

Although the close attention paid to evoking the plot limits the possibilities for the richly suggestive digressions included in later reviews, the article allows brief glimpses of Baudelaire's own aesthetics: his conviction that poetry should not be overtly philosophical, the importance of the imagination, his rejection of over-intellectualized mythological figures and, finally, his sensitivity to rhyme and his intense interest in words. The article's interest lies less in its evaluation of Ménard than in its indication of Baudelaire's early aesthetic thinking.

Champfleury (*Le Corsaire-Satan*, 18 January 1848)

Both friendship and a desire to understand a certain genre motivated Baudelaire's review of Champfleury's short stories. The three volumes discussed appeared in 1847, Baudelaire's article being printed early in the following year, at a time when the two men were very close friends. Their relationship dates from at least 1845[13] and, apart from an estrangement lasting from 1863 to 1865, seems to have continued throughout the poet's life, despite differences in their aesthetic ideals. They were particularly close in the first weeks of 1848 when, together with Charles Toubin, they produced the ephemeral *Salut public* (11, 1553ff.).

A prolific and controversial writer, Champfleury published numerous pantomimes, short stories, novels, translations and critical studies of literature and art. Indeed, there is something rather bizarre in the way in which he dashed off so many works on such wide-ranging subjects: one feels that he never allowed himself time to discover his true vein or to go deeply into questions which interested him. His close association with Courbet, Duranty and other Realists, at a time when for many critics Realism was synonymous with immorality, and the fact that several of his novels were totally banned or partially cut by the censors, meant that critics judging his works relied even more than was usually the case on their own political beliefs or aesthetic prejudices.[14]

On the one hand, young critics like Emile Chasles claimed that Champfleury was following in the 'tradition des romanciers sérieux', and Paul d'Ambly, rejecting charges of immorality, considered that the *Contes d'automne* were written 'à la bonne manière française, nettement, clairement, ironiquement'.[15] On the other hand, the crusty Cuvillier-Fleury, critic of the right-wing *Journal des débats*, wrote disdainfully that 'son histoire de *Chien-Caillou*, avec cette épigraphe: *Ceci n'est pas un conte* est en effet d'une vérité saisissante. Mais quelle vérité!' And that untiring opponent of Realism, Gustave Merlet, while allowing Champfleury 'le don précieux d'observer', protested that 'il l'exerce sur les infiniment petits'.[16]

Two points were frequently stressed by Baudelaire's contemporaries: on the one hand they claimed that Champfleury directed his undisputed gift of observation to things unworthy of attention; on the other, they accused his style of being vitiated by solecisms, a criticism very often made in order to ridicule a writer whose political or artistic views were incompatible with those of the critic. Champfleury's satirical evocations of provincial life were, however, generally admired, and several critics found in him affinities with Hoffmann, Diderot, Sterne and Balzac.

The few critics who reviewed *Chien-Caillou, Pauvre Trompette* and *Feu Miette* when they first appeared, emphasized, like Baudelaire, Champfleury's simplicity, charm and humour.

Champfleury had earned Baudelaire's gratitude by reviewing favourably his *Salon de 1845*, and by acceding to the injunction: 'PARLEZ des *Salons de Diderot*' (*C*I, 123): although Baudelaire's wish to respond, and the fact that Champfleury was a regular contributor to the *Corsaire-Satan*, for which the review was written, may have influenced his evaluation of the tales, his apparently high opinion of Champfleury was certainly shared, therefore, by several contemporary critics.

The article, which rapidly reviews individual tales[17] rather than isolating more general characteristics, shows signs of haste and inexperience. It has not the same degree of insight as the art criticism of 1846, nor the ability to penetrate to the heart of a writer's gifts that marks much of the later criticism. There are fewer reminiscences, fewer judgements based on tested aesthetic principles, more attempts to seize the reader's attention with unexpected juxtapositions or provocative judgements. Nevertheless, the article does reveal an ability to express in a few terse, dense phrases the essence of a work of art, and it indicates the increasing sureness with which Baudelaire perceives affinities between various writers.

Among the allusions to other novelists, a comment on 'Grandeur et Décadence d'une serinette' shows Baudelaire suggesting connections between writers while concisely recreating the predominant atmosphere of their works. For him, the tale reflects a deep-rooted affinity between Champfleury and 'quelques écrivains allemands et anglais' (II, 22: cf. II, 23), whose nature is a rich blend of irony and melancholy. Bouvier notes that Champfleury 'suivait à cette époque les cours de Philarète Chasles [. . .] et s'enthousiasmait pour les découvertes que faisait dans les littératures étrangères ce savant doublé d'un humoriste'.[18] Bouvier identifies the writers to whom Baudelaire alludes as Jean-Paul, Heine and Sterne. The name of Hoffmann would certainly need to be added to this list. To give only one example, Hoffmann has clearly influenced Champfleury in his creation of the organist Kreischmann who closely resembles Hoffmann's eponymous Kreisler and Krespel.[19] The link between Champfleury on the one hand and Sterne and Hoffmann on the other had, moreover, already been suggested by Champfleury's Fourierist homonym, J. Fleury, in an article published some six months before that of Baudelaire.[20] The dual qualities of melancholy and irony are, of course, present in Sterne, whom Baudelaire's preface to 'Révélation magnétique' describes as a 'romancier fort' (II, 247: cf. I, 554). Baudelaire may certainly be referring also to Heine, whom he quotes in his *Salon de 1846*, and to Jean-Paul, who was not well known at the time, but who is mentioned in the introduction to 'Révélation magnétique'.[21]

It is not merely by suggesting parallels but also by highlighting differences that Baudelaire etches more sharply Champfleury's particular talent. Thus, his brief tales form a stark contrast with the 'effroyables dysenteries de MM. Dumas, Féval et consorts' (ii, 21). The attack shows Baudelaire already emphasizing the advantages of brevity and the necessity for a writer to remain 'voué au travail' rather than rely on inspiration alone.

It is also by comparison with other novelists, in this case Balzac and Chennevières, that Baudelaire emphasizes Champfleury's awareness of the provinces as a rich source of theme and anecdote. In many of his early tales and later novels Champfleury does indeed draw on his intimate knowledge of provincial life and customs: tales such as 'Grandeur et Décadence d'une serinette', 'Simple histoire d'un rentier'[22] and 'Souffrances du professeur Delteil'[23] exploit the suffocating narrowness of life in a small village.

Throughout the review, Baudelaire throws into sharp relief Champfleury's presentation of an unadorned portrait of everyday life. He asserts that, from the outset, Champfleury has dared 'se contenter de la nature et avoir en elle une confiance illimitée' (ii, 21). The words *nature* and *vrai*, or their derivatives, appear at several points: like Chennevières, Champfleury is devoted to 'la religion de la nature' (ii, 21), and his works are described as 'naturelles' (ii, 22). Similarly, one of Champfleury's tales is described as an 'histoire vraie comme les précédentes' (ii, 22). Baudelaire's later criticism reveals a marked preference for the artificial over the natural, for the polished over the spontaneous, a preference adumbrated here both in the expression 'se contenter' and in the derogatory allusions to the extremely popular Dumas, Féval and Monnier.

As in several subsequent articles, the review borders on pastiche, the conscious echoing of stylistic techniques which Baudelaire exploits, occasionally for purposes of mockery, but more often to try his own hand at devices which have caught his attention. This is particularly noticeable in the choice of terms which have strong physical associations. The little dog in 'Pauvre Trompette', for instance, is poisoned with what Baudelaire describes as 'l'objet de ses convoitises', while the tale of 'Chien-Caillou' is 'crûment raconté' and the fecundity of Dumas and Féval is likened to 'effroyables dysenteries'. The clusters of adjectives and adverbs also recall Champfleury's style: in 'Une religion au cinquième', for example, he writes: 'les utopies ont été enterrées sournoisement, sans pompe, sans luxe, sans amis, sans ennemis pour suivre le corbillard'.[24] The opening sentences of Baudelaire's review in particular seem to echo this style: 'un jour parut un tout petit volume, tout humble, tout simple, au total, une chose importante, *Chien-Caillou*, l'histoire simplement, nettement, crûment raconté, ou plutôt enregistrée, d'un pauvre graveur' (II, 21).

The article has a threefold movement: it begins by carefully describing what Champfleury has achieved, asserts that more substance could have been extracted from the material chosen, and concludes by acknowledging that such criticism may after all be unfair: 'il ne faut forcer la destinée de personne' (II, 23). Perhaps Ménard's anger at the *Prométhée délivré* review has encouraged Baudelaire to express his reservations more discreetly. The charge that Champfleury does not delve deeply enough into the subjects he has chosen was already implicit in the remark that 'Carnaval' consisted of 'quelques notes précieuses' (II, 21): they assemble basic material rather than create an aesthetic whole. This criticism is not only valid but far-sighted, since Champfleury's realism is unsatisfying precisely because it remains superficial and because he fails to conjure up the 'magie suggestive contenant à la fois l'objet et le sujet, le monde extérieur à l'artiste et l'artiste lui-même' (II, 598). Baudelaire may, indeed, have had Champfleury in mind when, in his introduction to 'Révélation magnétique', he referred to 'les simples imaginatifs qui sont tout à fait indoués d'esprit philosophique, et qui entassent et alignent les événements sans les classer, et sans en expliquer le sens mystérieux' (II, 247–8). And in the notes headed 'Puisque Réalisme il y a', he wrote of Champfleury: 'Comme il étudie minutieusement, il croit saisir une *réalité* extérieure' (II, 58): for Baudelaire, the artist's task is to seize a reality which is both external and internal. Since Champfleury's later work is largely concerned with events rather than motives, descriptions rather than analyses, Baudelaire's early awareness of this tendency not only reveals his own interest in initial causes but also reflects considerably more critical perception than that shown by his contemporaries.

'Les Contes de Champfleury' is, in the best sense, criticism for a friend: it clearly conveys the writer's aims and achievements and yet it quietly suggests the direction he should follow in future.

The Secrets of Success: Pierre Dupont (Chants et Chansons, I (1851), preface)

It was in the bewildering, dangerous days of the Second Republic that Baudelaire published a preface to the works of another friend, the song-writer Pierre Dupont.

Later critics have approached the article with unease or suspicion. Jean Prévost is typical of many in suggesting that Dupont deserved it 'comme homme, non comme poète'[25] and Margaret Gilman describes it as 'one of the rare bits of Baudelaire's criticism which leave the reader cold'.[26] For Timothy Clark,[27] however, the preface shows Baudelaire 'praising Dupont for his simplicity, his political flair, his love of the Republic, and pouring scorn on the art that Dupont had supplanted'.[28] Finally, Lois Boe Hyslop insists that in Baudelaire's article, 'the sincerity of his pity for the downtrodden is still clearly obvious, and it is evident that his admiration for the proletarian poet was largely based on humanitarian considerations'.[29]

But to what extent is Baudelaire allowing external factors to affect his judgement? And is he praising Dupont as much as some critics suggest? There can be no doubting either the warmth of Baudelaire's friendship for Dupont,[30] or his intense awareness of the artistic and social questions being debated at the time. Yet to concentrate exclusively on those aspects is, I feel, to miss the point of Baudelaire's preface. As he makes perfectly clear from the opening paragraph, his focus is not the songs themselves, but the phenomenon of their success: 'je reste convaincu que le succès de ce nouveau poète est un événement grave' (II, 26). While it may be courtesy, friendship, or simply the fact that this is, after all, a preface to the poems discussed that leads Baudelaire to class Dupont's worth as 'très grande' (II, 26), it is certainly a keen desire to understand the reasons for popularity that makes him seek so minutely the logical link between historical phenomena and the song-writer's swift rise to fame. Moreover, there are at least three points in the article where Baudelaire reminds his reader that his focus is indeed Dupont's renown. He introduces his brief biography of Dupont by explaining that it reveals 'quelle admirable logique existe dans la genèse des faits matériels et des phénomènes moraux' (II, 28) just as later he mentions an event precisely because it forms part of 'la série des circonstances nécessaires pour créer un poète' (II, 30), and in discussing the poems themselves he makes it quite clear that he seeks 'éclaire[r] d'un grand jour le succès légitime, mais étonnant, de notre poète' (II, 33). By describing the success as 'étonnant', Baudelaire may simply be stressing that so rapid a rise to fame and such an overwhelming number of sales is unprecedented, but he may also be keeping his distance, attempting to understand rather than evaluate the success: it is certainly this attitude that gives the keynote for the preface.

That the question of success should dominate his thoughts is hardly surprising. The preface was written during a relatively productive period of Baudelaire's life, one in which he was seeking the best way of attracting public attention to his own works. Although, in a letter to his mother, he modestly claimed that the Dupont preface was of interest to her not for any intrinsic merit but only because it was her son who had written it (*C*I, 175), it is the first of his literary reviews to which he has obviously given much time and attention. No doubt he was spurred to greater effort partly by the knowledge that it would appear in more permanent form than the early articles, but the care taken also suggests very strongly that he seized on the opportunity for a searching analysis of the vital issue of popularity. After all, in *Le Spleen de Paris* it is that 'fausse déesse' who most nearly succeeds in corrupting the poet (1, 310).

Even a casual glance at the contemporary press confirms that, although his first publication, *Les Deux Anges*, met with little success when it appeared in 1844, Dupont did, indeed, become remarkably popular, leaping into the limelight in 1846 when, as he himself recalls, 'le bien-veillant Théophile Gautier donnant le branle, tout le monde chantait *Les Bœufs*'.[31] An unsigned review in *La Semaine* speaks of 'trente mille exemplaires de certains chants débités en peu de jours'[32] and the English critic Hayward mentions '"Les Ouvriers" for which a Paris publisher (Furne) gave 5,000f (£200), a conclusive proof of almost unprecedented popularity'.[33]

In the first six months of 1851,[34] Sainte-Beuve, Montégut and Cuvillier-Fleury, all highly esteemed Parisian critics, wrote favourably on Dupont's songs, while the irrepressible Hayward went so far as to claim that Dupont was 'not infrequently moved by [the indestructible love of nature] to more than beauty – to sublimity. Wordsworth himself was not more richly gifted in this respect.'[35] High praise indeed. And the French public was informed of the comparison by no less a light than the erudite Montégut. Montégut's article, to which Baudelaire seems, on occasion, to respond, admits that 'le mérite de ces chansons peut être discutable, mais non la vogue de popularité qu'elles ont obtenue. Ces chansons ont été bruyamment chantées dans la rue et accompagnées sur les élégants pianos des salons de Paris.'[36] The same ambiguous tone, together with the elegant pianos, reappears in Baudelaire's preface.

For the first time, therefore, Baudelaire is discussing a writer who needs little introduction to the public, a fact reflected in his article's tripartite structure. He begins by sketching in the background of the July Monarchy before sifting quickly through Dupont's biography, uncovering clues to the song-writer's future development. Finally, he examines not so much the songs themselves as their emotional impact.

The closing years of the July Monarchy saw a strong reaction against Romanticism, with the public turning its allegiance to novelists like Féval, dramatists like Ponsard, and song-writers like Dupont.[37] It is in attempting to understand this shift in opinion that Baudelaire paraphrases the main arguments of those critics most opposed to Romanticism. One cannot simply assume that these are necessarily his own opinions and evaluations. His reasoning seems to be as follows: since Dupont's success is best seen as a reaction, it can be fully understood only when the motives behind the public's rejection of Romanticism have been examined. Thus, when he speaks of 'l'insurrection romantique' (II, 26) his words echo those of critics such as L. Binault, who, in a violent attack on what he termed 'le romantisme déchu', declared that 'l'insurrection romantique contre la distinction des genres en littérature a eu les mêmes destinées que l'insurrection égalitaire contre la distinction des classes dans la société'.[38] Similarly, when Baudelaire mentions the materialism and sterility of Romanticism and its exclusion of 'la morale', he calls to mind Nisard's bellicose condemnation of a 'poésie toute en déception, toute matérielle [. . .], cette stérilité du cœur [. . .], cette philosophie sceptique à la suite'.[39] In the same way, when Baudelaire, surely one of the children in question, refers to Hugo's 'accents purement matériels, faits pour éblouir la vue tremblante des enfants' (II, 27), he may well be paraphrasing Louis Veuillot, who claimed that 'cette éloquence sauvage et coupable [. . .] a gâté tant de cœurs'.[40]

Furthermore, there is a suggestion of parody in the very language used when Baudelaire rather loftily describes Sainte-Beuve in Fourierist terms as an 'individualité maladive' (II, 27)[41] or when he ironically condemns the *littérateurs, antiquaires* and *versificateurs* who succeeded merely in lifting prosody 'presque à la hauteur d'une création' and in achieving 'des effets très surprenants' (II, 26). Moreover, the way in which Baudelaire ironically underplays the achievements of the Romantics recalls his arresting comment in 'Les Drames et les romans honnêtes', published a few months after the preface: there he refers to poets as a bourgeois might see them: 'tous ces gredins qui ont des dettes et qui croient que le métier de poète consiste à exprimer les mouvements lyriques de l'âme dans un rythme réglé par la tradition' (II, 39). Such parallels, echoes and paraphrases, which recall both the arguments and the language of contemporary criticism, make it highly likely that even if these comments are not entirely ironic they still cannot be taken merely at face value.

To a critic writing in 1851, then, neither Sainte-Beuve nor Hugo seemed to have attained lasting popularity: this, Baudelaire contends, was reserved for Auguste Barbier, whose poems, whatever their technical failings, asserted 'la sainteté de l'insurrection'. The conclusion is inescapable. If the public craves poetry that reflects its own concerns there can be no disputing the fact that art, to gain general popularity, must reflect the conventional wisdom and it must serve a clear purpose.

That Baudelaire is not at ease in conveying such an attitude is suggested by an occasional awkwardness of expression, particularly in the affirmation that 'le poète, placé sur un des points de la circonférence de l'humanité, renvoie sur la même ligne en vibrations plus mélodieuses la pensée humaine qui lui fut transmise' (11, 27). Possibly this is a specific reference, perhaps even a paraphrase or quotation from the socialist press.

Having established the literary background to Dupont's career, Baudelaire turns to an evocation of the political and social climate. In so doing he asserts that it would be 'curieux de raconter dans un livre impartial les sentiments, les doctrines, la vie extérieure, la vie intime, les modes et les mœurs de la jeunesse sous le règne de Louis-Philippe' (11, 27): one can detect the seeds that were to be transplanted to another decade and another country to become the plans for *Pauvre Belgique!*, minus, of course, the impartiality. The works of several of Baudelaire's contemporaries show their preoccupation with the July Monarchy, Nerval concisely evoking the atmosphere of the age in *Sylvie*, while Flaubert, in *L'Education sentimentale*, gives a precise and detailed depiction.[42] According to Baudelaire, it was a time of intense materialism, when the intellect was 'surexcité' and youth sought escape in 'lieux de débauche' and restaurants, places like the extravagantly elegant café described in 'Les Yeux des pauvres' (1, 318). Despite the depravity of the age, a few songs of moral purity and freshness managed to find favour. The 'jolies bouches' which Sainte-Beuve depicts singing Dupont's songs, and the 'élégants pianos des salons de Paris'[43] which, Montégut declares, accompanied them, have certainly influenced Baudelaire's choice of expression when he claims of the songs that 'les pianos bourgeois les répétaient avec une joie étourdie' (11, 28), the adjectives suggesting a degree of mockery. Baudelaire's opinions about the compatibility of art and the bourgeoisie are ambivalent: here, apart from such tiny sly touches, he keeps his feelings well in check, tracing the rise of Dupont's fame while leaving open the questions of his work's value and the worth of the public's appreciation of it.

Contemporary critics – Sainte-Beuve offering a striking example – often devoted a considerable part of their *feuilletons* to biography and anecdote. Although he follows accepted practice here, Baudelaire nevertheless explains and seeks to justify his approach. On the one hand, he claims that he is responding to the public's legitimate curiosity; on the other, he attempts to reveal connections between small details of a poet's life and the work he ultimately produces. He insists that public interest in the lives of the famous stems from 'un sentiment profond de l'égalité' (II, 28), a belief that such information contains an infallible key to genius and that any individual, once the knowledge is available, can achieve a similar 'perfectionnement'. How serious is this affirmation? The rather lofty language in which it is couched implies, to some extent at least, that Baudelaire is mocking the refusal of most men to accept their own lack of real ability. To express this as part of a general feeling of equality is, of course, to respond to the philosophies and echo the clichés of the time. The remark, moreover, recalls the deliberate irony of the projected prefaces for *Les Fleurs du mal*, in one of which, for example, he promises to tell:

> comment, appuyé sur mes principes et disposant de la science que je me charge de lui enseigner en vingt leçons, tout homme devient capable de composer une tragédie qui ne sera pas plus sifflée qu'une autre, ou d'aligner un poème de la longueur nécessaire pour être aussi ennuyeux que tout poème épique connu (I, 183).

As so often, Baudelaire's attitude towards his reader in this passage is ambiguous: torn between a desire to explain, and the twin convictions that 'ceux qui savent me devinent' (I, 182) and that those who do not respond automatically and intuitively cannot be taught, Baudelaire dashes hopes of a detailed exploration of the development of genius, merely producing the circular argument: 'l'enfance et la jeunesse de Pierre Dupont ressemblent à l'enfance et à la jeunesse de tous les hommes destinés à devenir célèbres' (II, 28). The expression 'destinés' prepares the theme of the interrelationship of fate and artistic success, a theme taken up later in the article in the unanswerable question: 'pourquoi le nom de celui-ci est-il dans toutes les bouches, et le nom de celui-là rampe-t-il encore ténébreusement dans des casiers de librairie, ou dort-il manuscrit dans des cartons de journaux?' (II, 33). The force of the language and the clarity of the images indicate the extent to which the fear of failure haunts the young writer's mind.

In this biographical passage, Baudelaire hints at two essential elements in the development of artistic genius: 'les sensations fraîches de la famille', however important, must be counter-balanced by some form of tyranny giving rise to the expression of revolt which will enable the poet to break the 'charme satanique' (II, 29). This clamping together of unexpected opposites not only underlines Baudelaire's delight in paradox but also emphasizes the ambivalence of his childhood memories. It is as if he feels that the myth of a lost but dangerous Golden Age must be renewed for each creative genius, leaving grief and yearning

which he seeks to express in his art. The passage has a very personal
ring: 'il est bon que chacun de nous, une fois dans sa vie, ait éprouvé la
pression d'une odieuse tyrannie; il apprend à la haïr!' (II, 29). The cry
wells up from Baudelaire's memories of a stepfather whose views were
incompatible with his own, the allusion becoming clearer still in a later
reference to a 'cruel et ponctuel militaire de l'Empire'.[44] Finally, one
notes the intensity of Baudelaire's expression here, the almost Balzacian
imagery in his insistence on the banking house as an 'étouffoir', and his
use of the term *explosion*: both words indicate an emotion so strong and
so forcibly held in check that it is hardly surprising that this conviction
should return again and again in the later criticism.

Baudelaire places particular emphasis on two biographical details.
Firstly, with obvious delight in the chance of twisting the usual meaning of *utile*, he insists that Dupont was able to force his Muse to play 'un
rôle utile, immédiat, dans sa vie' (II, 29): the proceeds from *Les Deux
Anges* enabled him to elude military service. Of course, Baudelaire's
precarious financial position underlies his ambivalent preoccupation
with the poet's need to make a living. Secondly, he underlines Dupont's
good fortune in being appointed a member of the staff preparing the
Academy's dictionary. This allusion to the dictionary shows the importance Baudelaire attached to 'la belle langue' even for writers of
popular songs: unlike Nerval, he is not interested in the simple,
colloquial language of the folk song.[45]

Although Dupont's fame began with *Les Paysans*, it was in writing
the more politically emotive 'Chant des ouvriers' that he discovered
his true talent. Recalling the hesitant manner in which Dupont offered
to sing the work to him, Baudelaire intimates that, however unaware
of his future success Dupont might have been, he himself was clear-
sighted enough to predict it (cf. II, 171). Whatever the truth of this
anecdote, it shows the importance Baudelaire attaches to a writer's
ability to gauge the needs and desires of his public, a point to which
he will return in reviewing *Madame Bovary*. While suggesting the historical logic behind Dupont's success, Baudelaire does not evaluate the
poem's worth, apart from the rather vague assertion that it is 'forte et
vraie' (II, 31), that is, that it presents real miseries with force and
conviction.

In predicting the continuing popularity of such poetry, however,
Baudelaire provides a clue to his own feelings, adopting a style so
rhetorical as to suggest either irony or embarrassment. There will come
a time, he prophesies, when 'l'exilé, l'abandonné, le voyageur perdu,
[. . .] quand il entendra cette forte mélodie parfumer l'air de sa senteur
originelle [. . .] pourra dire: je n'ai plus rien à craindre, je suis en France'

(II, 31). Given Baudelaire's opinion of the French public, that final phrase may very well be ironical, although the delight of the traveller returning to France may also echo Baudelaire's personal experience. I think it is when faced with a talent essentially different from his own that Baudelaire attempts a lofty form of imagery that is not always successful: his review of Hugo, while offering an example that does succeed, shows the same tendency: 'toujours il nous apparaît comme la statue de la Méditation qui marche' (II, 130).

Baudelaire tries his hand at Dupont's formula for fame in an admirable prose poem set into the texture of the article. It shows quite clearly that Dupont's solution would not have worked for Baudelaire. Dupont may have become closely associated with the Revolution, but his songs are relatively anodyne, appealing to a wide cross-section of the population. They were acceptable to the Left because, like the pastoral novels of George Sand, they gave a certain dignity to peasant life and labour. At the same time, they echoed the desires of the artisans and the lower bourgeoisie, seeking a fair day's pay for a fair day's work. Above all, their language is not that of the proletariat or the peasantry; it is a language whose roots are firmly grounded in respected literary tradition. No doubt, too, the less scrupulous members of the upper bourgeoisie pretended to take Dupont to their hearts in much the same way as Flaubert's M. Dambreuse bought and praised a tasteless progressive painting, when he believed that such a purchase could further his own financial ends.

Baudelaire was fully aware that Pierre Dupont's success depended on all these considerations. Yet, when he himself tries out the theme, it is patently obvious that even if he could have harnessed his talent to the motifs sought by the new Republic, the bourgeoisie would never have taken him to their hearts as they did Dupont. While Dupont tones down the suffering of the poor, investing it with a degree of nobility which renders it acceptable, Baudelaire presents it – as Zola was to do later in the century – with all its sharp edges, its inescapable physicality: with him it is

> cette multitude maladive respirant la poussière des ateliers, avalant du coton, s'impregnant de céruse, de mercure et de tous les poisons nécessaires à la création des chefs-d'œuvre, dormant dans la vermine, au fond des quartiers où les vertus les plus humbles et les plus grandes nichent à côté des vices les plus endurcis et des vomissements du bagne (II, 31).

The 'multitude maladive' with its physical ills stands in sharp and eloquent contrast to the 'individualité maladive' whose spiritual ills are described in *Joseph Delorme* and recalled earlier in the preface

(11, 27). There is an unwelcome reminder of the peasants' land hunger[46] and the workers' demands for equality in the lengthy glance bestowed on the sun and shade of the great parks. And there are unmistakable tones of irony and disbelief in the closing image, where 'pour suffisante consolation et réconfort' the multitude 'répète à tue-tête son refrain sauveur: *Aimons-nous!*' (11, 31).

In much the same way, Baudelaire takes up Dupont's lines:

Nous dont la lampe le matin
Au clairon du coq se rallume,
Nous tous qu'un salaire incertain
Ramène avant l'aube à l'enclume . . . (11, 31)

and reforges them in 'Le Crépuscule du matin',[47] stripped both of their incipient, conventional heroism, and of their banality to reveal a new, modern beauty, that of an urban dawn. Indeed, the provocation to create often springs from Baudelaire's feeling that others have not done full justice to a rich and potentially evocative theme (cf. *C*11, 245).

When he analyses the different aspects of the songs, Baudelaire, like Montégut, follows Dupont's own lead. In the preface to *La Muse populaire*, published in 1851, Dupont claimed that his lyre had 'trois cordes distinctes dont l'une rend le son simple, l'autre une note plaintive et pensive, la troisième un accord vibrant et presque guerrier'.[48] The very vocabulary shows Dupont to be far closer to Lamartine and Hugo than to the proletariat. With more simplicity than Dupont, Montégut mentions similar divisions: 'le petit volume de M. Dupont relève de trois genres divers: les chansons politiques, les chants populaires, les chants de fantaisie'.[49] Baudelaire likewise divides the songs into three similar groups: the pastoral, the social and the symbolic.

The first nine poems of *Chants et Chansons* are in fact arranged in the order in which Baudelaire has indicated the divisions, a pastoral poem like 'Les Bœufs' being followed by 'Le Chant des ouvriers' and the naively fantastic 'Belzébut', with its refrain: 'le monde subit la torture/ Du pouvoir infernal, / Le bien est l'esclave du mal'.[50] Baudelaire discusses the third type, the symbolic, only briefly. For him, it contains 'une philosophie un peu ténébreuse, une espèce de mysticité amoureuse' (11, 32). Similarly, but with more admiration, the anonymous critic of *La Semaine* notes in 'Belzébut' 'cette profonde pensée philosophique, que l'amour, pris dans son acception divine, doit vaincre un jour le génie du mal',[51] while Dupont himself claims to have developed 'une note plaintive et pensive' in 'les chants philosophiques et les légendes où l'auteur hasarde sa pensée et son sentiment: "Le Sauvage", "Belzébut", "La Comtesse Marguerite" etc.'[52] Given Baudelaire's opposition to overtly philosophical poetry, his reluctance to discuss this side of Dupont's work suggests either that Ménard's anger at the mocking review of *Prométhée délivré* has left its mark or that Baudelaire does not consider these poems as the cause of Dupont's success. In addition, they express a philosophy and adopt a style far removed from Baudelaire's own, depicting a world in which evil is overcome by simplicity, faith and love: thus, a child carried off by the Devil tranquilly proclaims:

> 'Je ne crois pas que vous teniez le monde'
> [. . .]
> Et de sa main traçant la mappemonde,
> Il écrivit sur le pôle: Aimez-vous!
> Le cheval noir devint un blanc squelette,
> Le vieux pommier croula sous un éclair,
> De Belzébut la grande silhouette
> En long serpent s'évanouit dans l'air.[53]

Dupont's optimistic, almost childlike, faith in the overthrow of evil through good presents Baudelaire, who had recently published such poems as 'Le Tonneau de la haine', 'De profundis clamavi' and 'La Cloche fêlée', with what he obviously considers a fascinating if distressing phenomenon: the writers who gain public favour are not those who suffer and who depict man's evil and folly, but those who find cause for hope and promise of love.

The pastoral poems also receive little attention. Earlier in the preface Baudelaire had evoked them lyrically as 'la fraîche source primitive qui filtre des hautes neiges' (II, 32) and had quoted four lines from 'La Chanson des prés': nevertheless, he referred to Dupont's 'amour fanatique de la nature', a particularly strong expression which may well reflect disapproval for what he saw as excessive. Here, moreover, he seems to reduce his commentary on the nature poetry to a transition between the fraternal love of the philosophical poems and the muted anger of the political songs. What he stresses, significantly enough, is their melancholy, just as, in the notice devoted to Banville, while depicting him as the poet who represents 'les belles heures de la vie' (II, 163), Baudelaire will nevertheless strongly bring out the darker side of life.

Baudelaire's discussion of Dupont's revolutionary songs experiments with the motif of civil strife, battle and war. Among his plans for prose poems are notes suggesting both that this was indeed a subject which tempted him and that his treatment of it would have been predominantly sardonic: 'Le canon tonne . . . les membres volent, . . . des gémissements de victimes et des hurlements de sacrificateurs se font entendre . . . C'est l'Humanité qui cherche le bonheur' (1, 371). The irony of this last sentence contrasts sharply with Dupont's conventional handling of the subject. The article, however, reveals a certain delight in the strident tones of trumpet and fife, and in the passion and suffering of battle. Similarly, in 'Mon cœur mis à nu' he proclaims that 'il n'y a de grand parmi les hommes que le poète, le prêtre et le soldat, l'homme qui chante, l'homme qui bénit, l'homme qui sacrifie et se sacrifie' (1, 693: cf. 1, 76, 684).

Baudelaire's attitude to armed struggle, however, is definitely two-sided: the enthusiasm with which he describes it in the passages just quoted is tempered by the sardonic remark that such things appeal to a 'nation militaire' like France (11, 33). Elsewhere, in listing the 'métaphores militaires' which abound in the language, he comments caustically: 'ces habitudes [. . .] dénotent des esprits, non pas militants, mais faits pour la discipline, c'est-à-dire pour la conformité' (1, 691). Indeed, he contends, at one remove, that Dupont himself has failed to give a sufficiently violent picture of war (11, 32-3), just as, in his later anthology notice, he admits that Dupont is not 'un de ces clairons guerriers comme les nations en veulent entendre dans la minute qui précède les grandes batailles' (11, 172).

The discussion of Dupont's political songs concludes with what I would suggest is a refutation of Montégut's accusation: 'le recueil de M. Dupont [. . .] n'a pas d'unité de sentiment'.[54] Baudelaire rightly insists that the common thread linking all Dupont's songs is 'l'amour de l'humanité' (11, 33).

This section of the preface closes with Baudelaire's posing, once again, the problem of Dupont's popularity. He concludes that the underlying reasons are to be found partly in the ability to reflect the mood of the Republic and partly in the joy the songs convey. Similarly, Montégut had pointed out that the poems 'respirent la joie de vivre, le bonheur de la vie domestique'.[55] Above all, the joy expressed in the works of certain writers and their ability to console the reader provide a clue to their popularity. Such writers are described, not as great or gifted, but as 'célèbres' (11, 34): it is their fame rather than their ability that has seized Baudelaire's attention here. He is forced to conclude that, given the public's craving for hope and consolation in works of art, his own intense and painful awareness of 'l'irréparable' (11, 34: cf. 1, 79), like that expressed by those great sufferers and dreamers, René, Obermann and Werther, cannot hope to win popular esteem. Here I disagree with the Pléiade note: 'il est remarquable que Baudelaire [. . .], sous l'effet du socialisme, s'illusionne sur la vraie nature de son génie. Le mot *Irréparable* deviendra le titre d'une pièce des

Fleurs du mal' (II, 1093). Surely the tone of bitter irony shows that Baudelaire is indeed fully aware of the nature of his own genius, but realizes only too keenly that that way popularity does not lie. He uses a technique which becomes more common in his later criticism, that of expressing as a question a point of view shared by many but which he himself does not hold: 'quand un poète vient affirmer des choses aussi bonnes et aussi consolantes, aurez-vous le courage de regimber?' (II, 34). The choice of the word 'courage' is surely significant. It is from the point of view of the public, therefore, that he rejects Romanticism in favour of a more optimistic, less individual literature.

In doing so, he introduces a highly dramatic style, studded with rich and deliberately incongruous imagery. He clearly delights in the virtuoso control of allusion and metaphor and there is certainly an element of play which should not be overlooked. Yet who is Baudelaire's butt, when he speaks of sheep returning to the enchanted forests whence they had been drawn by evil fairies, sheep which, like the Biblical swine plunging into the lake of Genezareth, are seized and shaken by Romantic vertigo? No doubt he is mocking those who have taken the ideals of Romanticism to excess, creating, not characters of stature equal to René, Werther and Obermann, but 'ombres fallacieuses' (II, 34). He may also be amusing himself at the expense of antagonistic critics, adopting their bombastic style and their mixed, tortuous metaphors. The final sentence: 'le génie de l'action ne vous laisse plus de place parmi nous' is similar in tone to, and, perhaps, as ironic in intention as, the dedication to the bourgeois in the *Salon de 1846*: 'vous n'avez jamais en aucune noble entreprise laissé l'initiative à la minorité protestante et souffrante, qui est d'ailleurs l'ennemie naturelle de l'art' (II, 416).

Like almost all the contemporary critics, Baudelaire insists on the importance of the musical accompaniment, arguing that it is essential to the enjoyment of Dupont's songs. Champfleury described it enthusiastically as 'une musique très neuve et très originale', Sainte-Beuve declared that 'au point de vue littéraire, les chants de M. Pierre Dupont perdraient à se séparer des airs' and the exuberant Hayward asserted that 'the effect of Dupont's singing is electrical'.[56] Baudelaire might also have mentioned the artistic presentation of the songs, the delicacy with which they were printed and the attractiveness of the lithographs accompanying them: a masterpiece of their kind, they represent a resounding success for their printer.

Adopting the actor Bignon's recently coined expression, Baudelaire urges those who sing Dupont's songs *'entrer dans la peau* de l'être créé' (II, 36; see also II, 1094). There may well be in this final paragraph a further clue, in addition to the irony and pastiche noted earlier, to the way in which Baudelaire has approached the review: he contends that 'il faut s'assimiler une œuvre pour la bien exprimer' (II, 36). Similarly, in his search for the causes of popularity, he himself has sought to assimilate both Dupont's songs and the mentality of those who admire them.

Just as the structure and substance of the article are highly polished, so is its expression. Appropriately, in a study of a poet who found such inspiration in the countryside, much of the imagery is drawn from nature: Dupont's songs stood out against the materialism of the July Monarchy like 'une oasis' (II, 28), a 'floraison' (II, 31), a 'fraîche source' (II, 32) running through the storm-racked mountains of the times, while the creations of late Romanticism now strike the public as 'brouillards du vide' (II, 34). Many of the images are very concrete. There are, for example, several metaphors connected with food: the 'saveur' of Dupont's poetry contrasts sharply with 'cette nourriture indigeste de crèmes et de sucreries dont les familles illettrées bourrent imprudemment la mémoire de leurs demoiselles' (II, 30). Several forceful images are drawn from the Bible – grief is necessary to the poet as a 'levain pour la pâte' (I, 29) and the Romantic heroes are to plunge like 'pourceaux dans le lac de Génézareth' (II, 34), – or from fairy-tales – 'les fôrets enchantées' and 'les fées ennemies' (II, 34). At one point, Dupont's own links with Romanticism are suggested in an image evoking novels in the Walter Scott vein: like a medieval knight, the song-writer, in breaking down the defences of Popularity, has 'coupé les chaînes du pont-levis de la forteresse' (II, 34: cf. II, 79). Finally, Baudelaire conveys the intensity of his feelings through the intensity of his language: 'explosion' (II, 29), 'discussions orageuses' (II, 30) and 'ébloui' (II, 31), expressions which recur in the later criticism and whose importance will be discussed in subsequent chapters.

In this preface, Baudelaire has eagerly seized an opportunity to explore a phenomenon of vital importance to his own career. It is a carefully worded study, which is neither an expression of beliefs nor a declaration of intent: Baudelaire is politely but firmly keeping his distance. Not only does he analyse Dupont's songs and the reasons behind his success, but he raises questions central to aesthetic debates and refers in passing to several of the foremost contemporary writers: Hugo, Barbier and Sainte-Beuve. His first attempt at making of literary criticism something more than a straightforward review is, therefore, an accurate if sardonic reflection of certain contemporary opinions, a sociological and aesthetic study which may not always be convincing but which shows that his ideas about criticism are already broader than those held by the great majority of his contemporaries.

The Dangers of Excess: 'Les Drames et les romans honnêtes' (*La Semaine théâtrale,* 27 November 1851) *and* 'L'Ecole païenne' (*La Semaine théâtrale,* 22 January 1852).

Two articles, published in 1851 and 1852 in the short-lived *Semaine théâtrale,* close the series of Baudelaire's early criticism. They are unique in that where the rest of Baudelaire's published literary criticism concerns individuals, they attempt to assess literary movements. These studies present particular difficulties to a twentieth-century reader: indeed, when Baudelaire sent them to his mother he commented: 'ils sont très *spécialement parisiens,* et je doute qu'ils puissent être compris hors des *milieux* pour lesquels et sur lesquels ils ont été écrits' (*C*I, 191). The reasons are both aesthetic and political.[57]

In 1843, the disastrous performance of *Les Burgraves* had brought Romanticism into disrepute, while Ponsard's *Lucrèce,* a pseudo-classical tragedy which extolled the virtues of wifely chastity and fidelity, was given an enthusiastic reception. This led to the formation of a group which acquired the sobriquet of 'l'école du bon sens'. Baudelaire gives his version of how the name came into being in a footnote to 'Les Drames et les romans honnêtes' (II, 40) and, much more pointedly, in his comments to Asselineau's preface (II, 98), but an anonymous article in *La Silhouette* of 7 December 1845 proffers a different suggestion: 'en raison d'un certain calme, d'une certaine modération dans l'exécution, qui caractérise leurs natures d'ailleurs si diverses, MM. Ponsard et Augier arrivèrent à croire qu'ils avaient réussi par la raison et le bon sens. De ce jour, l'*école du bon sens* fut fondée.' An epigram in *La Silhouette* sums the group up with equal accuracy and wit: 'c'est en littérature comme une société de tempérance'.[58]

The movement's ideals and methods constantly provoked a barrage of denunciations and eulogies. If Gautier was only half-serious when he claimed to find in the 'tendance à réhabiliter le mari au préjudice de l'amant' a 'grave symptôme [. . .] qui marque un changement dans l'esprit public',[59] Leconte de Lisle remarked with icy gravity in his preface to *Poèmes antiques*: 'une Ecole récente s'est élevée, restauratrice un peu niaise du bon sens public, mais qui n'est pas née viable, qui ne répond à rien et ne représente rien qu'une atonie peu inquiétante'.[60]

The rise of the school, as both Gautier and Baudelaire contend, was indeed symptomatic of political and social changes,[61] and Baudelaire is careful to point out that both sides, socialists as well as bourgeoisie, reveal the same feverish desire to preach and moralize. The year 1851 was one of counter-revolution, seeing the reassertion of bourgeois values, culminating in the December *coup d'état*, a plebiscite giving massive support to Louis-Napoleon, and the purge of the Republican opposition. A second symptom, relevant since it indicates Baudelaire's courage in printing what may seem a fairly anodyne, though lively, attack on governmental decisions, was the reimposition of strict censorship, lifted during the euphoric months following the February Revolution.[62]

Baudelaire's article puts both 'l'école du bon sens' and its turbulent background into a disconcertingly different perspective from that chosen by his contemporaries, whose windy arguments he calmly deflates by asserting that no one would seriously suggest that art should oppose 'les grandes lois morales' (11, 38). The question that must be asked, he claims, is not of principle but of technique: are the self-styled virtuous writers satisfactorily achieving their aim? Lois Hamrick has revealed similarities between the opening lines of Baudelaire's article and the first paragraph of the preface to *Mademoiselle de Maupin*: 'une des choses les plus burlesques de la glorieuse époque où nous avons le bonheur de vivre est incontestablement la réhabilitation de la vertu entreprise par tous les journaux'.[63] The comparison could be pursued much further if space permitted: both Gautier's preface and his novel have stamped their imprint on the ideas and tone of Baudelaire's criticism in general and these brief articles in particular.[64]

After the quiet start, the witty, rapier-like thrusts aimed at two 'drames honnêtes', Augier's *La Ciguë* and his *Gabrielle*, are all the more devastating.

La Ciguë, which established Augier's fame when it was performed in 1844,[65] incurs Baudelaire's wrath for three reasons. Firstly, he asserts that Augier might have created something worthwhile, 'quoique assez commun' (11, 38), had he made his hero turn from epicureanism to asceticism, instead of sliding into a conventional marriage. It is moreover with mocking sarcasm that Baudelaire terms Clinias a 'parfait épicurien', since his debauchery is as bourgeois as his subsequent reform:

> Comme, à l'écart des sots, et quoi qu'en ait envie,
> De festins en festins s'écoule notre vie!
> Pas de parents gênants; personne à ménager;
> De l'or, et l'appétit qu'il faut pour le manger;
> Une amitié sans fin et des amours sans suite.[66]

Secondly, Baudelaire sardonically suggests that Augier 'a voulu prouver qu'à la fin il faut toujours *se ranger*' (11, 38), that is, conform to conventional morality without accepting full personal responsibility either for the past or for the decision itself.[67] Above all, he insists that virtue itself is debased if it is made to accept, as in Augier's play, 'les restes de la débauche'. A similar expression appears in the play, the repentant hero asking:

> Qui voudrait accepter l'hymen d'un débauché,
> Et les restes d'un cœur par le vice séché?[68]

In a side-reference, Baudelaire pours scorn on the portrayal of 'filles publiques qui ont gardé je ne sais où une pureté angélique' (11, 40: cf. 11, 54), thus lampooning the theme of the rehabilitation of debauchees and prostitutes as well as the hackneyed picture of the golden-hearted whore. His mockery, of course, is not aimed solely at 'l'école du bon sens': the idea was also cherished by Hugo.

Turning to *Gabrielle*, first published in 1849, Baudelaire seizes with obvious delight on any clue suggesting that Augier has not thought out all the implications of his play. Although *Gabrielle* was enthusiastically received by the general public, critical reviews ran the full gamut, from S. Henry Berthoud's sententious welcome for 'la réhabilitation du mariage, écrite en vers charmants',[69] through the Fourierist Hennequin's regrets that despite 'ce vers léger [. . .], instrument plus souple que la plus agile prose', Augier 's'est borné à refléter les sentiments de son public, à faire retentir avec éclat toutes les maximes sûres',[70] to Vacquerie's sneering and predictable condemnation of 'le lyrisme du pot-au-feu'.[71] However varied the opinions expressed, Baudelaire's highly individual approach to the play, with his amusing pirouettes about the marquis de Sade and contraception, sets him apart from other critics. Moreover behind those pirouettes lies a very serious intent.

As Baudelaire and Vacquerie both point out, the play's success was due less to the ultimate victory of marital virtues than to the flattery offered to its middle-class audience. Vacquerie's censure is more corrosive even than Baudelaire's:

> quand on se résigne à convenir avec les notaires et les avoués épanouis dans leurs stalles qu'ils valent bien les poètes et qu'il n'existe pas au monde autre poème que le code, – c'est bien le moins que les avoués et les notaires répondent par un sourire au gracieux auteur qui se met aux genoux pour leur chatouiller la plante des pieds.

Baudelaire, too, is forced to admit that immediate popularity seems dependent on supporting the public's self-esteem against 'tous ces gredins qui ont des dettes et qui croient que le métier de poète consiste à exprimer les mouvements lyriques de l'âme dans un rythme réglé par la tradition' (II, 39). Yet while Vacquerie fulminates against the debasement of art, Baudelaire seems aware that his arguments will carry more weight if he places his emphasis on the school's lack of logic and its failure to achieve its goals.

The effect of the changing political situation on Baudelaire's literary criticism is reflected in the contrast between the suggestion in the Dupont preface that the bourgeois sought equality with the poet (II, 28), and his portrayal here of the public's desire to bring the poet down to their level and to wreak revenge on those who dare to out-shine them. He supports this claim by referring to a work which won its author considerable celebrity and to which a sequel had recently been published, Louis Reybaud's *Jérôme Paturot à la recherche d'une position sociale*.[72] This novel, which Baudelaire compares to the annual procession of aristocrats down the Courtille, during which time they mingled with, and were insulted and even assaulted by, the proletariat, is a superficial but amusing review of current social and artistic doctrines. Although Reybaud refrains from using his victims' names, they are instantly recognizable. Thus, Leroux is mercilessly lampooned in the account of Paturot's temporary infatuation with Saint-Simonian ideals,[73] while Proudhon, whom Baudelaire presents as 'un écrivain que l'Europe nous enviera toujours' (II, 41), is pilloried in the book's sequel: 'à ses yeux la propriété était une infâme; et quand il rencontrait un propriétaire sur son chemin, il fallait voir comme il le redressait'.[74] Hugo is an obvious target. Paturot, for example, complacently asserts:

je donnais dans l'enjambement, et c'est à moi que l'on doit ce sonnet célèbre qui disait:

> Toi, plus blanche cent fois qu'un marbre de Paros,
> Néère, dans mon cœur tu fais naître un paro-
> Xysme d'amour brûlant comme l'est une lave![75]

And Viollet-le-Duc, the last of those whom Baudelaire calmly defends against Reybaud, appears in the novel as 'un garçon ivre du passé et qui ressemblait moins à un Français du dix-neuvième siècle qu'à un Epiménide du moyen-âge'.[76] Baudelaire's quiet, but accurate, support for these men argues his continuing interest in social problems, his increasing admiration for Proudhon and his keen awareness of the value of Romanticism.

If *Jérôme Paturot* is included in this article, it is partly because the hero returns to the bourgeois fold after becoming disillusioned with all the other possibilities, and partly because it contains the destructive element that Baudelaire condemns in 'l'école païenne': it rejects all these experiments with considerable wit and broad humour, but uses no discrimination in doing so.

Another point of comparison between 'l'école du bon sens' and its rival, 'l'école païenne', lies in their abuse of language, leading to a corresponding perversion of thought. However much buffoonery it contains, Paturot's fatuous assertion that 'quiconque aspire au mieux est poète, car le mieux ici-bas est l'inconnu, l'idéal comme la poésie',[77] justifies Baudelaire's warning that 'la langue française périclite, et les mauvaises passions littéraires en détruisent l'exactitude' (II, 40). Once again he is twisting common clichés in applying the phrase *mauvaises passions* to literature and using it as a whip to beat the 'virtuous'. He contends that 'l'école païenne' has debased words rich in religious connotations by using them in inappropriate secular contexts. It is, as Baudelaire sardonically points out, particularly ridiculous for a poet to refer to his mistress as 'mon ange', for example, since 'généralement les maîtresses des poètes sont d'assez vilaines gaupes, dont les moins mauvaises sont celles qui font la soupe et ne payent pas un autre amant' (II, 40). The influence of *Mademoiselle de Maupin* can be felt once again, if one thinks of d'Albert remarking caustically: 'les poètes prennent habituellement d'assez sales guenipes pour maîtresses'.[78] The theme of the contrast between the poet's idealized image of woman and his flesh and blood mistress assumes far more concentrated form in such prose poems as 'La Soupe et les nuages' and 'La Femme sauvage et la petite-maîtresse', while the poem 'Je n'ai pas pour maîtresse' reveals that the reversal of the accepted vision of woman can itself become a cliché.[79]

Baudelaire's principal focus is not, of course, these lightweight dramas and novels, but the prickly and perennial problem of morality in art. It was a question Baudelaire's contemporaries debated at considerable length and with particular fervour. An anonymous review of a work entitled *Les Mauvais Livres*, for example, combined morality with mathematics in enumerating eight effects of evil literature, beginning with 'la corruption du cœur' and ending with suicide.[80] And in 1851 Montheau, writing for the aggressively right-wing *L'Assemblée nationale*, asked with heavy-handed irony: 'la morale? Qu'a-t-elle à démêler avec de pareils écrits? La morale? Elle affadirait le spectacle, elle glacerait le public', concluding that 'l'époux qui travaille, le père qui se sacrifie, prose et banalité tout cela; "poésie d'avoué ou de notaire tout au plus" comme on l'a si magistralement proclamée'.[81]

Among the plethora of such commentaries, two in particular seem to have fired Baudelaire's imagination: Gautier's *Mademoiselle de Maupin* and Balzac's reply to Castille's accusations that *La Comédie humaine* is immoral. Baudelaire, in fact, refers to two letters written by Balzac: I would suggest that he may be amalgamating the reply to Castille, published as a single letter, and the preface to *La Comédie humaine*, which Balzac uses to defend himself against just such an attack and to which he refers in the letter to Castille.[82] Baudelaire does not hesitate in setting aside Gautier's complete, if not entirely serious, rejection of the claims of morality in art. He clearly adheres to Balzac's assertion that 'moraliser son époque est le but que tout écrivain doit se proposer, sous peine de n'être qu'un *amuseur de gens*; mais la critique a-t-elle des procédés nouveaux à indiquer aux écrivains qu'elle accuse d'immoralité? Or, le procédé ancien a toujours consisté à montrer la plaie.'[83]

Above all, one notes the extremely concise way in which Baudelaire expresses so complex a problem: 'l'art est-il utile? Oui. Pourquoi? Parce qu'il est l'art. Y a-t-il un art pernicieux? Oui. C'est celui qui dérange les conditions de la vie' (II, 41). Here, as in his presentation of 'Révélation magnétique', and the *Salon de 1846*, he upholds his belief in 'l'unité intégral', insisting that nature is inherently good: 'le crime est-il toujours châtié, la vertu gratifiée? Non; mais cependant, si votre roman, si votre drame est bien fait, il ne prendra envie à personne de violer les lois de la nature' (II, 41). Later, of course, he grew increasingly convinced that the evil in man and in society was 'irréparable'. Finally, this cogent passage both reflects Balzac's declaration and points forward to the review of *Madame Bovary* when it says: 'étudiez toutes les plaies comme un médecin qui fait son service dans un hôpital, et l'école du bon sens, l'école exclusivement morale, ne trouvera plus où mordre' (II, 41).

Baudelaire's insistence that virtue is not best served by overt didacticism is given further force by a counter-example, provided by that execrably dull author of children's books, Berquin, whom Baudelaire claims not to have read as a child. His constant attempt to discover the seeds of future characteristics in early childhood is reflected in his claim that he himself had had 'le bonheur ou le malheur de ne lire que de gros livres d'homme' (II, 42). Significantly, Balzac himself declared in his reply to Castille: 'qui relit Berquin? Il faut la candeur de nos douze ans pour le supporter.'[84] The hypocrisy inherent in Berquin's offer of reward for virtue seems so obvious a target for Baudelaire's satire that it should be pointed out that he is not exaggerating his case. In *L'Ami de l'adolescence*, for example, the chastened Delphine exclaims in surprisingly adult terms: 'ô ma chère maman [. . .] si mon amour-propre venait jamais à s'aveugler, j'irais lui chercher des lumières dans votre prudence et dans votre amour'. And a child remarks in another Berquin tale: 'oh! c'est un bien honnête homme! Il m'a donné une poire superbe',[85] a materialistic version of *honnête* if ever there were one!

Public and governmental interference in the arts can of course encourage a similar form of hypocrisy. Baudelaire did not have to search far to discover examples. The baron de Montyon, for instance, founded several monetary prizes, among them one to be awarded to the work of literature judged to be the most useful to society, and another for an 'acte de vertu' performed by an indigent French citizen.[86] Several other critics rejected the idea of such a prize, Castille himself making the interesting if anachronistic assertion that:

> M de Monthyon [sic], en fondant des *prix de vertu* fit, sans le vouloir, la plus sanglante critique de l'interprétation de la vertu qui résulte de la charte de Louis-Philippe. Il alla plus loin que le maître, il prit la vertu dans son sens le plus général, le plus universel, et il se dit: récompensons la vertu.[87]

Gautier referred to the prize in derogatory tones in *Mademoiselle de Maupin*[88] and Eugène Pelletan expostulated: 'un prix de vertu, Dieu du Ciel! Il n'y a qu'un philanthrope pour avoir une pareille idée. Mais, la vertu, vous l'avez donc oublié, pèse dans l'humanité un poids si divin, qu'aucune somme humaine ne saurait faire équilibre dans l'autre plateau de la balance.'[89] Léon Faucher, a Greek scholar and an influential journalist who was given the portfolio of internal affairs in 1851, posed a far more serious threat in offering governmental support to writers whose works were overtly moralistic and consciously didactic. Since an attack on Faucher would be construed as an attack on the government and therefore a crime under the law, it was no doubt the fear of prosecution that reduced Baudelaire's remarks on Faucher to a passing, though virulent, reference and led to almost no discussion of the prize in contemporary art and drama reviews. In 1853 Calonne did, however, venture a criticism which timidly echoes Baudelaire's claim: 'c'était en quelque sorte une compensation offerte aux auteurs de talent qui se résignaient à abandonner les peintures scandaleuses du vice et de l'immoralité'.[90] Despite the brevity of his comments, Baudelaire succeeds in conveying the intensity of his feeling: Faucher's 'satanic' decree and all similar 'inventions du diable' have 'assassinated' virtue and 'mortally wounded' literature. Moreover, the terms 'satanique' and 'inventions du diable' (II, 43), recall the prose poem 'Le Joueur généreux' in which the Devil confesses to feeling fear for the first time when he heard a preacher proclaim: 'Mes chers frères, n'oubliez jamais, quand vous entendrez vanter le progrès des lumières, que la plus belle des ruses du diable est de vous persuader qu'il n'existe pas' (I, 326-7). Those who present the triumph of virtue as inevitable are clearly falling into this particularly subtle and diabolical trap. Once again, the use of such terminology indicates the extent to which religious questions fascinated and irritated Baudelaire and suggests that this may well lie at the heart of his outburst.

According to Baudelaire, the only prize a writer needs is the esteem of his peers – a version of the often repeated 'il n'y a que les poètes pour comprendre les poètes' – and a resounding financial success, a point which recalls the Dupont preface. There is also, no doubt, an echo of Gautier's claim in the preface to *Mademoiselle de Maupin* that a novel is useful, in part, because of the 'quelques mille francs qui entrent dans la poche de l'auteur'.[91]

The article shows signs of haste and is, perhaps, not very well-balanced, but it does convey in a particularly trenchant manner Baudelaire's opposition to conscious didacticism. He himself seems to have been pleased with the passages devoted to more general questions, since he includes a shortened version of them in his first study of Gautier.

The explicit didacticism of 'l'école du bon sens', its tendency to show poets as madmen, its determinedly philistine debasing of a lofty vision of art, all these are points liable to enrage Baudelaire: indeed, the only aspect he might have found in favour of the writers of this school was their occasional, but inconsistent, attempts to portray contemporary life.

The second part of the diptych formed by 'Les Drames et les romans honnêtes' and 'L'Ecole païenne', however, is less straightforward. One understands Baudelaire's irritation with those members of 'l'école païenne' who, spurning the beauty of modern life which Baudelaire had so emphatically stressed in his *Salon de 1846*, put in its stead stock images and stereotyped situations from the Ancients. Yet there is much in the article which makes one uneasy. After all, it concerns poets who, unlike Ponsard and Augier, possessed exceptional gifts: to *poetae minores* like Ménard, Deltuf and Laprade must be added Banville, Gautier, Nerval and Leconte de Lisle.[92] Is Baudelaire trying to forge a new aesthetic system, dismissing the excesses of both schools and purifying his own ideas of similar tendencies? Has he undertaken to write the two articles as a bet, wagering that he could attack with equal force and justice two of the main literary schools of the time? And how far is he mocking the *poncifs* and labels of contemporary criticism?

Since Banville's name is coupled with the tag 'l'école païenne' in Baudelaire's notes for the projected journal *Le Hibou philosophe* (II, 51), critics such as Eileen Souffrin have assumed that the pagan poet of whom Baudelaire gives a thumbnail sketch can be none other than Banville.[93] For Henri Peyre, whose annotated bibliography of Hellenism in France reveals the current fervour for Greece and Greek literature, the article 'semble viser L. Ménard, et peut-être aussi Th. Gautier et Th. de Banville'.[94] Other names could be added, but, as the notes to the Pléiade edition suggest (II, 1099), the neo-pagan can best be seen as a composite figure, exhibiting traits borrowed from several of Baudelaire's acquaintances and externalizing some of his own tendencies.

'L'Ecole païenne' not only develops some of the points raised in 'Les Drames et les romans honnêtes', but is also similar in construction: a brief opening paragraph sets the perspective, in this case that of paganism as symptomatic of the times;[95] this is followed by mocking illustrations of the school's beliefs, leading up to a more general discussion.

Although Baudelaire begins by seizing his reader's attention with an amusing anecdote, his technique is far removed from the glib journalism of a Monselet or a Houssaye, for whom an anecdote is merely an easy means of titillating the reader. The event he recounts, a toast proposed to Pan at a banquet commemorating the February Revolution, appears to him indicative of certain artists' confused reactions to political developments.

Baudelaire arouses and holds his reader's attention not only by the initial anecdote but also by the range of register and the variety of technical devices: as in the review of *Prométhée délivré*, more conventional analysis combines with pastiche and dialogue. Although he may possibly be drawing directly on Plutarch for his reference to the death of Pan, there seems to be a degree of pastiche when he echoes the solemn tones adopted by Rabelais in *Le Quart Livre*: 'je croyais qu'on avait entendu planer une grande voix au-dessus de la Méditerranée, et que cette voix mystérieuse, qui roulait depuis les colonnes d'Hercule jusqu'aux rivages asiatiques, avait dit au vieux monde: LE DIEU PAN EST MORT!' (II, 44). Rabelais tells how a strange voice had called out to an Egyptian ship's pilot: 'lors fait icelle voix plus haultement ouie, luy disant et commandant, quand il seroit en Palodes, publier et dire que Pan le grand Dieu estoit mort'.[96] Curiously enough, a review of Quinet's philosophy course published in 1840 reported that 'tandis qu'il faisait entendre cette voix gigantesque qu'on ouït dans les îles et qui allait en criant: "Le grand dieu Pan est mort!" j'ai vu des larmes couler de tous les yeux comme si chacun sentait qu'il avait aussi quelque grande mort à pleurer dans celle-là'.[97] The passage may possibly have been brought to Baudelaire's attention by Quinet's disciple Ménard, who later published a prose and verse collection entitled *Rêveries d'un païen mystique*.

The principal area of conflict, that between Baudelaire's demands for art to exploit 'le beau moderne' and the pagan's 'rêverie renouvelée des Grecs', in Nerval's phrase,[98] is summarized in the remark that the neo-pagan 'parlait du dieu Pan comme du prisonnier de Sainte-Hélène' (II, 44). An analogous technique appears in the review of *Prométhée délivré*, where the line 'Les dieux sont morts, car la foudre est à moi' (II, 10) is burlesquely rephrased in more modern terms as 'Franklin a détrôné Jupiter'. Similarly, the poet who believed Juno had looked favourably upon him is told mockingly that it was merely an actress who turned on him 'un véritable œil de *vache*' (II, 45), a cliché often used for comic effect.

The year 1851, which saw the toast to Pan, was one in which many poets, in whom the hopes aroused by the ideals of 1848 had been shattered, began to retreat into the past or the purely imaginary. One facet of this can be seen in the neo-pagan's claim that 'le Paganisme seul peut sauver le monde'. In the same way, the language of revolution blends with that of Hellenism in some of the poems published by Leconte de Lisle in the Fourierist press. Baudelaire's pagan goes on to claim that 'il faut revenir aux vraies doctrines, obscurcies *un instant* par l'infâme Galiléen' (II, 44). Similarly, the 1846 version of Leconte de Lisle's 'Les Ascètes' proclaims: 'ce culte s'éteint, et l'homme cherche encore, / Et pour user un Dieu vingt siècles ont suffi'.[99] There may also be echoes of Nerval: in a letter written towards the end of 1851, Baudelaire told Gautier that 'l'*incorrigible* Gérard prétend au contraire que c'est pour avoir abandonné le bon culte que Cythère est réduite en cet état' (*CI*, 180). And Gautier himself wrote in 1848 that 'la substitution des idées chrétiennes aux idées païennes nous paraît être la raison première de cette dégradation de la forme'.[100] Baudelaire's description of the Mardi Gras parade also recalls Nerval,[101] just as the suggestion that the actress Ernestine, in the role of Juno, 'lui a fait un œil plein de souvenirs' evokes not only Nerval's passionate love for the actress Jenny Colon, but also a passage in *Corilla*, where Marcelli, fatuously discussing with Fabio his romance with 'la divine Corilla' asks: 'Par Bacchus! vous avez bien remarqué les furieux clins d'œil que nous nous lançons?'[102]

The suspicion that Nerval is providing these traits of the neo-pagan poet is reinforced when Baudelaire traces this 'excès de paganisme' to an enthusiasm for Heine which is both exaggerated and based on misconceptions. Nerval translated and reviewed many of Heine's poems, and, if Baudelaire considered such poetry 'pourrie de sentimentalisme matérialiste', Nerval himself, in a review published in 1848, described Heine as 'un Voltaire pittoresque et sentimental'.[103]

It is above all the neo-pagans' alienation from the contemporary world which seems to arouse Baudelaire's scorn. He accuses them of being isolated from reality to the extent that their only comment on modern problems is: 'Comment voulez-vous que les femmes fassent de beaux enfants dans un pays où elles adorent un vilain pendu!' (II, 46). Further, when Paris is on the brink of a revolution, a time Baudelaire describes in a startlingly concise and evocative way in which the hurried actions of the populace recall certain Daumier cartoons, the neo-pagan pours over 'bouquins étranges et hiéroglyphiques' to uncover obscure details about the marriage of Isis and Osiris. Once again, Baudelaire's butt may well be Nerval, whose account of 'Le Temple d'Isis' was published in *La Phalange* in 1845. His attack also recalls Gautier's attitude, expressed in the preface to *Emaux et Camées* in 1853, but possibly made clear to his friends before that:

> Sans prendre garde à l'ouragon
> Qui fouettait mes vitres fermées
> Moi, j'ai fait *Emaux et Camées*.[104]

Baudelaire himself, on 20 March 1852, wrote to Poulet-Malassis that he was determined 'rester désormais étranger à toute la polémique humaine, et plus décidé que jamais à poursuivre le rêve supérieur de l'application de la métaphysique au roman' (*C*I, 189). And certainly the depoliticized Baudelaire of later years seems to share the neo-pagans' escapism, at least to some extent, when he writes in 'Paysage':

> L'Emeute, tempêtant vainement à ma vitre,
> Ne fera pas lever mon front de mon pupitre (I, 82).

However, this article is dominated by another side of Baudelaire's character, that which insisted that 'la vie parisienne est féconde en sujets poétiques et merveilleux' (II, 496). Moreover, it is both the exaggeration of 'l'école païenne' and their mocking rejection of Christianity which irritates him: he sees their actions as 'excès' and 'fanatisme'.

Baudelaire's delight in finding parallels between literature and the plastic arts is reflected in his reference to Daumier and the way in which the cartoonist lampooned the pretentiousness of the neo-pagans in a series of caricatures entitled *Histoire ancienne*. There, Daumier transformed the gods and heroes into bourgeois, and moved them to contemporary Paris. In a phrase which twists the often repeated demand that art be useful, Baudelaire describes Daumier's collection as both amusing and 'utile' (II, 47), since it provides a perspective which corrects distorted vision. This passage reappears, with variants, in 'Quelques caricaturistes français' (II, 555–6), the first version of which, according to Pichois (II, 1342), pre-dates 'L'Ecole païenne'. In the former article, Baudelaire stresses that Daumier's target is 'la fausse antiquité' whereas the literary review is more sweeping: 'Daumier s'est abattu brutalement sur l'antiquité et la mythologie' (II, 46). In addition, the reference to the 'poète lyrique et païen de mes amis' as being 'fort indigné' becomes considerably more insulting in the literary article, where the poet is no longer described as a friend and has been reduced to tears by Daumier's 'impiété'. Indeed, the 'malheureux' who 'avait encore besoin d'une religion' (II, 47), may well be Ménard, whom Baudelaire also described elsewhere as 'un homme de talent' (II, 11) just as here he is called 'un écrivain de talent' (II, 46) and who had ceased to be a friend since 1846, when the first draft of the essay on caricature may well have been written. Moreover, the fact that Ménard still felt the need of religion is proved by his espousal of a mystic syncretism.

Baudelaire summarizes his argument in a humorous yet vitriolic attack, based partly on literary grounds, partly on more prosaic preoccupations. With a barrage of impatient questions he seems to seize the neo-pagan by the neck and shake him in exasperation. In a mocking metaphor which may have its origins in such tales as Chamisso's *Peter Schlemil* and which prefigures the prose poem 'Perte d'auréole', he inquires: 'vous avez sans doute perdu votre âme quelque part, dans quelque mauvais endroit, pour que vous couriez ainsi à travers le passé comme des corps vides pour en ramasser une de rencontre dans les détritus anciens' (II, 47). Behind the humour lies a serious call for originality, for developing one's own *tempérament*, for resisting the temptation 'se faire [. . .] une âme d'emprunt' (II, 3). More prosaically, he questions the practicality of such art, in a paragraph which, with its 'côtelettes de Paros' and its 'bouillons d'ambroisie' (II, 47), is a comic *tour de force*, but which is so philistine and which comes so close to the perpetual demand for art to be useful that one wonders if he is not demolishing both the school and its critics at one blow. Nevertheless, it does have a precedent in the preface to Dupont's songs, where Baudelaire upholds Balzac's demand that a writer present 'une surface commerciale' (II, 30). Furthermore, the passage reveals yet again the unmistakable influence of *Mademoiselle de Maupin*: there, the exasperated

Gautier exclaims 'on ne se fait pas un bonnet de coton d'une métonymie, on ne chausse pas une comparaison en guise de pantoufle; on ne se peut servir d'une antithèse pour parapluie'.[105] Above all, Baudelaire has sandwiched between the humour expressions revealing an undertone of deadly seriousness: 'toutes ces statues de marbre seront-elles des femmes dévouées au jour de l'agonie, au jour du remords, au jour de l'impuissance?' (II, 47). 'Réversibilité', the manuscript of which dates from May 1853, offers several parallels with this brief but emotive passage, which, like *Les Paradis artificiels*, shows Baudelaire searching out the initial causes of patterns of thought or behaviour which imperceptibly become so ingrained as to be ineradicable.

The second half of Baudelaire's article consists of a more general argument based on questions posed by the very existence of 'l'école païenne': what use can one make of past discoveries, what differentiates an admiration for external beauty from a deeper comprehension of art and life, is beauty without truth sufficient for a work of art? As in 'Les Drames et les romans honnêtes', the problems of the usefulness and the truth of art, questions to which Baudelaire constantly returns, are debated with considerable vigour, but an obvious susceptibility to the very temptation he condemns makes the discussion a form of ironic self-analysis. The change of tone, from sardonic humour to bitter reproach, and the sudden density of minute detail, suggests that Baudelaire is attacking a problem which is intimately connected with his own personality and poetry.

Baudelaire implies that 'l'école païenne', by rejecting passion, reason, the efforts of Christianity and the discoveries of philosophy, has isolated itself from 'les moyens de perfectionnement' (II, 47). Philarète Chasles, in a review of Chénier's poetry, had recently expressed a similar belief: 'il ne faut procéder ni par destruction et dénigrement, ni par élimination et critique, mais par adoption du passé, en continuant ses conquêtes et poussant plus loin son progrès'.[106] The Dupont preface shows Baudelaire using the word *perfectionnement* in a somewhat ironic sense (II, 28), but 'L'Ecole païenne' as well as the projected prefaces for *Les Fleurs du mal* (I, 182) implies that the artist can, by his own endeavours, perfect his gifts. Similarly, a letter dated 30 August 1851 emphasizes that Balzac, however unexceptional his early writings may have been, 'est parvenu à avoir, *à se procurer*, pour ainsi dire [. . .] immensément d'esprit' (*C*I, 177).

A further danger lurks in the neo-pagan's enthusiasm for 'les séductions de l'art physique', in his preoccupation with beauty in a very restricted sense of the word. Where Baudelaire sought 'transformer [sa] volupté en connaissance' (II, 786), the neo-pagan, in responding to the world, makes no effort to understand 'les ressorts qui le font se mouvoir' (II, 47). Nature, for him, is no more than rhythms and forms, whereas, for Baudelaire and for Delacroix, it is the basic matter of a work of art, which the artist's sensitivity and intelligence must transform into his painting or poem. In his notes on Realism, Baudelaire rejects the approach of Champfleury and Courbet for similar reasons; they, too, have failed to realize that 'ce monde-ci' is a 'dictionnaire hiéro-glyphique' (II, 59). This belief achieves its most striking formulation in the *Salon de 1859*: 'tout l'univers visible n'est qu'un magasin d'images et de signes auxquels l'imagination donnera une place et une valeur relative; c'est une espèce de pâture que l'imagination doit digérer et transformer' (II, 627). Champfleury himself echoes Baudelaire's con-demnation in *Les Aventures de Mademoiselle Mariette*, which appeared in 1853:

> ils [un peintre et un poète de l'histoire] ont étudié la sculpture et la poèsie grecques et n'en ont pris que la surface. A quoi cela répond-il de notre temps? Est-ce que nous avons besoin de nous plonger dans l'antiquité? N'avons-nous pas d'autres passions, d'autres mœurs, d'autres vices? Encore s'ils avaient compris le fond de la poésie et la sculpture grecques! mais ils n'en ont pris que la forme, les Vénus, les Io Pœan, des bêtises![107]

In Baudelaire's eyes, the exclusive passion for outward beauty brings with it 'de grandes chances de perdition' (II, 47): particularly forceful is the word 'perdition', with its religious implication of the soul's destruction. Peyre points out that 'nos païens modernes repoussent, à leur insu parfois, consciemment le plus souvent, les notions de la perversité naturelle de l'homme et de la nécessité de la grâce et de la rédemption'.[108] This may well lie at the root of Baudelaire's anger, since by clinging to external beauty, the pagans refuse to recognize and represent the corruption suppurating beneath the surface.

In yet another passage which, as the notes to the Pléiade edition point out, could be applied to himself, Baudelaire reveals the miseries awaiting 'tout enfant [. . .] dont les sens seront journellement caressés, irrités, effrayés, allumés et satisfaits par des objets d'art' (II, 48). 'Mon cœur mis à nu' contains the following often quoted note: 'glorifier le culte des images (ma grande, mon unique, ma primitive passion)' (I, 701), and in *Le Salon de 1859* he remembers that 'très jeunes, [ses] yeux remplis d'images peintes ou gravées n'avaient jamais pu se rassasier', adding: 'je crois que les mondes pourraient finir, *impavidum ferient*, avant que je devienne iconoclaste' (II, 624). In 'L'Ecole païenne', however, he claims to understand, if not to share, 'les fureurs des iconoclastes et des musulmans contre les images' (II, 49). The precocity of the child described – 'à douze ans il retroussera les jupes de sa nourrice' – recalls the boy in Baudelaire's prose poem 'Les Vocations' who has discovered the softness of his nurse's skin and the perfume of her hair (i, 333), and offers obvious parallels not only with the reference in 'Fusées' to his own 'goût précoce des femmes' (i, 661) but also with the note in his plans for novels and short stories: 'tout jeune, les jupons, la soie, les parfums, les genoux des femmes' (i, 594). There are further echoes of Gautier's *Mademoiselle de Maupin* in the important eleventh chapter of which d'Albert confides: 'par une espèce de réaction in-stinctive, je me suis toujours désespérément cramponné à la matière, à la silhouette extérieure des choses, et j'ai donné dans l'art une très grande place à la plastique. – Je comprends parfaitement une statue, je ne comprends pas un homme.'[109] The materialism, the importance placed on the plastic arts, the escapist tendencies, the failure to add intellectual exploration to emotional response, all these are points made by both authors and in each case condemnation is finely balanced by temptation. Further, just as Baudelaire stresses the importance of the *juste* and the *vrai*, which are submerged by 'la passion féroce du beau', Gautier debates the role of truth, with d'Albert insisting that 'il faut laisser le champ tout à fait libre à l'auteur et que la fantaisie doit régner en souveraine'.[110]

The concatenation of personal references, the breathless intensity and the forceful expressions, suggest very strongly that this passage is less a part of his argument than a moment of merciless self-investigation, an attempt to understand the initial causes of his own later charac-teristics. Once again, moreover, the image of nature vindicating herself – 'il a banni la raison de son cœur, et, par un juste châtiment, la raison refuse de rentrer en lui' (ii, 48) – implies a belief in universal harmony, a total set of laws whose logic man's intelligence should be capable of penetrating. And once again, as so often, Baudelaire gives a physical form to abstract concepts, picturing Nature sending 'la douleur' and 'la misère' as instruments in her war against 'ces rebelles'.

In his final paragraphs, Baudelaire returns to 'l'école païenne', illustrating the inhumanity of their vision of art and life by two anec-dotes which, however serious their implications, serve to lighten the tone. The first, concerning an artist who keeps a false coin in order to give it to a beggar, reappears in *Le Spleen de Paris* as 'La Fausse Monnaie'. The second, which depicts artists refusing to give money to beggars who are not aesthetically clad, is not only similar in tone to 'Les Yeux des pauvres', but also recalls a poem by Desbordes-Valmore[111] and a passage in *Mademoiselle de Maupin*: 'je donne plus volontiers aux mendiants dont les haillons et la maigreur sont pittoresques'.[112]

Finally, Baudelaire calls on art 'marcher fraternellement entre la science et la philosophie', to use all available 'moyens de perfectionnement' in order to 'retremper ses forces dans une atmosphère meilleure' (II, 49). In making this demand, Baudelaire is taking up once again ideas proposed in the *Salon de 1846* with its call for modernity and the creation of a new form of beauty.

It is the intensity of Baudelaire's expressions which makes this brief article so arresting: the reader is constantly made uneasily aware that behind the pirouettes and the pyrotechnics the analysis is of vital importance. The words he chooses are often devastatingly forceful: 'congédier la passion et la raison, c'est tuer la littérature [. . .], c'est se suicider' (II, 47), 'c'est créer de grandes chances de perdition' (II, 47). 'La plastique' – the very word gives him gooseflesh (cf. II, 130) – has 'empoisonné' the child whose senses have been inflamed by art (II, 48), and a frenetic love of art is 'un chancre qui dévore le reste'. It is not only the extreme physicality of the term 'chancre' which shocks the imagination, but its unexpected juxtaposition with the love of art, the material and the intellectual clamped irrevocably together. The 'effrayant rappel à l'ordre' which alone offers hope underlines the need for an explosive event to destroy the satanic dependence, just as in the Dupont preface Baudelaire stresses the importance of a 'fécondante discipline' which drives the 'pauvre et généreuse nature' 'fai[re] son explosion' (II, 29).

However arresting it may be, the article is not an easy one for a present-day reader to understand. Several of the allusions are obscure and the intensity of the arguments sometimes makes them less convincing than those expressed in a more matter-of-fact tone. Nevertheless, the fact that the neo-pagans' derogatory remarks about Christianity and their 'immensité d'orgueil et d'égoïsme' (II, 49) seem to have aroused such irritation in him is important for the comprehension of his psychological development, particularly since the growth of *orgueil* and *égoïsme* is the central temptation in *Les Fleurs du mal* and *Les Paradis artificiels*. In addition, it is noticeable that the temptation exerted over him by external, unanalysed beauty appears all the more powerful because of the force of his attack on it. Above all, this vigorous, amusing, yet profoundly serious review underlines Baudelaire's conviction that childhood greatly influences the artist's adult creation, his desire to forge a new form of literature, which would benefit from all that was best in the modern world, and, finally, the necessity for the artist not to let his emotional response swamp his intellectual understanding.

2

❧ *The Life and Works of Edgar Allan Poe*

Thus far, it has been possible to study Baudelaire's reviews in chronological order: in turning to the many notes and articles on Edgar Allan Poe, however, it will be necessary both to go back to 1848 and to move forward almost to the end of Baudelaire's life. Nevertheless, although they reveal changing centres of interest, these commentaries offer sufficient homogeneity to allow them to be considered as a whole.

The evidence points to the year 1847 as the date when Baudelaire first read Poe. Much later he described this first encounter as producing a 'commotion singulière' (*C*1, 676) which drove him to seek out Americans in Paris in the hope of borrowing Poe's complete works and gleaning information about his life and personality.[1] 'Et alors', he confided to Fraisse, 'je trouvai [. . .] des poèmes et des nouvelles dont j'avais eu la pensée, mais vague et confuse, mal ordonnée, et que Poe avait su combiner et mener à la perfection' (*C*1, 676). Nevertheless, Baudelaire's correspondence suggests that the realization of affinities between himself and Poe was less instantaneous than the letter to Fraisse implies. The first substantial reference to Poe does not occur until 1852, when Baudelaire wrote to his mother: 'j'ai trouvé un auteur américain qui a excité en moi une incroyable sympathie' (*C*1, 191). It was not until 1854 that he specifically mentioned 'la ressemblance intime, quoique non positivement accentuée, entre mes poésies propres et celles de cet homme, déduction faite du tempérament et du climat' (*C*1, 269). Later he came to the bitter realization that where he perceived an affinity, inimical critics saw a plagiarized source. By February 1865, he was writing: 'j'ai consacré beaucoup de temps à Edgar Poe, parce qu'il me ressemble un peu' (*C*11, 461), and, three days later, he complained: 'j'ai perdu beaucoup de temps à traduire Edgar Poe, et le grand bénéfice que j'en ai tiré, c'est que quelques bonnes langues ont dit que j'avais emprunté à Poe *mes* poésies, lesquelles étaient faites dix ans avant que je connusse les œuvres de ce dernier' (*C*11, 466–7).

The articles follow a similar pattern, with the introduction to 'Révélation magnétique' in 1848 being brief and rather tentative despite its insights, the study written in 1852 based very closely on the available

American sources, a handful of translator's notes between 1852 and 1856 picking out points of resemblance between himself and Poe, and the 1856 preface representing a climax, its forceful exposition and cogent expressions thrusting similarities into the foreground. By 1857 Baudelaire seems disillusioned with the possibility of establishing Poe's reputation in France: his article paraphrases or translates Poe's aesthetic writings as much as it analyses and debates them, and it alienates the public by violently attacking society with apparently uncontrolled anger. Later references speak of Poe as 'le maître de l'horrible' (1, 428), one of the stars in Romanticism's sombre heaven, indubitably a genius, but no longer quite so akin to Baudelaire himself.

It was in July 1848 that the Republican paper, *La Liberté de penser*, which included in its staff Marie d'Agoult, Renan, Michelet and Baudelaire's schoolmate Emile Deschanel, published Baudelaire's first translation of Poe, 'Révélation magnétique'. The choice of this discursive and rather dull narrative has been criticized (11, 1204–5), but W. T. Bandy reminds us of Baudelaire's long-standing enthusiasm for Mesmerism,[2] and it seems to me that some influence may have been exerted by the editorial staff of the paper, which is sub-titled 'revue philosophique et littéraire'.

The introductory note to 'Révélation magnétique', in which Baudelaire returns to problems discussed in his earlier reviews, has received short shrift from Baudelaireans. Margaret Gilman asserts that 'Poe is hardly mentioned; Baudelaire is hard away on his novelists', and Patrick Quinn, who emphasizes that Poe is presented as an 'illuminist', considers Baudelaire's strategy 'based chiefly on an association of Poe with other more familiar names'.[3] Nevertheless, this brief introduction strikes me as at once broader and more central than these remarks imply.

Firstly, in defining Poe's talent by comparison and contrast, Baudelaire is not only continuing a practice adopted in earlier reviews, but exploiting a traditional device whose popularity continues. Indeed, the technique was so well established that certain names, titles and quotations become so familiar as to leap, almost unbidden, from the critic's pen. A case in point is Hoffmann, whom Baudelaire mentions in his 'Présentation', and who is surely one of those in whom he discerns 'la préoccupation d'un perpétuel surnaturalisme' (11, 248). Hoffmann's exploration of the fantastic, whose roots, plunged in 'les plus lointaines impressions de l'enfance' (11, 248), Baudelaire detected and Freud examined, was considered by many French critics as having blazed a trail for Poe. Both Philarète Chasles and Emile Deschanel were to speak of the 'Hoffmann américain', and Edouard Thierry developed the comparison by claiming that whereas 'les visions d'Hoffmann ne lui appartiennent pas, c'est lui qui leur appartient', Poe remains 'le maître et l'impresario de ses sombres acteurs'.[4] The other novelists mentioned in the 'Présentation' are rarely included in contemporary studies of Poe and reflect more closely Baudelaire's eclectic reading.

Two further points should be made in considering the charge that Baudelaire refers to the other novelists merely in order to project on Poe the glory of more familiar names. On the one hand, two of those names could hardly have been expected to project much favourable light at all. At the time, Jean-Paul was not well known[5] and Laclos, if mentioned at all, was cited as an example of a particularly perverse form of literature. Given his projected study of Laclos, it is especially interesting to find Baudelaire mentioning him so early and to see how eager he is to rehabilitate the novelist as a writer and thinker worthy of high regard.[6] On the other hand, the two main propositions debated here have been central to Baudelaire's criticism and reflect a desire for comprehension all the more urgent since he hoped that the year 1848 would enable him to turn his hand to 'la création d'œuvres d'imagination pure, – le Roman' (*C*I, 145). In this article he isolates the basic requirements for a novelist before discussing what directions are available once this base is firmly established.

Baudelaire considers essential to any type of novelist a personal method deeply rooted in the individual *tempérament* (II, 247). The idea is a familiar one, appearing as early as the Chennevières review (II, 3) and the *Salon de 1845* (II, 382). The 1846 *Salon* delves more deeply into the idea: indeed, David Kelley considers *tempérament* one of the *Salon*'s key words.[7] Baudelaire uses the word far less frequently after 1848, although a letter written in May 1865 reveals that it still carries much weight: he writes that Manet will never overcome 'les lacunes de son tempérament' adding: 'mais il a *un tempérament*, c'est l'important' (*C*II, 501). The term replacing it in the later criticism is *sui generis*: Baudelaire, groping towards a clearer and more satisfactory description of the essence of a writer's work, may have seized on this expression when reading J. M. Daniel's review of Poe: 'the few things that this author has written which are at all tolerable, are coins stamped with the indubitable die. They are of themselves – *sui generis* – unlike any diagrams in Time's Kalaidescope [sic], – and gleam with the diamond hues of eternity.'[8]

Baudelaire asserts that once a novelist has established a method based on his own temperament two vast fields are open to him: on the one hand, he can delve into the mysteries of the world man inhabits, seeking out 'le ressort' which commands the human psyche (11, 248: cf. 11, 587); on the other, he can explore the possibilities of other worlds and imagine different forms of existence. Both demand the 'esprit primitif de *chercherie*' which denotes the 'romanciers *curieux*' (11, 248). Without this 'manie philosophique' they would succumb to the mimetic reproduction of unexamined details. According to Baudelaire, Poe, like Balzac, combines these two approaches, seeking a unifying thread and revealing his 'rêve caressé' of a 'système unitaire et définitif'. Once again, therefore, Baudelaire insists that natural laws do exist and may be discovered not only by 'les têtes savantes' but also by 'la tête des poètes'.[9]

Surely this is a fruitful approach to Poe, who is brought to life for contemporary French readers by the references to writers they knew. While it is not always easy to follow the line of argument, the article does not digress from its subject, nor are the other novelists mentioned irrelevant to the discussion. It emphasizes Poe as novelist and thinker, to which dual role Baudelaire is soon to add those of poet and critic, and it serves as a provocative guide to anyone reading 'Révélation magnétique' for the first time.

As W. T. Bandy has discovered, the study entitled 'Edgar Allan Poe, sa vie et ses ouvrages', published in the *Revue de Paris* in March and April 1852, is based on two articles which first appeared in the *Southern Literary Messenger*.[10] Because this pillaging of John M. Daniel and John R. Thompson has led to accusations of plagiarism[11] four points should be strongly stressed. Firstly, such borrowing was not only rife among Baudelaire's contemporaries but was considered with none of the opprobrium it might encounter today. Stendhal, of course, is a case in point,[12] and Jean Richer's collection *Nerval par les témoins de sa vie* shows how widespread the practice was. Secondly, unlike many contemporaries in similar circumstances, Baudelaire makes it quite clear that he is drawing on American sources. He frequently alludes to the articles, and if the critics' names are not mentioned this is surely because they would mean nothing to French readers. Thirdly, many French critics reviewing *Histoires extraordinaires* drew substantially and unashamedly on Baudelaire's preface.[13] Finally, as Claude Richard has revealed, Daniel's article itself plagiarizes Griswold's obituary notice.[14] Surely this amusing discovery will at last silence the anachronistic condemnations of immoral plagiarism! What could more justly be seen as unfair in Baudelaire's use of his sources is that he sometimes attributes to them, with little cause, the beliefs and attitudes he most despises in the American approach to life and art.

Both Bandy and Richard pinpoint most of what Baudelaire added, altered or omitted in adapting the American reviews. Nevertheless, a brief classification of these changes may clarify Baudelaire's pre-occupations and techniques as a literary critic.

Several additions have an obvious structural purpose. He begins and ends the article by raising the question of preordained fate, thus carefully selecting the light in which the reader is led to judge Poe and his achievements. Moreover, he is careful to explain why certain aspects of Poe's life and work demand detailed analysis, justifying, for example, Daniel's discussion of Poe's physical features (II, 267) and the long translation from 'William Wilson' (II, 257–8).

Secondly, as in his preface to 'Révélation magnétique', he has clearly attempted to make Poe more comprehensible to his audience through comparisons with French authors. Balzac's recent death, for example, provides a parallel with Poe's struggle against misfortune (II, 268) and there is a sly allusion, in the following contrast, to the numerous caricatures in which Hugo is given an exorbitantly bulging forehead: 'non qu'il rappelât les proportions ridicules qu'inventent les mauvais artistes, quand, pour flatter le génie, ils le transforment en hydro-céphale' (II, 268).

Clearly, he is already well aware of the 'valeur de circonstance' that he was later to mock Crépet for ignoring (*C*II, 46). Among the most valuable of Baudelaire's additions to his sources are the analyses of facts, in which he tries to determine underlying causes or elaborates on suggestions put forward by the American studies. Not content to follow Daniel in merely quoting from 'William Wilson' he inserts a paragraph of sharply detailed examination, where enthusiasm for Poe and a desire to arouse a like response in his reader combine with dark memories of hated school days and interpretations of childhood experiences in the light of later developments. Furthermore, he suggests an exceptionally interesting interpretation of William Wilson's double, the 'compagne inséparable' of his life, presenting him as a personification of 'la douleur' (II, 258). Although many of the comments on childhood are a direct translation of his sources,[15] the way in which he has meditated on his subject, and the extent to which he subscribes to those beliefs, are not only evident but, in a contemporary context, surprising. Thus, he introduces his comments on childhood – a rare subject at the time – as a matter of course and is clearly seeking something much more profound than anecdote when he writes: 'si tous les hommes qui ont occupé la scène du monde avaient noté leurs impressions d'enfance, quel excellent dictionnaire psychologique nous posséderions!' (II, 253). Moreover, where Daniel simply records Poe's physical prowess in his youth,[16] Baudelaire claims that even this should be considered in the context of his general approach to life: 'cela', he remarks, 'rentrait en peu dans son talent: calculs et problèmes' (II, 268). As in the Dupont preface, therefore, he perceives a logical link between physical and moral phenomena. And, in a passage revealing Baudelaire's fascination with science and the emphasis he places on will power, he asserts that 'l'air est raréfié dans cette littérature comme dans un laboratoire. On y contemple sans cesse la glorification de la volonté s'appliquant à l'induction et à l'analyse.' The way in which he highlights Poe's love of 'l'explication rationnelle' (II, 283) suggests yet another affinity with his own search for initial causes. The importance he gives, both here and in the earlier 'Présentation', to the *calculs et problèmes* side of Poe's tales, rather than to the macabre, largely determined the way in which they were appreciated by the general public. In addition, the expression shows Baudelaire pursuing his earlier interest in things as they might be: he is evidently searching for a suitable term, trying *chercherie* in the 'Présentation' and here introducing the rather clumsy neologism *conjecturisme* and a word borrowed from casuistry but given a new meaning, *probabilisme*.[17]

Three tales are chosen to illustrate Poe's exploration of *probabilisme*: 'The Gold Bug', 'A Descent into the Maelström' and 'The Murders in the rue Morgue'. The first of these enables Baudelaire to linger on the description of a wonderfully rich and copious treasure and to suggest, fleetingly, a striking contrast between Poe's technique and his own: '*ce n'était point un rêve*, comme il arrive généralement dans tous ces romans, où l'auteur vous réveille brutalement après avoir excité votre esprit par des espérances apéritives' (II, 275). Once again, he clamps together the metaphysical ('espérances') with the physical ('apéritives'). It is the latter method of course that Baudelaire himself adopts in 'La Chambre double' and 'Rêve parisien', where a vision of deep happiness or great beauty is brought to an abrupt and brutal end. What seems to have seized his attention in Poe's tale is the fusion of the natural and the supernatural, the contrast between the scientifically accurate search and the dreamlike abundance of the treasure.

'A Descent into the Maelström' had been discussed by E. D. Forgues in an article published in 1846, and Baudelaire's brief comment may well have been provoked by one of Forgue's statements:

> nous n'affirmerons pas que la vraisemblance vulgaire soit ici tout-à-fait respectée, ni qu'une théorie de la pesanteur ait jamais pu être improvisée par un grossier paysan dans une situation qui semble exclure tout exercice des facultés mentales [. . .]; mais [. . .] on peut admettre que l'extrême péril développe chez un homme à qui la certitude de la mort a rendu tout son sang-froid, une lucidité particulière de l'intellect.[18]

Baudelaire seems inclined to agree with Forgues, asking rather tentatively: 'ne pourrait-on pas descendre dans un gouffre dont on n'a pas encore trouvé le fond, en étudiant d'une manière nouvelle les lois de la pesanteur?' (11, 276).

'The Murders in the rue Morgue' is another tale upholding the supremacy of the intellect. Baudelaire points out that through his intelligence Dupin is able 'surprendre la loi de la génération des idées' (11, 276), a phrase recalling both his reference in the 'Présentation' to the existence of logical laws governing nature, and the 1848 review of Champfleury, in which Balzac is portrayed as 'un naturaliste qui connait également la loi de génération des idées et des êtres visibles' (11, 22). Clearly, then, Baudelaire perceives close affinities between Balzac and Poe: one might almost say that they are beginning to amalgamate to form a paradigm of the ideal novelist, one who reveals and explores initial causes and the laws governing logical development.

By *conjecturisme* Baudelaire seems to mean, on the one hand, that meditation on metaphysical questions which produces such tales as 'Mesmeric Revelation' or 'The Conversation of Eiros and Charmion', and, on the other hand, the exploitation of the fantastic, 'à la manière d'Hoffmann' (11, 277). Once again, Baudelaire forges a link between Poe and Hoffmann, briefly discussing the tale, 'The Man of the Crowd', which, as several critics have pointed out, has much in common with Hoffmann's 'Des Vetters Eckfenster' and with Baudelaire's own prose poem, 'Les Foules'.[19] Poe's tale, moreover, so fascinated Baudelaire that he returned to it in 'Le Peintre de la vie moderne', where he altered the emphasis, no longer highlighting the strange individual followed throughout the night from one centre of human activity to another, but focusing instead on the curiosity experienced by the narrator himself, this curiosity being seen, significantly, as the spur to creative activity (11, 689–90).

The analysis of 'The Black Cat' is striking above all for exemplifying the movement that so often takes place in Baudelaire between literary criticism and self-investigation. It reveals how imperceptibly the seeds of the future are sown: the 'manière douce et innocente' which marks the beginning of the hero's married life is gradually corrupted both by economic failure and by elements of his own character. Expressions such as 'les dangers de l'eau-de-vie et du genièvre' and 'l'habitude du poison' (11, 277) do not merely stem from the impersonal interest of a critic but well up from an imperious creative need – 'Du Vin et du hachisch' dates from this same year – and echo the bitterness of personal experience: 'que la vie sombre de la taverne, que les heures silencieuses de l'ivresse morne sont bien décrites!' (11, 277). 'Sombre', 'silencieuses', 'morne': these epithets with their mournful nasals and the sinister hissing of their sibilants are Baudelaire's, not Poe's and nowhere in the narrative does Poe make more than a fleeting reference to tavern life. It is significant, too, that Baudelaire has chosen to insert the entire passage in which Poe analyses 'l'esprit de PERVERSITE' (II, 278), an analysis clearly very close not merely to Baudelaire's art but to his own personality. And the intensity with which his mind transforms the written word into images that sear themselves on the brain is revealed by the abrupt, tense, unforgettable closing sentence of this sequence, a sentence which once again owes little to Poe: 'un cri profond, lointain, plaintif se fait entendre; l'homme s'évanouit; la justice s'arrête, abat le mur, le cadavre tombe en avant, et un chat effrayant, moitié poil, moitié plâtre, s'élance avec son œil unique, sanglant et fou' (II, 279).

Apart from *conjecturisme* and *probabilisme*, a third type of tale explores 'les maladies de l'esprit' (II, 279), a type illustrated by 'Berenice', of which Baudelaire published a translation in 1852. His summary of the tale is extremely detailed, suggesting that he was working on his translation at the same time as he prepared his article, but also reflecting his own curiosity about mental disorders. This curiosity reappears, of course, in such prose poems as 'Mademoiselle Bistouri', 'La Corde' and 'Le Crépuscule du soir' (I, 311). What fascinates him here, as in the prose poems, is the way in which it is something very trivial, 'invariablement puéril' (II, 280) which takes on such exaggerated, hypnotic significance. He is careful to insist that the tale is not merely a flight of black fantasy, affirming that, on the contrary, 'rien n'est plus logique et possible que cette affreuse histoire' (II, 280); once again, the emphasis is on the logical and the possible.

A few dense, taut paragraphs, inspired in part by Daniel's review but containing much that is original, define the style and atmosphere that make Poe's tales so distinctive.[20] Like his sources, he stresses the sparseness of the tales, the suppression of all that is not central, and particularly the vagueness of the background, but, unlike his sources, he seeks out the reasons dictating Poe's technique. He concludes that 'grâce à cette sobriété cruelle, l'idée génératrice se fait mieux voir' (II, 282).

In turning to the mode of narration and to Poe's passion for the horrible, Baudelaire's article shows signs of haste, repeating the rather clumsy formula 'quant à' (II, 282). Significantly, a letter to his mother, written while he was working on the study, complains that his time is devoured by the 'confection d'articles maladifs faits à la hâte pour gagner quelque argent' (*C*I, 190): the allusion is probably to 'Les

Drames et les romans honnêtes' and 'L'Ecole païenne'. Nevertheless, this section does include a startling, pre-Freudian, passage in which Baudelaire suggests a close link between a writer's interest in the horrible and his sublimated passion, repressed sensitivity or accumulated energy for which there is no other outlet.[21] Moreover, there is a veiled and fleeting criticism of the lack of variety in Poe's narratives: his 'méthode de narration' is described as 'simple', based 'presque toujours' on a first person narrative, and very often exploring 'l'horrible' (II, 282).

According to Baudelaire, Poe stands out against his contemporaries by opposing to their fatuous, idolatrous preoccupation with earthly love an 'infatigable ardeur vers l'idéal' (II, 283). The word *ardeur* and its derivative *ardemment* appear three times in this brief section, underlining Baudelaire's desire to emphasize Poe's unique intensity. The link between Poe and Balzac as philosopher-novelists seeking their ideal of unity, eager to discover a harmonizing principle governing the physical as well as the intellectual world, a link discussed in the 1848 'Présentation', is expressed even more forcibly here, elucidating Baudelaire's claim in 'L'Ecole païenne' that 'le temps n'est pas loin où l'on comprendra que toute littérature qui se refuse à marcher fraternellement entre la science et la philosophie est une littérature homicide et suicide' (II, 49). There is a further parallel between these passages and Baudelaire's assertion to Poulet-Malassis, in a letter dated 20 March 1852, that he will henceforth pursue 'le rêve supérieur de l'application de la métaphysique au roman' (*C*I, 189).

As a counterbalance to such tales of induction and analysis, with their rarefied atmosphere and unearthly characters,[22] Baudelaire translates the lengthy passage from *The Narrative of Arthur Gordon Pym of Nantucket* which is quoted in Daniel's review. His rather inapt description of the novel as 'purement humain' seems to me to be based on a misunderstanding or perhaps a rejection of Daniel's comment, a point not noted in Bandy's edition. Daniel had written: 'he was entirely incapable of producing a novel presenting human life and character in any of its ordinary phases; but his chief fictitious work, the "Narrative of Arthur Gordon Pym" has been unjustly disparaged and neglected'.[23]

As Bandy points out, Baudelaire had not yet read 'Eurêka' and his evaluation of it is very dependent on Daniel's interpretation. He was not content, however, merely to reproduce Daniel's judgements. Daniel, for example, contends that 'Eurêka' is an attempt to discover the process which brought the world into being and which 'must evidently reduce all things to the vague, imperceptible, immaterial chaos of pure matter or spirit from which it arose'.[24] Baudelaire has obviously compared Daniel's résumé with the works of Poe to which he did have access for he points out that a pantheistic view of the world would contradict those tales – he is probably thinking of 'Morella' and 'The Colloquy of Monos and Una' – which imply a 'hiérarchie des êtres' and the 'permanence des personnalités' (II, 287). However dependent on his sources he may have been, he cannot be accused of accepting them uncritically.

Baudelaire gives his article a flavour distinctly his own by bringing to the fore three points, in addition to the search for unity, which are of special interest to him: the problems posed by Poe's addiction to alcohol, the question of destiny, and the theme of maternal love.

The pressure of fate, to which Baudelaire gives the less elegant term *guignon*, poses a problem which recurs throughout Baudelaire's creative and critical writing and which is frequently debated in contemporary literature: Borel's *Madame Putiphar*, the prefatory poem to Barbier's *Il Pianto*, and above all Gautier's poem 'Ténèbres' hover in the background of the review's opening paragraph.[25] Even here, despite the restrictions imposed by close adherence to the American critics, he has been able to introduce the perplexing questions of social progress as opposed to individual misfortune, to contrast predestination with personal responsibility and to set the problem of fate against that of obsessive self-destruction.

Society's role is mercilessly pilloried, in terms reminiscent of 'Bénédiction', and Baudelaire suggests, fleetingly, that Poe's alcoholism, so violently castigated by the Americans, is a means of escape rendered necessary by their very persecution. A second twist to the screw is given when Baudelaire shows that 'malgré son masque bienveillant de liberté' Democracy seems at times to crush the individual, while 'la toute-puissance de l'industrie' (II, 252), striding forward with such apparent progress, allows no compassion towards those who cannot bear its yoke.

Predestined misfortune as opposed to personal responsibility is mentioned twice. In an image which recalls the poem 'Le Rebelle', Baudelaire pictures 'l'Ange aveugle de l'expiation' seizing certain men and beating them 'à tour de bras pour l'édification des autres' (II, 249). Several of Baudelaire's contemporaries also used this image of the spirit of destiny and vengeance armed with a whip: Leconte de Lisle concluded his sonnet, 'Les Planètes damnées' with the following lines:

Mais toi, que le Destin flagelle à tour de bras,
Jamais, jamais, jamais tu ne t'endormiras
O troupeau haletant des mondes lamentables![26]

and Asselineau's review of *Les Fleurs du mal* asks: 'pourquoi ce fouet sanglant, que l'auteur des *Iambes*, le dernier, a manié avec tant de vigueur et de franchise, ne viendrait-il pas nous rappeler que le poète n'est pas nécessairement un douceâtre et un thuriféraire?' (I, 1205). Later, Delacroix was to give plastic form to the allegory in one of the murals he painted for Saint-Sulpice (see II, 731). The fleshing out of such metaphysical concepts by concrete imagery is a device Baudelaire often employs: one might compare 'Les Dons des fées', 'Les Bienfaits de la lune' and 'Laquelle est la vraie?' as well as the personification of *Ennui* in 'Au Lecteur'.

Predestination can also be considered on a less remote level, that of the formation in early childhood of immutable habits which shape the life of the adult: in an important addition to Daniel's review Baudelaire states that 'le caractère, le génie, le style d'un homme est formé par les circonstances en apparence vulgaires de sa première jeunesse' (II, 253), an assertion similar to that in the Dupont preface: 'la jeunesse de tous les hommes destinés à devenir célèbres [. . .] explique l'âge suivant' (II, 28–9), and to the exploration in 'L'Ecole païenne' of the fate awaiting a child whose senses have been constantly inflamed by plastic beauty.

The theme of the *guignon* and that of Poe's alcoholism intertwine in the third aspect of fate to which Baudelaire refers in this article. Once again, as in 'L'Ecole païenne', Baudelaire struggles to discover how such characteristics develop and whether they can be explained logically. Has some 'Providence diabolique' – the antithesis is distinctively Baudelairean – deliberately driven Poe to seek relief in alcohol by placing him in such uncongenial surroundings? Or is this tendency part of an obsessive urge towards self-destruction? A third cause is also possible: Poe may have considered alcohol as an artistic stimulant. It is this solution which, adumbrated here (II, 271–2), swells into the vital 'art mnémonique' passage of the 1856 preface.

In sharp contrast to the dark power of fatality, Baudelaire evokes the guiding light of maternal love. The highly personal nature of this section (II, 266–7) has been recognized by several critics (see II, 1207), who also quote a letter to his mother in which Baudelaire, referring to the article, mentions 'quelques lignes d'une très extraordinaire sur-excitation' (CI, 191). A mother's affection and her faith in her son's genius can, according to Baudelaire, overcome fatality by restoring his reputation in the eyes of posterity. Addressing Maria Clemm, Baudelaire writes ecstatically: 'ton image quasi divine voltigera incessamment au-dessus du martyrologe de la littérature' (II, 267). Not only the central image, but also the religious terminology, recall very strongly the poem 'L'Aube spirituelle', thought to have been sent to Madame Sabatier in 1853:

Forme divine, Etre lucide et pur,

Sur les débris fumeux des stupides orgies
Ton souvenir plus clair, plus rose et plus charmant,
Pour mes yeux agrandis voltige incessamment (*CI*, 224).

The study closes with a meditation which, as so often, takes the form of a prose poem incorporated within the criticism. Poe's fate – or at least Baudelaire's conception of it – has inspired a more general question, a question underlying the studies on intoxicants: 'quelle est donc cette loi fatale qui nous enchaîne, nous domine, et se venge de la violation de son insupportable despotisme par la dégradation et l'amoindrissement de notre être moral?' (11, 287–8). As in 'Les Drames et les romans honnêtes' and even more in 'L'Ecole païenne' Baudelaire insists with angry incomprehension that all excess brings its own penalty. Nevertheless, from such excess, he insists, springs a literature far more moving than that of a Goethe or a Walter Scott, each so 'calme et *vertueux*'. Once again, virtue is rejected as an adequate criterion for assessing art. Moreover, the language Baudelaire uses here is highly personal, with the frustration of the longing for the infinite momentarily assuaged by the 'affreux soulagement' of 'le vin de la débauche' (11, 288); it is also drawn very much from the vocabulary of orthodox Catholic dogma, with its references to the catechism, to the reversibility of suffering, and to the intercession of saints. The language of all the reviews published in 1851 and 1852 suggests strongly that for Baudelaire this was a time of intense spiritual questioning.

However dependent on his sources Baudelaire may have been, therefore, he has not allowed them to restrict his exploration or determine his interpretations. Above all, the article is remarkable for its enthusiasm and for Baudelaire's eager desire to kindle in his reader a similar emotion.

In various translator's notes published over the next three years Baudelaire reasserts or subtly reworks the main points raised in his 1852 article. The introduction to 'Bérénice', for example, is a concentrated résumé of the earlier study, eulogizing again the devotion of Mrs Clemm and highlighting Poe's 'redoutable destinée' (11, 289) through the familiar analogy with Balzac and Hoffmann. Once again, society is accused of persecution. Nevertheless, far more importance is given to the belief that Poe chooses those subjects which are '*seuls dignes de l'attention d'un homme spirituel*', the emphasis lying as before on Poe's fascination with *calculs et problèmes*. This is an element that many contemporaries threw into sharp relief. In 1846 E. D. Forgues had described Poe as a 'pourchasseur de vérités abstraites, amoureux des plus excentriques hypothèses, des calculs les plus ardus'.[27] Other critics seem to take their lead from Baudelaire, L. Cartier speaking of Poe's 'lucidité de *Visionnaire*' and E. Thierry claiming that 'c'est l'algèbre dans la fantaisie, l'invention scientifique combinée avec l'intention littéraire'.[28] Finally, L. Etienne, whose review owes much to Baudelaire, speaks of 'l'invasion de l'esprit mathématique dans le roman et dans la poésie'.[29]

This brief introduction is interesting, too, in that it shows Baudelaire twisting the conventional use of the word *utilité*, a technique he exploits in several of his later studies. Here he insists that: 'c'est l'idée opiniâtre d'utilité, ou plutôt une curiosité enragée, qui distingue M. Poe de tous les romantiques du continent, ou, si vous l'aimez mieux, de tous les sectaires de l'école dite romantique' (ii, 289). The stress placed on Poe's curiosity, moreover, echoes and intensifies the earlier reference to his 'esprit primitif de *chercherie*' (ii, 248).

The year 1852 saw another of Baudelaire's commentaries on Poe in the form of an introductory note to 'La Philosophie de l'ameublement'. The opening paragraph of this brief introduction forms an evocative prose poem based on the pleasure inherent in conjuring up an 'appartement modèle, un domicile idéal, un *rêvoir*' (ii, 290). Not only do Baudelaire's own 'Rêve parisien' and 'La Chambre double' remodel the poet's surroundings in much the same way as 'La Philosophie de l'ameublement', but Poe's blend of prose poem and criticism is further exploited in some of Baudelaire's later reviews.

The other face of Poe's article, the sneering mockery of American taste, is quickly revealed by his translator, eager to launch a further attack on the New World. 'Impartial ou non', he explains, 'cet article nous a paru une bonne curiosité, et il divertira nos lecteurs' (ii, 291). Despite a certain *engouement* for American aims and ideals, contemporary writing shows a degree of amusement and, at times, a more violent attitude towards the Americans. Alfred Assollant was only one of several writers who poked rather envious fun at 'ce pays de loups et de chasseurs de dollars'.[30] Baudelaire, therefore, was probably correct in predicting that his contemporaries would find 'La Philosophie de l'ameublement' amusing, although he no doubt felt that Poe's strictures applied equally to Parisians.

In 1854 Baudelaire published a dedication to Maria Clemm, into which he weaves several threads which are to reappear, strengthened and embellished, in later studies. Firstly, as in previous notes, Poe is linked with other writers, their common quality being cosmopolitanism, by which Baudelaire means both their ability to respond to all forms of beauty, and the way in which their works appeal to readers of all nationalities. Secondly, Poe's tales are described as 'éblouissantes végétations', 'le produit d'une terre volcanisée' (11, 291). This image is more sharply etched in the 1856 introduction, where 'la galanterie' is described as 'cette fleur volcanique et musquée pour qui le cerveau bouillonnant des poètes est un terrain de prédilection' (11, 312). Finally, where the emphasis in the earlier studies had lain on his hatred of America, Baudelaire now explicitly broadens his attack to encompass not only the bourgeois-based 'Républiques marchandes' but also 'les Sociétés physiocratiques' (11, 292) which sought a return to an economy based on agriculture: Baudelaire's ideal society seems based on individual freedom and an aristocracy of the intelligent.

A commentary to the translation of 'The Unparalleled Adventures of one Hans Pfaal' appeared in April 1855. Although it is largely a summary of Poe's own note, Baudelaire has added several comments of his own. For the first time he abandons the tone of high seriousness usually adopted in discussing Poe: 'je permets au lecteur de sourire, – moi-même j'ai souri plus d'une fois en surprenant les *dadas* de mon auteur' (11, 295). More importantly, there is an indication that Baudelaire is less captivated than before by Poe's exploitation of science: 'il est réellement singulier de voir un cerveau, tantôt si profondément germanique et tantôt si sérieusement oriental, trahir à de certains moments l'américanisme dont il est saturé' (11, 295). The hoax in the story is based on a considerable knowledge of scientific theories concerning gravity. What seems to have aroused Baudelaire's attention in this tale, as in 'Mesmeric Revelation', is the attempt to fuse the fantastic and the scientific, to give to the fireworks of the imagination the aura of scientific verisimilitude. The last lines of this commentary are rich in suggestion and masterly in their controlled imagery and finely graduated shading: 'qui donc entre nous [. . .] aurait osé, a vingt-trois ans [. . .] enfourcher imperturbablement le *dada* ou plutôt l'hippogriffe ombrageux de la *verisimilitude*?' (11, 295). As with Banville, Baudelaire is amazed and slightly envious of such calm precociousness. Nevertheless, he reveals a degree of amusement in the long adverb 'imperturbablement' and the repeated, colloquial term '*dada*', and there is a hint of mockery – directed at the reader more than at Poe – in the expression 'hippogriffe ombrageux' which recalls 'Metzengerstein' and suggests not science but the free-moving imagination.

When, in 1856, Michel Lévy brothers published *Histoires extraordinaires*, Baudelaire radically revised his 1852 article, which he had originally intended to use as a preface. By that time, of course, he had not only become familiar with a much larger selection of Poe's works, but had also discovered additional biographical documents.[31] Moreover, the preceding year had seen the publication of three detailed and carefully wrought articles, Baudelaire's review of the Exposition universelle, his analysis of laughter, and his assessment of the actor Philibert Rouvière: the experience gained in preparing them, as well as the application of several ideas gleaned from Poe's own writings, combine with Baudelaire's additional knowledge to produce a far more forceful introduction.

Baudelaire's increased awareness of how best to highlight essential points is obvious from the opening passage of the study. Although his early reviews show that he was already considerably skilled in the *entrée en matière*, it is likely that he benefited from one of Poe's theoretical pronouncements:

> how many good books suffer neglect through the inefficiency of their beginnings! It is far better that we commence irregularly – immethodically, – than that we fail to arrest the attention; but the two points, method and pungency, may always be combined. At all risks, let there be a few vivid sentences *imprimis*, by way of the electric bell to the telegraph.[32]

'Method and pungency' could well serve to illustrate Baudelaire's own achievements as a literary critic.

Whereas the 1852 article opened with a statement supported by an anecdote, the preface reverses the anecdote and the conclusions drawn from it, so that the reader is first enticed by the unusual, concrete fact of the tattooed criminal, and then encouraged to see this as a metaphor of far wider implication.

A second structural alteration to the 1852 study also demonstrates a theory Baudelaire may have developed from Poe's writings: that everything in a tale or poem – and, by extension, a critical review (*C*1, 538) – must prepare the final impression so that the total effect is one of complete unity. In 'The Philosophy of Composition', Poe had written: 'it is only with the *dénouement* constantly in view that we can give a plot its indispensable air of consequence, or causation, by making the incidents, and especially the tone at all points, tend to the development of the intention'.[33] Where before Baudelaire had been obliged to follow his sources closely, by 1856 his additional knowledge and greater mastery of the medium enable him to present all his facts and analyses so that they build up inexorably to the final image of Poe as a heroic martyr dogged by fate, crushed by society, yet constantly striving to create beauty.

Stylistically, too, the preface is more impressive than the earlier review. Firstly, Baudelaire has obviously sought for conciseness. He removes, for example, most of the comparisons with other writers.

Such allusions may well have been among the most original sections of the 1852 article, but they were often little more than picturesque touches which diverted attention from the central figure: a case in point is the fleeting reference to Lesage (11, 260). Even sentences which have been lifted almost unchanged from the earlier review have been tautened, increasing their emotive power. Thus, the weakening clause 'on dirait que' is omitted from the suggestion that the blind angel of vengeance has seized those who are destined to suffer (11, 296). Secondly, he has increased the article's intensity by choosing quotations of greater force: the passage from Gautier's 'Ténèbres', for instance, has been exchanged for one which insists less on earthly treachery than on the impossibility of escaping preordained fate. In addition, sections such as Baudelaire's attack on America are pinned more firmly to the central discussion by being presented as Poe's own opinions (11, 299). And, finally, many of the earlier images have been revised to present essential arguments with the greatest possible power. Thus, the cry: 'bouchons toutes les issues, fermons la porte à double tour, calfeutrons les fenêtres' (11, 250) becomes the yet more forceful, almost panic-stricken: 'ces âmes de choix [. . .] perfectionneront la prudence, boucheront toutes les issues, matelasseront les fenêtres contre les projectiles du hasard' (11, 297). Many more examples could be chosen, but all Baudelaire's alterations share the desire to burn more deeply into the reader's memory the picture of a harassed and yet ultimately triumphant Poe.

The central arguments are similar to those made in the 1852 review or in the subsequent translator's notes: the saving power of maternal love, the crushing weight of destiny, the perennial conflict between the poet and society, the deeper problem of Poe's use of alcohol. The presentation of Poe's death as 'almost' a suicide was also adumbrated in the early discussion of the urge to self-destruction.

Maria Clemm, with her efforts to enhance Poe's reputation both as man and as artist, had already assumed the characteristics of the woman who, in *Les Fleurs du mal*, guides the poet 'dans la route du Beau' (1, 43). In the 1856 preface the analogy is strengthened by two arrestingly physical images. She is the 'soleil moral' of Poe's life (11, 309), a 'flambeau et foyer allumé par un rayon du plus haut ciel' (11, 308), just as Baudelaire says of 'l'Ange gardien, la Muse et la Madone' that 'son fantôme dans l'air danse comme un flambeau' (1, 43). The comparison suggests that Baudelaire is indeed making of Poe, as has often been suggested, a screen on to which he can project his own needs and desires.[34]

The role of destiny is again thrown into sharp relief. The idea that what we perceive as fate may be the result of inherited or acquired characteristics was tentatively proposed in the 1852 version (II, 262), with its allusion to Poe's 'mauvais démon né de son sang et de ses douleurs antécédentes': here, however, it is given greater weight and increased physicality when Baudelaire says of those who seem ill-starred that 'leur destinée est écrite dans toute leur constitution, elle brille d'un éclat sinistre dans leurs regards et dans leurs gestes, elle circule dans leurs artères avec chacun de leurs globules sanguins' (II, 297). The passage might almost serve as an epigraph to *Les Rougon-Macquart*. The extent to which the poet's life follows a predestined pattern is further underlined by the repetition of two words which are particularly suggestive in Baudelaire's vocabulary: 'irrémédiable' and 'irréparable' (II, 304, 308, 312). Nevertheless, where fate had served as the Ariadne's thread through the labyrinth of borrowings and originality of the 1852 review, by 1856 it is only one strand in a far more complex pattern.

This change of emphasis is seen, for example, in the attempts to solve the enigma posed by Poe's drunkenness. The search for historical precedents is abandoned. Instead, Baudelaire elaborates his earlier suggestion that Poe sought through drink to recapture 'les visions calmes ou effrayantes qui sont déjà ses vieilles connaissances' (II, 272). In a striking passage anticipating Proust, he declares that alcohol served as a stimulant to, or a relaxation after, Poe's artistic creation, becoming 'un moyen mnémonique', a means of rediscovering those 'enchaînements de rêves' and 'séries de raisonnements' which alcohol intensifies and of which a work of art is the distillation. Where Baudelaire's theory foreshadows the ideas of Proust is in his suggestion that the dreams induced by drink are analogous to

> ces impressions fugitives et frappantes, d'autant plus frappantes dans leurs retours qu'elles sont plus fugitives, qui suivent quelquefois un symptôme extérieur, une espèce d'avertissement comme un son de cloche, une note musicale, ou un parfum oublié, et qui sont elles-mêmes suivies d'un événement semblable à un événement déjà connu et qui occupait la même place dans une chaîne antérieurement révélée (II, 315).

Baudelaire's 'Poème du hachisch' examines similar attempts to rediscover lost visions, forgotten insights, half-remembered intimations of unity. To the best of my knowledge, however, none of Poe's works proposes such a method: it would seem, therefore, that Baudelaire's conclusions are based on personal experience or at least spring from his own meditations.

As in the earlier articles, it is the sudden profusion of tiny, realistic details and the physicality of the imagery that suggest that Baudelaire's criticism has suddenly become self-analysis.[35] That the passage debates problems on which Baudelaire has often meditated, both in order to find a personal solution and to explore their more general application to the creative mind, is suggested by the number of parallels with his other works, above all *Les Paradis artificiels*. Both there and in the preface Baudelaire examines the mentality of the man who has discovered, through stimulants, visions so splendid that to regain them he will risk even the subjugation of his own free-will.

More prosaically, he suggests, as he did in the earlier article, that alcohol offered Poe an escape from 'rancunes littéraires, vertiges de l'infini, douleurs de ménage, insultes de la misère' (ii, 314). The poet's inability to adapt to his society is thus portrayed even more starkly than before and the analogies with Baudelaire's own life are further emphasized. The tyranny exerted by democracy, now amusingly debased from a physiocracy to a zoocracy, is likened to that of 'l'idole de Jaggernaut [sic]' (ii, 298); an image almost certainly, I suggest, inspired by *Melmoth the Wanderer*.[36] The assertion that 'Poe et sa patrie n'étaient pas de niveau' (ii, 299) is reinforced by examples drawn from Poe's *Marginalia* and from 'Philosophie de l'ameublement'. Once again, however, the butt of Baudelaire's attack is as much France as America, since what Baudelaire considers contemporary follies, such as the rejection of the essential beliefs in Hell and original sin, provoke a bitter condemnation of journalists like Girardin, 'le philosophe du chiffre' (ii, 300), and 'la théologienne du sentiment' (ii, 300), George Sand. Once again Baudelaire has bracketed sharply contrasting ideas, philosophy and money, theology and sentiment: it is this unexpected pairing which gives his mockery its particularly biting edge.

The aesthetic blindness endemic to modern society stands in such opposition to a 'vision implacable du vrai' (ii, 300) and an 'amour insatiable du beau' that Baudelaire can only marvel that Poe could '*durer* aussi longtemps'. Here he may well have been influenced by Barbey d'Aurevilly's characteristically pungent exclamation:

> rien n'était plus hostile au génie natif d'Edgar Poe que sa société et sa race, et les modifications que devaient naturellement lui imprimer ces deux tortionnaires de son génie devaient être si profondes qu'on s'étonne qu'elles n'aient pas été de véritables destructions, – la mort même de ses facultés![37]

Baudelaire, however, goes further than Barbey: he claims that this torture not only withered Poe's artistic faculties but drove him to seek physical annihilation. The idea that Poe's death was indeed a conscious act of self-destruction is proposed only tentatively: 'cette mort est presque un suicide, – un suicide préparé depuis longtemps. Du moins, elle en causa le scandale' (II, 305). Baudelaire seems wary of formulating or following up this idea, seizing rather on the opportunity to set down his thoughts on suicide in general, a desire rendered more pressing and poignant by the recent anniversary of Nerval's death. It is significant that, whereas he pruned the digressions from his earlier article, this discussion, although only tenuously attached to Poe, has actually been added. As so often, Baudelaire's criticism has become the forum of a more wide-ranging debate.

Suicide was not just a theoretical problem: it appears in Baudelaire's thought as a personal temptation. Thus, the 1856 preface refers to the 'compagnie de fantômes déjà nombreuse, qui nous hante familièrement, et dont chaque membre vient nous vanter son repos actuel et nous verser ses persuasions' (II, 307). The impression that this is not just a figure of speech is strengthened by Baudelaire's confession to his mother: 'je vois toujours devant moi le suicide comme l'unique et surtout la plus facile solution de toutes les horribles complications dans lesquelles je suis condamné à vivre depuis tant, tant d'années' (CII, 201). Finally, the importance the question held for him is reflected by his fiery rejection of the critical response to his preface: 'je remarque, à propos de tous ces monstres de gratte-papier, démocrates, napoléoniens surtout, qu'aucun ne veut aborder franchement la question de la misère et du suicide' (CI, 346).

Just as the presentation of Poe's alcoholism, his reaction to society, and his death has been altered by Baudelaire's increased knowledge of Poe's beliefs, so his heightened awareness of Poe's style and technique affects the assessment of the tales and essays.

As in the 1852 review (II, 273), Baudelaire admires Poe's critical writing, but attaches less importance than formerly to the method, emphasizing rather the overall impression, the 'vivacité', 'netteté', 'sévérité' (II, 302) and above all 'cette lucidité qui est un de ses privilèges' (II, 305). This movement away from detailed description of Poe's critical style – a movement which contrasts sharply with the desire to analyse more precisely the poetry and the tales – perhaps shows Baudelaire somewhat uncomfortably aware that his own ideas about criticism are far removed from Poe's fiery, idiosyncratic swashbuckling, with its amusing but condescending and sometimes pedantic attention to style and grammar.

In 1852, according to Bandy, Baudelaire had known at most four of Poe's poems,[38] and his remarks about them certainly suggest that he was not yet capable of appreciating English prosody. Where his tendency had been to embellish Daniel's account, heightening praise and disregarding criticism, he damped down Daniel's verbal fireworks in praise of the poetry and condemned 'To Helen' as a pastiche (II, 259). Perhaps he felt it too dependent on Classical trappings, too far removed from his demands for poets to exploit 'le beau moderne'. His remarks on three more poems by Poe, 'The Bells', 'Ulalame' and 'Annabel Lee', are no more than platitudes (II, 274), while his commentary on 'The Raven' follows Daniel's very closely, adding, however, the evocative sentence comparing the student's thoughts to 'un fleuve de souvenirs qui se répand dans la nuit froide et désolée' (II, 274). Yet even in these brief allusions, he emphasizes once again the centrally important question of success and celebrity.

By 1856, Baudelaire had not only acquired Hannay's edition of the poems but was also more capable of appreciating them. His comments remain brief, but they are more just: 'pour qui sait sentir la poésie anglaise', he writes, the *caveat* revealing that he is now aware of the problem, they express 'l'accent extraterrestre, le calme dans la mélancolie, la solennité délicieuse, l'expérience précoce [. . .] qui caractérisent les grands poètes' (II, 302). His reading of the poems has caused him to alter his earlier assertion that Poe scorns the love of woman in favour of 'l'infatigable ardeur vers l'idéal' (II, 283). Now he insists that the poetry is saturated with 'la divine passion': nevertheless, he points out that the atmosphere of the love poems is that of many of the tales, an 'irrémédiable mélancolie', and he implies that love for a mortal in no way contradicts the yearning for the ideal, since Poe's female characters 'brillent au sein d'une vapeur surnaturelle' and there is no hint of sensual pleasure (II, 312). Despite its brevity, this description not only adequately conveys the ethereal, one might say bloodless, quality of Poe's female characters, but also reflects a sharp difference between them and Baudelaire's vision of woman, which presents her as a very physical, animal entity.

Nevertheless, Baudelaire's central interest in Poe's work concerns neither the criticism nor the poetry, but the tales and philosophical sketches. As the publication of *Histoires extraordinaires* made summaries of the tales unnecessary, Baudelaire takes the opportunity to include a deeper study of them than in any of his earlier reviews.

His former interest in *calculs et problèmes* seems to have decreased, and in this study he decides against exploring the reasons which drive Poe 'se jouer avec une volupté enfantine et presque perverse dans le monde des probabilités et de conjectures' (II, 316). In a comment which I suggest refers to a remark made by Thalès Bernard, he adds: 'personne ne niera que Poe ne soit un jongleur merveilleux'. Bernard is the first critic I have found using the word 'jongleur' in reference to

Poe: he wrote in 1853 that: 'toute la question consiste à savoir s'il y a eu dans l'esprit du poète mis en cause une véritable sincérité, si les élévations à Dieu qui sortent de sa plume sont une ignoble jonglerie ou une secrète protestation de l'âme contre les faiblesses de la vie matérielle'.[39] In a letter written to Sainte-Beuve in March 1856, Baudelaire asserted: 'on fera semblant de ne vouloir considérer Poe que comme *jongleur*, mais je reviendrai à outrance sur le caractère surnaturel de sa poésie et de ses contes. Il n'est Américain qu'en tant que *Jongleur*' (*C*I, 345). He does, therefore, seem to be reacting to Bernard's challenge, stressing that Poe's greatest works are indeed a protestation against 'les faiblesses de la vie matérielle'. Nevertheless, the choice of the term is also a very deliberate provocation: as so often, Baudelaire sets out to shock his readers by using a word usually associated with condemnation in a context which is clearly a eulogy.

A second category of tales examined in the 1852 article, those that explore exceptional mental states, still fires Baudelaire's enthusiasm. He refers admiringly to 'ce tempérament unique' which allows Poe to portray 'd'une manière impeccable, saisissante, terrible, *l'exception dans l'ordre moral*' (11, 316). This fascination for disturbed mental states is obvious, too, in many of the prose poems in *Le Spleen de Paris* and in the delight he takes in Asselineau's short story, 'La Jambe', reviewed in January 1859.

In this preface, however, Baudelaire concentrates less on listing the various types of tale than on highlighting the motivating force and unifying factor they all share: Poe's 'amour du beau'. By choosing this wider perspective, he is able to direct his attention to a close study of the tails, giving an impression of harmony where the earlier review had suggested a degree of fragmentation.

Baudelaire begins by extolling Poe's ability to seize the reader's attention from the outset and to hold it throughout his 'entraînantes déductions' (11, 317). Here Baudelaire can be seen using his criticism as a means of training his own creative skills: one cannot help thinking of his own control of the *entrée en matière* which allows him to begin so many of *Les Fleurs du mal* with such compelling opening lines. Nevertheless, his judgement of Poe is, I feel, valid for certain tales and certain readers only, for whereas tales like 'The Pit and the Pendulum', with its rousing opening sentence – 'j'étais brisé, – brisé jusqu'à la mort par cette longue agonie' (Poe, 358) – or 'Bérénice', which begins with the deceptively simple 'le malheur est divers' (Poe, 327) might pull one relentlessly with them, 'Mesmeric Revelation' and 'The Colloquy of Monos and Una' (despite the arresting '*Ressuscité*?' with which it opens (Poe, 461)) might well exert less power. Baudelaire's contemporaries, however, seem to have agreed with him, a quotation from L. Cartier showing, in addition, how widespread was the unacknowledged pilfering from Baudelaire's article that was mentioned at the beginning of this chapter: 'l'intérêt éveillé s'empare de vous, ne vous lâche plus, vous harcèle, vous entraîne, vous tient haletant jusqu'à la conclusion'.[40]

The themes and atmosphere of Poe's tales are evoked in so poetical a manner in this section of the preface that such commentators as J. Crépet and Pichois have concentrated on the resonances set up with Baudelaire's own poetry rather than on testing the passage's validity by comparison with Poe's works. It is, of course, undeniable that these paragraphs contain as much of Baudelaire as of Poe, yet it is less than just to Baudelaire's critical gifts not to point out that each motif mentioned is indeed explored in the tales.

The 'ardeurs de curiosité' (ii, 317) felt by the convalescent are, of course, examined in 'The Man of the Crowd': later Baudelaire was to note a similar curiosity in Guys, and to present it as 'le point de départ de son génie' (ii, 689). The debilitating effect of certain seasons, of the 'temps chauds, humides et brumeux, où le vent du sud amollit et détend les nerfs [. . .], où les yeux se remplissent de larmes' (ii, 317) is eloquently described in 'Le *Confiteor* de l'artiste' and in 'Ciel brouillé', in such lines as:

> Tu rappelles ces jours blancs, tièdes et voilés,
> Qui font se fondre en pleurs les cœurs ensorcelés,
> Quand, agités d'un mal inconnu qui les tord,
> Les nerfs trop éveillés raillent l'esprit qui dort. (i, 49)

Poe, too, was keenly sensitive to atmospheric changes: in the brief work entitled 'Shadow', for instance, with its reference to 'ce terrible mode d'existence que subissent les gens nerveux' (Poe, 478), Poe's narrator suffers from the 'pesanteur dans l'atmosphère' and bemoans the way in which 'l'esprit particulier des cieux' affects 'les âmes, les pensées et les méditations de l'humanité' (Poe, 478).[41]

Hallucinations, a *topos* which Baudelaire mentions in his preface, explores in his 'Poème du hachisch' and brings terrifyingly alive in 'Les Métamorphoses du vampire' (i, 159), also form the subject of several of Poe's tales, notably 'Ligea' and 'Metzengerstein'.

The strange logic of the absurd, mentioned as a further theme of Poe's work, can be found in 'The Imp of the Perverse', as well as in Baudelaire's own prose poems, notably 'Le Mauvais Vitrier' and more specifically in 'Les Dons des fées', while the destructive power of hysteria is not only central to poems such as 'La Voix', in which the poet is indeed 'désaccordé au point d'exprimer la douleur par le rire'

(II, 317) – 'c'est depuis ce temps que [. . .] je ris dans les deuils et pleure dans les fêtes' (I, 170) – but it is also present in the voice of Oinos in 'Shadow': 'un poids mortel nous écrasait. [. . .] Cependant, nous poussions nos rires, et nous étions gais à notre façon, – une façon hystérique' (Poe, 478).

The parallels between the two poets, or at least between Baudelaire and what he highlights in Poe's works, are so strong that some critics have been drawn to propose an analogy which I consider false. When Baudelaire seeks to explain Poe's preoccupation with the grotesque and the horrible, he compares it to 'la volupté surnaturelle que l'homme peut éprouver à voir couler son propre sang' (II, 317). This particular delight, which calls to mind the writings of several of the *petits romantiques* as well as Flaubert's letters, is not present in Poe – Baudelaire is not, of course, suggesting that it is – nor do I believe that it is shared by Baudelaire himself. The prevailing mood of 'La Fontaine de sang', with which the passage has been compared (II, 1233), is not of sensual pleasure but of terror:

> J'ai demandé souvent à des vins captieux
> D'endormir pour un jour la terreur qui me mine;
> Le vin rend l'œil plus clair et l'oreille plus fine! (I, 115)

The evocation of the atmosphere in Poe's tales is also more skilfully developed here than in the 1852 article. Where Baudelaire had earlier asserted that the suppression of all that was not central to Poe's theme rendered more obvious 'l'idée génératrice' (II, 282), he now realizes that 'les fonds et les accessoires [. . .] sont appropriés aux sentiments des personnages' (II, 317: cf. I, 655). Moreover, by stressing a positive, rather than a negative function he can draw parallels between Poe and another of those he most admires, Delacroix.[42] To describe the beauty of the scenery in Poe's tales, Baudelaire chooses terms which, once again, recall his own poetry, in particular, the opiate dreams of 'Rêve parisien'. The description, however, is equally applicable to such works of Poe as 'A Tale of the Ragged Mountains', where opium's power 'revêtir tout le monde extérieur d'une intensité d'intérêt' (Poe, 226) is suggested in a powerful passage to which Baudelaire alluded in his review of the Exposition universelle (II, 596).

When Baudelaire refers in his preface to the 'échappées magnifiques, gorgées de lumière et de couleur' with their 'architectures, vaporisées par la distance' (II, 318), he probably has in mind 'The Domain of Arnheim': 'le visiteur [. . .] est ravi et stupéfait à la fois par le large globe du soleil couchant [. . .] qui maintenant se présente en face de lui et forme la seule barrière d'une perspective immense qui s'ouvre à travers une autre fente prodigieuse séparant les collines' (Poe, 954). And when, finally, 'tout le paradis d'Arnheim éclate à la vue' it is 'une masse d'architecture moitié gothique, moitié sarrasine, qui a l'air de se soutenir dans les airs comme par miracle' (Poe, 956).

Lastly, Baudelaire defines the characters in Poe's novels as reflections of their creator and he sketches a portrait of the writer which is, in many ways, an idealized image of Baudelaire himself. The incurable melancholy, the insatiable love of beauty, the hyperintensity of the faculties, the nerves stretched almost to breaking point: all these have their counterpart in Baudelaire. But Poe is also, according to Baudelaire, 'l'homme dont la volonté ardente et patiente jette un défi aux difficultés' (11, 318): in highlighting this side of Poe's character Baudelaire is clearly attempting to screw up his own courage, to use his critical faculties as a personal call to arms. This aspect of his criticism becomes increasingly important in his later articles, but it can be detected as early as the Dupont review and it is very much present in his letters.

Baudelaire's preface to *Histoires extraordinaires* is a cogent, convincing and sympathetic introduction to a writer who aroused considerable interest among contemporary critics and whose works the public greeted with unusual warmth. Yet, the preface to *Nouvelles Histoires extraordinaires*, completed by January 1857 (11, 1233), is a blistering attack on materialism, progress and contemporary literary criticism in which Baudelaire's irritation has spilled over in an acid condemnation which could result only in an erosion of both his own and Poe's position. The reasons behind this lack of control are no doubt complex and may never be fully understood. Doubtless the separation from Jeanne in September 1856 affected him deeply, while Flaubert's impending trial for 'offense à la morale publique' in January and February 1857 cannot have failed to fortify his conviction that society's values were radically perverse. Besides, he was absorbed in the preparation of *Les Fleurs du mal*, the manuscript of which was given to his publisher in February 1857. He complained, too, of the financial and intellectual difficulties he was experiencing in writing the preface, lamenting: 'je n'accouche que douloureusement' (C1, 361) and confiding to his mother that 'la préface a traîné interminablement par suite de mes interminables embarras d'argent' (C1, 366). Psychological factors cannot be ruled out either, the twin desires to create and destroy being among the contradictory tendencies he himself noted in his personality (1, 684). Finally, it seems possible that the preface reacts directly against various comments made in the critical response to *Histoires extraordinaires*.

At first glance, one might have expected Baudelaire to be delighted with the reviews: if several brows were raised at the neologisms, this traditional means of mocking an opponent seems a mere cavil compared with the general admiration and enthusiasm. His preface, moreover, moulded French opinions of Poe to an extent which must have been immediately obvious to him. Poe's ability to capture and hold the reader's attention, the mathematical preciseness of his exposition, the absence of sensuality, are among points made by Baudelaire and echoed in similar terms by other critics. Yet the assertions which are most deeply rooted in his own nature are all either ignored, rejected or distorted. The implacability of American society towards Poe was not generally accepted: Pontmartin, for instance, scoffed that 'ni l'Amérique d'Edgar Poe, ni la France de Gérard de Nerval ne sont responsables de ce léger grain de folie qui, mêlé chez quelques-uns à des facultés supérieures, chez un grand nombre à des facultés médiocres, explique le désordre des uns, les prétentions des autres, le malheur de tous'. Several critics twisted Baudelaire's attack on society, turning it against Poe himself: according to Cartier, 'Edgar Poe est le produit naturel, spontané, d'une démocratie pressée, qui n'a pas le loisir de s'arrêter aux théories du sentiment, aux lenteurs de la passion'.[43] Baudelaire's attempt to explain Poe's alcoholism as a 'moyen mnémonique' was either ignored or derided: 'le beau', sneered Fournel, 'ne se cherche pas dans l'ivresse et les révélations de l'alcool'.[44] The theme of suicide was left all but untouched,[45] and Poe's exploration of exceptional psychic states seems to have been beyond the comprehension of most critics. As Lemonnier says, 'cette peinture de l'horreur et de l'exception morbide qui avait charmé les lecteurs romantiques indigna les critiques bourgeois'.[46] Poe himself was seen as ill, as an 'esprit maladif',[47] suffering from 'une hallucination vigoureuse'.[48] Baudelaire had set out to 'faire hurler' (*C*1, 341): what he provoked was not howls so much as distorted echoes and deafening silences. No wonder that in 'Notes nouvelles' he allowed his control to slip, and railed against his *bêtes noires* in a manner verging on hysteria.

The new preface begins – as do so many of Baudelaire's reviews – by establishing the perspective in which Poe is to be judged; that of a poet who, in protest against the mediocrity and materialism of his society, retreats into a world of dream and imagination. Baudelaire accepts the frequently made comparison between Poe and the French Romantics but rejects the accusation of decadence levelled at Romanticism by those he derisively calls 'ces sphinx sans énigme qui veillent devant les portes saintes de l'Esthétique classique' (11, 319). As so often, he reveals in this metaphor his astonishing ability to express abstractions in terms which are both memorably concrete and amusingly apt. Although the popularity of Ponsard's *Lucrèce* in 1843 had led many critics gleefully to certify as dead the old quarrel between Romantics and Classicists, skirmishes continued and the lament that Romanticism had resulted in the decadence of French literature, a lament voiced at great length by Nisard,[49] was echoed throughout the 1840s and 1850s. Baudelaire responds by suggesting, in a passage developed from the 1856 study (II, 318) and subsequently transformed into 'Le Coucher du soleil romantique', that a declining literature may have the same poignant beauty as a setting sun. He has three other grounds for refuting the accusation. Firstly, he personifies Classical literature as a 'matrone rustique [. . .] *ne devant rien qu'à la simple nature*' (II, 319); the works he most admires, on the contrary, are portrayed as a female version of the perfect dandy. This argument closely resembles the opening paragraphs of *Mademoiselle de Maupin*, in which Gautier imagines virtue as a bespectacled grandmother, to whom he naturally prefers 'quelque petite immoralité bien pimpante, bien coquette, bien bonne fille'.[50]

Baudelaire's rejection of the term *décadence* in regard to Romanticism is based on something deeper than a mere difference in taste: he argues that to speak of a 'littérature de décadence' is to posit the existence of a preordained scale of literary sub-types; to accuse a writer of decadence is, therefore, to condemn him for carrying out the role he has been predestined to fulfil. Clearly, the theme of fate as compared with creative freedom has lost none of its importance, although the emphasis has changed, and once again Baudelaire sets out to shock and provoke his reader by ridiculing an accepted critical standard.

Thirdly, Baudelaire twists the attack, asserting that it is the decadence not of literature but of society itself with its false view of progress and its debased democratic ideals that has forced Poe to write as he does. It is this view of Poe – as a clear-sighted lampooner of contemporary follies who is intensely aware of evil – that Baudelaire throws into sharp relief in the following section of 'Notes nouvelles'. Most of this part of the preface is more interesting for what it reveals about Baudelaire's state of mind than for its merits as literary criticism, but it does debate an issue suggested in the earlier reviews, that of material progress as opposed to individual responsibility, and it explores a theme frequently analysed by Poe himself, that of perversity.

In examining the motif of perversity, Baudelaire gives a succinct summary of the tale which opens *Nouvelles Histoires extraordinaires*, 'Le Démon de la perversité', in which Poe studies one of the 'mobiles primordiaux' (Poe, 271) of the human psyche, one moreover which he claims to have been overlooked by moralists and phrenologists, and which Baudelaire emphasized in his 1852 essay on Poe. Baudelaire in turn portrays this force in numerous prose poems, notably 'A une heure du matin', 'Une Mort héroïque', and above all in 'Le Mauvais Vitrier'. Under the influence of perversity, Poe contends, 'nous agissons sans but intelligible; ou [. . .] sous son influence nous agissons par la raison que *nous ne le devrions pas*' (Poe, 272). Even Baudelaire's childhood letters, with their precocious awareness of the gulf between intention and action, show how deeply Poe's statement would have affected him. Indeed, Poe illustrates his claim with several examples which seem to summarize with uncanny precision the temperament of Baudelaire himself (Poe 273–4). The affinity between the two writers in this regard seems beyond dispute, particularly if one compares the tales with such poems as 'L'Héautontimorouménos'. Moreover, 'Le Démon de la perversité' is less a tale than a prose poem, and both its subject-matter and its movement from general considerations to specific examples leading to an unexpected conclusion may have influenced Baudelaire in his creation of *Le Spleen de Paris*. Yet, whereas Poe's analysis is wryly sarcastic and makes no mention of the Devil, Baudelaire's summary is far more pessimistic and decidedly Manichean. It is possible that he did not fully understand – or chose to ignore – the difference between the words *demon* and *devil*, since the French doublets may both refer to Satan, while English reserves *demon* for lesser forces. Similarly, in the title, Baudelaire translates Poe's term 'imp' by the more highly charged word 'démon'. The conclusion he draws certainly owes little to Poe:

> l'impossibilité de trouver un motif raisonnable suffisant pour certaines actions mauvaises et périlleuses, pourrait nous conduire à les considérer comme le résultat des suggestions du Diable, si l'expérience et l'histoire ne nous enseignait pas que Dieu en tire souvent l'établissement de l'ordre et le châtiment des coquins; – *après s'être servi des mêmes coquins comme de complices!* tel est le mot qui se glisse, je l'avoue, dans mon esprit comme un sous-entendu aussi perfide qu'inévitable (II, 323).

In this case at least, Baudelaire has clearly manipulated Poe, making of a psychological study a theological debate.

The third and fourth sections of 'Notes nouvelles' are closely linked to Poe's theoretical works, *Fifty Suggestions*, *Marginalia* and 'The Philosophy of Composition'. As so much of this part of the article derives from Poe's own writings, Baudelaire has once again been accused of plagiarism. A comment in Poe's *Marginalia*, with which the author of *La Fanfarlo* would surely have agreed, may serve to shed some light on the subject:

> the poetic sentiment implies an abnormally keen appreciation of poetic

excellence, with an unconscious assimilation of it into the poetic entity, so that an admired passage, being forgotten and afterwards reviving through an exceedingly shadowy train of association, is supposed by the plagiarizing poet to be really the coinage of his own brain.[51]

Three important points are raised in the third section of the preface: the power of the imagination, the demands and restrictions of the short story, and the possibility of creating a new genre, the purely poetical tale.

Using an image he is to repeat in the *Salon de 1859*, Baudelaire claims that, for Poe, 'l'imagination est la reine des facultés' (11, 328: cf. 619). Although the expression has been attributed to Poe himself, it seems to be Baudelaire's own, that of the American being similar but not identical. In *A Chapter of Suggestions*, for example, Poe emphasizes the power of imagination in the following terms: 'that the imagination has not been unjustly ranked as supreme among the mental faculties, appears from the intense consciousness, on the part of the imaginative man, that the faculty in question brings his soul often to a glimpse of things supernal and eternal – to the very verge of the *great secrets*'.[52] Similarly, in his *Salon de 1859*, Baudelaire claims that it is imagination which has 'enseigné à l'homme le sens moral de la couleur, du contour, du son et du parfum' and he insists that 'elle est positivement apparentée avec l'infini' (11, 621).

From his brief discussion of imagination, Baudelaire turns to examine the aims and ideals of Poe's short stories. The genre is presented not as the highest area of literary endeavour, that honour being reserved for poetry, but as one capable at least of great variety. The conciseness of the tale is seen as a particular advantage, compared with the more ample proportions of the novel. Here Baudelaire seems to be applying to prose works Poe's conviction that brevity is essential to poetry: in *The Poetic Principle*, for instance, he claims: 'that degree of excitement which would entitle a poem to be so called at all, cannot be sustained throughout a composition of any great length. After the lapse of half an hour, at the very utmost, it flags – fails – a revulsion ensues – and the poem is, in effect, and in fact, no longer such.'[53] Besides, the tale's brevity allows greater unity – the quality which Poe describes as a 'vital requisite in all works of art'.[54] According to Poe, 'in the tale proper [. . .] mere *construction* is, of course, far more imperatively demanded than in the novel. Defective plot, in this latter, may escape observation, but in the tale, never.'[55] Similarly, Baudelaire insists that 'si la première phrase n'est pas écrite en vue de préparer cette impression finale, l'œuvre est manquée dès le début' (11, 329).

However much Baudelaire's account of Poe's aesthetic opinions may seem a mere paraphrase, the need for unity of effect was expressed in embryonic form in his very early 'Conseils aux jeunes littérateurs', where the self-confident young critic declared that 'aujourd'hui, il faut produire beaucoup; – il faut donc aller vite; [. . .] il faut donc que tous les coups portent, et que pas une touche ne soit inutile' (I, 17). In the same way, a letter to Calonne confides: 'je suis un de ceux (et nous sommes bien rares) qui croient que toute composition littéraire, même critique, doit être faite et manœuvrée en vue d'un dénouement' (CI, 538). Similar ideas were, of course, expressed by other contemporary writers: Flaubert, for example, wrote: 'tu me permettras dans ma critique d'avoir toujours en vue l'*intention générale*, l'effet d'ensemble à produire et non telle petite intention particulière et locale qui souvent y nuit'.[56] What is more original in Baudelaire is the insistence that *every* part of a work must lead to the final effect. Once again, Baudelaire appears to be giving special prominence to the points on which he and Poe are in full agreement.

Finally, Baudelaire briefly discusses the greater liberty and the corresponding dangers of the short story's freedom from constraints of rhythm. As in his earlier studies, it is evident that he believes the different genres have clearly defined functions which should be exploited but never abused: 'l'auteur qui poursuit dans une nouvelle un simple but de beauté ne travaille qu'à son grand désavantage, privé qu'il est de l'instrument le plus utile, le rythme' (II, 330). This is at once a carefully worded criticism of some of Poe's works and an indication that he himself is seeking out the ideal genre for his own experiments. His concluding sentences, as J. Crépet has suggested,[57] seem to reflect his own doubts about his prose poems:

> je sais que dans toutes les littératures des efforts ont été faits, souvent heureux, pour créer des contes purement poétiques; [. . .] mais ce sont des luttes et des efforts qui ne servent qu'à démontrer la force des vrais moyens adaptés aux buts correspondants, et je ne serais pas éloigné de croire que chez quelques auteurs, les plus grands qu'on puisse choisir, ces tentations héroïques vinssent d'un désespoir (II, 330).

Baudelaire may well have in mind not only Poe and perhaps himself but also Gautier, whose *nouvelle poétique* he will discuss in his essay of 1859 (II, 121).

Some of the ideas explored in the final section of the preface are repeated and developed in the later criticism and will, therefore, be discussed in subsequent chapters. Four points, however, should be examined here: they are the dual necessity of inspiration and work, the appropriation of the means to the total effect in a work of art, the need for both symmetry and surprise, and the question of overt didacticism.

In showing that Poe's achievements derive not merely from inspired writing but from a combination of genius and hard work, Baudelaire is once again making of his critical writing a personal call to arms, an appeal to himself to emulate Poe in seizing and profiting from the rare moments of 'santé poétique' (II, 331: cf. I, 401–2). A 'génie jeune et vigoureux' (I, 401), however, does not suffice to create great art. In his 'Conseils aux jeunes littérateurs', under the heading 'Du travail et de l'inspiration', Baudelaire had already woven variations around the theme that 'l'inspiration est décidément la sœur du travail journalier' (II, 18). In the preface he insists that Poe, too, not only regards work as an essential adjunct to inspiration, but also stresses the need to understand inspiration, placing it under the microscope of his analytical mind. The theoretical work in which Poe most fully develops these ideas is *The Philosophy of Composition*, with its unabashed demolition of what Baudelaire would term 'les partisans de l'inspiration' (II, 335). Baudelaire's phrase no doubt refers to writers like Musset, accused in 1860 of totally failing to understand 'le travail par lequel une rêverie devient un objet d'art' (CI, 675). In Poe, on the contrary, Baudelaire discovers a poet who is always in control of his inspiration, striving, like the true dandy, to banish spontaneity and 'simuler le sang-froid et la délibération' by paying extremely close attention to every point of his poem, no matter how minor.

The problem of how best to convey emotion in a work of art, of whether the artist should remain aloof or become emotionally involved, is a perennial question in aesthetic debates: no doubt the position adopted in Diderot's art criticism and his 'Paradoxe du comédien'[58] helped to shape Baudelaire's thinking in this regard well before he encountered Poe, and his interest in the problem is reflected both in the review of *Madame Bovary* (II, 80) and in that of *Les Martyrs ridicules* (II, 186).

It is in 'The Philosophy of Composition' that Poe shows how he chooses the best means of conveying the required total effect. Rhyme, refrain, rhythm, memory, vocabulary and sentiment must all, according to Baudelaire's interpretation of Poe, be thoroughly understood and controlled. The passage, despite its Baudelairean emphasis, does follow Poe very closely. Poe, for example, claims: 'having chosen a novel, first, and secondly a vivid effect, I consider whether it can best be wrought by incident or tone [. . .] afterward looking about me (or rather within) for such combinations of event, or tone, as shall best aid me in the construction of the effect'.[59] He discusses 'l'usage de la rime' in a passage describing 'novel effects, arising from an extension of the

application of the principles of rhyme and alliteration' and 'le perfectionnement du refrain', of particular significance for 'The Raven', is
analysed in the following terms: 'I determined to produce continuously
novel effects, by the variation *of the application* of the *refrain*'.[60] Although
Baudelaire also mentions 'l'adaptation du rythme' (II, 335) to the
emotion the poet wishes to evoke, Poe does not, in fact, see much
possibility of variety in what he calls 'mere *rhythm*' and insists that
'Melancholy [. . .] is [. . .] the most legitimate of all the poetical tones',[61]
suggesting that any rhythm can be made to recreate this sentiment.
Despite the parallels, however, Poe is being subtly remoulded; this
passage awakens so many echoes with statements made elsewhere in
Baudelaire's writing that it seems less a description of Poe than an
indication of what Baudelaire sought in an ideal artist.

Poe's demand for 'the combination of the two elements, Equality and
Unexpectedness'[62] is undoubtedly one of those ideas whose truth
Baudelaire had recognized before reading Poe but which he discovered
fully formulated in Poe's theoretical writings. As early as 1845 Baudelaire had insisted on 'le mérite de l'inattendu' (II, 390) and in his
Journaux intimes he contends that 'l'irrégularité, c'est-à-dire l'inattendu, la surprise, l'étonnement sont une partie essentielle et la
caractéristique de la beauté' (I, 656). In his letters as well as in his
criticism he often refers to the joy of causing surprise: in 1855 it is
mentioned as 'une des grandes jouissances causées par l'art et la
littérature' (II, 578) and in 1859 beauty is described as '*toujours* étonnant'
(II, 616).[63]

Finally, in paraphrasing Poe's castigation of the 'heresy of the
didactic',[64] Baudelaire chooses to throw man's stupidity into sharper
relief than does Poe. And, where Poe is content merely to indicate his
contemporaries' tendency towards overt didacticism, Baudelaire, as
usual, delves for the underlying causes, isolating them as hypocrisy on
the one hand and the unintelligence and baseness of men's minds on the
other. Poe's argument is that it is impossible to reconcile 'the obstinate
waters of Poetry and Truth':[65] Baudelaire treats the question differently,
insisting not on the impossibility but on the undesirability of such a use
of poetry. In order to clarify this assertion he adds to his examination of
The Poetic Principle the claim that although poetry does indeed lift its
readers 'au-dessus du niveau des intérêts vulgaires' (II, 333), it should
not, 'sous peine de mort ou de défaillance, s'assimiler à la science ou à
la morale': similarly, the closing sentence of 'L'Ecole païenne' called on
art, not to assimilate itself to 'la science et la philosophie' but to walk
fraternally between them, that is, to take from them all that can
strengthen the sinews of a work of art, but to maintain the indepen-

dence essential to art. Baudelaire's position has not altered as radically as the Pléiade notes suggest; in discussing Poe he reasserts his own ideas in the terminology that Poe himself uses.

Although 'Notes nouvelles' contains many forceful expressions, the tension and anger, which racked Baudelaire when he wrote it and which can be detected in the loose structure of his sentences with their frequent dashes,[66] prevent it, in my view, from being among his best critical assessment, however illuminating it may be.

The introduction to 'La Genèse d'un poème', published in 1859, is at once calmer and more convincing. Once again, Baudelaire insists that work must support inspiration and adds that, according to Poe, originality can be learnt, if not taught. The similarity of this last suggestion to ideas expressed in the first study on Dupont and in the projected prefaces for *Les Fleurs du mal* is inescapable; one of the planned prefaces, for instance, includes the note: 'comment, par une série d'efforts déterminée, l'artiste peut s'élever à une originalité proportionnelle' (I, 183). Baudelaire also returns to Poe's love of analysis, *combinaisons* and *calculs* (II, 343): the surprisingly slight emphasis that contemporary critics placed on Poe's tendency towards the macabre is no doubt due in part to Baudelaire's constantly focusing attention on Poe's imaginative explorations. He also asserts, as in other articles, the preference for the artificial over the natural, using terms which are, in part, a way of avoiding the unfortunate and provocative word *jonglerie*: 'après tout, un peu de charlatanerie est toujours permis au génie, et même ne lui messied pas. C'est, comme le fard sur les pommettes d'une femme naturellement belle, un assaisonnement nouveau pour l'esprit' (II, 344). Expressed in this way the idea may also reflect Baudelaire's continuing interest in Hoffmann: the 'charlatanerie' which Baudelaire permits in a poet is personified in Hoffmann's Celionati, the dominant character in *Prinzessin Brambilla*, who consciously controls the action in the same way as an artist creates situations in a play or novel.

In a brief, extraordinarily dense paragraph, Baudelaire analyses 'The Raven', throwing into stark relief the terrible despair he finds exemplified in the poem. The word 'désespoir' is twice repeated, the second time intensified by the highly suggestive epithet 'irrémédiable'. Poe, in discussing the mood he sought to create, uses the word 'melancholy' and makes it clear that the emotion is not unalloyed with pleasure. For Baudelaire, however, the word *nevermore* is mysterious and terrible. The mouths which have repeated it down the ages are 'crispées', an epithet which is at once sharply visual and suggestive of deep emotion. The idea that the living will never again see those who have died has filled to the brim 'l'immensité fécondée par la destruction': as a result, humanity is willing even to accept the concept of Hell in order to escape the remorseless consequences of mortality.

In many ways, Baudelaire's final word on Poe, an 'Avis du traducteur' which seems to have been written towards the end of 1864, crystallizes the central points made in the previous articles. Poe's multiple, often antithetical, characteristics are calmly reviewed and concisely conveyed. The earlier parallels with Balzac are recalled in the description of Poe as 'conteur visionnaire' (II, 347), his analytical and philosophical bent is again stressed, while his insistence on verisimilitude half-mockingly termed his 'dada' in 1855 (II, 295), and his frequent *canards*, whose value Baudelaire had expressed rather clumsily in 'Notes nouvelles' (II, 321), are described in loftier words: 'toujours philosophe et analyste, amateur de la magie de l'absolue vraisemblance, amateur de la bouffon-nerie la plus désintéressée' (II, 347). Baudelaire renounces his earlier ambition of adding to the image of Poe as a tale-writer and 'subtil dialecticien' that of the poet and the literary critic. In the preamble to 'La Genèse d'un poème', he lamented that 'dans le moulage de la prose appliqué à la poésie, il y a nécessairement une affreuse imperfection' (II, 344): here he is even more adamant, claiming modestly that 'ma très humble et très dévouée faculté de traducteur ne me permet pas de suppléer aux voluptés absentes du rythme et de la rime' (II, 347). The choice of the powerfully evocative word 'voluptés' underlines the physiological intensity of Baudelaire's reaction to poetry in general and Poe in particular, although the poems he mentions as being available in translation and capable of suggesting 'les merveilles du pur poète' would demand all the powers of 'ceux qui savent beaucoup deviner'. The possibility of translating Poe's criticism is also rejected. Baudelaire claims that this criticism would have little appeal for the frivolous Parisians, and doubtless he felt he did not have the time needed to devote to such a task, but it is also likely that Baudelaire himself did not accept Poe's method. As I have suggested, his own criticism is far removed from the fault-finding, half-mocking approach of his American counterpart.

For the first time, in a study intended for publication, Baudelaire specifically refers to the resemblances between himself and Poe, giving the similarities as one of the reasons for his many translations. Yet his principal motivation is undoubtedly that of exploring and revealing, as much for his own sake as for that of his readers, 'un genre de beauté nouveau' (II, 348). It is this desire, I feel, which dominates his criticism of Poe and this perspective which has allowed him to reveal so much of Poe's strange and difficult genius, while at the same time reflecting so many of his own beliefs and aspirations. The studies show Baudelaire exploiting with increasing mastery a genre he uses ostensibly to introduce to the public a gifted writer, but, perhaps more profoundly, to increase his own skills and to spur his will to create, through the inspired analysis of a mind he much admires.

3
✣ Self-Defence and Self-Analysis

Madame Bovary (*L'Artiste*, 18 October 1857)

For five years Baudelaire abandoned his criticism of his French contemporaries to devote himself to *Les Fleurs du mal* and his translations
and studies of Poe. Yet, in 1857, the year in which he published his
volume of poetry and in which both he and Flaubert were accused of
committing 'une offense à la morale publique' as well as 'une offense à
la morale religieuse', he reviewed *Madame Bovary*. No doubt the
publication of *Les Fleurs du mal* and the completion of most of the
translations gave him more time for literary criticism, but his decision
to champion Flaubert certainly seems to have been motivated by more
positive reasons, and, above all, by an intense personal need.

Firstly, he and Flaubert were on terms of friendship. Although
documentary evidence is slight, the letters that do exist indicate warm
and mutual comprehension. Baudelaire twice mentions Flaubert as one
of the few men with whom he has anything in common, and as one of
the rare modern writers whose work he values (*C*II, 254 and 611).
Furthermore, there is no contradiction between the sentiments expressed in letters to Flaubert himself and those in Baudelaire's other
correspondence. Flaubert's letters not only praise Baudelaire's poetry
and his 'Poème du hachisch', but also offer, modestly but without
reticence, some pertinent criticism: he rejoiced above all that Baudelaire had discovered 'le moyen de rajeunir le romantisme' and that he
was able 'chante[r] la chair sans l'aimer, d'une façon triste et détachée'.[1]

Secondly, Flaubert's novel had rapidly achieved considerable success.
Anxiously watching the sales of *Les Fleurs du mal*, Baudelaire uses his
review to pose yet again the questions which dominate the Dupont
preface: why does the public respond to some works while remaining
indifferent to others and how can a writer best seduce the fickle siren of
popularity?

Thirdly, because *Madame Bovary* had been accused and acquitted of
immorality, Baudelaire's review could return to the perennial problems
of morality in art, upholding the artist's freedom to choose subject and

method. Official disapproval in itself, of course, posed a serious threat to unbiased discussion of the novel: whether the charges levelled at him were merely an excuse, as Flaubert himself felt, to attack the left-wing *Revue de Paris* in which *Madame Bovary* was first serialized,[2] or whether, as F. W. J. Hemmings asserts, the authorities feared the 'mere example of frank reporting and fearless analysis',[3] obviously any critic reviewing the work, and any journal publishing such a review, would need to tread carefully. Indeed, Baudelaire claimed that he himself had 'failli être poursuivi pour l'article sur *Mad[ame] Bovary*' (*C*I, 436).

Finally, I suggest that Baudelaire planned to publish the review before his trial, using it to defend *Les Fleurs du mal* and to reject the court's right, or indeed ability, to judge art. In a letter written to Flaubert in August 1857, he regrets that his article has been delayed 'encore de quelques jours' (*C*I, 424). Although in other letters Baudelaire describes articles as completed when they existed only in note form or indeed merely in his imagination, a second detail tends to confirm that at least part of the review had in fact been completed at that date; early in his article (II, 78) he mentions Custine as though he were still alive. As the notes to the Pléiade edition point out, Custine's death, which occurred on 25 September, would almost certainly have provoked some comment (II, 1121), had the passage been written at a later date. The surprising brevity of the final section, comparing *Madame Bovary* and *La Tentation de Saint Antoine*, suggests that, because he had been unable to complete the article before the trial and because he had been convicted, his inspiration and enthusiasm may have flagged. Alternatively, he may have been rushing to meet a deadline and unable to develop a comparison which clearly interested him. It is, of course, also possible that he saw in the review a means of retaliation after the trial and used it to underline the discrepancy between Flaubert's acquittal and his own conviction.

Whatever the reasons motivating the review, the attention Baudelaire devoted to it is beyond doubt. Apart from the rushed final section, the structure reveals considerable care. The concise opening passage, outlining his intentions, prepares the way for a discussion of the legal issues and Flaubert's acquittal. The third part, which sketches in the literary and social background, suggesting the reasoning behind Flaubert's choice of theme and approach, leads up to the detailed analysis of the heroine. The closing paragraphs, and possibly the study of Emma Bovary, seem to me to have been written either later or under pressure: the smooth control of the earlier parts has crumbled and Baudelaire jots down a series of richly suggestive ideas which he might have been expected to examine at greater length. Nevertheless, he does manage to convey much in a very limited space, employing a considerable variety of techniques: straightforward analysis is interspersed with quotations, interior monologue, and personal reminiscences. The review is certainly one of those which best demonstrate Baudelaire's ability to modulate from extremely personal references to general aesthetic principles.

Essential to the structure is a series of paradoxes: the critic who reviews a work much later than his colleagues is at once at greater liberty and under more restraints than they; the magistrates, although their province is truth and justice, have shown an awareness of beauty; Flaubert's situation was simultaneously good and bad; the French public reject literature but vaunt material possessions; the heroine does not need to be a heroine, *stricto sensu*; and Emma combines qualities which Baudelaire defines as both masculine and feminine. The review's structural unity derives both from the repeated use of paradoxes and from such classical allusions as the reference to Pasiphaë and the Minotaur.

The review opens with Baudelaire's description of himself as an 'écrivain retardataire' (II, 76), a position in which he discerns a 'charme paradoxal': since the novel has aroused such interest he has no need to assess all its aspects nor to enlist in any debate, either in condemnation or defence. He insists that his article is based solely on his own reactions to the novel and to the criticisms levelled against it, reactions motivated uniquely by a love of beauty and justice. These opening paragraphs are especially interesting for their exploration of criticism in general and Baudelaire's own position in particular. Yet one cannot help suspecting that he protests too much: three times in this brief passage he refers to himself as 'l'écrivain retardataire', 'l'écrivain en retard', 'seul comme un traînard' (II, 76), apologies he did not feel constrained to make in reviewing *Prométhée délivré* after a delay of two years. Although the majority of reviews of *Madame Bovary* were published in May or June, Barbey d'Aurevilly's article appeared only a few weeks before that of Baudelaire, while a handful of critics waited until 1858. Baudelaire may well have hoped that these claims would divert attention from his central purposes: the assertion that one cannot apply to art the morality of daily life, and the corresponding vindication of his own poetry. Above all, he strives to convince officialdom that he writes 'sans autre excitation que celle de l'amour du Beau et de la Justice' (II, 76): there is a particularly mordant irony in the final noun.

Indeed, his reflections on the acquittal are carefully presented in the guise of an afterthought: 'puisque j'ai prononcé ce mot splendide et terrible, la Justice, qu'il me soit permis, – comme aussi bien cela m'est agréable, – de remercier la magistrature française de l'éclatant exemple d'impartialité et de bon goût qu'elle a donné dans cette circonstance' (II, 76–7). The lines might almost have been written by the councillor Lieuvain, who opened Yonville's agricultural show with the following words: 'qu'il me soit permis d'abord (avant de vous entretenir de l'objet de cette réunion d'aujourd'hui, et ce sentiment, j'en suis sûr, sera partagé par tous), qu'il me soit permis, dis-je, de rendre justice à l'administration supérieure, au gouvernement, au monarque'.[4] Under a thin veneer of praise for the magistrates' faithful and impartial judgements, Baudelaire staunchly supports not only *Madame Bovary* but, implicitly, *Les Fleurs du mal*, since each work explores, in a similarly impartial and faithful manner, 'un champ, banal comme tous les champs, flagellé, trempé, comme la nature elle-même, par tous les vents et tous les orages' (II, 77). Far from agreeing that Flaubert's novel is in any way offensive, therefore, Baudelaire insists that Flaubert has drawn his theme from among the most common of experiences, rendering his statement all the more provocative both by adopting a tone which simply takes such a conception for granted, and by selecting such unexpected, richly connotative terms as 'flagellé', 'trempé' and 'holocauste'. The paradoxical contrast between the corruption of the accusers and the beauty of the accused, which, according to Baudelaire, should have shielded the novel from recriminations, is repeated in an irate attack on 'cette société qui a définitivement abjuré tout amour spirituel' (II, 77). With calculated provocation, therefore, Baudelaire twists the common accusation that the physical love portrayed in *Madame Bovary* is immoral, contending in strongly physiological terms that such an attack merely reveals that the public itself 'n'a plus cure que de ses viscères' (II, 77).

Behind the mask of praise for the magistrates, Baudelaire insinuates that, because their task is limited to truth and justice, they should have no jurisdiction over art, whose primary concern is the creation of beauty. Even more ironic is the claim that the acquittal represents the permanent victory of art over narrow bourgeois morality: this throws into harsh relief the inconsistency of those who, after proclaiming Flaubert's innocence, affirmed Baudelaire's guilt.

Baudelaire abruptly discounts any accusation that 'le livre a dû son immense faveur au procès et à l'acquittement' (II, 77): the stress placed on the 'immense faveur' offers a clue to part of Baudelaire's interest in the novel, just as later he mentioned Flaubert as having 'trouvé un repos d'esprit suffisant pour accomplir [. . .] une fort belle œuvre et devenir célèbre d'un seul coup' (CI, 458). Several critics did indeed trace the novel's success to the publicity given by the trial, among them Cuvillier-

Fleury, who claimed that 'cette aventure de police correctionnelle lui donne un air de fruit défendu qui ne nuit pas à un livre',[5] and the pugnaciously moralistic Pontmartin, according to whom, '*Madame Bovary* s'est présentée au public dans les conditions les plus favorables, unissant, à son profit, les immunités d'une innocence officielle à l'appât d'un scandale entrevu'.[6] Barbey d'Aurevilly, whose attitude to the novel remained uneasily ambiguous, remarked that 'rien n'a manqué à sa fortune; ni la pointe du scandale, qui est le sel d'un livre en France, ni l'intérêt dramatique d'un procès'.[7] And Flaubert himself declared dryly: 'le procès [. . .] m'a fait une réclame gigantesque' and he attributed to it 'les trois quarts de [son] succès'.[8]

The influence of external circumstances on the creation and subsequent popularity of the novel is suggested in two further remarks. Firstly, Baudelaire refers to *Madame Bovary*'s serialization in the *Revue de Paris*. As in the prefaces to Poe he insists on the importance of the total effect made by a work of art, contending that this means of publication vitiated the essential harmony. Sainte-Beuve had made the same point, declaring that 'si saisissantes qu'en fussent les parties, [le roman] devait y perdre, et surtout la pensée générale, la conception devait en souffrir'.[9] Secondly, Baudelaire asserts that the novel's nature was determined by the way in which Flaubert's genius succeeded in reconciling the two opposing forces facing him at the time he created *Madame Bovary*. To explain why Flaubert's situation was at once excellent and unfavourable, he examines the contemporary social and literary climate. The technique is similar to that adopted in the Dupont preface and reappears in much of his later criticism. The notes on *Les Liaisons dangereuses*, for example, insist that 'le grand homme n'est jamais aérolithe' (11, 69), and when he declined to devote to Maturin 'un travail critique et biographique', he explained that: 'dans un pareil travail, il faudrait expliquer ce que c'est que Maturin, quel rang il occupe dans l'histoire de la littérature moderne, ce que c'est que la littérature satanique, par où il touche à Byron, etc., etc.' (*C*11, 467).

Paradoxically, Baudelaire insists that Flaubert's position was excellent precisely because, since the death of Balzac, interest in the novel had ebbed, clearing the way for a powerful novelist to seize the public's attention and win its favour. As in the Dupont preface, Baudelaire thus implies that to be successful an artist must be alert to current trends.

To depict more clearly Flaubert's position, he evokes the central characteristics of a small band of novelists who, while failing 'forcer le seuil branlant de la Popularité' (11, 79) have nevertheless made valiant attempts to do so. On the one hand he singles out those writers – Custine, Barbey d'Aurevilly, Champfleury and Barbara – who appeal to a small minority and the very nature of whose talent and aims prevents them from enjoying widespread popularity: indeed, Baudelaire ironically affirms that they encounter 'toute la mauvaise fortune que méritait [leur] talent' (11, 78). Each of these writers, in his own way, is too interested in the exceptional to appeal to the majority (cf. 11, 106). On the other hand, Féval, Soulié and Sue, more concerned to create a breathtaking series of adventures than subtle depictions of character, have failed 'accomplir le léger et soudain miracle de cette pauvre petite provinciale adultère, dont toute l'histoire, sans imbroglio, se compose de tristesses, de dégoûts, de soupirs et de quelques pâmoisons fébriles arrachés à une vie barrée par le suicide' (11, 79).[10] Baudelaire is able to express the novel's basic themes and essential atmosphere with such vigour, partly by the force of the nouns: the unexpected use of 'miracle' is intensified by its conjunction with the adjectives 'léger' and 'soudain', the latter recalling his frequent description of the moment of inspiration as an 'explosion', and an additional dimension is given to 'tristesses' and 'dégoûts' by putting them in the plural to imply monotonous repetition. The forceful expression is also due in part to the conciseness of the participial phrases with the energetic 'arrachés' and 'barrée', and in part to the string of alliterative adjectives in 'pauvre petite provinciale adultère'.

The failure of other writers to seize public attention may have been in Flaubert's favour, but Baudelaire contends that he was at the same time handicapped by the increasing apathy and materialism of contemporary readers, a claim he is to repeat with growing astringency in the later criticism. The contemporary materialism is evoked all the more intensely by the metaphor 'budget d'enthousiasme', with its insistence on money and avarice. The earlier suggestion that Baudelaire saw similarities between the way in which Dupont and Flaubert profited from current emotions and opinions is strengthened by the claim here that 'les dernières années de Louis-Philippe avaient vu les dernières explosions d'un esprit encore excitable par les jeux de l'imagination' (11, 79). The bitterness of his attack and the physicality of such expressions as 'abrutie et goulue', with the implication that intelligence has ceded to animality, suggests that Baudelaire finds his situation as a poet in such a society all but intolerable. His admiration for Flaubert's ability to turn such a situation to his own advantage and his desire to discover the reasons behind the novelist's aesthetic decisions no doubt represent both a desire to understand and an attempt to whip up his own flagging energy and courage, just as later his reading of *Salammbô* aroused 'un sentiment d'envie fortifiante' (*C*11, 238).

Although he obviously enjoys and generally succeeds in the *tour de force* which consists in the epigrammatic indication of a writer's genius, Baudelaire seems to me less successful in this instance when he tries to link his contemporaries to the wider literary background of Dickens on the one hand and Byron and Bulwer Lytton on the other. Those following in Dickens's footsteps are clearly Champfleury, Barbara and Féval, with their interest in the detail of everyday life, while d'Aurevilly's studies of passion might be compared to Byron's. Bulwer Lytton's painstaking evocation of past ages hardly seems appropriate: possibly Baudelaire is confusing him with Walter Scott and suggesting a parallel between the latter and Custine, whose *Romuald* begins in the Isle of Man, which Custine places in the Outer Hebrides.

In the studies devoted to Poe, the artist features as juggler (11, 316) or charlatan: in the review of *Madame Bovary* he becomes a fencer, for whom the problem of seizing the public's attention represents an intellectual tournament. Baudelaire's image of Flaubert assessing current trends and rationally deciding how best to turn them to advantage bears the indisputable influence of Poe's 'The Philosophy of Composition', with its equally unemotional manipulation of sentiment and language, and with its degree of *pince-sans-rire* leg-pulling.[11] According to Baudelaire, Flaubert concludes that, because his readers are insensitive to greatness and nobility, his subject must of necessity be trite. Given their embarrassment in the face of undisguised passion, he will maintain an icy impersonality no matter how rousing the events he relates. Thirdly, Baudelaire suggests that Flaubert has deliberately chosen to exploit the current confusion caused by the Realists: while appearing to conform to their manifesto – 'nous serons, comme dit l'école, objectif et impersonnel' (11, 80) – he transcends it, for whereas the Realists attempt a banal representation of the trivial, the power of Flaubert's novel derives in part from the tension between word and meaning, achieved by expressing what is generally considered important in terms usually reserved for the commonplace, and by cloaking banality in a language which is 'nerveux, pittoresque, subtil, exact' (11, 80).

With this extraordinarily condensed and appropriate evocation of Flaubert's style, and the advanced insight into the creation of *Madame Bovary*, Baudelaire subtly disarms the many critics who condemned Flaubert for precisely these characteristics. While they bemoaned or castigated his supposedly impersonal representation of a world they felt beneath their notice, Baudelaire, revealing yet again his interest in method, quietly points out that Flaubert has thus discovered 'une méthode nouvelle de création' (11, 80). Sainte-Beuve, in contrast, although forced to admit that Flaubert's analysis is 'profonde, délicate,

serrée', could not set aside time-worn standards, asking: 'est-ce moral?
est-ce consolant? L'auteur ne semble pas s'être posé cette question; il ne
s'est demandé qu'une chose: Est-ce vrai?'[12] Similarly, Mazade, voicing
in the *Revue des deux mondes* his paper's opposition to Realism,[13] stated
haughtily that Flaubert possessed 'un certain don d'observation
vigoureuse et âcre; mais il saisit les objets pour ainsi dire par l'extérieur
sans pénétrer jusqu'aux profondeurs de la vie morale'.[14] While Baudelaire reveals the reasons behind Flaubert's so-called impersonality and
Sainte-Beuve, despite reservations, considered it 'une grande preuve de
force', Cuvillier-Fleury was far more typical of contemporary beliefs
when he complained that 'Flaubert y met du sien le moins qu'il peut: ni
imagination, ni émotion, ni morale'.[15]

In describing Flaubert's style as subtle and exact, however, Baudelaire was closer to current critical opinion. Barbey d'Aurevilly, torn
between admiration for Flaubert's technical skills and disapproval of his
subject, considered the language of *Madame Bovary* 'colorée, brillante,
étincelante et d'une précision presque scientifique'.[16] E. Texier likewise
emphasized 'le charme du style, la vigueur de l'expression'.[17] Mazade
and Cuvillier-Fleury, however, were enraged, the first objecting to 'ses
néologismes étranges et barbares', while the second condemned a
'style si étrangement mêlé de vulgarité et de prétention'.[18]

It is through the same lucid process which selected theme and
approach, according to Baudelaire, that Flaubert has chosen the setting,
characters and principal events of the novel. If he has placed his novel
in the provinces, it is because life there is stifled by stupidity and
dominated by minor civil servants who exercise just enough power to
give them an inflated idea of their own importance and to render them
intolerant of anyone unable to conform. In describing these officials,
Baudelaire disdainfully repeats the epithet 'petits' (II, 80) just as he later
defines Emma as 'très sublime [. . .] dans son petit milieu et en face de
son petit horizon' (II, 83).

Turning to Flaubert's choice of adultery as his central theme,
Baudelaire appeals to the reader's sophistication, deflating the furore by
reversing the rhetoric, quietly recalling that this is the most trivial of
subjects. It is not only the theme that is commonplace: in Flaubert's
imagined monologue, he asserts that the heroine herself need not be
unusual. Provided that she is 'suffisamment jolie, qu'elle ait des nerfs, de
l'ambition, une aspiration irréfrénable vers un monde supérieur, elle
sera intéressante' (II, 81). The phrase 'une aspiration irréfrénable vers
un monde supérieur' recalls many passages in the criticism, notably the
preface to *Histoires extraordinaires*, in which Baudelaire described Poe's
heroines as being marked by an 'amour insatiable du Beau' (II, 318). It

also reflects Baudelaire's own longing for a world beyond, his desire to achieve 'une tension des forces spirituelles vers le ciel' (I, 401). Clearly, the Emma Baudelaire describes is as much his own creation as that of Flaubert.

Baudelaire, influenced no doubt by the fascination with *calculs et problèmes* he shared with Poe, sees Flaubert's novel as a *tour de force*, a carefully planned response to a series of artistic challenges. In his eyes, Flaubert, through analysis and logic, has proved, as Hugo tried to prove in several prefaces, notably those to *Cromwell* and *Les Orientales*, that 'tous les sujets sont indifféremment bons ou mauvais, selon la manière dont ils sont traités' (II, 81). Flaubert himself insisted that 'on peut intéresser avec tous les sujets. Quant à faire du Beau avec eux, je le pense aussi, [. . .] mais j'en suis moins sûr.'[19]

Having revealed the logic underpinning the novel, Baudelaire returns to the important question of morality in works of art. In what J. Gale justifiably sees as a direct attack on Sainte-Beuve,[20] he recalls that 'plusieurs critiques avaient dit: cette œuvre, vraiment belle par la minutie et la vivacité des descriptions, ne contient pas un seul personnage qui représente la morale, qui parle la conscience de l'auteur' (II, 81). This is a precise summary both of Sainte-Beuve's guarded enthusiasm for Flaubert's style and of his complaint that 'le bien est trop absent; pas un personnage ne le représente'.[21] Pontmartin, too, sneered that 'le côté moral [. . .] n'y brille que par son absence'.[22] Nonetheless, Baudelaire's main target is not literary critics alone: when he paraphrases their demand for a character personifying a 'réquisitoire', and angrily denounces this 'éternelle et incorrigible confusion des fonctions et des genres', his shafts are aimed, however obliquely, at the magistrates, those men 'dont les facultés ne sont mises en réquisition que pour le Juste et le Vrai' (II, 77), but who nevertheless presume to judge art. Baudelaire's literary criticism bears trenchant witness to the ire aroused in him by the attempt to force literature to perform tasks alien to its main function: already present in the review of *Prométhée délivré*, the idea is explored in 'Notes nouvelles' and taken up again in the essay on Gautier. Flaubert himself was in full agreement with Baudelaire that 'la morale de l'art consiste dans sa beauté même'.[23] In Baudelaire's eyes, 'la logique de l'œuvre suffit à toutes les postulations de la morale, et c'est au lecteur à tirer les conclusions de la conclusion' (II, 82). This is very similar to Balzac's protestation, which Baudelaire quotes from memory in 'Les Drames et les romans honnêtes': 'malheur à vous, messieurs, si le sort des Lousteau et des Lucien vous inspire de l'envie!' (II, 42). Despite his reservations, Sainte-Beuve made an analogous claim: 'le livre, certes, a une moralité: [. . .] il ne tient qu'au lecteur de la tirer et même terrible'. Although he is close to Sainte-Beuve here, one should not underestimate Baudelaire's courage in rejecting the competence of his judges and in running counter to powerful critics on whose goodwill depended, in large measure, the success of *Les Fleurs du mal*.

The fifth section of the review (II, 84) pugnaciously returns to the question of literature and morality, launching a two-pronged attack on those who have sought to condemn *Madame Bovary* on moral grounds. On the one hand, he insinuates that a Christian society, given the example of Christ and the adultress, is totally unjustified in such hypocritical censure. On the other hand, he calmly points out that being cuckolded is hardly a world-shattering tragedy. In poking fun at the moral codes of the bourgeoisie, Baudelaire, having compared Emma to a 'bizarre Pasiphaé' (II, 84), refers to the deceived husbands as 'minotaurisés'. The allusion here is to Balzac's *Physiologie du mariage*: 'quand une femme est inconséquente, le mari sera, selon moi, *minotaurisé*'.[24] The reference to the 'vitesse rotatoire des sphères', however, reflects Baudelaire's preoccupation with Poe's *Eurêka* and its theorizing on the creation of the universe. Both examples reveal the eclectic nature of his reading and the way in which he drew on it to invigorate his literary criticism.

In his review of *Madame Bovary*, Baudelaire tries to turn attention away from the moral question, emphasizing the way in which art has transformed something grotesque and repugnant. Once again, in defending Flaubert, Baudelaire protects himself. The final sentence of this indignant paragraph is as appropriate to *Les Fleurs du mal* as to the novel, the word 'contagieuse', moreover, providing a further key to his motivation in writing the review:

> il est temps qu'un terme soit mis à l'hypocrisie de plus en plus contagieuse, et qu'il soit réputé ridicule pour des hommes et des femmes, pervertis jusqu'à la trivialité, de crier: haro! sur un malheureux auteur qui a daigné, avec une chasteté de rhéteur, jeter un voile de gloire sur des aventures de tables de nuit, toujours répugnantes et grotesques, quand la Poésie ne les caresse pas de sa clarté de veilleuse opaline (II, 84).

Similarly, in his essay on Gautier, Baudelaire will assert that Balzac is able 'revêtir, à coup sûr, de lumière et de pourpre la pure trivialité' (II, 120). For Flaubert, the light is semi-translucent, appropriate to the delicacy and sombreness of his analysis: for Balzac it is a triumphant blaze of colour and light, which leaves nothing hidden. Thus, while critics such as Dumesnil were berating Flaubert as a *voyeur* and condemning the novel as 'un des plus immoraux que je connaisse',[25] while Barbey d'Aurevilly failed to see in Flaubert's approach anything but insensitivity,[26] Baudelaire provocatively changes the focus, emphasizing that the novel's language, far from being crude or salacious, lends value and dignity to his theme.

This non-didactic evaluation of the novel also dominates Baudelaire's account of the way in which Emma was created: she, too, is part of the *gageure*, a vital component of Flaubert's *tour de force*. Yet, according to Baudelaire, if Flaubert succeeded in producing 'une merveille' it is precisely because he failed 'se dépouiller [. . .] de son sexe'. For Baudelaire, Emma unites 'toutes les séductions d'une âme virile dans un charmant corps féminin' (II, 81). Sainte-Beuve, on the contrary, answered his question: 'comment la définir?' with the simple reply: 'elle est femme'.[27] It is surely Baudelaire's interest in the androgynous which has determined his appreciation of Emma. This interest can also be detected in 'L'Art philosophique', on which he may have started working as early as 1857 (II, 1377). Referring to Janmot's series of paintings entitled *Le Poème de l'âme*, he explains that, since each painting contains both a boy and a girl, he wondered whether the 'pensée intime du poème n'était pas [. . .] l'histoire du double élément mâle et femelle d'une même âme' (II, 604). Moreover, a passage interpolated into his version of De Quincey's confessions claims that

> l'homme qui, dès le commencement, a été longtemps baigné dans la molle atmosphère de la femme [. . .] y a contracté [. . .] une espèce d'androgynéité, sans [laquelle] le génie le plus âpre et le plus viril reste, relativement [. . .] incomplet (*MO*, 224–6).

The curiosity about the androgynous was shared by many of Baudelaire's contemporaries, notably Gautier who exploited the theme in *Mademoiselle de Maupin*, while Leconte de Lisle, in the preface to *Poèmes et Poésies*, contended that 'le monde moderne ne réussit à concevoir des types féminins, qu'à la condition d'altérer leur essence même, soit en leur attribuant un caractère viril, comme à lady Macbeth, ou à Julie, soit en les reléguant dans une sphère nébuleuse et fantastique, comme pour Béatrice'.[28]

In presenting Emma as a blend of masculine and feminine traits, Baudelaire, perhaps unconsciously, makes her resemble himself, both as he was and as he would have liked to be. This passage has been seen as a possible origin of Flaubert's putative statement: 'Madame Bovary c'est moi'.[29] Nevertheless, Barbey d'Aurevilly's conclusion is closer in expression than Baudelaire's to the statement Flaubert is said to have made.[30] 'M. Flaubert', he wrote, 'est la Madame Bovary de son livre.'[31] For Barbey, however, this represents a failing on Flaubert's part: Baudelaire may, therefore, be responding to Barbey's censure by showing the extent to which Emma's masculinity can be seen as a proof of the novel's strength.

Emma, Baudelaire provocatively insists, is unlike most women, who are controlled by 'ce qu'on appelle le cœur' (II, 82), in that her dominant quality is imagination. The contrast between *imagination* and *cœur* is also present in 'L'Art philosophique', which warns against confusing 'la sensibilité de l'imagination avec celle du cœur' (II, 604, cf. II, 11). In the trio of *imagination, cœur, raison*, therefore, imagination reigns supreme and must be distinguished from the products of reason and the senses or emotions. As the Pléiade notes point out (II, 1123), the passage suggests the kind of reverie on imagination which culminates in the masterly passages of the *Salon de 1859*. Indeed, Baudelaire's pre-occupation with the theme has to some extent determined the per-spective in which he sees Emma, although the importance of her imagination was thrown into relief by most contemporary critics. Sainte-Beuve, for example, depicted her as 'rêveuse et sensible à l'excès', adding that 'elle a un défaut grave, elle n'a pas beaucoup de cœur; l'imagination de bonne heure a tout pris et absorbé'.[33] Sainte-Beuve's reference to the *cœur*, with its conventional overtones of bourgeois sweetness as the ideal quality for women, may well have provoked Baudelaire's sardonic expression: 'ce qu'on appelle le cœur'. Pontmartin, whose literary judgements are often shaped by his right-wing political convictions, asserted: 'Madame Bovary, c'est l'exaltation maladive des sens et de l'imagination dans la démocratie mécontente.'[34] And Cuvillier-Fleury castigated her for possessing nothing but 'de l'imagination et des sens, des besoins de luxe et des appétits de plaisir'.[35]

Baudelaire's eagerness to emphasize both those qualities which make Emma approach his ideal and those which have a counterpart in his own nature can be seen in the second of her so-called masculine traits: 'énergie soudaine d'action, rapidité de décision, fusion mystique du raisonnement et de la passion, qui caractérise les hommes créés pour agir' (II, 82). The judgement is valid only to a certain extent. Emma's decisions to remove Berthe from the nurse, to visit Rodolphe at 'La Huchette' in the early days of their affair, and to poison herself, are indeed rapidly reached and instantaneously acted upon. Nevertheless, other episodes serve rather to underline her tendency to vacillate: she is, for example, equally unable to welcome or discourage Léon's unspoken longing for her, and when she yields to Rodolphe, it is not only after considerable hesitation on her part, but also as the result less of her own conscious decision than of submission to his desire. Here it seems to me that Baudelaire sees Emma as half-reflecting, half-contrasting with the paradoxes of his own nature: certainly, these characteristics are examined in the review of *La Double Vie* with its lament for 'l'intention laissée en route' (II, 87), and in such prose poems as 'Le Mauvais Vitrier' with its analysis of 'une espèce d'énergie qui jaillit de l'ennui et de la rêverie' (I, 285). Above all, Baudelaire stresses the urgent need for constant, practical activity as opposed to the febrile bursts which characterize his own personality.

Thirdly, Baudelaire describes as masculine Emma's 'goût immodéré de la séduction' and its resulting *dandysme*. Many slight touches throughout *Madame Bovary* do indeed create this image of Emma. Flaubert frequently stresses that her fingernails are fastidiously manicured, she often gazes at herself in the mirror, insists that her lingerie be immaculate, and covers her face with cold cream. And, like the dandy, she is constantly acting. In the final stages of her affair with Léon she reveals her 'goût immodéré de la séduction' when she becomes the dominant member of the relationship, and she showers both Rodolphe and Léon with presents, a characteristic more commonly associated with men than with women. Yet, once again, it could be argued that Baudelaire isolates the elements which serve to emphasize his own image of art and the outside world. Surely it is largely Baudelaire's admiration for the ideals of the dandy which leads him to highlight in Emma a rare example of feminine *dandysme*, where most readers might find the more commonplace traits of vanity and the desire to capture and hold a lover's attention. And does she possess that essential quality of the dandy: 'une quintessence de caractère et une intelligence subtile de tout le mécanisme moral de ce monde' (II, 691)? Baudelaire, moreover, introduces a distinctly personal note in examining Emma's desire to dominate others: the way in which it is her illusions which lead her to give herself to men unworthy of her. Here, Emma becomes very much a reflection of Baudelaire himself, since it is 'les sophismes de son imagination' which lead her astray, and she abandons herself 'd'une manière toute masculine' to 'des drôles qui ne sont pas ses égaux, exactement comme les poètes se livrent à des drôlesses'. There are obvious parallels with his own experience and with 'Les Drames et les romans honnêtes', with its claim that 'les maîtresses des poètes sont d'assez vilaines gaupes' (II, 40: cf. II, 1123).[36]

He finds further evidence of Emma's 'qualité toute virile' (II, 82) in that she suffers less from Charles's outward provincialisms than from his inner 'absence totale de génie', giving as an example her wrath when his operation to cure Hippolyte's club foot fails so humiliatingly. Baudelaire's vigorous description of Emma's fury relies on memory. He recalls, in onomatopoeic words and brief, tense phrases which echo the breathlessness of anger, that 'une colère noire, depuis longtemps concentrée, éclate dans toute l'épouse Bovary; les portes claquent' (II, 82). Flaubert had in fact written:

– Assez! cria-t-elle d'un air terrible.
Et s'échappant de la salle, Emma ferma la porte si fort, que le baromètre bondit de la muraille et s'écrasa par terre.[37]

Baudelaire conflates this episode with an earlier incident when he makes Emma cry out: 'Ah! que ne suis-je *au moins* la femme d'un de ces vieux savants chauves et voûtés, dont les yeux abrités de lunettes vertes sont toujours braqués sur les archives de la science!' Much earlier in Flaubert's novel, Emma had watched Charles fall asleep over a medical journal: 'que n'avait-elle, au moins, pour mari un de ces hommes d'ardeurs taciturnes qui travaillent la nuit dans des livres, et portent enfin, à soixante ans quand vient l'âge des rhumatismes, une brochette en croix'.[38] Here, as elsewhere, Baudelaire reveals his ability to recreate episodes from memory, bringing them alive with telling expressions: in this case, the scholars are brought into sharp focus with the expression 'chauves et voûtés' and by the reference to their 'lunettes vertes', while the intensity of concentration is suggested by the more unusual word 'braqués'.

In emphasizing Emma's frustrated ambition for her husband, and the confused longing for inner qualities which outweighs her irritation with external faults, Baudelaire faithfully reflects the duality of Flaubert's vision, insisting, as he does, on the stereotyped nature of Emma's ideals. Yet there is more to the intensity of Baudelaire's style here, with the contrast between physical and spiritual characteristics being forcefully etched in through the strongly-worded opposing pairs: 'défectuosités extérieures visibles', 'provincialismes aveuglants' on the one hand, and 'absence totale de génie', 'infériorité spirituelle bien constatée' (II, 82) on the other. Once again, the barely contained anger in the language probably springs from Baudelaire's intense preoccupation with personal problems. Certainly he seems to be drawing clear parallels between Emma's situation and his own relationship both with society at large and with a woman incapable of comprehending and responding to his genius.

Similarly, in insisting that Emma revealed from her early school days an 'aptitude étonnante à la vie', Baudelaire superimposes on the fictional character not only his own image of the ideal artist but also emotive personal recollections of his own childhood (cf. I, 680). It is no doubt these memories that lead him to claim that Emma 'se gorgeait de la musique solennelle des vêpres': Flaubert was in fact far more sardonic, referring merely to 'pacifiques compositions qui lui laissaient entrevoir, à travers la niaiserie du style et les imprudences de la note, l'attirante fantasmagorie des réalités sentimentales'.[39] And when he refers to Emma's delight in the 'teintes orientales que les longues fenêtres ouvragées jetaient sur son paroissien de pensionnaire' (11, 83), Baudelaire certainly seems to be drawing on his own childhood memories: Flaubert makes no mention at all of stained-glass windows. Once again, the precision of the small details, the 'longues fenêtres ouvragées', the 'teintes orientales', the 'paroissien de pensionnaire', create the denser texture which seems to indicate personal reminiscence. Finally, one might compare to these experiences the *volupté* felt by the child in 'Les Vocations' who describes his vision of God with 'une inexprimable expression d'extase et de regret' (1, 333).

In like manner, Baudelaire's insistence on Emma's 'hysteria' is both closely linked to Flaubert's own interest in the interdependence of physiological and psychological factors and also reflects essential aspects of Baudelaire. Not only is 'hysteria' frequently mentioned in *Madame Bovary*, but the description Baudelaire gives of it as 'une boule ascendante et asphyxiante' recalls Emma's symptoms when she discovers that Rodolphe has left her:

> — J'étouffe! s'écria-t-elle en se levant d'un bond. Mais, par un effort de volonté, ce spasme disparut; puis:
> — Ce n'est rien! dit-elle, ce n'est rien! c'est nerveux![40]

'Hysteria' exerted an ambiguous fascination over Baudelaire for both personal and artistic reasons. Not only in the well-known passage in 'Hygiène' (1, 668), but also in parts of *Le Spleen de Paris* and *Les Paradis artificiels*, it poses a constant threat. The narrator of 'Le Vieux Saltimbanque', for example, feels his throat gripped by 'la main terrible de l'hystérie' (1, 296) and its power is forcibly portrayed in 'Le Mauvais Vitrier' through an examination of 'cette humeur, hystérique selon les médecins, satanique selon ceux qui pensent un peu mieux que les médecins, qui nous pousse sans résistance vers une foule d'actions dangereuses ou inconvenantes' (1, 286). Doctors of the time, as Gérard Wajeman points out, were indeed fascinated by 'hysteria', which they saw as the affliction *par excellence* of women. As Wajeman indicates, however, it was 'une affection [. . .] jusqu'au milieu du xixe siècle rejetée vers la marge d'un savoir impuissant à en rendre compte'.[41] It may well have been this refusal to analyse 'hysteria' that led Baudelaire both to insist on the intrinsic interest of this affliction, and to suggest that much more could be drawn from it, that it could form 'le fond et le tuf d'une œuvre littéraire' (11, 83). Furthermore, he strengthens the parallels he has constantly drawn between himself and Emma by affirming that 'hysteria' in woman has as its counterpart in 'les hommes nerveux' 'toutes les impuissances' and 'l'aptitude à tous les excès'. Curiously enough, Briquet's *Traité clinique et thérapeutique de l'hystérie*, published in 1859, is, according to Wajeman, the first work to prove the existence of hysteria in men, and it was not until the end of the century that doctors began to consider it, not as a malfunction of the uterus, but as a disorder of the nerves. Through their insight into human nature, their reading of such writers as Brierre de Boismont, and, above all, through their own personal experience, Flaubert and Baudelaire seem to have revealed intuitively truths which scientific research was not to discover for some time.

Emma's 'hysteria' was seldom mentioned by contemporary critics. Texier, however, described her as 'l'hystérique Madame Bovary', and asserted ambiguously that Flaubert had 'une façon de voir les sentiments à un point de vue physique dont la brutalité vous blesse et ne vous déplaît pas toujours'. Texier, in fact, is one of the rare critics to suggest a connection between the physical and the mental and to go beyond the usual view of Flaubert as a medical student misusing his scalpel. Even he, however, advises Flaubert 'oublier, dans une certaine mesure, ses études physiologiques quand il écrira un roman nouveau'.[42]

Appearing to yield to public opinion, in order to oppose it all the more strongly, Baudelaire admits that Emma may well seem ridiculous (cf. 11, 155). Certainly Mazade described her as such, referring with heavy-handed irony to 'la figure resplendissante' of the novel's heroine.[43] Barbey d'Aurevilly, on the contrary, insisted like Baudelaire that 'le grand mérite de ce roman est dans la figure principale, qui est toute la pensée du livre et qui, quoique commune, cesse de l'être par la profondeur avec laquelle elle est entendue et traitée'.[44] For Baudelaire, Emma is certainly ridiculous to some extent, but: 'qu'importe? disons-le, avouons-le, c'est un César à Carpentras; elle poursuit l'Idéal' (11, 84).[45]

Baudelaire's view of Flaubert's creation is summed up in a deliberately provocative statement: 'toutes les femmes *intellectuelles* lui sauront gré d'avoir élevé la femelle à une si haute puissance, si loin de l'animal pur et si près de l'homme idéal' (11, 83). Where most critics sought to emphasize Emma's depravity, contrasting her sharply with their comfortable, spun-sugar image of woman, Baudelaire challenges his reader to see Emma as Flaubert has created her, caught between the animality of 'la femelle' and the intellectuality of 'l'homme idéal'.

His enthusiasm for the novel in general and the heroine in particular is evident from the taut style, the breathless interpolation of questions and exclamations, and the highly original metaphors with which the passage is studded. He himself comments, 'si je m'abandonnais sur cette pente analytique, je n'en finirais jamais avec *Madame Bovary*; ce livre, essentiellement suggestif, pourrait souffler un volume d'observations' (II, 84).[46] In thanking Baudelaire for his review, Flaubert took up this statement, remarking: 'si vous trouvez mon livre suggestif, ce que vous avez écrit dessus ne l'est pas moins'.[47] Both saw creative and critical literature as a springboard for more far-reaching questions and meditations.

Two further aspects of this 'livre suggestif' seem to Baudelaire to have been 'ou négligés ou vitupérés par les critiques' (II, 84). Firstly, he defends the episode of the disastrous operation, which most critics left unmentioned or condemned as an unnecessary excrescence destroying the harmony of the novel's structure. Baudelaire, on the contrary, perceived that it 'sert à mettre en vive lumière tout le caractère de la personne' (II, 82). Secondly, in what appears to be a response to Barbey d'Aurevilly's accusations, he extracts from the scene in which Emma seeks help from the *curé* not only its structural importance but also its emotive power. Where Sainte-Beuve refers only briefly to the incident and Barbey sees no more than 'une intention de caricature', a further example of Flaubert's failure to give his work the 'puissante variété que les grands romanciers doivent faire abonder dans leurs œuvres',[48] for Baudelaire it is an 'épisode [. . .] véritablement *moderne*', revealing both the Church's failure to help Emma and the way in which she is left with no further course than to plunge into 'les eaux tourbillonnantes de l'adultère', a phrase which parodies the language of moralistic critics. Baudelaire recounts the interview, relying on memory, and introducing a strongly suggestive personal reminiscence as well as a direct appeal to the reader's own experience. He asks: 'quel est celui de nous qui, dans un âge plus naïf et dans des circonstances troublées, n'a pas fait forcément connaissance avec le prêtre incompétent?' (II, 85). Once again, what Baudelaire seeks to emphasize is how commonplace is an episode which has aroused such widespread anger.

The article concludes with a surprisingly brief comparison between *La Tentation de Saint Antoine* and *Madame Bovary*. Despite its brevity, the comparison manages to convey much detail with great sensitivity. Although, when he wrote the review, *La Tentation* was still available only in uncollected fragments, Baudelaire has evidently found in it characteristics and insights which have deepened his appreciation of *Madame Bovary*. Significantly, the two qualities he most admires in both works are irony and lyricism. In his private diaries, he singles out 'deux qualités littéraires fondamentales: surnaturalisme et ironie' (I, 658), and, although *surnaturalisme* and *lyrisme* may not be synonymous, Baudelaire's use of the former term suggests that he associates it with moments of great intensity (cf. I, 659), among which are to be numbered the instants of poetical fervour which give rise to lyricism.

Baudelaire contends that not only do the two works share their modes of expression, but *Madame Bovary* is a transposition, into bourgeois, contemporary terms, of *La Tentation*, the demons harassing Emma being those of illusion and heresy, combined with the torments of material desires. And although *La Tentation* is remote in time and place, Saint Antoine is indeed 'harassé par toutes les folies qui nous circonviennent' (II, 85).

According to Baudelaire, the clue to *La Tentation* is 'cette faculté souffrante, souterraine et révoltée, qui traverse toute l'œuvre'. This sentence, which sheds light on Baudelaire's approach to literature as much as it puts into relief Flaubert's aesthetics, is also a commentary on both *Le Spleen de Paris* and *Les Fleurs du mal*. Clearly, the aspects he chooses to mention in discussing both works are those which have most bearing on his own situation and which can, therefore, suggest to him ways in which he can transform personal preoccupations into works of art.

Baudelaire's understanding of Flaubert, which may be intuitive, but which may spring from their conversations, is fully revealed by his assertion that Flaubert 'a volontairement voilé dans *Madame Bovary* les hautes facultés lyriques et ironiques manifestées sans réserve dans la *Tentation*'. In his letters to Louise Colet, Flaubert confessed that *Madame Bovary* was 'loin de [sa] manière naturelle' while in *La Tentation de Saint Antoine*, he says, 'j'étais chez moi'.[49]

Baudelaire's review drew from Flaubert the following delighted response: 'votre article m'a fait le plus grand plaisir. Vous êtes entré dans les arcanes de l'œuvre, comme si ma cervelle était la vôtre' (*LAB*, 153). Margaret Gilman considers it 'the best of all Baudelaire's criticism'.[50] Nevertheless, and bearing in mind Baudelaire's declaration that his article aspires in no way to completeness, there are several surprising omissions.

Although Emma's character is analysed with obvious enjoyment, Bournisien, Charles, Léon and Rodolphe are only fleetingly examined, albeit with insight and freshness. Given Baudelaire's pleasure in graphic caricature, it is remarkable that Homais is not even mentioned. This is all the more surprising – or perhaps all the more comprehensible – since many contemporary critics devoted much ink to the pharmacist. Sainte-Beuve, for example, saw him as 'le M. Prudhomme de la demi-science'.[51] Similarly, Denys, who was warmly enthusiastic about the novel, admiring its 'pages éblouissantes d'audace et de vérité', defines Homais as a 'Joseph Prudhomme de province'.[52] Finally, Barbey d'Aurevilly claimed that Flaubert's 'pharmacien Homais, trop vanté, est une variété spéciale de l'éternel Prudhomme, le type universel dont le fantôme plane actuellement sur tous les esprits, si peu aptes au comique, du dix-neuvième siècle'.[53] It is significant that so many contemporary critics saw Monnier's Prudhomme as a great creation. Baudelaire, however, argues in 'Quelques caricaturistes français' that 'au lieu de saisir entièrement et d'emblée tout l'ensemble d'une figure ou d'un sujet, Henri Monnier procédait par un lent et successif examen des détails' (II, 557). It is regrettable that Baudelaire did not examine the link between Prudhomme and Homais, although it may perhaps be that the pharmacist was too remote from Baudelaire's own nature greatly to interest him. Nevertheless, Flaubert's virulent satire of Homais should have appealed to Baudelaire, precisely because the pharmacist's views are a quintessence of what he himself most despised in his contemporaries.

In addition, the review makes only an oblique reference to what Thibaudet has called the other end of the 'chandelle ridicule' that Emma burns:[54] after all, it is her passion for 'beautiful' and expensive objects which leads her so far into debt that she poisons herself. The only allusions to this are in Baudelaire's description of Emma as a *dandy* and in his comparison between *Madame Bovary* and *La Tentation de Saint Antoine*, where Baudelaire lists as one of Emma's temptations the 'lubricités de la matière environnante'. The intensity of the vocabulary here is certainly revealing: 'lubricités' suggests the kind of connection between profligacy and prodigality that Freud was to discuss fifty years later, and it indicates the tumult and guilt of Baudelaire's own complex reaction to money. Perhaps Emma's condition is so analogous to Baudelaire's – he, too, knowing the overwhelming desire to possess the beautiful and the shame and despair of being mercilessly dunned – that an analysis of this aspect would be too painful.

Finally, there is no mention of Flaubert's 'chosisme', his practice of making objects mentioned only in passing sum up a character or predict his future development. The omission may well be linked to Baudelaire's reluctance to discuss stylistic details at length and to his conviction that the public was not prepared to follow an examination of the finer points of art.

The article is remarkable not only for the depth of its insight and the variety of its presentation, but also for the power of its metaphors. Among the crisp definitions of writers, two are particularly arresting. In a gifted pastiche of his style, Barbey d'Aurevilly is depicted as 'chantant, pleurant et criant au milieu de l'orage, planté comme Ajax sur un rocher de désolation'. To Balzac comes the honour of the most daring of metaphors, it, too, a pastiche of the novelist's language: he is 'ce prodigieux météore qui couvrira notre pays d'un nuage de gloire' (II, 78). Many of the images are based on a disorientating use of classical allusions. Emma's combination of masculine characteristics in a woman's body is compared to the birth of Pallas Athene, produced, fully armed, from the brain of Zeus, and her attempt to find her ideal in the shoddy cafés of Rouen makes her appear as a 'bizarre Pasiphaé'. Baudelaire's use of classical mythology is very similar to that of Daumier in *Histoire ancienne*, interpreting it in solid bourgeois terms both to suggest the timelessness of Flaubert's theme and to mock conventional bourgeois morality. There may well be a further reason for Baudelaire's reference to the Pasiphaé myth. In a recent article, Anne Green points out that 'an exchange of letters [. . .] dating from the middle of 1857, when Flaubert was planning his Carthaginian novel, suggests that the initial inspiration was formed by the myth of Pasiphaé'.[55] I would suggest that Baudelaire may have heard directly or through friends both about Flaubert's plans, and his interest in the myth, and that he used these references to suggest the unity of Flaubert's thought, just as he underlines the parallels between *Madame Bovary* and *La Tentation de Saint Antoine*.

In Flaubert, Baudelaire discovered a writer whose preoccupations closely resemble his own, allowing him to offer a detailed and suggestive investigation of the novel and to examine in more general terms the many vital questions it raises. His review poses once again the problem of sudden success, discusses the role of morality in art, stresses that it is not the subject but the way in which it is treated which must be used as the touchstone in judging art, and rejects the conventional stereotype of woman and her relationship with men. With far greater insight than his contemporaries, not excluding Sainte-Beuve, he takes up the main objections to the novel and demolishes them, provocatively challenging his reader to reconsider not only *Madame Bovary*, but also those assumptions about art and human nature on which Flaubert himself throws considerable doubt.

La Double Vie (L'Artiste, 9 January 1859)

When, in September 1858, Baudelaire wrote to the journalist Paul Mantz, apologizing for the delay in completing his essay on Gautier and mentioning that his articles on caricature were still at the press, he nevertheless added: 'je tiens vivement à me charger du livre d'Asselineau

(*La Double Vie*)' (*C*i, 515). One might wonder why he was so eager to review an unexceptionable but second-rate collection of tales at a time when so many other projects jostled for attention. The answer is probably threefold. Firstly, Asselineau had reviewed *Les Fleurs du mal* with warmth and understanding and Baudelaire doubtless welcomed this opportunity to repay the debt (see i, 1197–205). Secondly, the two men had been close friends since they first met in 1845 and, although Baudelaire must occasionally have been amused or exasperated by Asselineau's somewhat philistine attitude to art (see *C*i, 667), their friendship continued throughout the poet's life. Moreover, Baudelaire's willingness to do all in his power to help his friends has been evident from his earliest articles and letters. In particular, he collaborated with Asselineau on the preface to *La Double Vie*, offering witty and cogent comments on expression and thought. As this preface reveals, the two had much in common, sharing an admiration for Romanticism,[56] a desire to comprehend the mechanisms of the mind, particularly in regard to dreams, and a preoccupation with questions of fate and individual liberty. Asselineau's preface to *Le Roman bourgeois*, a work in which Baudelaire claims to have immersed himself (*C*i, 333), underlines their community of mind. This preface, which emphasizes the bad luck that dogged Furetière and describes a world in which sensitivity brings its own punishment and certain men must expiate the faults of others, recalls several passages in Baudelaire's articles on Poe. 'Ne serait-ce pas qu'il y a une damnation particulière sur la vie du satirique?' asks Asselineau, adding: 'ces âmes inflammables, auxquelles la nature donne de si vigoureuses colères contre le vice, de si éloquents ressentiments de l'injustice, portent en elles le châtiment de leur propre délicatesse, et sont destinées à expier dans leurs personnes les vices qu'elles châtient'.[57] Not only the beliefs but also the expressions, especially the phrase 'le châtiment de leur propre délicatesse', seem very close to Baudelaire. Above all, however, *La Double Vie* seems to have stimulated Baudelaire's imagination, provoking meditations on man's duality, the logic of dreams, and the conflict between the ideal and the real.

Structurally, the review follows the pattern of that devoted to Champfleury and the 1852 discussion of Poe's tales. An introductory passage isolating the collection's unifying theme is followed by a brief discussion of each tale in turn, with a final paragraph describing the atmosphere and analysing the style. Compared with the earlier studies, however, the article reveals both greater sureness of touch and a growing concern with the total effect: the meditation of the opening paragraph, for instance, not only introduces themes expanded in the body of the review but also uses several terms to which Baudelaire returns in the concluding paragraph, playing on their resonances to suggest his reservations and Asselineau's limitations.

In emphasizing the power of suggestion in the title, Baudelaire illustrates an assertion he made in reviewing the Exposition universelle of 1855: 'il m'arrivera souvent d'apprécier un tableau uniquement par la somme d'idées ou de rêveries qu'il apportera dans mon esprit' (II, 579). Among contemporary critics, the ardent Babou also applauded the title, insisting that 'ce recueil de nouvelles est bien nommé: l'idée qui le traverse et l'éclaire se résume parfaitement dans le titre du livre'.[58] Cherbuliez, on the contrary, complained petulantly: 'qu'est-ce que la double vie? L'auteur ne le dit pas et laisse au bon public la tâche de se torturer l'esprit pour deviner cette énigme. Nous avons vainement lu son volume d'un bout à l'autre sans y réussir.'[59]

From the outset Baudelaire unmistakably but tactfully conveys certain criticisms. The stories are described as 'petites' and referred to as 'morceaux': the implication that they are too short is reinforced by the repetition of 'petit' in the final paragraph, where the description of the work as a 'charmant petit volume', together with the phrase 'élégant et éloquent volume' (II, 87), suggests both its nature and its limitations. A few weeks after the publication of the review, Baudelaire congratulated Asselineau on his short story 'Lucien S.', but voiced the criticism which his article merely implies: 'voilà de l'énergie pour le coup! et quelle haine! mais toujours trop court, mon ami, toujours trop court. C'est encore un roman abrégé. Tel que c'est, cependant, c'est d'une grande distinction' (CI, 543). Even in his letter, however, Baudelaire is careful to sandwich tactful criticism between words of warm encouragement. Nevertheless, as in his 'Notes nouvelles', Baudelaire warns that although conciseness is essential in a short story, it is still a 'défaut' to make it 'trop courte' (II, 329).

The brevity of the tales formed the main focus of criticism for the few contemporaries who reviewed them. Cherbuliez asserted that Asselineau 'a de l'esprit, de l'imagination, du style, et ne réussit en général avec tout cela qu'à faire des ébauches fort incomplètes. Les données les plus ingénieuses et les plus fécondes restent sous sa plume à l'état d'embryons, faute d'un plan et d'un but.'[60] Eugène Lataye agreed that La Double Vie represented 'plutôt une série d'esquisses et de plans qu'une suite de nouvelles complètement développées', while for Babou, it was 'par excès de précision' that Asselineau restricted himself to 'les limites d'une ébauche'.[61] Finally, Cuvillier-Fleury took up the refrain with his description of 'une collection de nouvelles dont quelques-unes sont de simples ébauches d'une touche assez fine, mais trop peu accusée pour que le critique, s'il n'a de très bons yeux, ait rien à y voir'.[62]

Although Baudelaire suggests reservations through several fleeting touches, he clearly believes that the critic's main task is 'donner une idée de l'esprit qui anime l'ouvrage' (II, 87). To do so, he addresses the reader directly, asking the question which both Asselineau's volume and a chapter heading of Buffon have summoned up with the intensity of an obsession: 'qui parmi nous n'est pas un *homo duplex*?' Although, as so often, he suggests the wider literary background to *La Double Vie* by mentioning Buffon, his admiration for whom he defends in 'Les Bons Chiens' (I, 360), it is obviously the chapter's title, rather than its content, which has sparked off his reverie. The force of the word 'précipité', with its suggestion of physical violence and the implication that the reaction is beyond Baudelaire's control, is reinforced by such strongly physical words as 'provoquer' and 'confronter'.

Just how central the theme of duality is to Baudelaire's thought becomes immediately clear with the brusque intervention of the personal 'nous', the appeal to the reader, and the sudden burst of detail which, as in 'L'Ecole païenne', the review of *Madame Bovary*, and the studies on Poe, seems to indicate self-analysis rather than objective criticism. With an allusion to De Quincey he defines his ideal readers as 'ceux dont l'esprit a été dès l'enfance *touched with pensiveness*' (II, 87).[63] The duality of those 'touched with pensiveness', and in particular those who are artists, is thrown into sharp relief in 'De l'essence du rire', where what is 'essentiellement humain' is shown to combine 'une grandeur infinie' with 'une misère infinie' (II, 532). More importantly, Baudelaire's description of the man who is constantly torn between 'action et intention, rêve et réalité' is not only a résumé of the central themes of *La Double Vie* and a reflection of his own character as it appears in *Les Fleurs du mal* and *Les Paradis artificiels*, but also a seedbed of future prose poems. The longing to travel felt by those who fail to recognize 'la douceur du foyer' (I, 95), for example, recalls both the 'Poème du hachisch', with its reference to the eager questions put by those who 'n'ont jamais quitté le coin de leur feu, quand ils se trouvent en face d'un homme qui revient de pays lointains et inconnus' (I, 408), and the insistent 'Et puis, et puis encore?' of 'Le Voyage' (I, 132). And there are further parallels with the daydreaming of the narrator in 'Les Projects' and the opening sentences of 'Anywhere out of the World': 'cette vie est un hôpital où chaque malade est possédé du désir de changer de lit. Celui-ci voudrait souffrir en face du poêle et celui-là croit qu'il guérirait à côté de la fenêtre' (I, 356). The voyagers who would willingly exchange their adventurous lives for a quiet existence, 'enfermée dans un espace de quelques mètres' (II, 87) reflect Baudelaire's own reaction to his voyage to La Réunion and recall the com-

plaints of the passengers in 'Déjà!' (I, 338), while the joys of the 'vie
casanière' are depicted in such prose poems as 'Les Projets'. Besides,
there are echoes of Gautier's poem 'Destinée':

> Eh bien! celui qui court sur la terre était né
> Pour vivre au coin du feu: le foyer, la famille,
> C'était son vœu; mais Dieu ne l'a pas couronné.
>
> Et l'autre, qui n'a vu du ciel que ce qui brille
> Par le tour du volet, était le voyageur.
> Ils ont passé tous deux à côté du bonheur.[64]

Even the more precise examples of the gulf between plan and action,
however closely linked to *La Double Vie*, seem to draw substance from
Baudelaire's own procrastinations and his desire to transform dream
into reality. The 'rêve oublié dans un auberge' refers both to Asselineau's
tale 'L'Auberge' and, doubtless, to Baudelaire's numerous abandoned
schemes, while 'le projet barré par l'obstacle' suggests 'Le Mensonge'
and 'Les Promesses de Timothée' in Asselineau's collection, but also
recalls the constant frustrations Baudelaire encountered in achieving his
own ambitions. Finally, the reference to misfortune and illness following hard on the heels of success conjures up not only the tale 'L'Enfer
du musicien' but also Baudelaire's view of the fate of writers such as
Hoffmann and Balzac.

The passage is marked by a sub-current of irony: this is Baudelaire's
fruitful period and it is clear that he fears – not without justification –
that things may go wrong. The tone of regret tinged with irony which
pervades this passage is certainly that of many of the tales, but it also
stems from Baudelaire's often repeated longing for a different kind of
existence and the attendant knowledge that this, too, would inevitably
be marred by boredom and discontent.

The image drawing together the disparate threads of *La Double Vie*
insists, through the very materialism of its expression, on the dominance
of everyday reality over the world of dreams: 'l'incessant mécanisme
de la vie terrestre, taquinant et déchirant à chaque minute l'étoffe de la
vie idéale' (II, 87). The image seems to me to have been inspired, in
part, by Balzac's *La Peau de chagrin*, a work which also left its mark on
'Le Poème du hachisch', published in 1860. The mechanism to which
Baudelaire refers, moreover, forms the pivot of 'La Chambre double'
and 'Rêve parisien'.

The dense and suggestive opening passage of Baudelaire's review
concludes with a brief description of Asselineau's style, emphasizing its
intimacy and delicate sincerity. Because of the work's genre, a blend of

monologue and private letter, its unstudied style is not openly condemned. Thus, although Baudelaire attacked George Sand for writing
her novels on letter paper (11, 283), he implies that Asselineau's inborn
reserve enables him to avoid *le style coulant*. Nevertheless, he does very
tactfully suggest the work's limitations through such words as 'abandon'
and 'lettre intime'. Certainly the epithet 'exquis' with its implications of
delicacy and over-refinement subtly conveys Baudelaire's reservations
and the nature of the collection itself.

Turning to a discussion of the individual tales, Baudelaire not only
shows how each one illustrates the central theme of duality, but also
introduces other ideas which Asselineau explores. And, as is so often
the case, Asselineau is very decidedly being presented through the
curved mirror of Baudelaire's own personality. Significantly, two tales,
'Le Plus Beau Temps de la vie' and 'Le Presbytère', both very much
below the standard of the others, are left unmentioned: similarly,
Babou's study admits that 'dans ce livre plein d'unité, quoique très
divers, c'est à peine si quelques pages d'agrément, "Les Promesses de
Timothée", "Le Plus Beau Temps de la vie" et "Le Presbytère" sem-
blent compromettre l'unité de la pensée'.[65] If Baudelaire includes the
first of these in his review it is undoubtedly because his attention is
gripped by its application to his own experience.

As the lengthy and accurate quotation from 'La Jambe' reveals,
Baudelaire did have *La Double Vie* to hand. Nevertheless, the review
provides ample proof of his ability to compress even the most loosely
constructed of tales. 'Le Cabinet des sabliers', for instance, is a rambling
piece content to describe the outings of two young men without
attempting to draw from them anything of general validity or interest.
Baudelaire's résumé, however, stresses the general relevance of the
situation, presenting the central characters as seizing moments of
tranquillity from a life of turbulence, misfortune and despair. To do so,
moreover, he has altered the perspective of the tale, for where Asselineau emphasizes 'le paysage horizontal des rivières', to use Baudelaire's
evocative phrase, he throws into equal relief the other side of the coin,
the 'vie tumultueuse des rues'. Thus his own increasing sensitivity to
noise and bustle (1, 351) has obviously coloured his presentation of the
tale.

Baudelaire examines in more detail 'L'Auberge', a tale in which
Asselineau places particular emphasis on the contrast between possibility and reality. Asselineau's rather banal claim that 'les voyages ont
cela de bon qu'ils sont comme une parenthèse ouverte au milieu des
ennuis de la vie ordinaire',[66] is transformed by Baudelaire's taut
description of the voyager returning 'vers le cercle où l'enferme sa

fatalité', the term 'cercle' suggesting Dante and 'fatalité' underlining Baudelaire's continuing interest in questions of predestination. Asselineau, moreover, stresses the contrasts between travel and daily life: a voyage, in his eyes, is 'cette vie magique entée sur les peines journalières',[67] much as Baudelaire presents the interplay of dream and reality in his prose poems. Asselineau, however, conveys a more positive approach than that shown by Baudelaire to the opposition of the ideal and the real: he speaks of 'le besoin d'échapper à soi-même et de se retremper en tout temps par l'opposition des contrastes'.[68] This is nonetheless very similar to the way in which Baudelaire draws inspiration from paradox and contrast.

In describing the traveller's reaction when his hostess suggests that he marry her daughter, Baudelaire reveals himself to be as much a moralist as a literary critic: where Asselineau was content to depict the voyager's laughter as the 'plus bel éclat de rire qui fût jamais sorti de [son] gosier',[69] Baudelaire tersely describes it as 'inhumain'. The essay on laughter, reprinted some fifteen months before this review, established a firm link between cruelty and comedy, insisting that 'le comique est un des plus clairs signes sataniques de l'homme et un des nombreux pépins contenus dans la pomme symbolique' (II, 530): the adjective 'inhumain', therefore, seems highly ironic in this context. Similarly, where his study on humour showed laughter to be indicative of a highly civilized mind, one which is induced by pride to consider itself superior to others, so he repeats here that the traveller is 'un lettré'.

Laughter also provides a focus for the evaluation of 'Mon Cousin Don Quixote'. As in the essay on laughter (II, 530–1), Baudelaire admits that 'le rire provoqué par une infirmité sublime [est] presque la condamnation du rieur' (II, 89), but suggests that the comic effects in this tale result rather from the discrepancy between the hero's ideals and those of the age: this humour, no doubt because it depends on feelings of identification rather than superiority, is described as 'attendrissant'. There is also a political side to Baudelaire's pleasure in the tale: he can by this time feel sympathetically amused by the heroism and vanity of those who dream of 'bonheur universel' (cf. II, 22: 'Une religion au cinquième'). Although I would not want to push the comparison too far, it is possible, too, that Baudelaire sees Don Quixote as an image of the artist, shown very much as he appears to the average bourgeois. Certainly he presents the tale as giving ample rein to 'les deux grandes qualités de l'auteur [. . .] le sentiment du beau moral et l'ironie qui naît du spectacle de l'injustice et de la sottise' (II, 88). The emphasis placed on 'injustice' and 'sottise' recalls the review of *Madame Bovary*, as does the counterbalancing term 'beau moral' with its implications of a search for the ideal.

'Les Promesses de Timothée' seems to delight Baudelaire principally by its twisting of conventional beliefs. In this tale, Asselineau explores the paradox that if the promises of a friend prove empty, help may often be obtained from 'un de ceux que le monde appelle des mauvais sujets, ou même des chenapans'. The fact that the tale awakened precise personal memories as well as literary echoes is suggested by the intensity of the vocabulary – the struggle is 'abominable', the man who does not honour his promises is 'ce voleur' – and by the repetition of 'souvent': 'il en est souvent ainsi', 'plus souvent qu'on ne veut le reconnaître' (II, 88). This is certainly one of the moments when Baudelaire seems to admit to Asselineau: '*Thou art the man!* Voilà mon confesseur!' (II, 91).

In a brief commentary on the insipid tale 'Le Roman d'une dévote', Baudelaire repeats the term 'monologue' used in the introductory passage, and suggests the work's limitations by indicating that its audience will consist of 'plus d'une vieille femme'. The compassion which marks 'Les Petites Vieilles' underlies the reference to the smiles and tears the story will provoke among elderly women.

'Le Mensonge', a tale dedicated to Poulet-Malassis, is presented almost as an emblem of the entire volume, aptly illustrating the 'préoccupation générale du livre' which Baudelaire defines as '*l'Art d'échapper à la vie journalière*', an art explored by many of his own prose poems as well as his studies on stimulants, and, of course, *Les Fleurs du mal*. Baudelaire draws a comparison between this story and pictorial art, recalling the many dreams of happiness caught by artists and authors in the 1840s and 1850s, but reminiscent above all of Gautier's novel *Fortunio*: 'les seigneurs turcs commandent quelquefois à nos peintres des décors représentant des appartements ornés de meubles somptueux, et s'ouvrant sur des horizons fictifs' (II, 89). Similarly, in 'Le Poème du hachisch', those who seek 'créer le paradis par la pharmacie' may be compared to 'un maniaque qui remplacerait des meubles solides et des jardins véritables par des décors peints sur toile et montés sur châssis' (I, 403). One notices yet again the value Baudelaire places on luxurious furnishings, something he longed to acquire and which forms the basis of many of his images. Nevertheless, he retains his sense of irony in pointing out the artifice of the canvasses being rolled up 'comme une carte géographique'. In like manner, the hero of 'Le Mensonge' decorates and populates his life with falsehoods. 'Qu'est-ce qu'un mensonge?', Asselineau's protagonist asks, answering: 'de l'imagination à la deuxième puissance'[70] and he justifies his habitual lying in the following terms: 'le temps vous attriste; l'ennui du présent vous jette dans la défiance de l'avenir, dans le dégoût du passé; [. . .] vous fermez alors les yeux, et, dans votre cerveau, clos comme la chambre noire d'un jeu d'optique viennent se refléter pour un instant les images des Eldorados bâtis en songe'. The imagery here resembles Baudelaire's, particularly the expression 'la chambre noire de votre cerveau', while the reference to Eldorado recalls the 'Eldorado promis par le destin' in 'Le Voyage' (I, 130), and the whole sentence echoes 'Paysage':

> Et quand viendra l'hiver aux neiges monotones,
> Je fermerai partout portières et volets
> Pour bâtir dans la nuit mes féeriques palais (I, 82).

Moreover, in reviewing the tale, Baudelaire concludes that 'il faut bien payer son bonheur' just as the prose poem 'Le Mauvais Vitrier' admits that 'ces plaisanteries nerveuses ne sont pas sans péril, et on peut souvent les payer cher' (I, 287). Baudelaire follows the text closely; his expression 'délire systématique' resembles Asselineau's own description of Jules as one of the 'faiseurs de systèmes',[71] and his account of the hero's decision not to destroy his fictional world in order to gain happiness in the real world faithfully echoes the sense of Jules's explanation that 'les seuls biens que je possède [sont] l'Illusion et l'Espérance'.[72] However, Baudelaire's images and the force of the language he uses suggest that, unlike Asselineau, he seeks to present Jules and his predicament as an allegory of the artist: 'démolir une fiction, se démentir, détruire un échafaudage idéal, même au prix d'un bonheur positif, c'est là un sacrifice impossible pour notre rêveur!' (II, 89). The punning use of 'démentir' in this expression highlights Baudelaire's delight in twisting the usual meanings of words in order to create a richer, more provocative language.

The tale 'La Jambe', although it solicits yet again the epithet 'petite', earns Baudelaire's praise for its study of 'la légitimité de l'absurde et de l'invraisemblable', particularly in the reproduction of 'les étranges raisonnements du rêve' (II, 89). Not only does Baudelaire's interest in 'ce voyage aventureux de tous les soirs' (I, 408) dominate numerous passages in his critical and creative writing, but it was to Asselineau that he described a dream which Butor has imaginatively analysed.[73] Asselineau perceives two kinds of dreams: those in which 'l'impossible se mêle au réel' and those which seem to indicate 'des facultés ou [. . .] des notions d'un ordre particulier, et étrangères à notre monde'.[74] Baudelaire likewise distinguishes between the 'rêve naturel' which is 'l'homme lui-même', and a hieroglyphic dream which represents 'le côté surnaturel de la vie' (I, 408). Although the lengthy quotation which he inserts to illustrate Asselineau's recreation of the dream world may seem a form of padding, it does allow him to vary his critical means and to demonstrate what he sees as an apparent paradox, in which Asselineau's style, a 'procès-verbal cru et net', nevertheless attains 'un grand effet poétique'. The quotation reveals how it is the very prosaic logicality of the style which throws into such sharp relief the absurd reasoning of dreams: possibly Baudelaire took advantage of this realization when he came to write 'Les Tentations' and 'Le Joueur généreux'.

The evaluation of the two main tales, 'La Seconde Vie' and 'L'Enfer du musicien', underlines how closely Asselineau's view of the artist coincides with Baudelaire's. Indeed, one wonders whether he himself did not suggest a fable epitomizing the artistic condition which Asselineau then developed. The creation of a personal mythology to explain apparent deviations from the standard pattern of humanity is very much a part of Baudelaire's own artistic method: one thinks above all of 'Les Dons des fées' and 'Les Bienfaits de la lune'.

The synopsis of each of these tales follows the originals closely, Baudelaire's main contribution being threefold. Firstly, he draws a comparison between the hero of 'La Seconde Vie' and the exiled Ovid, an analogy in which his admiration for Delacroix's painting may well have a place (see also 1, 77 and 983–4). Secondly, he coins the expression 'une médecine énergique' to define the role of love in 'L'Enfer du musicien'. Thirdly, and most importantly, he lays particular stress on the disproportion between man and the external world: but, as he was to insist in 'Le Poème du hachisch', published in 1860, 'tout homme qui n'accepte pas les conditions de la vie, vend son âme' (1, 438). A similar awareness and a more intense meditation on this theme occur in the final section of the first full-length study of Poe.

The choice of the laconic quotation which concludes the résumé is certainly significant: 'le péché d'orgueil a été racheté par l'amour' (11, 91), since the theme of pride recurs with almost obsessive frequency in 'Le Poème du hachisch' and *Les Fleurs du mal*.

As in the reviews of *Prométhée délivré* and Champfleury's short stories, Baudelaire leaves his main stylistic analysis until the end of his article, although he has indicated his opinion and suggested his reservations in the earlier sections, particularly in the introductory paragraph. Once again, he emphasizes that his criticism is written for an ideal reader, a 'lecteur intelligent' who is able to add flesh to the dry bones of a brief review. In referring to the choice of subject, he highlights 'l'esprit de recherche qui anime le travail' (11, 91): Asselineau's interest in the fantastic and in abnormal mental states, an interest also emphasized by Babou, has perhaps suggested a connection with the 'romanciers *curieux*' whose 'esprit primitif de *chercherie*' Baudelaire examines in the presentation of 'Révélation magnétique' (11, 248). The verb *animer*, also used in the first paragraph, is part of a subtle conceit in which Baudelaire refers in turn to the skeleton, the flesh, and the soul of a work of literature. The flesh of the book, by which Baudelaire seems to mean the form and the tone, is described as 'bonne, douce, élastique au toucher': the rather imprecise terminology may possibly suggest a certain reticence, detectable, too, in the way in which he immediately insists that it is 'l'âme intérieure' which merits the closest attention.

Once again, the collection is described as 'petit' and there is a further fleeting note of criticism when Baudelaire calls it 'personnel, excessivement personnel': his résumés of the tales tend to imply a general appeal lacking in the original. The words 'monologue', 'sincérité' and 'négligé', all used in the opening paragraph, are repeated here. Sincerity was certainly a quality Baudelaire valued; he noted that any tales written for *Le Hibou philosophe* should be in a 'style dégagé, vrai et plein de sincérité' (11, 51), the *Salon de 1846* asserts that the principal failing of the artists is a lack of 'naïveté et [. . .] sincérité' (11, 444), and he suggests that the critics' task is 'commander à l'artiste la naïveté et l'expression sincère de son tempérament' (11, 419).

In describing Asselineau's 'négligence féminine' Baudelaire may imply a further comparison with the careless prolixity of George Sand or Musset, the latter being depicted in 'Théophile Gautier' as 'féminin et sans doctrine' (11, 110). Nevertheless, although he admired what he considered to be the masculinity of Poe's prose, judged to be 'tout à fait anti-féminine' (11, 282), he also valued De Quincey's 'manière pénétrante et *féminine*' (1, 447). It seems, therefore, that the use of the terms 'mâle' and 'féminin' in regard to a writer's manner does not necessarily signify either praise or condemnation: indeed, he insists in his adaptation of De Quincey that without 'une espèce d'androgynéité [. . .] le génie le plus âpre et le plus viril reste [. . .] un être incomplet' (*MO*, 225–6).

Baudelaire is aware of the discrepancy between his usual tastes and his enjoyment of *La Double Vie*. He asks: 'affirmerez-vous que vous aimez toujours, que vous adorez sans répit ces livres dont la pensée, tendue à l'outrance, fait craindre à tout moment au lecteur qu'elle ne se rompe, et le remplit, pour ainsi dire, d'une trépidation nerveuse?' (11, 91). This seems to refer to Poe, whose reader, 'lié par le vertige, est contraint de suivre l'auteur dans ses entraînantes déductions' (11, 317). This willingness to admit apparent discrepancies in his response to different works of literature is a characteristic reappearing in later articles, particularly in the notice on Marceline Desbordes-Valmore.

The idea of duality and the air of confession are further points to which Baudelaire alludes in his opening passage and takes up again here, once more addressing the ideal reader, a 'lecteur pensif', capable, like De Quincey, of seeing a work of art as a mirror and of crying out to the writer: 'Thou art the man!' (*MO*, 179). Despite the fleeting mockery in the exclamation: 'heureux l'auteur qui ne craint pas de se montrer en négligé!', Baudelaire, while himself unable to publish anything which had not been prepared with minute attention, certainly saw the advantages, in terms of freshness and an impression of sincerity, of Asselineau's spontaneity.

Like Baudelaire's review of Champfleury's early volumes, this analysis of *La Double Vie* is very much criticism for a friend: it suggests possible improvements, underlines achievements and balances praise with caution while indicating quite clearly to the reader the nature and merit of the tales. Although it called for considerable tact and tolerance – gifts rarely encountered among Baudelaire's contemporaries – the review offered Baudelaire an excellent opportunity for self-investigation, at a time when he had completed *Les Fleurs du mal* and was contemplating new experiments in creative writing.

4

❧ *The Magician and the Meteor*

Gautier (*L'Artiste,* 13 March 1859)

For many modern readers, Gautier's poetry is obscured by the shadow of subsequent poets such as Baudelaire and Mallarmé who, recognizing in him a guide and master, built on and extended his discoveries. It is this overshadowing that makes Baudelaire's assessment of Gautier, both in the two articles devoted to him and in the famous dedication to *Les Fleurs du mal*, so remote from present-day evaluations that several critics, following in the wake of Gide, have accused him of cynically setting out to curry favour with a powerful and respected journalist.[1] In a letter asking Hugo for a preface to the 1859 essay on Gautier, Baudelaire fuels their fire with the following frequently quoted assertion:

> relativement à l'écrivain qui fait le sujet de cet article, et dont le nom a servi de prétexte à mes considérations critiques, je puis vous avouer *confidentiellement* que je connais les lacunes de son étonnant esprit. Bien des fois, pensant à lui, j'ai été affligé de voir que Dieu ne voulait pas être absolument généreux. Je n'ai pas menti, j'ai esquivé, j'ai dissimulé (*C*1, 597).[2]

Yet the statement applies to almost all Baudelaire's criticism: indeed, what reviewer of contemporary art could not admit the same of his own work? And if Baudelaire is right in considering Gautier unknown as a poet, then surely he is justified in drawing attention to the 'étonnant esprit' rather than concentrating on the lacunae. Besides, why should Baudelaire's letter to Hugo be considered more sincere than his study? Since he is begging a favour, it would hardly be surprising if he should both seek to flatter Hugo by seeming to confide in him, and take pains not to appear to value Gautier more highly than Hugo.

To put Baudelaire's article in perspective, one should first try to picture French literature before the appearance of the complete *Fleurs du mal* and then follow the chronological development of Baudelaire's friendship with Gautier. Although he is included among Baudelaire's 'secondes liaisons littéraires' (1, 785), Baudelaire knew Gautier's *feuilletons* from as early as 1838 (see *C*1, 58). Certainly his poetry, from the early to the late work, is rich with reminiscences of Gautier's creative and critical writing.

If the satirical 'Comment on paie ses dettes' of 1845 speaks of Gautier as not only 'gros, paresseux et lymphatique' but also as bereft of ideas, knowing only how to 'enfiler et perler des mots en manière de colliers' (11, 8),[3] the *Salon de 1845* more justly contends that 'M. Th. Gautier, quand les œuvres vont bien à son tempérament et à son éducation littéraires, commente bien ce qu'il sent juste' (11, 355). The implication that there are definite limits to Gautier's comprehension of art reappears in attenuated form in Baudelaire's article on caricature, published in 1857, but conceived much earlier: there, referring to Gautier's 'excellent article' on Goya, Baudelaire considers him 'parfaitement doué pour comprendre de semblables natures' (11, 567). The 'Conseils aux jeunes littérateurs' of 1846 describe Gautier's reviews as 'souvent médiocres' (11, 18–19) but the *Salon* of that year, while lamenting that he has not been sufficiently discriminating, admires in him 'un esprit excellent, large et poétique' (11, 463). As early as 1852 Baudelaire considered writing an 'appréciation générale des ouvrages de *Th. Gautier*' (11, 50), presenting him as epitomizing 'l'école plastique' (11, 51): his wary interest in this side of Gautier's poetry is also reflected in 'L'Ecole païenne'. By 1857 their friendship had strengthened, with Baudelaire attempting to persuade Poulet-Malassis to reprint *Le Roman de la momie* (*C*1, 395–6): his letter concludes: 'j'espère que vous comprendrez, que, vu mes relations avec Théophile et les services que je lui dois, il me serait douloureux de lui présenter moi-même un refus' (*C*1, 396). By 1859 Gautier's *feuilletons* on Rouvière are recommended as 'ce qui a été écrit de meilleur' on the actor's gifts (11, 63), and he is ranked with Balzac, Poe and Hoffmann among the great writers of the short story (*C*1, 537). Later letters place him even higher, referring to him as a creator of '*littérature pure*' (*C*11, 225), and one of the very few with whom Baudelaire feels in sympathy (*C*11, 522 and 611). That Baudelaire should mention him in such terms in a private letter and at a time when bad health and misfortune had combined to sour many of his earlier convictions argues the very real warmth of his admiration for Gautier both as a poet and as a friend.

Of course Baudelaire was not blind to Gautier's quirks and limitations. Of course the early articles poke fun at the reviewer, giving full rein to Baudelaire's delight in shock technique and in undermining *idées reçues*. Yet there can be little doubt that Gautier's work affected him deeply from an early stage, leaving its mark both on *Les Fleurs du mal* and on his criticism.

The essay on Gautier[4] was written in a particularly stimulating period of Baudelaire's life. In 1858 and 1859 he not only reprinted his articles on caricature and published literary reviews, but was also at work on the 'Poème du hachisch', 'Les Aventures d'Arthur Gordon Pym' and many of his notices for the Crépet anthology. Moreover, a letter of November 1858 bristles with projects, including his version of De Quincey's *Confessions*, an article entitled 'Les Peintres qui pensent', his collection of prose poems, and the additional *Fleurs du mal* needed to fill the gaps left by the censor's scissors (*C*i, 522). If one considers Baudelaire immersed in all this activity and caressing plans for future work, as well as trying to arrange his affairs so that he could, eventually, live tranquilly at Honfleur, it is hardly surprising that the article took longer than his editor, Edouard Houssaye, might have liked. To conclude that Baudelaire's procrastinations indicate hesitancy about undertaking the article, or difficulty in writing it, as critics such as J. Crépet and Margaret Gilman have done,[5] is to ignore both the poet's temperament – his correspondence abounds in pleas for just a little more time – and the welter of other works demanding his attention. Besides, despite the essay's length, both the structure and the language show considerable care, suggesting that Baudelaire saw in it far more than a sop to a powerful critic.

Typographically, the article is divided into six sections. The first, revealing yet again Baudelaire's pleasure in irony and in reversing accepted modes of thought, begins by justifying the decision to study in detail a writer apparently well-known to the reading public, and points to the ambiguity of popularity. There follows the obligatory evocation of Gautier's personality, to which Baudelaire gives a different emphasis from biographies written by his contemporaries, concentrating on characteristics illuminating the work, just as biographical details are included in *Un Mangeur d'opium* only if they offer a 'clef à la fantasmagorie tout individuelle de l'*Opium*' (*C*i, 522). The third section, after placing Gautier in the context of recent French literature, examines the perennial and thorny problems of beauty, morality and utility in art. The following segments deal with Gautier's prose works, both fiction and journalism, and with his poetry. A concluding passage parries criticisms commonly levelled at Gautier and reveals some of Baudelaire's own reservations. This carefully constructed article is, therefore, certainly very far from being marked, as J. R. Kane would have us believe, by a 'disorderly manner'.[6]

Binding the essay together are such recurring themes as that of fate and the artist (ii, 104, 116), the insistence on Gautier as both famous and, paradoxically, an *inconnu* (ii, 105, 106), the links with other writers (ii, 107, 110, 117), the personal, strongly suggestive, reminiscences drawn both from Baudelaire's own life and from his knowledge of Gautier (II, 107, 118), the repeated use of the term *idée fixe* (II, 104, 111, 117) and, running through the whole article as a constant undercurrent, the idea of beauty as the unique source of Gautier's art.

Into this clear but flexible framework, Baudelaire introduces various tightly controlled digressions as well as several passages of self-quotation which examine in particularly telling formulations questions which constantly recur in contemporary criticism. The essay's liveliness stems partly from the variety of critical techniques, partly from the tiny details provided by Baudelaire's own experience, partly from invented words such as 'philosophaillerie' (II, 111) and 's'emphilistiner' (II, 106), and partly from Baudelaire's handling of the *entrée en matière*, illustrated by the direct, disarming appeal to the reader with which the article opens, the abrupt lament: 'Hélas! la France n'est guère poète non plus' (II, 124) and the frank assertion of the final section: 'j'ai essayé (ai-je vraiment réussi?) d'exprimer l'admiration que m'inspirent les œuvres de Théophile Gautier, et de déduire les raisons qui légitiment cette admiration' (II, 127). The use of the word 'admiration', recalling the essay's opening lines, further serves to tauten the structure.

The essay is one of the very few in Baudelaire's literary criticism (cf. II, 192, 296) to open with an epigraph. Taken from Gautier's own *Caprices et Zigzags* it confesses: 'nous voudrions bien de temps en temps vomir un crapaud, une couleuvre et une souris rouge, ne fût-ce que pour varier; mais cela n'est pas en notre pouvoir' (II, 103). Although it could be interpreted to imply that Gautier dwells on the conventionally beautiful to the exclusion of the ugly and the evil, it probably applies principally to the perfection of Gautier's style. Baudelaire does not refer directly to the quotation, but there is a subtle allusion to it in the final sentence, where Gautier is described as 'un diamant de plus en plus rare dans une époque ivre d'ignorance et de matière' (II, 128), recalling the claim: 'nous ne pouvons ouvrir la bouche sans qu'il en tombe aussitôt des pièces d'or, des diamants, des rubis et des perles' (II, 103).

The study's opening sentence, with its reference to the difficulties posed by admiration, sets the tone while acting as a *captatio benevolentiae*. As in his review of *Madame Bovary* and, later, in the anthology notice on Marceline Desbordes-Valmore, Baudelaire poses the problem of an instinctive rather than an analytical reaction to literature, a dichotomy Valéry was to explore in his discussions on sequential and simultaneous appreciations of art. As if to rebuke those who contend that he was moved mainly by thoughts of friendship, Baudelaire specifically rejects the idea that 'l'ignoble respect humain' (II, 103) is the root cause of his embarrassment. What he fears is that he may fail to express that admiration in a 'manière suffisamment noble'.

Mocking those who attach more importance to the man than the work, Baudelaire dismisses the purely biographical approach to literary criticism, claiming that Gautier's life consists of 'rien qu'une immensité spirituelle' (II, 104) bereft of 'cette variété matérielle qui réduit la tâche d'un écrivain à celle d'un compilateur'.[7] Such fleeting touches suggest both his opposition to certain accepted critical methods and his desire to provoke his reader by setting aside extraneous events, giving sharper relief to the wonderful visions of the imagination. The solemnity of these visions is suggested here by his preferring to the more humble term *tête* the expression 'coupole de son cerveau' (II, 104). Both the idea and the image are present even in the early criticism, the *Salon de 1846* claiming of Delacroix, for example, that 'les révolutions et les événements les plus curieux se passent sous le ciel du crâne, dans le laboratoire étroit et mystérieux du cerveau' (II, 429). Besides, 'coupole' evokes the Academy, its use here preparing the later suggestion that Gautier should be accorded greater official recognition. The central aim of his study, Baudelaire concludes, should be the definition and the analysis of the dominant force in Gautier's life, his *idée fixe*. Deriding the stock biography, therefore, he dismisses the importance of birthdates and childhood successes and points to those whose childhood successes have not been followed up in maturity. Obviously Baudelaire is still worrying away at the paradoxes posed by destiny and at the importance of certain aspects of childhood for a poet's future development.[8]

Although Gautier did produce his *Portraits contemporains* and his *Portraits et Souvenirs*, Baudelaire's assumption that he would not choose to 'remuer ce fatras de lycéen' was no doubt based on a mocking passage from *Les Jeunes-France*: 'j'ai été nourri par ma mère, et sevré à quinze mois; puis j'ai eu un accessit de je ne sais quoi en rhétorique; voilà les événements les plus marquants de ma vie'. And in *Portraits contemporains* he insists: 'diverses notices me font naître à Tarbes, le 31 août 1808. Cela n'a rien d'important, mais la vérité est que je suis venu dans ce monde où je devais faire tant de copie, le 31 août 1811.'[9] Nevertheless, it would appear that once again Baudelaire's image of Gautier is moulded by his own beliefs, since it is the painstaking author of *Les Fleurs du mal* much more than the exuberant *feuilletoniste* of *La Presse* or even the poet of *Emaux et Camées* whom the following lines evoke: 'il n'y a pas d'homme qui pousse plus loin que lui la pudeur majestueuse du vrai homme de lettres, et qui ait plus horreur d'étaler tout ce qui n'est pas fait, préparé et mûri pour le public, pour l'édification des âmes amoureuses du Beau' (II, 104). Perhaps the phrase 'pudeur majestueuse' was suggested by 'Le Roi Candaule', discussed later in the essay. In addition, by dismissing the importance of the 'couronnes puériles' offered to promising school children, Baudelaire justifies his own relatively limited success at school. I would also propose that the phrase *'enfants sublimes'* alludes to Chateaubriand's reputed description of Hugo as a child.

Baudelaire insists that by analysing Gautier's *idée fixe*, rather than repeating biographical details, he will bring to the public's notice a well-known writer who is nonetheless unknown. Similarly, the article written for Crépet's anthology reaffirms that 'Gautier, feuilletoniste très accrédité, est mal connu comme romancier, mal apprécié comme conteur de voyages et presque *inconnu* comme poète' (II, 151). Once again, therefore, Baudelaire's mind is stimulated by paradox, and once again he attempts to shake the public's lethargic acceptance of widely-held beliefs. Finally, the public's blindness to many of Gautier's gifts suggests another familiar theme, the seeming injustice of fate and a critic's duty to redress the balance.

To illustrate the public's ignorance of Gautier's poetry Baudelaire abandons conventional critical style, adopting a satirical, semi-dramatized narration, in which the reader is whisked into a middle-class drawing-room, where coffee is served with the inevitable condiment of aesthetic conversation. Baudelaire allows full rein to his gift of parody, drawing attention to it by sardonically deploring the 'détestable et risible argot auquel la plume devrait se soustraire' (cf. *C*I, 298 and I, 181).

The widespread aesthetic obtuseness at this time is emphasized by the term 'couronnes banales' which echoes the 'couronnes puériles' to suggest, as did the review of *Madame Bovary*, that criticism is the task of an élite. Thus, in bourgeois circles Gautier is accorded the empty accolade of possessing two talents Baudelaire despises in literature, 'esprit' and a *style coulant* (II, 105). The blend of wit and facility, however, is indeed characteristic of Gautier's *feuilletons* and some of his short stories: with remarkable conciseness, therefore, Baudelaire sums up one aspect of Gautier's work and, by placing the judgement in the mouths of the bourgeoisie, implies that these are gifts on which he himself places little value. The ironic subtlety of the attack shows how greatly his mastery of the genre has increased since the overtly damning review of *Prométhée délivré*.

According to Baudelaire, any reference to Gautier not as reviewer but as poet provokes incredulity and embarrassment, since none of the fashionable readers remembers those 'échantillons de la plus pure beauté française', *Albertus*, 'La Comédie de la mort' and *España*. Similarly, the anthology notice laments, in a metaphor tightening the parallels between Gautier's situation and Baudelaire's own, that 'peu de personnes ont daigné étudier ces fleurs merveilleuses' (II, 150). Whereas other critics might argue that the general ignorance of these works proves Gautier's failure, Baudelaire sees it as a further indication of contemporary insensitivity and asserts, paradoxically, that unpopularity argues a degree of perfection beyond the comprehension of the average reader.

Baudelaire insists that it is not sufficient for a critic merely to lament the public's neglect of Gautier's poetry: he must also seek out the underlying causes. The most obvious explanation is simply that the public has lost the ability to appreciate great works of literature. Although an extremely common assertion, constantly furnishing material for critics *en mal de copie*, Baudelaire's claim is formulated with an energy springing from strongly personal motives. Nevertheless, he considers the solution incomplete, noting that those poets who have overcome the resistance of public apathy have succeeded only by injecting into their work an element of immediate appeal or practical utility to contemporary readers (cf. I, 184). Those poems depicting permanent and timeless beauty, on the contrary, arouse no enthusiasm, so that even the widely-acclaimed Hugo is incompletely known and Barbier's renown depends on his first volume of poetry alone. This is certainly true of Barbier, whose later works failed to arouse the universal interest accorded to the *Iambes*. Hugo's work inspired such a barrage of commentary that the reaction of the general public is difficult to determine.

Gautier, however, will not stoop to adulterate his art for the sake of mere celebrity, a claim Baudelaire couches in characteristically culinary images, the 'condiment' in Gautier's verse being 'du choix le plus exquis et du sel le plus ardent' (II, 106: cf. I, 284). The idea that immediate popularity comes only to those who debase themselves becomes a commonplace in Baudelaire's later criticism: nevertheless, the reader is also made frequently aware of Baudelaire's exasperated conviction that the public ought to be able to comprehend what he considers self-evident. Once again, Gautier is cast in the role of ideal poet, or rather, Baudelaire seeks to explain his lack of success by attributing it to the kind of conscious decision that the ideal poet alone could make.

That fame is the spur, Baudelaire never seems to doubt and both the ambiguous importance he attaches to it and his attempts to explain the relative renown or obscurity of other writers, both here, in prose poems such as 'Les Tentations' and in many of his other literary reviews, have an important bearing on his poetry. Moreover, he seems convinced that the kaleidoscope of time, constantly altering social values, may even end by meting out true justice. In a misanthropic comment, he highlights the paradoxical nature of such a situation: 'on peut tout attendre de la bizarrerie humaine, même l'équité, bien qu'il soit vrai de dire que l'injustice lui est infiniment plus naturelle' (II, 107). Not only does the sardonic use of 'même' recall the tone of many of the prose poems, but the theme of justice recurs in the anthology notice, in which Baudelaire predicts that, should civilization be destroyed, Gautier's poems will be justly appreciated by future scholars as an indication of the beauty and complexity of the lost French language (II, 151).

This opening section concludes with the wry comment that Gautier has been judged as overrated by one of those very journalists who have sought distinction by pandering to the public's debased concept of art: he punningly describes this critic as an 'écrivain politique', emphasizing the cunning sensationalism of such writers. The reference is to Théodore Pelloquet's reviews in the witty but superficial *Gazette de Paris* (see II, 1132). Pelloquet's articles epitomize contemporary attitudes to Gautier. Thus, when he praises the poet's scintillating language, he does so in order to throw into sharper relief the claim that Gautier's style 'se pare de tant de bijoux étincelants dans les occasions les plus simples, que le lecteur étonné y cherche parfois un sens profond et caché, audacieux et redoutable, quand il s'agit de fort peu de chose'.[10] And Pelloquet, like the young Baudelaire, insists that 'dans les plateaux des balances de M. Gautier, tous les artistes pèsent du même poids'.[11] Indeed, since there is much in Pelloquet's review which echoes Baudelaire's earlier evaluation of Gautier, his irritation may be all the more pronounced partly because he recognizes beliefs he no longer considers valid, and partly because Pelloquet remains insensitive to Gautier's achievements in poetry.

If the petty details of Gautier's life are considered unimportant, the second section of the essay implies that his personality can nevertheless shed light on his work. Inserting the kind of reminiscence common to contemporary criticism, Baudelaire recalls his first meeting with Gautier. Gautier's joy at being presented with a volume of poetry – he who must have received so many – seems to Baudelaire to reveal the quality he describes as 'enfantine'. This is an important word in Baudelaire's critical vocabulary, since genius, so he declares in *Un Mangeur d'opium*, is 'l'enfance nettement formulée, douée maintenant, pour s'exprimer, d'organes virils et puissants' (*MO*, 222). Baudelaire was obviously pleased with the formula, since he used it again, almost textually, in his study on Guys (II, 690). Gautier's curiosity about what Baudelaire calls the '*non-moi*' (II, 107) is yet another facet of the genius, that which makes him 'l'homme des foules': of Guys, Baudelaire says that 'la *curiosité* peut être considérée comme le point de départ de son génie' (II, 689). As in the article on Poe, it is clear that curiosity and conjecture are central both to Baudelaire's vision of literature and to his ideas about criticism. Nevertheless, certain reservations are implied by the phrase 'curiosité facile' (II, 107): although his reviews are addressed to the 'curieux' (II, 3), although he admires the 'esprit primitif de *chercherie*' (II, 248) which marks the 'romanciers *curieux*' (II, 248), the word, particularly combined with the epithet *facile*, is not without ambiguity. Curiosity in *Les Fleurs du mal* and *Le Spleen de Paris* causes anguish (I, 302) and torment (I, 130): moreover Baudelaire is well aware that 'qui trop embrasse mal étreint'. This, therefore, may well be a subtle expression of regret for the fragmentation of Gautier's talent, coupled with an acute sympathy for its causes.

Baudelaire uses Gautier's reaction to the verse offered for his inspection as a means of emphasizing his respect for traditional form in poetry, just as the anthology notice declares that he always obeyed the 'règles les plus sévères de la langue que sa naissance lui commandait de parler' (II, 152). With clarity and simplicity Baudelaire deliberately introduces technical details at this point, swiftly acknowledging Gautier's devotion to 'la règle de la quadruple rime' (II, 108): thus, although aware that even the élite who read *L'Artiste* might be alienated by a close discussion of technique, Baudelaire can introduce them succinctly and easily into his argument. It is noticeable that Baudelaire, whose *Fleurs du mal* contain several 'sonnets libertins', neither condemns nor praises Gautier's attitude, merely expressing it as the poet's own point of view.

Gautier's veneration for a vast vocabulary is illustrated by an anecdote which in turn illuminates Baudelaire's own ideas on poetry. Turning from the verse in question to his young visitor, Gautier asks him, 'comme pour m'éprouver', as Baudelaire recalls, whether he enjoys reading dictionaries. Baudelaire's answer not only indicates his long-standing passion for words but also portrays him as eager to earn the esteem of another writer: 'par bonheur, j'avais été pris très jeune de lexicomanie' (II, 108), the coining of *lexicomanie* suggesting a degree of mild self-mockery. Gautier's wide-ranging vocabulary aroused admiration among many contemporary critics, Labitte, for example, claiming in an apt metaphor that: 'le vocabulaire est pour M. Th. Gautier un véritable sérail où il commande en maître'[12] and Mirecourt insisting more prosaically that 'de tout temps, les dictionnaires ont été et sont encore la lecture favorite de Gautier. Il en a cinquante sur le premier rayon de sa bibliothèque, à portée de sa main.'[13] Gautier himself announced provocatively: 'je ne lis que les préfaces et les tables, les dictionnaires et les catalogues'.[14]

It is in describing as indispensable an unfailing command of language that Gautier incurs Gide's scorn: 'l'écrivain qui ne savait pas tout dire [. . .] n'était pas un écrivain'. Baudelaire repeats Gautier's maxim, in a slightly different form, in his anthology notice: 'à lui seul peut-être il appartient de dire sans emphase: *Il n'y a pas d'idées inexprimables*' (II, 152). It is only in the later article that Baudelaire gives precise expression to a related idea implicit in the essay: 'Pour [Gautier] l'idée et l'expression ne sont pas deux choses contradictoires qu'on ne peut accorder que par un grand effort ou par de lâches concessions' (II, 152). The question of whether idea and form are in opposition or whether the distinction is false aroused much contemporary debate, particularly among creative writers such as Flaubert and Hugo: here Baudelaire seems to be saying that writers should not strive to force a predetermined idea into an adequate form, but rather that the two should arise together, inextricable and in harmony.

Gautier's first conversation with Baudelaire touched not only on intellectual aspects of a poet's development, but also on more practical considerations, in particular, the need for rigid self-discipline. Although Baudelaire's diaries certainly indicate the importance he attached to discipline, the discussion here is highly reminiscent of Gautier's account of his own first meeting with Balzac.[15] Indeed, Gautier's essay on Balzac could well have been on Baudelaire's desk as he wrote. Certainly he always associated Balzac with prodigious powers of self-control, and it is in this essay that he includes his longest and most suggestive passage on the novelist. Perhaps, therefore, he attributed Balzac's practical philosophy to the writer whom he uses to convey his own convictions.

Theories of progress, which Gautier ridicules in the preface to *Mademoiselle de Maupin* and which provided a further topic of conversation, provoke the kind of scorn one would expect from the Baudelaire of the late 1850s. Although Gautier's reviews between 1848 and the early 1850s follow contemporary fashion in vaunting the advance of civilization, Baudelaire is remembering the Gautier who insisted: 'je ne pense même pas qu'après un siècle de progrès, au train dont nous y allons, aucun amoureux soit capable de renouveler le treizième travail d'Hercule',[16] and who published the travel journal from which Baudelaire takes the following quotation: 'il est trois choses qu'un civilisé ne saura jamais créer: un vase, une arme, un harnais' (II, 108).[17] Similarly, the study of Delacroix uses a very contemporary image to show the artist ridiculing 'le ballon-monstre de la perfectibilité et du progrès indéfinis' (II, 759). The very fact that Baudelaire sent Hugo, that arch-priest of progress, a review in which he so forcefully denounces the 'fatuité du siècle' (II, 108) shows how little he is affected by thoughts of 'le respect humain'.

In describing Gautier's mind as a 'miroir cosmopolite de beauté', Baudelaire introduces a further motif which becomes increasingly important in his criticism, that of the artist's ability to respond to beauty wherever he finds it. The point is reinforced, but with a double edge, in the anthology notice, where Gautier is hyperbolically described as: 'heureux homme! homme digne d'envie! Il n'a aimé que le Beau; il n'a cherché que le Beau' (II, 152).

The joy Baudelaire experiences in recording this meeting springs not merely from the harmony of thought that existed between himself and Gautier, but also from a gift he values highly and frequently praises: that of conversation. Delacroix's conversation is 'un mélange admirable de solidité philosophique, de légèreté spirituelle et d'enthousiasme brûlant' (II, 611), Leconte de Lisle's is 'solide et sérieuse' (II, 176), that of Le Vavasseur 'nourrissante, suggestive' (II, 181) and that of Poe 'des plus remarquables' (II, 313). Similarly, in a letter to Sainte-Beuve he claims that the latter's article, 'Des prochaines élections à l'Académie', recreates 'toute votre éloquence de conversation, avec son bon sens et ses pétulances' (CII, 219). Finally, it was one of the pleasures he most missed in Belgium, and he complained to Ancelle: 'quant à la conversation, ce grand, cet unique plaisir d'un être spirituel, vous pourriez parcourir la Belgique en tous sens sans trouver une âme qui *parle*' (CII, 409).[18]

In a metaphor which captures Gautier's style both in the detail of its imagery and in the insistence on the rapid flight of time, Baudelaire sighs: 'depuis cette petite fête de ma jeunesse, que d'années au plumage varié ont agité leurs ailes et pris leur vol vers le ciel avide' (II, 109). Despite the pastiche, the bitter appropriateness of the final epithet is distinctly Baudelairean.

Baudelaire justifies the inclusion of what may seem an impertinent personal memory by declaring that Gautier himself encouraged such easy intimacy, much as the sages of antiquity delighted in the company of the young. The comparison not only serves to introduce one of the essay's main themes – Gautier's role as guide and inspirer – but also shows Baudelaire establishing a correspondence between human nature and elements of the external world: 'ces braves gens illustres de l'anti-quité, qui aimaient la société des jeunes, et qui promenaient avec eux leur solide conversation sous de riches verdures, au bord des fleuves, ou sous des architectures nobles et simples comme leur âme' (II, 109).

Similarly, Baudelaire conveys the abstract notion of mind or imagination in such concrete terms as 'sa chambre spirituelle' (II, 109: cf. II, 86) or 'la chambre secrète de son esprit' (II, 332). Finally, in apparently justifying himself to those who may find him 'un peu *parvenu* de parler sans façon [. . .] de [son] intimité avec un homme célèbre', Baudelaire obliquely mocks the current trend for critics to seize the slightest opportunity to claim friendship with the famous.

In the third section of his essay, Baudelaire sets Gautier in historical context in order to explain his artistic development. When portraying the essential features of Gautier's predecessors, he throws into sharpest relief two related qualities: their creative power and their ability to infuse new life into the nation's poetry. Although nostalgia for the exciting early days of Romanticism[19] is a familiar theme, whatever reservations may have been aroused by later developments, Baudelaire succeeds in describing the 'crise féconde' with particular vigour, especially in his apt evocation of Chateaubriand as 'un Athos qui contemple nonchalamment le mouvement de la plaine' and in the amusing reference to Dumas's plays, 'où l'éruption volcanique était ménagée avec la dextérité d'un habile irrigateur' (II, 110).

According to Baudelaire, Gautier's main contribution in his early years was twofold. Firstly, he exploited an element which had previously been rare in French literature: a 'filon de riche jovialité', 'le sentiment du grotesque' (II, 110). Secondly, such works as *Les Jeunes-France* embodied a vision of youth with its '*beauté du diable*'. This collection of tales, moreover, proved Gautier alert to the excesses of Romanticism, follies and pretences which are mercilessly pilloried in such tales as 'Onuphrius Wphly'. As in his attacks on Realism and 'l'école païenne', Baudelaire's condemnation is aimed not so much at beliefs as at excesses.

The work which best illustrates Gautier's *idée fixe* and over which, therefore, Baudelaire lingers most, is the coruscating *Mademoiselle de Maupin*. Contemptuously dismissing claims that the novel merely represents adolescent passions, Baudelaire insists that it be read as an allegory depicting a higher passion: 'l'amour exclusif du Beau'. Although mentioned in any general review of Gautier, *Mademoiselle de Maupin* received little precise evaluation in the 1850s: Baudelaire may be referring here to an accusation commonly expressed in society rather than in the press. Nevertheless, Mirecourt's biography of Gautier described the novel as 'le véritable livre à craindre, le livre dont chaque phrase est un sophisme et qui pose la débauche en reine au milieu des pompes littéraires les plus éclatantes'.[20] Clément de Ris, for whom Gautier was merely 'un Delille romantique', considered *Mademoiselle de*

Maupin 'un livre dont la lecture doit attrister profondément ceux que la littérature intéresse encore, et qui pensent que l'art d'écrire ne devrait être employé que comme un sacerdoce'.[21] In describing the novel as a hymn, not to the senses but to beauty, Baudelaire obviously has in mind his own 'Hymne à la beauté', published in 1860, a poem in which abstract notions of good or evil are shown as irrelevant compared with the power of beauty which can make 'l'univers moins hideux et les instants moins lourds' (1, 25). There may also be an echo from the preface to *Fortunio*, a work Gautier describes as 'un hymne à la beauté, à la richesse, au bonheur, les trois seules divinités que nous reconnaissons'.[22] Although Baudelaire may well be sincere in discounting the potent eroticism of *Mademoiselle de Maupin*, it is more likely that here, as in the review of *Madame Bovary*, he has chosen to disarm criticism by emphasizing aesthetic rather than thematic issues. And, just as in reviewing *Madame Bovary* he played down the moral aspects and underlined Flaubert's 'chasteté de rhéteur' (11, 84), so he highlights Gautier's exclusive love of beauty, insisting that it was this which made the work 'un véritable événement'. He is certainly justified in stressing the importance Gautier devoted to the language of *Mademoiselle de Maupin*, one of the rare novels of the period to pay close and perspicacious attention to style.

The study of *Mademoiselle de Maupin* introduces a long meditation inspired by Gautier's works and closely connected with his theories, but serving principally to elaborate Baudelaire's own aesthetics: Baudelaire is clearly using this essay, as he explained in his letter to Hugo, as a 'prétexte à [ses] considérations critiques' (*CI*, 597). The statement is an extremely important elucidation of his idea of criticism, underlining the very conscious way in which he seized on literary reviews as a means of exploring and refining central problems.

According to Baudelaire, the idea of beauty as the sole criterion of art, a principle which was formerly widely accepted, has recently been obscured by 'je ne sais quelle lourde nuée, venue de Genève, de Boston ou de l'enfer' (11, 111). The plastic quality of this image makes me feel that Baudelaire may be referring to a specific caricature, perhaps one of those he considered for his study of the comic. The denigration of Boston and its moralistic outlook has been a commonplace in Baudelaire's criticism since his articles on Poe and seems fully justified if one refers to Boston's reaction to that poet, or the *North American Review*'s appreciation of *Madame Bovary* in 1857. The allusion to Geneva and the repressive morality of Calvinism recalls a passage from Gautier's article 'Du beau antique et du beau moderne', originally printed in Hugo's journal *L'Evénement* in 1848: 'l'esprit protestant a prévalu.

Cette doctrine bourgeoise, économe et chicaneuse, s'accorde bien avec les sentiments envieux de notre temps. La crainte de l'examen critique et l'absence d'autorité a singulièrement intimidé les développements extérieurs de la civilisation.'[23]

The doctrine of the 'indissolubilité du Beau, du Vrai et du Bien' (II, III), which Baudelaire laments as having perverted public thought and which he discussed at length in the studies on Poe, is connected above all with Cousin, whose predilection for watching over the morals of others Baudelaire holds up for scorn in his article on the celebrations in memory of Shakespeare (II, 229). Despite his earlier reference to 'le respect humain', therefore, Baudelaire is nothing loth to attack both energetically and accurately 'la philosophaillerie moderne'. Although the doctrine is not, of course, the product of the nineteenth century, the importance Cousin and his followers placed on it made it appear new to Baudelaire's contemporaries. Baudelaire condemns it principally because the mingling of the three aspects – beauty, truth and goodness – demands that several faculties be brought into play simultaneously, leading to a loss of purity and to a weakening of the individual faculties. According to him, truth, the basis of knowledge, demands intellect; the good is the desire and domain of the moralists; to create beauty is the sole aim of good taste. Gautier's *Mademoiselle de Maupin*, although demanding of its author both taste and truth, owes its existence to an enthusiasm which is unalloyed, that for beauty. That any other criterion be used to judge the novel, Baudelaire not only condemns but also considers an imperfect understanding of aesthetics.

The point is developed in a passage borrowed from Baudelaire's preface to *Histoires extraordinaires*, the self-quotation indicating that Baudelaire considers this to be the finest formulation of his 'éternelle thèse' according to which 'la *morale* cherche le *bien*, la science, le *vrai*, la *poésie* et quelquefois le roman, ne cherchent que le *beau*' (*C*I, 537). Although a detailed analysis of these paragraphs would exceed the confines of this study, several points should be stressed, and, above all, it should be remembered that much of the passage is closely based on Poe's theoretical studies.

Firstly, as in 'Les Drames et les romans honnêtes', Baudelaire, who denied in a projected preface that any 'respect humain' could lead him 'confondre l'encre avec la vertu' (I, 181), rejects once again 'l'*hérésie de l'enseignement*' (II, 112). He is not, of course, referring to the effect of a poem, but to the poet's intention: although it would be absurd to claim that poetry cannot 'élever l'homme au-dessus du niveau des intérêts vulgaires' (II, 113), Baudelaire asserts that 'si le poète a poursuivi un but moral, il a diminué sa force poétique'. The logical result is that poetry cannot 's'assimiler à la science ou à la morale'. Although this statement has often been held to contradict the conclusion reached in 'L'Ecole païenne', that 'toute littérature qui se refuse à marcher fraternellement entre la science et la philosophie est une littérature homicide et suicide' (II, 49), Baudelaire is not suggesting that poetry cannot fruitfully draw substance from 'la science' or 'la morale', but rather that a work of literature which fully adopts the aims or techniques of either of these two modes of knowledge ceases to be poetry. However where the first statement has literature walking between science and philosophy, the sentence structure of the second keeps them apart, suggesting a desire to make the point with absolute clarity.

Secondly, in elaborating several ideas jotted down in the notes Baudelaire gave his lawyer for the trial of *Les Fleurs du mal*, the passage develops in particular the suggestion that:

> il y a plusieurs morales. Il y a la morale positive et pratique à laquelle tout le monde doit obéir.
> Mais il y a la morale des arts. Celle-ci est tout autre, et depuis le commencement du monde, les Arts l'ont bien prouvé (I, 194).

Here he suggests that vice, for 'certains esprits poétiques', is that which infringes 'le rythme et la prosodie universels' (II, 113: cf. II, 334): similarly, in 'Les Drames et les romans honnêtes', pernicious art is defined as that which 'dérange les conditions de la vie' (II, 41). Baudelaire's assertion that vice disturbs 'le rythme et la prosodie universels' recalls many contemporary discussions about universal harmony, particularly those of the Fourierists, as well as Baudelaire's own use of the expression in his art criticism (see especially II, 575, 685) and 'L'Héautontimorouménos':

> Ne suis-je pas un faux accord
> Dans la divine symphonie (I, 78).[24]

For Baudelaire, the sense of beauty is an instinct, inherent rather than learnt. It is, moreover, this sense which allows man to see the world as 'une *correspondance* du Ciel', just as art permits him to see, however dimly, 'les splendeurs situées derrière le tombeau'. The statement is closely linked to the note in his diaries which presents *surnaturalisme* as essential to art (I, 658). Yet even this ideal has two sides, for it is the longing aroused by beauty which leads man to turn to inappropriate means in his attempt to seize here and now 'un paradis révélé'. The parallels with *Les Paradis artificiels* and the fact that the passage first appeared in a study of Poe not only suggest that Baudelaire arrived at this conclusion as a result of his attempts to understand Poe's alcoholism, but also underline the links he perceived between intoxication and moments of intense artistic sensitivity.

In a passage drawn, with slight changes, from 'Les Drames et les romans honnêtes' Baudelaire claims that, by insisting that conventional morality rather than beauty should be the principal aim of poetry, modern thought has given undue prominence to writers whose talent is meagre but whose ideas accord with contemporary morals or enthusiasms. Although he has condensed his earlier article, he does add a detailed commentary on the line 'ô poète je t'aime', underlining the idiocy of such an expression and emphasizing, half in anger, half in amusement, the muddle about what constitutes a poet. He seizes once again the opportunity to mock feminine reasoning, denying woman the ability 'approprier les mots à leur usage'. And he sardonically delights in the paradox created by the confusion of morality and art: 'car le talent de composer des vers parfaits nuit évidemment aux facultés de l'époux, *qui sont la base de toute poésie!*' (II, 115).

Nor is this false reasoning limited to the self-styled didactic writers, since 'le vent du siècle est à la folie; le baromètre de la raison moderne marque tempête' (II, 115). The metaphor is borrowed from Hoffmann and appears, although with a different meaning, in *Les Paradis artificiels* (I, 378, 401). Baudelaire's butt here is Michelet and his astonishing marriage manual entitled *L'Amour*, in which woman is described as an invalid and her husband as a constant nurse, always having regard for her inherent weaknesses. To the husband falls the task of educating his wife and of caring for her spiritual needs, his love for her creating, according to Michelet, something more splendid than poetry. Once again, therefore, concepts which are by nature separate are being confused and thus debased.

The importance Baudelaire accords to *L'Amour* and his brutal description of Michelet as a 'vieillard sans majesté, fébrile et féminin, jouant à la poupée, tournant des madrigaux en l'honneur de la maladie, et se vautrant avec délices dans le linge sale de l'humanité' (II, 116) certainly suggests that some intense irritation, probably based on sentimentalized conceptions of woman, has made him lose sight of his central topic. Nevertheless, given contemporary critical methods and the lengthy digressions of such critics as Sainte-Beuve, this brief side-track hardly constitutes a proof that Baudelaire was embarrassed by the need to evaluate Gautier's worth. Indeed, although he refers to it as a 'chemin de traverse', it is firmly attached to the central assertion of beauty as standing apart both from bourgeois virtue and from passion, being guided solely by imagination.

Baudelaire builds on this firm foundation of general principles when he turns to Gautier's literary qualities, specifically limiting his study to the products of the imagination (II, 116). Within this domain, Baudelaire insists, Gautier is 'l'écrivain par excellence', because he conceives of art as a duty and has sacrificed to it his liberty. Yet, in depicting Gautier as 'l'esclave de son devoir', as Mallarmé, in 'Toast funèbre' was to refer to a 'devoir idéal', Baudelaire may well be suggesting certain reservations, implying, perhaps, a lack of conscious effort on Gautier's part. The relationship between fatality and creativity has, of course, been a central question in his criticism since the first Poe studies: nevertheless, in asserting that beauty is for Gautier a *fatum*, Baudelaire does seem to me to be hinting that he has achieved less because he has not been obliged to struggle in recreating beauty. Later, the facility of a Banville arouses a similar blend of envy and suspicion. The claim that Gautier 'a retrouvé tout de suite la grande voie' (II, 117) certainly conveys a degree of envy similar to that expressed in the Dupont preface and in the review of *Madame Bovary*: nevertheless, such envy can be 'fortifiante' (*C*II, 238), driving Baudelaire both to seek out the reasons behind the success and to emulate it.

It is this focus which leads Baudelaire to epitomize the dominant trait of various writers who have aroused general acclaim. In Chateaubriand he finds melancholy and *ennui*, in Hugo the paradoxically harmonious conflict of the elements, in Balzac the struggles and ambitions of society. The stress on what is unique to an author is paralleled in the art criticism by the desire to isolate what is *sui generis* in an artist (see II, 561, 596, 636) while the essay on Wagner likewise insists that 'un artiste, un homme vraiment digne de ce grand nom, doit posséder quelque chose d'essentiellement *sui generis*, par la grâce de quoi il est *lui* et non un autre' (II, 806). Gautier not only possessed qualities which are indeed *sui generis*, but, whereas the preoccupations of other great writers are reflected in the lesser poets of their age, in him alone can be found the 'amour exclusif du beau' (II, 117).

Yet, however eager he may be to evoke Gautier's unique gifts, Baudelaire feels forced to admit that he himself lacks 'cette connaissance de la langue qui n'est jamais en défaut' (II, 117), at least in so far as a detailed discussion of style is concerned. His unusual awareness of this problem will be examined in my conclusion. He is, however, able to convey much of the essence of Gautier's poetry, particularly its linguistic precision and the aptness of the metaphors. These metaphors, according to Baudelaire, are so appropriate precisely because Gautier possessed 'une immense intelligence innée de la *correspondance* et du symbolisme universels' (II, 117). Here, as elsewhere, Baudelaire highlights the degree to which such insights are inherent, underlining the poet's unique position among men. Similarly, he will throw into sharp relief Hugo's ability to draw on 'l'inépuisable fonds de l'*universelle analogie*' (II, 133). Once again, however, there is a degree of ambiguity in the claim that Gautier's success is achieved 'sans fatigue comme sans faute', the alliteration serving to put the point with greater force. Baudelaire's letter to Armand Fraisse gives particularly cogent form to his frequently expressed belief in the importance of 'le travail par lequel une rêverie devient un objet d'art' (*CI*, 675).

Baudelaire insists that if Gautier has been able to express so brilliantly his awareness of the outside world and its meaning for mankind, it is through his magical use of language, the sorcerer's power of evocation. Not only do the terms *magie* and *sorcellerie* frequently recur in *Les Paradis artificiels*, reinforcing the parallels already noted, but in his diaries Baudelaire depicts as an 'art magique' the 'évocation de l'inspiration' and jots down the note: 'de la langue et de l'écriture, prises comme opérations magiques, sorcellerie évocatoire' (I, 658). *Les Fleurs du mal* themselves of course are dedicated to the 'parfait magicien ès lettres françaises'. In his literary criticism, Baudelaire describes reality when transmuted by art as having the 'magie de la vraisemblance' (II, 121: cf. II, 347), speaks of 'l'effet magique' of Hugo's poetry (II, 139), evokes the 'magie hyperbolique' (II, 165) of Banville's landscapes and characters, and says of Poe that 'aucun homme [. . .] n'a raconté avec plus de magie les *exceptions* de la vie' (II, 317). Although the comparison between art and magic obviously acquires great importance in Baudelaire's aesthetics, he does not begin to express it in his criticism until 1856: nevertheless, the idea can be detected as early as the presentation of 'Révélation magnétique', where he speaks of art as permitting a mystic fusion of the known and the possible. This mystic quality of art is further stressed in the essay on Gautier, where, with an obvious religious reference, Baudelaire exchanges the usual expression *le mot* for the biblical *le verbe* and insists that poetry possesses 'quelque chose de *sacré*' (II, 118).

It is through Gautier's magical use of language that 'la couleur parle, comme une voix profonde et vibrante; que les monuments se dressent et font saillie sur l'espace profond; que les animaux et les plantes [. . .] articulent leur grimace non équivoque; que le parfum provoque la pensée et le souvenir correspondants; que la passion murmure ou rugit son langage éternellement semblable' (II, 118). As with several passages in the studies of Poe, the parallels with Baudelaire's own thought and poetry are so striking that the reader may well wonder to what extent Gautier, in whom he undoubtedly saw a predecessor, is being reforged in the fire of Baudelaire's own ideals. Nevertheless, his comments do indeed apply to Gautier's work, particularly to the description of visions inspired by hashish and opium. The poetic possibilities of synaesthesia, for example, are explored in several prose works: 'mon ouïe', Gautier claims in 'Le Hachich', 's'était prodigieusement développée; j'entendais le bruit des couleurs' and it is under the influence of opium that 'les monuments [. . .] font saillie': he sees 'des maisons rechignées, accroupies au bord du chemin comme de vieilles filandières, des clôtures en planches, des réverbères qui avaient l'air de gibets à s'y méprendre'.[25] The reference to passion, murmuring its 'langage éternellement semblable' may also reflect Baudelaire's reading of *Madame Bovary*, with its illustration of 'l'éternelle monotonie de la passion qui a toujours les mêmes formes et le même langage'.[26] Nevertheless, it also conforms to Gautier's attitude in *Mademoiselle de Maupin* and it strengthens Baudelaire's increasingly precise presentation of the dichotomy between passion and imagination. Above all, one notes the intensity of his comments, the density of the tiny details and the degree to which Gautier's work has become part of the texture of Baudelaire's memory.

The fourth section of this essay examines the way in which Gautier's search for beauty has led him to choose certain genres, a focus which allows Baudelaire to debate the various merits and problems of different art forms. He sees the principal value of the novel and the short story as lying in their suitability for conveying a wide variety of themes and for addressing many different sections of the public. The questions of prose as opposed to rhymed verse, of brevity versus development, of a genre appealing to the general public or one written for an élite, have obviously been occupying his thoughts since his studies on Poe. Here he seems torn between the short story, the brevity of which intensifies the total effect, and the novel, whose broad canvas and general popularity promise freedom and fortune.

While Gautier is undoubtedly being used to focus a wider aesthetic debate, this general discussion offers a very skilful introduction to his short stories. Although Baudelaire rightly emphasizes the mastery with which Gautier has exploited a wide variety of themes and styles, his enthusiasm is aroused above all by what he terms 'la nouvelle poétique' and which he defines by contrast, describing first the genre most removed from it, the *roman de mœurs*, which Balzac so successfully developed.

Compared to the world depicted in the *roman de mœurs*, 'la muse de Théophile Gautier habite un monde plus éthéré' (II, 120–1). Elaborate descriptions of a poet's muse are so commonplace in contemporary criticism that Baudelaire may well be mocking the convention by parodying it, or, as in many of his pastiches, developing it in his own way.[27] Moreover, the personification provides yet another means of varying critical technique. According to Baudelaire, Gautier's muse breaks away from 'le tracas ordinaire des réalités présentes' in four ways: by the settings of the tales, by the remoteness of the age in which they take place, by the characters and by the choice of language. However general the analysis, it is sufficiently precise to call to mind specific works, indicating not only that Baudelaire is soaked in Gautier's writing but that he also expects his ideal reader to recognize and respond to the briefest allusions.

Despite his admiration, Baudelaire subtly introduces a warning, not unexpected in a writer who sought to depict 'le beau moderne': the *nouvelle poétique* runs the risk of not being sufficiently 'visible et tangible' (II, 121). Significantly *Spirite*, Gautier's last tale of the fantastic, does abandon the visible and the tangible for the nebulous regions of the spirit world and in so doing loses much of the 'magie de la vraisemblance'. Baudelaire's insight is all the more impressive in this regard in that contemporary critics saw Gautier rather as being too plastic, too concerned with the sensual world. Desnoiresterres, for example, claimed that 'M. Th. Gautier est le poëte de la sensation, de la sensation extérieure avant tout. L'âme est quelque chose; mais le corps!', and Cuvillier-Fleury fulminated: 'M. Gautier n'est pas seulement un poète sensualiste: il est le sensualisme en chair et en os'.[28] And Pontmartin protested that Gautier:

> saisit d'un regard et décrit d'un mot le ton de la chair, le grain de la peau, les lignes du visage, les contours de la taille: mais ce qui vit, pense, sent, sous cette enveloppe matérielle, il ne le sait pas, il ne veut pas le savoir, et sa tâche finit là où commence celle du véritable écrivain.[29]

As with his review of *Madame Bovary*, then, Baudelaire quietly takes the heat from a contemporary quarrel by showing that the converse of an accepted opinion might be equally or indeed more valid.

To illustrate these points Baudelaire analyses the tale 'Le Roi Candaule'. The choice of a detailed and specific example is rare in Baudelaire's criticism, the only other important exceptions being Poe's tales and Asselineau's 'La Jambe'. Although faithful to Gautier's intention, the interpretation of this tale illuminates above all Baudelaire's own approach to literature. In his 'Notes nouvelles' he insisted that the writer of short stories, 's'il est habile, n'accommodera pas ses pensées aux incidents, mais, ayant conçu délibérément, à loisir, un effet à produire, inventera les incidents, combinera les événements, les plus propres à amener l'effet voulu' (II, 329). With 'Le Roi Candaule', as with *Madame Bovary*, Baudelaire seeks out the logic dictating the choice of theme and style, presenting the tale as a series of aesthetic challenges. With intentional provocation, he depicts Gautier and Flaubert deliberately choosing 'un sentiment vulgaire, usé' (II, 122), which they invest with nobility and meaning. In both cases, too, he diverts attention from moral issues by insisting that it is the interpretation, rather than the theme itself, which the critic must evaluate. He asserts that Candaule's wife, Nyssia, has elevated modesty to the status of a religion – one might almost say an *idée fixe* – the very exaggeration of which saves it from banality. In this 'culte de la femme pour elle-même' it is impossible not to see a form of Baudelaire's own *dandysme* and a parallel with his vision of Emma Bovary. One notices not only his amusement at the way Gautier deliberately magnifies his themes, pushing possibilities to their extreme limit, just as Balzac gave his works 'un relief puissant et une grimace saisissante' (II, 120), but also the insistence on Nyssia as 'une véritable fleur de serre, harem ou gynécée': Baudelaire's initial interest in the story may have been heightened on the one hand by personal reminiscences of his journey to La Réunion, and on the other by Gautier's accounts of travels in the Middle East, Nerval's *Voyage en Orient* and, above all, by Delacroix's *Femmes d'Alger*. He emphasizes, too, the way in which Candaule appears as a symbol of the artist, the man dominated by his nerves, who is blessed with a vision of great happiness but whose temperament drives him to share his vision with others, despite his awareness that he thereby risks its destruction. This need is described by Baudelaire as 'un sentiment aussi impérieux que bizarre', one to which 'l'homme nerveux et artiste' must inevitably succumb. The literary criticism frequently spotlights the physical nature of the artist's temperament, the way in which reason is dominated by nerves. Emma, for example, resembles 'le poète hystérique' in that she transforms the orthodox image of God into one more conducive to her fantasies, 'par un paradoxe dont tout l'honneur appartient aux nerfs' (II, 83). Similarly Poe is 'l'écrivain des nerfs' (II, 316) and Rouvière's talent is 'fait de raisonnement et d'exagération nerveuse, ce dernier élément l'emportant généralement' (II, 241: cf. II, 636). Above all, Baudelaire admires in Gautier's tale the search for motives, the 'analyse des sentiments qui ont engendré les faits': this preoccupation with causes rather than effects is a general tendency evident from Baudelaire's earliest criticism.

To conclude his study of Gautier's short stories, Baudelaire indulges in an amusing pastiche of the novelist's style, highlighting two points which his contemporaries failed to appreciate: the great variety of subject-matter and the importance placed on Greek and Roman antiquity. Pastiche is used here both as an exercise of Baudelaire's own skills and as a subtle, if playful, form of flattery. Not only does the ease with which Baudelaire mimics Gautier's style argue a great familiarity with his works, but the application to Gautier of the lines written by Poe (II, 122), demonstrates yet again the way in which he emphasizes in a poet those elements which most closely correspond to his vision of the ideal writer.

From the tales, Baudelaire turns again to that most ephemeral form of imaginative writing, the critical *feuilleton*. In doing so, he reveals his mastery of the art of transition, leading easily from Gautier's love of perfection in creative art to his ability to define and judge the achievements of other artists.

Two aspects of Gautier's criticism attract Baudelaire's attention. Firstly, he praises Gautier's ability to extract from a work of art all its beauty, regardless of the grief, horror or degradation it may portray: he may well be thinking here of the evocations of Spanish art included in the travel journal *Tra los montes* and in many of the poems. Secondly, he emphasizes the way Gautier subsumes his own individual and national identity in appreciating beauty in all its guises. He could 'immédiatement britanniser son génie' (II, 123) when faced with the paintings of the English school in 1855 just as he enjoys the art of all countries through which he travels. The importance of cosmopolitanism becomes increasingly pronounced in Baudelaire's literary criticism. Although the term appears as early as the *Salon de 1846*, where the artist is depicted as a 'voyageur enthousiaste', an 'esprit cosmopolite qui préfère le beau à la gloire' (II, 470: cf. II, 538, 546), it becomes a central theme only in the mid 1850s: in 1854, Poe is described as 'un écrivain qui, comme les Hoffmann, les Jean-Paul, les Balzac, est moins de son pays que cosmopolite' (II, 291) and in 1855 cosmopolitanism is described in curiously religious terms as 'cette grâce divine' (II, 576). The word has already appeared twice before in the Gautier essay: Gautier's muse is 'cosmopolite' (II, 122) and his mind is a 'miroir cosmopolite de beauté' (II, 108). Similarly, the study devoted to Leconte de Lisle claims, in a passage linking the poet to Gautier, that 'ces deux esprits se plaisent également dans le voyage; ces deux imaginations sont naturellement cosmopolites' (II, 177). Finally, Shakespeare is 'un poète que sa grandeur (comme celle de plusieurs autres grands poètes) rend cosmopolite' (II, 225). This 'cosmopolitan' approach and response to art and beauty is essential for artists as well as for writers: the *Salon de 1859*, for example, emphasizes that quality which allows the creative mind 'saisir les parcelles du beau égarées sur la terre, de suivre le beau à la piste partout où il a pu se glisser à travers les trivialités de la nature déchue' (II, 650). Not only, therefore, is this a vital concept in Baudelaire's critical vocabulary, but the frequency with which the term is applied to Gautier's *feuilletons* shows how radically Baudelaire's earlier assessment of his criticism has altered.

What Baudelaire stresses in evaluating Gautier's criticism is its role in forming the knowledge and sensitivity of the young: he claims, indeed, that it is through Gautier that a whole generation has become aware of art. Clearly, the impact Gautier's *feuilletons* made on him as an adolescent has left memories tenacious and vivid enough to reveal their overall importance, even if individual comments or reviews seem to use insufficient critical judgement. Moreover, in comparing him to Hugo, whose *Notre-Dame* urged the French public to respect its architectural heritage, Baudelaire subtly implies through his choice of language that Gautier was the more successful: 'Théophile Gautier leur a donné l'amour de la peinture, comme Victor Hugo leur avait conseillé le goût de l'archéologie' (II, 124). The importance of Gautier's art criticism[30] is sometimes anachronistically overlooked, but before the widespread reproduction of works of art the graphic powers of Gautier's prose, his talent for the *pittoresque* and his ability both to describe a painting and to convey the joy art can give, must have played a vital part in presenting art to the public.

Gautier's art criticism is all the more important since, as contemporary critics and Baudelaire himself constantly lament, the general public is not, or at least is no longer, 'naturellement artiste' (II, 124). In words recalling the notes for 'L'Art philosophique', on which he was working at the time, and which develop his earlier discussion of truth, beauty and goodness, Baudelaire declares that 'où il ne faut voir que le beau, notre public ne cherche que le vrai. Quand il faut être peintre, le Français se fait homme de lettres.' Similarly, he condemns 'l'art philosophique' as 'un art plastique qui a la prétention de remplacer le livre, c'est-à-dire de rivaliser avec l'imprimerie pour enseigner l'histoire, la morale et la philosophie' (II, 598). Once again, therefore, it is above all the confusion of genres in the minds of both the public and the artists that he condemns, just as in the early review of *Prométhée délivré*.

Moreover, Baudelaire deplores the way in which the French judge 'successivement, analytiquement' whereas other races 'sentent [...] tout à la fois, synthétiquement', a passage he repeats in the *Salon de 1859* (II, 616). The questions of whether art can be appreciated instantaneously or only after a slow process of individual responses, and whether an analytical or a synthetic approach is more creatively successful recur in Baudelaire's art criticism and are further debated in his notices on Hugo and Banville.

Thus, although Baudelaire defines Gautier's prose style, evokes the atmosphere of his tales, and evaluates his criticism, he also eagerly seizes on the opportunity to raise broader questions regarding creative and critical writing, and to deplore once again the obtuseness of the public. This final thread – a frequent complaint among his contemporaries – is taken up again, much more briefly, in the anthology notice, which laments the 'répugnance native des Français pour la perfection' (11, 150).

The fifth section of Baudelaire's essay opens with a clever transition, contending that the French public's insensitivity to painting is paralleled by its lack of response to poetry. As before (11, 106), the images used are drawn from the very physical domain of food: 'quelque politique que soit le condiment le Beau amène l'indigestion, ou plutôt l'estomac français le refuse immédiatement' (11, 125).

However artistically insensitive the public may be, Baudelaire has no doubts about the ability of the country's poets: 'nos voisins disent: Shakespeare et Goethe! Nous pouvons leur répondre: Victor Hugo et Théophile Gautier!' Although this claim may sound exaggerated, I do not think it insincere: the names of Hugo, Balzac and Gautier were frequently linked in contemporary criticism and such comparisons with great writers of other countries are commonplace. The parallel between the two poets is tightened in the anthology notice where Baudelaire insists that any study of the 'resplendissantes poésies' of Hugo must be complemented by a knowledge of Gautier's poetry, which, while less magnificent, never leaves the realm of pure poetry: 'quelques-uns observent même que pendant que le majestueux poète était entraîné par des enthousiasmes quelquefois peu propices à son art, le poète précieux, plus fidèle, plus concentré, n'en est jamais sorti' (11, 152). Although there is some irony in the placing of his judgement in the mouths of the vague 'quelques-uns' and although the word 'précieux' is ambiguous, suggesting artifice as well as achievement, Baudelaire certainly preferred Gautier's concept of art for art's sake to the didacticism of some of Hugo's writing.

Having led up so carefully to Gautier's poetry, the genre which 'fait [son] principal honneur', Baudelaire, as on previous occasions, stops short of a detailed analysis. Once again, he seems torn between the desire to kindle in his readers the spark of understanding, and the impossibility of explaining poetry to those not intuitively responsive to it. Moreover, there is the problem, already raised earlier in the essay (11, 117), of finding a language adequate for such an explanation. This preoccupation with forging a style precise yet subtle enough to convey a certain range of ideas may reflect a similar search, resulting in the prose poems. Finally, he uses the unanswerable argument he will invoke in reference to Marceline Desbordes-Valmore: 'il en est des vers comme de quelques belles femmes en qui se sont fondues l'originalité et la correction; on ne les définit pas, on les *aime*' (II, 125), an argument reinforcing his earlier reference to a synthetic and immediate approach to art.

Although technical analysis seems impossible, Baudelaire does attempt to classify the poems he most admires and to assess Gautier's general contribution, firstly, by showing the tradition to which he belongs and which he develops, and secondly, by indicating his innovations. On the one hand, he sees Gautier as continuing the Romantic tradition of melancholy initiated by Chateaubriand (see also II, 635), but, whereas the latter's *ennui* is characterized by having no obvious cause, that of Gautier is 'd'un caractère plus positif, plus charnel et confinant quelquefois à la tristesse antique'. Similarly, Baudelaire claimed of Delacroix that he possessed 'une qualité *sui generis*, indéfinissable et définissant la partie mélancolique et ardente du siècle' (II, 596–7). The poems mentioned as revealing this quality, 'La Comédie de la mort', 'Deux Tableaux de Valdès-Léal' and 'A Zurbaran', suggest that for Baudelaire Gautier's melancholy derives from a constant awareness of decay in beauty and death in life, the transience of earthly things and the deception of sensuous pleasures, 'les secrets de la mort et de la sépulture'.[31] This kind of general view is close to Baudelaire's own, the affinity being reinforced when 'La Comédie de la mort' is shown to express 'le vertige et l'horreur du néant', a combination of opposing reactions similar to Baudelaire's famous confession: 'tout enfant, j'ai senti dans mon cœur deux sentiments contradictoires, l'horreur de la vie et l'extase de la vie' (I, 703). The antithesis, as well as the choice of the word 'vertige' in the article, may well have been inspired by 'A Zurbaran', in which the artist's monks are depicted in the following terms:

Le vertige divin, l'enivrement de foi
Qui les fait rayonner d'une clarté fiévreuse,
Et leur aspect étrange, à vous donner l'effroi.[32]

Finally, Baudelaire mentions a poem of melancholy that has obviously haunted him: 'Ténèbres'. In his studies of Poe, it is from this poem that he quotes to illustrate the apparent tenacity of fate (II, 250, 296, 297), and in the preamble to 'La Genèse d'un poème' it is concisely and evocatively defined as 'ce chapelet de redoutables concetti sur la mort et le néant, où la rime triplée s'adapte si bien à la mélancolie obsédante' (II, 344). In 'Ténèbres' Gautier does, indeed, make brilliant use of the *terza rima* to suggest, through the anticipation of the repeated rhyme, the inevitability of death. The melancholy dominating Gautier's poetry is further examined in Baudelaire's anthology notice, in which he exclaims: 'que de fois il a exprimé, et avec quelle magie de langage! ce qu'il y a de plus délicat dans la tendresse et dans la mélancolie!' (II, 150). The affinity between Baudelaire and Poe is very clear in this regard: in 'The Philosophy of Composition' Poe asserts that, if 'le Beau est le seul domaine légitime de la poésie' (Poe, 987), then 'la mélancolie est [. . .] le plus légitime de tous les tons poétiques' (Poe, 988). In the well-known definition of beauty in 'Fusées', Baudelaire writes: 'je ne prétends pas que la Joie ne puisse pas s'associer avec la Beauté, mais je dis que la Joie [en] est un des ornements les plus vulgaires; – tandis que la Mélancolie en est pour ainsi dire l'illustre compagne' (I, 657–8). Similarly, his uncompleted letter to Janin describes melancholy as 'toujours inséparable du sentiment du beau' (II, 238).

In a strangely double-edged conclusion to this analysis Baudelaire insists that 'il arrive même à ce poète, accusé de sensualité, de tomber en plein, tant sa mélancolie devient intense, dans la terreur catholique' (II, 126). Once again Baudelaire challenges the critical clichés, stressing the spiritual in contrast with the physical. And once again there seems an element of self-confession on the part of the poet convicted of 'offense à la morale publique'.

If Baudelaire sees Gautier as 'un écrivain d'un mérite à la fois *nouveau et unique*' (II, 117), it is partly because he has introduced into poetry 'la consolation par les arts, par tous les objets pittoresques qui réjouissent les yeux et amusent l'esprit'. Melancholy, therefore, is counterbalanced by the skilful and harmonious evocation of plastic beauty. Once again, Baudelaire epitomizes Gautier's style through an evocation of his muse: 'sa poésie, à la fois majestueuse et précieuse, marche magnifiquement, comme les personnes de cour en grande toilette' (II, 126). Behind this praise of Gautier's harmonious lyricism lies a further sign of Baudelaire's own search for a *prose poétique* expressing the 'soubresauts de la conscience' as well as the 'ondulations de la rêverie' (I, 276): true lyric poetry, he insists, avoids 'la précipitation et la saccade', its movement being 'élastique et ondulé'. Baudelaire's love of the rhythmical movement he describes as undulating can be found in his attitude to women, to pictorial art and to prose, as well as to poetry. One thinks, for example, of the 'ondulation de ce corps musculeux' evoked in 'Le Masque' (I, 23), of the graceful gait of the woman in 'Le Serpent qui danse', of Baudelaire's marked preference for 'une harmonie ondoyante de lignes' (II, 373) in the plastic arts, and his profound admiration for the thought of De Quincey which is not merely 'sinueuse; le mot n'est pas assez fort: elle est naturellement spirale' (I, 515). No doubt

Gautier's poetry offered him an example of the way in which this delight can be captured in a work of art and his assessment of Gautier's skill allowed him not only to render homage but also to sharpen his own artistic awareness.

Far from claiming that Gautier has always found satisfactory solutions to the problems posed by such a vision of poetry, Baudelaire merely depicts him as fully aware of them, and asserts that *Emaux et Camées* provides sufficient proof of his preoccupation with all questions connected with rhetoric and form, a statement underlining Baudelaire's own interest in such problems.

The last sentence of the essay's fifth section offers adequate proof that Baudelaire had conquered not only the problem of the arresting opening sentence but also that of the resounding conclusion. In a brief, firm assertion that seems to stifle all argument, he insists of *Emaux et Camées* that 'quiconque aime la poésie les sait par cœur' (II, 126). Interestingly, Baudelaire's comment that Gautier has introduced 'la majesté de l'alexandrin dans le vers octosyllabique' (II, 126) may perhaps have influenced Valéry, who attempted, in 'Le Cimetière marin', 'porter [le] *Dix* à la puissance du *Douze*'.[33] Yet there is a hint of criticism when Baudelaire concludes that, in *Emaux et Camées*: 'là surtout apparaît tout le résultat qu'on peut obtenir par la fusion du double élément, peinture et musique, par la carrure de la mélodie, et par la pourpre régulière et symétrique d'une rime plus qu'exacte' (II, 116). The intermingling of different art forms is a technique Baudelaire frequently attacks, particularly in the unfinished review of Janin's *Le Gâteau des rois*, where the combination is far less skilful than in *Emaux et Camées*. Nevertheless, it was a question over which he seems to have hesitated, recognizing both the value and the disadvantages of the *nouvelle poétique* and seeing in his own prose poems the possibility of forging a new genre. The reference to 'la pourpre régulière et symétrique d'une rime plus qu'exacte' is somewhat ambiguous, since, although he emphasizes the pleasure the human mind receives from symmetry, Baudelaire himself considers that surprise, a break in the pattern, increases that pleasure: 'ce qui n'est pas légèrement difforme a l'air insensible; – d'où il suit que l'irrégularité, c'est-à-dire l'inattendu, la surprise, l'étonnement sont une partie essentielle et la caractéristique de la beauté' (I, 656). Finally, his reference to 'cette série de petits poèmes de quelques vers' recalls his belief that poetry can be too short as well as too long, and his admiration of 'le souffle'.

Whatever doubts he may have – and his criticism reveals that he very often responded with immediate enthusiasm to a work whose faults he realized later without necessarily rejecting the work or denying his initial pleasure – Baudelaire is able to evoke with astonishing precision and brevity the essence of *Emaux et Camées*. Their resemblance to sculpture, flowers and jewelry, their glowing colours and their form, which, in its perfection, rivals objects of marble or crystal; all these are points which Baudelaire admires, even if forced to admit that, taken as a whole, the poems are merely 'intermèdes galants ou rêveurs'. Certainly, his brief analysis is both more accurate and more evocative than that of many contemporaries: the antagonistic Cuvillier-Fleury, for instance, described the poems as 'verroteries d'un scintillement si étrange, d'un éclat si faux, d'une enluminure si chargée, d'un mauvais goût si franc et si lâché'; Dufaï, having amused himself with a grossly insensitive attack on Gautier's pantheism, wrote disdainfully of the volume: 'on ne le vendait guère, on le lisait encore moins, il ne faisait de mal à personne, et très-assurément personne ne lui eût cherché chicane, sans les hyperboliques et grotesques éloges dont ont voulu le combler de trop dangereux camarades'.[34] Gautier's colleague Limayrac, however, declared that, in *Emaux et Camées*, 'Gautier est à la fois peintre, sculpteur, poète; il est artiste des yeux, de la tête, du cœur', and emphasized that where the earlier works had lacked sentiment, 'dans ce volume, au milieu d'une forme de plus en plus éblouissante, le sentiment perce à maint endroit'.[35]

In concluding his essay, Baudelaire characteristically insists that his motivation has been twofold: not content merely to express his admiration, he has sought out 'les raisons qui légitiment cette admiration' (II, 127), insisting, as so often, on the twin poles of immediate response and intellectual investigation.

In a series of carefully balanced sentences, he declares that the current, misguided judgement of Gautier will be rectified by posterity: later generations will judge him a 'maître écrivain'. The point is made again, almost belligerently, in the second article: 'parmi les vivants clairvoyants, qui ne comprend qu'on citera un jour Théophile Gautier, comme on cite La Bruyère, Buffon, Chateaubriand, c'est-à-dire comme un des maîtres les plus sûrs et les plus rares en matière de langue et de style?' (II, 152).

From his general assertion of Gautier's coming fame, at least as far as his style and language are concerned, Baudelaire turns to a brief evocation of the warmth and helpfulness of the man and then calmly demolishes several common criticisms of his work.

Firstly, he denies that Gautier is insensitive to politics and religion, arguing somewhat obliquely that he is protected from error in this regard by a longing for order and a sense of 'universelle hiérarchie': similarly, in his first study on Poe, Baudelaire emphasized the writer's 'idées sur la hiérarchie des êtres' (II, 287). Perhaps he is once again fusing Poe and Gautier into an idealized poet. The expression 'universelle hiérarchie' is Fourierist in origin: in *L'Esprit des bêtes*, for example, a work Baudelaire described in 1856 as *'absolument instructif'* (*CI*, 336), Toussenel refers to 'l'échelle de l'universelle hiérarchie'.[36]

Secondly, Baudelaire rejects the claim that Gautier lacks humanity. This criticism was certainly among the most common: Labitte insisted that 'les personnages des romans de M. Gautier vivent par les sens et ne vivent pas par le cœur', Limayrac asserted that 'dans son culte ardent pour la forme' Gautier neglected 'le côté intérieur de l'art, le côté du sentiment'[37] and Pontmartin derided 'ce singulier cerveau en qui les tons et les contours tiennent la place des sentiments et des pensées'.[38] Baudelaire chooses to reject this criticism firstly by insisting that it is not applicable since a poet's function is 'extra-humaine' – a point prepared by the earlier statement that 'la muse de Théophile Gautier habite un monde plus éthéré' (II, 120–1: cf. II, 304) – and secondly by arguing that Gautier's coldness, far from revealing a lack of emotion, springs from intense sensitivity. Gautier, according to Baudelaire, has made a conscious decision to escape 'le spectacle désolant' of his fellows' folly and cruelty. This claim is similar to one made in 1856 by E. Eggis, according to whom Gautier is 'épris de la forme, parce que le fond l'a trompé, comme un artiste qui ne veut plus aimer que la *robe* parce qu'il a appris que lorsqu'on aime la *femme* le cœur saigne'.[39] The anthology article makes a spirited attack on the same criticism, defending Gautier this time not by philosophical arguments but by proving through quotation that he does indeed possess 'cette fameuse qualité que les badauds de la critique s'obstinent à lui refuser: le sentiment' (II, 150). This quotation, by revealing Baudelaire's irritation with contemporary critics, proves his awareness of what they were writing. Baudelaire insists that the underlying reason for the criticism lies in the very perfection of Gautier's style and the current conviction that 'un ouvrage *trop bien* écrit *doit* manquer de sentiment' (II, 150). Certainly Gautier's poetry hardly deserves the vitriolic censure it incurred on the grounds of its insensitivity; indeed, one could argue that much of *Emaux et Camées* is *too* sentimental. The attack appears to have become so much a part of critical analyses of Gautier that it may well have been repeated without thought or conviction.[40]

Having thus demolished common criticisms of Gautier, Baudelaire suggests some of his own, softening the blow by showing that he understands why Gautier has transgressed. Just as the apparent 'froideur' hides despair, so his conviction that it is impossible 'corriger qui que ce soit', has led him 'accorder par-ci par-là quelques paroles laudatives à monseigneur Progrès et à très puissante dame Industrie' (11, 128). Baudelaire shares this sense of defeat in the face of the public's stupidity: one of his 'projets de préface' admits: 'tâche difficile que de s'élever vers cette insensibilité divine! Car moi-même, malgré les plus louables efforts, je n'ai su résister au désir de plaire à mes contemporains, comme l'attestent en quelques endroits, apposées comme un fard, certaines basses flatteries adressées à la démocratie' (1, 183–4). In accusing Gautier of contemporary follies, Baudelaire tries to keep the tone light by the parody evident in the personification of Monsignor Progress and Dame Industry, and by insisting that Gautier praises them only because he wearies of trying to reveal the falsity of such convictions. The heavy-handedness of Baudelaire's attempt at humour is sufficient indication of his weary recognition that belief in this 'fanal obscur' (11, 580) is too deep-seated to be removed by reason. Although, in the early 1840s, Gautier deplored the lack of beauty in industrial machinery and architecture, the euphoria preceding the Revolution and his later appointment to *Le Moniteur universel* led him to vaunt 'l'imprimerie, la vapeur, l'électricité, tous ces moyens merveilleux de communication presque instantanée' and to suggest the possibility of 'un monde nouveau tout resplendissant d'acier et de gaz, aussi beau dans son activité que [le monde antique] dans sa rêverie séreine'.[41] Whether Baudelaire is right in suggesting that, far from being sincere in his praise, Gautier shared the conviction that industry and progress were 'despotiques ennemis de toute poésie' (11, 128: cf. 11, 618) is a question which cannot be dealt with here.[42]

Baudelaire's conclusion to his essay confirms Gautier as 'l'égal des plus grands dans le passé' (11, 128), establishes him as a model for future poets – a role Gautier obviously played for Baudelaire himself – and a unique contrast to the prevailing ignorance and materialism of the present.

Throughout this essay, therefore, Baudelaire has quietly suggested lacunae in Gautier's talent, visible to those who 'savent y voir clair dans le crépuscule' (11, 128), but his principal aim has been to emphasize those gifts of which the public seemed unaware: his skilful control of language, his extensive vocabulary, his evocation of melancholy and despair, the graphic precision of his art criticism and the wide range of his creative and critical works. As L. J. Austin points out, in his preface to *L'Art romantique*, Gautier is one of those poets who permitted Baudelaire to discover himself, and this essay explores Gautier's gifts not merely in order to present them to the public, but above all to extract from his poetry ideas and techniques which Baudelaire himself could exploit and develop. Perhaps more than any of his other reviews, it reveals an artist exploring art with all the knowledge, insight and intensity that stem not from a desire to teach or judge, but from an urgent personal need to understand in order to create.

Balzac

Baudelaire's essay on Gautier reveals his mastery not only of the *entrée en matière* and the resounding conclusion, but also of the skilfully controlled digression, which, however peripheral it may seem, still develops or consolidates a central argument. His critical articles frequently allude to Balzac in fleeting phrases or terse sentences: here he has obviously seized on a splendid opportunity to analyse Balzac's art in greater detail while remaining within the framework of an exploration of the novel.

In his abundantly documented survey of Balzac criticism in the second half of the nineteenth century, D. Bellos contends that this passage 'marks a very sudden break with all that Baudelaire had previously written about the novelist'.[43] He claims that this radical change of mind was provoked by Taine's celebrated essay of 1858. The suggestion is not new: in 1934 a swashbuckling comparative study by R. Hughes noted that: 'dans ses traits essentiels et même dans certaines allures de sa phraséologie, cette appréciation de Baudelaire rappelle singulièrement celle de Taine [. . .]. Est-ce que Baudelaire, ayant lu l'étude de Taine, en a gardé l'empreinte? Cela n'est pas le moins du monde improbable.'[44] Nor is it at all improbable that Baudelaire's attitude was affected by other contemporary assessments. In particular, since his most detailed commentary appears in a study of Gautier, the latter's own *Honoré de Balzac*, published in *L'Artiste* in 1858, may well have influenced him. Restrictions of length, however, have prevented both Hughes and Bellos from providing the detailed chronological survey needed to determine the nature and trace the vicissitudes of Baudelaire's appreciation of Balzac in the light of contemporary criticism.

Baudelaire's 'notices bio-bibliographiques' include Balzac among the 'premières liaisons littéraires' (1, 784): according to Prarond, the two met while out walking, recognized each other immediately as kindred spirits and 'cheminèrent ensemble, causant, discutant, s'enchantant, ne parvenant pas à s'étonner l'un l'autre'.[45] Whatever the truth of this anecdote, it is undeniable that Baudelaire's earliest articles establish Balzac's position in his small gallery of highly admired novelists. Indeed, in his very first literary review, he chooses to emphasize the talent he perceives in Chennevières by declaring that one of his tales is not unworthy of Balzac (II, 3).

A few weeks after the Chennevières review, Baudelaire published an amusing sketch entitled 'Comment on paie ses dettes quand on a du génie'. Although a pastiche, it is firmly rooted, like all good examples of the genre, in a sure knowledge of the themes and techniques of the author whom it parodies. Baudelaire revels, for example, in echoing the importance Balzac places on physiological signs for the interpretation of emotions: 'il était triste, à en juger par ses sourcils froncés, sa large bouche moins distendue et moins lippue qu'à l'ordinaire, et la manière entrecoupée de brusques pauses dont il arpentait le double passage de l'Opéra. Il était triste' (II, 6). In referring to the passage by name, moreover, Baudelaire mirrors Balzac's preoccupation with creating an exact portrait of Paris, while the repetition of 'il était triste' and, in the next paragraph, 'c'était bien lui', echoes his emphatic style, his desire to drive his points thoroughly home. That a person's temperament and mood can be judged by his walk is of course a further idea of Balzac's that Baudelaire copies. He strikes a further resonance on this note when he adds that, once the problem has been solved, Balzac walks with 'un pas sublime et cadencé' (II, 7). Significantly, Proust's pastiche of Balzac also emphasizes 'la sonorité spéciale du pas des hommes supérieurs'.[46] Moreover, in describing Balzac as 'le cerveau poétique tapissé de chiffres comme le cabinet d'un financier' Baudelaire is echoing not only Balzac's idiosyncratic use of *poétique* and his fascination with riches, but also his predilection for similes which abound with physical detail: one might compare, for example, his description of an elderly princess who 'avait dans le parchemin de sa cervelle tout celui du cabinet des chartes'.[47] Stylistic parody is also present in Baudelaire's hyperbolical description of this 'homme aux faillites mythologiques' (II, 6) and in the series of questions, with their insistence on the twin pivots of Balzac's universe, 'l'or et le plaisir'. Balzac's habit of presenting his protagonists as embodiments of their dominant characteristic, his interest in social class, and his analyses of older women are captured in what Pichois terms a 'visible et excellent pastiche' (II, 1081): 'quelque princesse, approchant de la quarantaine, lui avait-elle jeté une de ces œillades profondes que la beauté doit au génie?' (II, 6). Not only such novels as *La Peau de chagrin*, *Le Père Goriot*, *César Birotteau* and *Illusions perdues*, but also Baudelaire's own experience, hover behind the reasons given for Balzac's sudden flash of genius: 'en ces sortes de cas, il arrive parfois que, pressé, accablé, pétri, écrasé sous le piston de la nécessité, l'esprit s'élance subitement hors de sa prison par un jet inattendu et victorieux' (II, 7). The language used here, with its machine-age imagery and its clustered adjectives, recalls not only Balzac but also many passages in Baudelaire's later literary criticism, where the sudden creative outburst is described as a 'jaillissement', an 'explosion'. One thinks above all of his assertion in 'Fusées' that 'il y a dans l'engendrement de toute pensée sublime une secousse nerveuse qui se fait sentir dans le cervelet' (I, 661).[48] Even at this early stage, therefore, Baudelaire is steeped in Balzac's style and thought, and delighted to try his hand at both in a half-mocking, half-admiring pastiche.

Yet the anecdote poses problems of interpretation. Is Bellos right in suggesting that Baudelaire ridicules, albeit sympathetically, Balzac's obsession with money? To some extent, of course, the article is indeed a piece of literary gossip which at times borders on the malicious. Nonetheless, the tone is less of ridicule than of glee, of intense amusement at the novelist's crafty hoodwinking of 'un commerçant riche et prospérant'. And underlying the laughter, there is a constant note of admiration for Balzac's ability not merely to dream but also to act. Certainly Enid Starkie's interpretation is too prim, too firmly based on a moral code to which Baudelaire would not have subscribed:

> this is an attack on Balzac's way of commissioning hacks to write articles which he then signed, in order to make money to pay his debts. Baudelaire, who, in other respects, was one of Balzac's most fervent admirers, and who, himself, was also crushed by debts, did not approve of this way of solving a difficulty and never, even in his most penurious days, resorted to it himself.[49]

On the contrary, it is difficult to imagine Baudelaire being anything but delighted at Balzac's triumph of organization. Furthermore, the final paragraph, added in August 1846, insists that it should not be seen as 'un attentat à la gloire du plus grand homme de notre siècle': had it constituted an attack, Baudelaire would probably have sought to cover himself by including the *caveat* in the first version.

More importantly, the sketch contains the germ of several ideas which come to fruition in later articles. Firstly, it touches both on the significance of the artist's own *tempérament* and on the perplexing problem of creativity and predestination: Balzac's blend of qualities and faults is described as 'cette incorrigible et fatale monstruosité' (II, 6). In addition, Baudelaire's later references to the swift, destructive passage of time are adumbrated in the image of the genius who, with one eye on the clock, 'sent la nécessité de doubler, tripler, décupler ses forces dans la proportion du temps qui diminue, et de la vitesse approchante de l'heure fatale' (II, 7).

Above all, the article contains the first of a series of passages in which Baudelaire insists on the degree to which Balzac's characters spring from his own personality. He, therefore, is 'le plus curieux, le plus cocasse, le plus intéressant et le plus vaniteux des personnages de la *Comédie humaine*' (II, 6). Similarly, in the following year Baudelaire concluded his *Salon* with the triumphant affirmation that:

> les héros de l'*Iliade* ne vont qu'à votre cheville, ô Vautrin, ô Rastignac, ô Birotteau, – et vous, ô Fontanarès, qui n'avez pas osé raconter au public vos douleurs sous le frac funèbre et convulsionné que nous endossons tous; – et vous, ô Honoré de Balzac, vous le plus héroïque, le plus singulier, le plus romantique et le plus poétique parmi tous les personnages que vous avez tirés de votre sein! (II, 496).

Once again, this extravagant, enthusiastic eulogy is, in part, a pastiche of Balzac's own style. Baudelaire's admiration is expressed with greater intensity here than in the earlier article. There is no longer the hint of reservation implied by 'cocasse' and 'vaniteux', and Baudelaire strengthens his picture of Balzac as a writer profoundly modern in his Romanticism and a hero in his own right. The need to find a modern form of heroism underlies much of the *Salon*, Balzac's character Raphaël de Valentin typifying a heroic modern suicide (II, 494), while in the 1852 study on Poe Balzac himself is described as descending into 'le gouffre final en poussant les nobles plaintes d'un héros qui a encore de grandes choses à faire' (II, 252).[50]

In the precocious 'Conseils aux jeunes littérateurs', published in April 1846, Baudelaire expresses one of his rare censures of Balzac: 'on dit que Balzac charge sa copie et ses épreuves d'une manière fantastique et désordonnée. [. . .] C'est sans doute cette mauvaise méthode qui donne souvent au style ce je ne sais quoi de diffus, de bousculé et de brouillon, – le seul défaut de ce grand historien' (II, 17). The attack seems based on the way in which such a method destroys the unity, both of individual passages and of the work's overall structure. In 1855 he refers again to 'les *épreuves* arachnéennes de Balzac' (II, 295), but this time the tone is neutral. His journals and notes reveal an increasing awareness that the ability to write is in itself valuable, whatever the disadvantages of the method adopted: 'travail immédiat, même mauvais', he tries to convince himself, 'vaut mieux que la rêverie' (I, 672). Baudelaire's contemporaries also referred to Balzac's cluttered galley proofs, A. de Belloy noting that 'le roman achevé n'était qu'une espèce de brouillon qu'il refaisait encore sur les épreuves, et plus d'une fois'.[51] George Bell asserted enthusiastically that 'les corrections, les ratures sans nombre qui les couvrent seraient la meilleure des leçons à donner aux jeunes gens amoureux d'entrer dans la carrière des lettres'.[52] And, with a characteristic flight of fancy, Gautier compared the galleys to 'le bouquet d'un feu d'artifice dessiné par un enfant' (*HB*, 81).

The passage in 'Conseils' describes Balzac as a great historian: at this stage, therefore, Baudelaire sees him principally as an observer and recorder of facts. A further reference, which Pichois dates from the same year, tends to confirm this view: Baudelaire claims that the most important contribution that Gavarni and Daumier can make is to complete Balzac's observations by their own studies of modern Parisian types (II, 560). Balzac's passion for realistic detail is mentioned again in the *Salon de 1846* where Baudelaire ridicules 'un poëte ordinaire de la Comédie-Française' (II, 481) for expressing disgust at what he considered the earthiness of Balzac's novels. Finally, Baudelaire's account of another exhibition which took place in 1846 casts Balzac in the same light: he claims that all the details in David's painting of Marat are 'historiques et réels, comme un roman de Balzac' (II, 409: cf. II, 547).

When he reviewed Champfleury's short stories in January 1848 Baudelaire added several new shades to his portrait of Balzac. Firstly, he insisted that the great novelist had 'triomphalement démontré' (II, 21) how rich are the provinces in literary inspiration. The idea, first expressed in the article on Chennevières, is developed in the study of *Madame Bovary*. More importantly, perhaps, Baudelaire emphasizes the quality of Balzac's method, which he urges Champfleury to examine: 'c'est un grand homme dans toute la force du terme; c'est un créateur de méthode et le seul dont la méthode vaille la peine d'être étudiée' (II, 22). The intensity of the terms is particularly remarkable. Several critics indeed have found in *La Fanfarlo* proof that Baudelaire himself followed Balzac's method closely.[53] His attention may have been drawn to Balzac's technique by Eugène Pelletan who, in 1846, asserted that 'dans la méthode [du romancier] la réflexion domine l'inspiration', adding that 'de tous les romanciers, il est le seul, peut-être, qui ait une méthode. Il n'écrit pas une ligne qui ne soit pesée, calculée, préméditée; il a mis la tactique dans la poésie.'[54] The tantalizing brevity of Baudelaire's statement makes it impossible to decide whether he would have agreed with Pelletan's interpretation of Balzac's method, but his subsequent criticism of Champfleury's failure 'tirer de[s] conclusions' and 'épuiser un sujet' (II, 23), together with the high value he himself placed on the unity of every element in a work of art, suggest part of what he had in mind.

In the Champfleury review, Balzac is no longer presented purely as a historian: he is 'un romancier et un savant, un inventeur et un observateur' (II, 22). The order of the nouns is, I think, significant; the emphasis still falls on the 'observateur' but Balzac's creative side is beginning to attract Baudelaire's attention.

Later in 1848 Baudelaire, in the introduction to his translation of
'Révélation magnétique', returns to the idea of Balzac as novelist and
sage, describing him as one of the 'romanciers forts' who are 'tous plus
ou moins philosophes' (II, 247). Unlike the 'simples imaginatifs' he is
not content merely 'entasse[r] et aligne[r] les événements sans les
classer, et sans en expliquer le sens mystérieux' (II, 248). In some,
according to Baudelaire, one finds 'la préoccupation d'un perpétuel
surnaturalisme' while others 'examinent l'âme à la loupe'. Balzac, however, is one of the writers who 'cherchent à fondre ces deux systèmes
dans une mystérieuse unité'. Already he is being presented as both a
'naturaliste enragé' and a seer: although the word *voyant* or *visionnaire* is
not used the concept is certainly implicit.

The introduction to Poe's tale also refers to 'l'idée de l'unité' to which
both Poe and Balzac adhere; Baudelaire insists that Balzac, whom he
describes as 'ce grand esprit dévoré du légitime orgueil encyclopédique,
a essayé de fondre en un système unitaire et définitif différentes idées
tirées de Swedenborg, Mesmer, Marat, Goethe et Geoffroy Saint-
Hilaire' (II, 248). The belief that a system capable of explaining all
aspects of man's existence could be discovered is one which the young
Baudelaire shared and which he seems to have abandoned with considerable reluctance. This passage does much to explain what Baudelaire means in his call in 'L'Ecole païenne' for literature to walk fraternally between science and philosophy.

Balzac's 'rages de science', to which Baudelaire refers again in 1851
(II, 283), and his dual role as philosopher and novelist, aroused the
interest of several critics in the 1840s and 1850s. Philarète Chasles's
obituary notice introduced a new term into criticism devoted to Balzac
when he truculently asserted that 'ce n'est pas un analyste; c'est mieux
ou pis, c'est un voyant'.[55] In 1854, the antagonistic Pontmartin wrote
scornfully: 'l'analyse se change en alchimie, l'observateur en maniaque
et le *voyant* en visionnaire'.[56] Balzac as 'observateur' is, however, a far
more common figure: in 1842, Paul de Molènes, whose short stories
Baudelaire admired (II, 215–16), and who wrote many critical reviews,
claimed that 'il a reçu au plus haut degré un don sans lequel on n'écrit
ni livre de morale ni livre de poésie, le génie de l'observation', and in
1850 Jacob Cohen referred to 'l'esprit d'observation, l'intelligence
profondément analytique, cette sorte d'anatomie morale qui ont fait
la réputation européenne de Balzac'.[57]

Balzac's death in 1850 moved Baudelaire deeply. Much later he was
to write that the death of Delacroix awoke in him again 'cette dépres-
sion d'âme, [. . .] cette sensation de solitude croissante que nous avaient
fait déjà connaître la mort de Chateaubriand et celle de Balzac' (II, 769).

Many of his comments about Balzac in the years after the novelist's death are darkened by a sense of despondency and loneliness, deepened by an awareness of the injustice of fate. In the study on wine and hashish, published in 1851, Baudelaire laments that 'notre cher et grand Balzac' had to wait until he was near death before he saw 'briller l'aurore boréale de ses plus anciennes espérances' (I, 379). The metaphor recalls the prose poem, 'Any Where Out Of The World', in which the poet suggests to his soul that they go to the frozen North: 'là, nous pourrons prendre de longs bains de ténèbres, cependant que, pour nous divertir, les aurores boréales nous enverront de temps en temps leurs gerbes roses' (I, 357). It can also be seen as a first draft of the more elaborate simile in the review of *Madame Bovary*: there, Balzac is 'ce prodigieux météore qui couvrira notre pays d'un nuage de gloire, comme un orient bizarre et exceptionnel, comme une aurore polaire inondant le désert glacé de ses lumières féeriques' (II, 78).

Despite his sorrow at Balzac's death, Baudelaire attempted to draw from *La Comédie humaine* inspiration for his own approach to literature and indeed to life in general. Thus, in his first preface to Dupont's songs he agrees with Balzac that 'le poëte doit vivre par lui-même; il doit [...] offrir une surface commerciale' (II, 30). Balzac made the comment in a letter to the editor of *La Presse* in August 1839; there he raised the problem of copyright in regard to the illicit Belgian publications. Suggesting that the state take the matter in hand, he asked: 'après tout, que contrefait la Belgique? Les dix ou douze maréchaux de France littéraires, selon la belle expression de M. Victor Hugo, ceux qui font œuvre, collection, et qui offrent à l'exploitation une certaine surface commerciale.'[58] I suggest that Baudelaire's reference, which slightly alters the sense of Balzac's letter, is based on a review by Charles de Mazade, published in the *Revue des deux mondes* in 1850: Mazade refers to 'cette [...] pensée qu'un grand écrivain, un *maréchal* littéraire, comme il l'appelait, était celui qui offrait une certaine surface commerciale'.[59]

Similarly, Baudelaire throws into sharp relief the joy Balzac's works convey, a joy which seems independent of the author's personal misery. Here, as in much of his criticism, the review is used not only to shed light on a writer but also to screw Baudelaire's own courage to the sticking point. Further evidence of this tendency, and the important role Balzac played in shaping Baudelaire's image of the ideal artist, is provided by a letter written to Madame Aupick in August 1851. Describing his impressions of Balzac's early works and unpublished papers, in which he was particularly interested at the time (see *C*II, 931), he claims that: 'personne ne pourra jamais se figurer combien ce grand homme était maladroit, niais, et BETE dans sa jeunesse. Et cependant il est parvenu à avoir, *à se procurer*, pour ainsi dire, non seulement des conceptions grandioses, mais encore immensément d'esprit. Mais il a TOUJOURS travaillé' (*C*I, 177).

November 1851 saw the publication of 'Les Drames et les romans honnêtes', in which Baudelaire praises Balzac's answer to a criticism levelled by H. Castille, according to whom *La Comédie humaine* gives immoral emphasis and colour to vice. Baudelaire's sharp memory of Balzac's reply, together with the later reference to it in the notes for his lawyer (I, 194), reflects the intensity of the impression it made on him. His commentary is characteristic:

> après avoir énuméré tous les châtiments qui suivent incessamment les violateurs de la loi morale et les enveloppent déjà comme un enfer terrestre, il adresse aux cœurs défaillants et faciles à fasciner cette apostrophe qui ne manque ni de sinistre ni de comique: 'Malheur à vous, messieurs, si le sort des Lousteau et des Lucien vous inspire de l'envie!' (II, 42).

Baudelaire is quoting from memory: Balzac's words were: 'Si, lisant la *Comédie humaine*, un jeune homme trouve peu blâmable les Lousteau, les Lucien de Rubempré, etc., ce jeune homme est jugé.'[60] The parallels with the *Madame Bovary* review – 'c'est au lecteur à tirer les conclusions de la conclusion' (II, 82) – are obvious. The enumeration of the punishments meted out to wrong-doers exists only in Baudelaire's memory: Balzac, on the contrary, insists that the writer's task is merely to contrast vice with virtue, to oppose a Nucingen to a Birotteau, a Camusot to a Popinot. The intensity and physicality of the images Baudelaire attributes to Balzac are also distinctly Baudelairean, recalling the note on *Les Liaisons dangereuses*, which asserts that 'la détestable humanité se fait un enfer préparatoire' (II, 69) and his lines in 'Au lecteur': 'quand nous respirons, la Mort dans nos poumons / Descend, fleuve invisible, avec de sourdes plaintes' (I, 5).

The 'amères récriminations des hypocrites' (II, 42) – the phrase points forward to the review of *Madame Bovary* – constantly recur in contemporary journals. Chaudes-Aigues, for example, castigated Balzac for depicting 'des mœurs ignobles et dégoûtantes, ayant pour seul mobile un intérêt sordide et crapuleux'.[61] Weill asserted that he 'n'a d'élan que pour le ridicule, de poésie que pour le vice, de dévouement que pour la sottise'.[62] And Janin claimed that: 'l'on n'entend, dans ces pages martelées sur l'enclume de fer, que le ricanement strident et perverti d'un talent qui s'agite dans le vide et d'un esprit qui se perd dans l'excommunication active et permanente de ce qui est bon, honnête et pur'.[63] In 'Edgar Allan Poe, sa vie et ses ouvrages', Baudelaire disdainfully lays bare what he sees as the reasons behind the critics' onslaught on both Poe and Balzac:

> il n'est sorte de reproches qu'on ne lui ait plus tard jetés à la figure, à mesure que son œuvre grossissait. Tout le monde connaît cette longue kyrielle banale: immoralité, manque de tendresse, absence de conclusions, extravagance, littérature inutile. Jamais la critique française n'a pardonné à Balzac *le Grand homme de Province à Paris* (II, 273–4).

Certainly critics such as Lerminier justify such an accusation, asserting that Balzac 'faisait de la vie littéraire une peinture désespérée, hideuse: il représentait la réputation comme une prostituée'.[64] That particular simile, of course, is one Baudelaire himself uses, both in his review of *Madame Bovary* (II, 79) and in his prose poem 'Les Tentations'. The terse list of the accusations made by critics antagonistic to Balzac, coupled with the damning suggestion that *Illusions perdues* is an accurate reflection of the journalist's mentality, is not only a resounding *tour de force* but also indicates that Baudelaire was acutely aware of current critical opinion, provocatively turning it to his own advantage.

'Les Drames et les romans honnêtes' concludes with a brief reference to yet another aspect of Balzac's work, and a promise to discuss further, at a later date, the 'tentatives qu'ont faites pour rajeunir le théâtre deux grands esprits français, Balzac et Diderot' (II, 43). Among the proposals for *Le Hibou philosophe* is an article on '*Balzac*, auteur dramatique' (II, 50), a plan which was as unfruitful as his later attempts to have Diderot's *Est-il bon? Est-il méchant?* performed in Paris (*C*I, 298–9). As elsewhere, Baudelaire reveals in these plans his particular enthusiasm for the artist capable of all types of literature and his own ambition to seize celebrity through the theatre. Not only did the theatre command considerable prestige and offer a tempting path to fame and fortune, but Balzac's plays were frequently discussed, denigrated and defended by contemporary critics.[65] The views of three critics seem particularly relevant. Nerval sees two main causes of Balzac's failure in this genre: 'la prévention du public, qui n'admet pas facilement qu'on réussisse en divers genres' and 'l'esprit de routine des théâtres, qui craignent tout ce qui est hardi ou inconnu'.[66] Gautier, for his part, suggests cautiously: 'les ébauches scéniques de Balzac, qui n'ajoutent rien à sa gloire dès à présent fondée sur d'indestructibles bases, offrent un très grand intérêt d'art et de philosophie'.[67] Most interesting of the contemporary comments is that of Lerminier, for whom Balzac's approach to the theatre reveals a response to the kind of *gageure* in which Baudelaire himself saw a spur to creativity:

> le roman et le drame ont entre eux de telles affinités et de telles différences,

qu'il y a autant de raisons pour motiver les succès du même écrivain dans les deux genres que pour les empêcher. Il y avait donc là un problème littéraire digne de la curiosité de ceux qui s'inquiètent encore de l'art et de ses destinées.[68]

Baudelaire's review of *Madame Bovary*, moreover, returns to Balzac's theatre with a reference to 'la jeune fille laide, ce type tant jalousé par Balzac (voir le vrai *Mercadet*)' (II, 78). The parenthetical reference is, of course, a pastiche of one of Balzac's devices. While many critics bemoaned the ugliness of Balzac's characters, Baudelaire, like Gautier, sees in ugliness an aesthetic challenge: according to Gautier, Balzac 'sait donner [. . .] à la laideur une touche si fière, [que l'ouvrage] est à la fois réel et fantastique, condition indispensable de l'art'.[69]

Balzac's prodigious appetite for work and his endless energy, which enabled him both to write his plays and to supervise their production, are among the characteristics to which Baudelaire returns in 'Edgar Allan Poe, sa vie et ses ouvrages'. Several references in this study throw into sharp relief the contrast between Balzac's capacity for working intensely for long periods and the way in which his premature death robbed him of the fruits of his labour, but the most forceful commentary is that in which Baudelaire examines the three ambitions Balzac cherished:

> une grande édition bien ordonnée de ses œuvres, l'acquittement de ses dettes, et un mariage depuis longtemps choyé et caressé au fond de son esprit; grâce à des travaux dont la somme effraye l'imagination des plus ambitieux et des plus laborieux, l'édition se fait, les dettes se payent, le mariage s'accomplit. [. . .] Mais la destinée malicieuse, qui lui avait permis de mettre un pied dans sa terre promise, l'en arracha violemment tout d'abord (II, 250).

The succinct phrasing and the balance achieved by the three brief clauses 'l'édition se fait, les dettes se payent, le mariage s'accomplit' not only underline the irony of Balzac's fate but also show how acutely Baudelaire feared that he, too, was destined to be cheated of fame by an early death.

Baudelaire's enthusiasm for Balzac, as the 1851 study on Poe suggests, was inspired not only by his creative writing, but also by his criticism. His interest in Balzac's uncollected papers had brought to his attention a review of Custine's *Le Monde comme il est* (CII, 528–9). Although the study rejects an idea upheld by Baudelaire, that of suicide as a noble escape from a world in which 'tout tend à étouffer les gens de cœur et d'esprit', it shares Baudelaire's belief that 'la souffrance est l'apprentissage des grandes volontés humaines'.[70] It may well have been this article which led Baudelaire to reflect on Balzac's ideas about criticism. Balzac contends that certain passages of *Le Monde comme il est* 'forceront les penseurs, les âmes solitaires, les gens désabusés ou ceux qui s'abusent encore, à poser le livre et à s'abîmer dans la rêverie que l'auteur provoque'.[71] The role of a work of art in stimulating reverie is emphasized in Baudelaire's account of the Exposition universelle of 1855, where he describes Balzac's reported reaction to a painting of a winter countryside, dotted with huts and peasants: 'Que c'est beau! Mais que font-ils dans cette cabane? à quoi pensent-ils, quels sont leurs chagrins? les récoltes ont-elles été bonnes? *ils ont sans doute des échéances a payer?*' (11, 579). The similarities with Baudelaire's own critical approach – if not his own appreciation – are striking. As he himself points out: 'il m'arrivera souvent d'apprécier un tableau uniquement par la somme d'idées ou de rêveries qu'il apportera dans mon esprit' (11, 579).

Up to 1858, therefore, Baudelaire had seen in Balzac a novelist and a dramatist, a critic of literature and of society who was both 'observateur' and 'inventeur' and who commanded admiration above all for his appetite for life and work.

In 1858 there appeared two full-length appreciations of Balzac: that of Hippolyte Taine was published in *Le Journal des débats* in February and March, and in book form later in the year; Gautier's *Honoré de Balzac*, subsequently included in the volume containing Taine's study, first appeared in *L'Artiste* during March, April and early May. In 1859 Poulet-Malassis reprinted Gautier's analysis in a version Baudelaire knew, since he describes it as being marred by printing errors (*C*1, 604).

Taine considered that Balzac's central preoccupation was with money: 'l'argent partout, l'argent toujours: ce fut le persécuteur et le tyran de sa vie' (*NE*, 53). It is this obsession, Taine contends, that makes Balzac so modern and enables him to represent 'la vie que nous menons', adding: 'il nous parle des intérêts qui nous agitent, il assouvit les convoitises dont nous souffrons' (*NE*, 54). Like so many contemporary critics, Taine considers Balzac's style 'pénible, surchargé' (*NE*, 59), a 'chaos grotesque' (*NE*, 91). Nevertheless, he shows how this style is intimately connected with the ideas it seeks to convey and he concludes, albeit a little grudgingly, that 'évidemment cet homme, quoi qu'on ait dit et quoi qu'il ait fait, savait sa langue: même il la savait aussi bien que personne; seulement il l'employait à sa façon' (*NE*, 95). In analysing 'le monde de Balzac', Taine emphasizes not only his treatment of Parisian society but also his portrayal of 'les gens de métier et de province': 'jadis ils n'étaient que des grotesques [. . .]. Balzac les décrit sérieusement' (*NE*, 98). In Taine's eyes, Balzac is at once 'peintre', 'médecin' and 'philosophe' (*NE*, 58). Moreover, 's'il est fort, c'est qu'il est systématique; [...] le philosophe en lui s'ajoute à l'observateur. Il voit, avec les détails, les lois qui les enchaînent' (*NE*, 70). Although this conclusion is characteristic of Taine's scientific, teleological approach, it is very similar to remarks made ten years earlier by Baudelaire, both in his introduction to 'Révélation magné-tique', where he emphasizes Balzac's longing for unity and his search for the laws governing man's existence, and in the review of Champ-fleury's tales, in which he describes Balzac as 'un naturaliste qui connaît également la loi de génération des idées et des êtres visibles' (11, 22). Although Taine places so much importance on Balzac's 'talent d'obser-vateur' (*NE*, 103), he concludes that 'sa nature et son métier l'ob-ligeaient à imaginer et à croire, car l'observation de romancier n'est qu'une divination' (*NE*, 134). For him, as for Chasles, therefore, the novelist is a *voyant*, possessing an 'imagination enthousiaste et inépuis-able' (*NE*, 63–4).

Gautier's essay, with its characteristic flights of fancy, its sparkling language and its gentle good humour, contrasts sharply in style with that of Taine. Nevertheless, many of the points he raises are similar to those emphasized by the philosopher. Like Taine, he throws into high relief 'la modernité absolue' of Balzac's genius (*HB*, 128), his 'profonde compréhension des choses modernes' (*HB*, 130). And like Taine, he stresses Balzac's awareness that 'la vie moderne qu'il voulait peindre était dominée par un grand fait – l'argent' (*HB*, 63). In terms likely to arouse Baudelaire's attention, he describes money as 'ce héros métal-lique' (*HB*, 62). Gautier rejects the common condemnation of Balzac's style, insisting that it was the novelist's vision of life which forced him 'se forger une langue spéciale, composée de toutes les technologies, de tous les argots', and that he thus created 'le style nécessaire, fatal et mathématique de son idée!' (*HB*, 110). The use of the epithet 'mathé-matique' is interesting in that it recalls a sentence in Baudelaire's essay on Gautier: 'il y a dans le style de Théophile Gautier une justesse qui ravit, qui étonne, et qui fait songer à ces miracles produits dans le jeu par une profonde science mathématique' (11, 118). According to Gautier, the embodiment of the central idea Balzac sought to convey demanded not only Balzac's 'mérite d'observateur' and his 'perspicacité de physiologiste' (*HB*, 37) but also a 'puissante faculté d'intuition' (*HB*, 38): like Chasles and Taine, Gautier concludes that 'Balzac fut un voyant' (*HB*, 38).

The essay makes three further points likely to interest Baudelaire. Not only does Gautier admire Balzac's 'haute faculté critique' (*HB*, 81) but he also studies at some length Balzac's experiments with the theatre, laughing gently at the novelist's idiosyncratic approach, but claiming that 'il s'en est fallu de bien peu que *La Marâtre* [. . .] ne fût un chef-d'œuvre' (*HB*, 118–19). Finally, he refers to Balzac's list of 'figures irréprochables comme vertu' (*HB*, 130). Baudelaire had seen in this device a reflection of Balzac's 'bonhommie naïve et comique' (11, 42) and Gautier likewise describes it as revealing 'une ingénuité qui sied bien à un grand homme' (*HB*, 130). Above all, he castigates as a 'dernière injure de la médiocrité impuissante et jalouse' the accusations of immorality, asserting staunchly that 'l'auteur de la *Comédie humaine* non seulement n'est pas immoral, mais c'est même un moraliste austère' (*HB*, 130).

The two studies have much in common, and both also draw widely on earlier evaluations. Although they give more prominence to Balzac's imagination than do their predecessors, Taine and Gautier were certainly not the first to see it as an essential source of Balzac's genius. In 1853, for example, Clément de Ris reinterpreted Chasles's basically negative judgement:

> l'on admire beaucoup l'observation de Balzac, et l'on tombe, selon moi, dans une grave erreur. Sans être dépourvu de cette précieuse faculté, ce qui domine surtout chez lui, c'est l'imagination. Honoré de Balzac a beaucoup plus deviné qu'il n'a observé, et monsieur Ph. Chasles a pu très justement dire de lui que c'était un voyant.[72]

Baudelaire may well have known Taine's study and almost certainly read the first version of Gautier's essay, not only because he respected his critical judgement, but also because the work appeared in *L'Artiste*, a review which printed several of Baudelaire's own poems and articles in the years 1857 to 1859. To what extent, then, have they influenced the paragraphs on Balzac which appear in Baudelaire's study of Gautier?

The passage in question is sparked off by a more general discussion on the novel. As in so many articles, Baudelaire's focus is on the nature and causes of success. He believes that, of all the types of novel and short story, the *roman de mœurs* is the most favoured, achieving its popularity by taking for its subject its own public. Using an image common to Hoffmann and Stendhal, Baudelaire comments dryly that 'la foule se complaît dans les miroirs où elle se voit' (11, 119–20). But the *roman de mœurs*, he cautions, demands sure taste if it is to avoid mediocrity. Reversing the hackneyed use of the term *utile*, much as Gautier himself does in the preface to *Mademoiselle de Maupin*, Baudelaire insists that the novel will be useless if the novelist fails to invest it with a certain nobility. No doubt he felt the intensity of this claim needed some justification, at least in the eyes of an exponent of the practical utility of art; in his letter to Hugo, therefore, Baudelaire affirms: 'en un temps où le monde s'éloigne de l'art avec une telle horreur, où les hommes se laissent abrutir par l'idée exclusive d'utilité, je crois qu'il n'y a pas grand mal à exagérer un peu dans le sens contraire' (*C*I, 597). According to Baudelaire, Balzac has avoided the pitfall by projecting his whole personality into his works, thus making them 'une chose admirable, toujours curieuse et souvent sublime' (II, 120): a fleeting note of reservation is suggested in the careful contrast between 'souvent sublime' and 'toujours curieuse', but, as usual, Baudelaire sandwiches the suggestion of criticism between words of praise.

Seizing the opportunity to reassert his admiration for Balzac, Baudelaire intensifies his earlier depiction of the novelist as 'un inventeur et un observateur' (II, 22), using words which resemble those of Clément de Ris: 'j'ai mainte fois été étonné que la grande gloire de Balzac fût de passer pour un observateur; il m'avait toujours semblé que son principal mérite était d'être visionnaire, et visionnaire passionné' (II, 120). The apparent change of emphasis from the earlier articles seems to me to spring less from a reading of Taine, or for that matter of Gautier, than from Baudelaire's gradual realization of the value of imagination. As Margaret Gilman has pointed out,[73] his early works rarely use the term: the celebrated apotheosis of imagination as the 'reine des facultés' (II, 585) does not appear until 1855 and the long meditation on the theme came as late as 1859. Nevertheless, the idea of Balzac as *visionnaire* is adumbrated in the Champfleury review and is implicit in the presentation of 'Révélation magnétique' with its assertion that: 'il est certain que ces esprits spécialement littéraires font, quand ils s'y mettent, de singulières chevauchées à travers la philosophie. Ils font des trouées soudaines, et ont de brusques échappées par des chemins qui sont bien à eux' (II, 248). According to Baudelaire, Balzac's gifts as a *visionnaire* enable him to reveal devotion, patience, joy or cunning with far greater intensity than they appear in the everyday world.

Balzac's characters are here reduced by Baudelaire to the expression of their *idée fixe*, a theme which is essential to the thought of both writers and which also establishes a link other than that of genre between Balzac and Gautier. Taine may possibly have influenced Baudelaire to emphasize the way in which Balzac draws his characters from all social classes, 'depuis le sommet de l'aristocratie jusqu'aux bas-fonds de la plèbe' (II, 120). Nevertheless in insisting that all Balzac's characters are 'doués de l'ardeur vitale dont il était animé lui-même', Baudelaire is returning to another familiar theme; it is the complement of a much earlier statement that Balzac is the most heroic of all his characters.

Contemporary criticism frequently referred to Balzac's determination, Gautier claiming in 1851 that 'Balzac a conquis son talent par des travaux énormes, par la plus terrible dépense de volonté qu'ait jamais faite un cerveau humain'.[74] In his 1858 essay, Gautier emphasizes once again Balzac's 'volonté surhumaine' (*HB*, 82), while Clément de Ris insisted: 'je connais peu d'exemples aussi frappants que M. de Balzac de ce que peuvent la force de caractère, l'énergie et la suite de volonté'.[75] Although Baudelaire does not use the word *volonté* in earlier references to Balzac, the idea is certainly implicit both in 'Edgar Allan Poe, sa vie et ses ouvrages' (II, 250) and in the letter he wrote to his mother in 1851, admiring Balzac's boundless capacity for work and his unquenchable determination to achieve genius. In 1860 Baudelaire twice refers to Balzac's will power. In the article devoted to Moreau he is 'une de ces volontés aux prises avec l'adversité' (II, 160) and in 'Le Poème du hachisch' he is described as 'le théoricien de la *volonté*' (I, 439): Gautier's study also mentions 'le précieux manuscrit' entitled *Le Traité de la volonté* which was confiscated in Balzac's school days and whose themes are taken up again in *Louis Lambert*.

Not content merely to establish *volonté* as the dominant feature of Balzac's characters, Baudelaire, typically, pushes further, attempting to discover and demonstrate why they must be presented in the manner Balzac has chosen. He concludes that, like his fictional characters, Balzac is extravagant in his aims; he wants 'tout voir, [. . .] tout faire voir, [. . .] tout deviner, [. . .] tout faire deviner' (II, 120). Both Taine and Gautier remark on Balzac's tendency to exaggerate in creating his characters. Taine, despite reservations, exclaims: 'quelle saillie et quel relief l'interminable énumération donne au personnage! comme on le connaît dans toutes ses actions et toutes ses parties! comme il devient réel!' (*NE*, 69). For him, Balzac's technique is essential to a full understanding of mankind: 'l'homme intérieur laisse son empreinte dans sa vie extérieure, dans sa maison, dans ses affaires, dans ses gestes, dans son langage; il faut expliquer cette multitude d'effets pour l'exprimer tout entier' (*NE*, 69). Gautier remarks that

> les hommes n'ont pas tant de muscles que Michel-Ange leur en met pour donner l'idée de la force. Balzac est plein de ces exagérations utiles, de ces traits noirs qui nourrissent et soutiennent le contour; il imagine en copiant, à la façon des maîtres, et imprime sa touche à chaque chose (*HB*, 114).

Neither explanation is really like that proffered by Baudelaire, who, emphasizing the value of 'la totalité d'effet' (II, 329), sees Balzac's extravagant marking of the 'lignes principales' as evidence of the desire 'sauver la perspective de l'ensemble' (II, 120). This important assessment casts particular light on Baudelaire's idea of the method Balzac used and the aims he pursued.

Baudelaire insists yet again on the artist's freedom to explore his own temperament, emphasizing that Balzac's style and method result from his 'étonnante disposition naturelle'. He truculently brushes aside the many critics for whom this tendency to exaggerate represents a weakness: 'pour mieux parler c'est justement là ses qualités'. The remark shows considerable insight into Balzac's genius, developing the earlier realization that if certain defects were removed, the powerful whole would be vitiated.

In addition, Baudelaire sees Balzac as having developed a method which allows him 'revêtir, à coup sûr, de lumière et de pourpre la pure trivialité' (11, 120). Here, I believe, lies Baudelaire's greatest originality as a critic of Balzac. Whereas other critics lamented or defended Balzac's choice of subject and style, Baudelaire seeks out the reasons dictating this choice, and as in his review of *Madame Bovary* he signals the triumph of elevating the trite to the heroic.

Although contemporary critics may well have directed Baudelaire's attention to certain aspects of Balzac's genius, and although Taine and Gautier in particular do seem to have influenced some of the formulations of the 1859 study, Baudelaire's image of Balzac was firmly etched by 1851 and subsequent remarks merely develop and add force to the earlier statements. In all these passages, Baudelaire is seeking out in Balzac, both as man and as novelist, those qualities and techniques which have enabled him not only to seize popularity but also to develop his innate talent, through will power and work, to the point of genius.

5
❧ *The Colossus: Victor Hugo*

If Baudelaire admired Poe's dogged worrying away at *calculs et problèmes* (11, 268), his own criticism suggests a similarly determined response to the puzzling questions posed by literary history. Hugo, above all, set him a complex series of thorny problems which he repeatedly struggled to untangle. How can one solve the dilemma created by a writer in whose works one has been immersed from an early stage but whose later development contains elements of which one cannot approve? How resolve the tricky antithesis of conscious indebtedness and a desire for individuality, a dislike of political pontificating in art and an admiration for a poet who rebelled both politically and artistically? Baudelaire's published articles moreover reveal him facing the challenge of offering his readers an accurate assessment of an outstanding writer while still indicating, albeit *sotto voce*, his points of disagreement with the man.

His reaction to Hugo evolved and fluctuated over the years, reflecting the influence of Hugo's publications, of political events and of Baudelaire's private life. Roughly speaking, his evaluation of Hugo follows a curve reaching its zenith around 1859, with the publication of the scintillating *Légende des siècles*, but plunging down again with the appearance of *Les Misérables*. This curve, suggested by L. J. Austin,[1] has been examined at greater length by L. Cellier,[2] whose findings this chapter will attempt to assess in the light of a broader study of Baudelaire's literary criticism.

Baudelaire's correspondence reveals that from adolescence he knew and admired Hugo's work: in 1837, he asked for *Les Derniers Jours d'un condamné* (C1, 48), and the following year, in a mood of premature world-weariness, he confided: 'il n'y a que les drames, les poésies de Victor Hugo et un livre de S[ain]te-Beuve (*Volupté*) qui m'aient amusé' (C1, 61). In 1840, he wrote Hugo an admiring letter in praise of *Marion Delorme*. Three remarks call for special attention. Firstly, the young Baudelaire claims, with an amusing if not very convincing attempt at modesty: 'il me semble, (peut-être est-ce bien de l'orgueil) que je comprends tous vos ouvrages' (C1, 81). Unless it is a totally insincere piece of flattery, this would indicate that Baudelaire, like so many of his generation, is steeped in Hugo's early writing. Secondly, in a comment that contrasts sharply with the convictions of the more mature Baudelaire, he asserts: 'je vous crois bon et généreux, parce que vous avez entrepris plusieurs réhabilitations' (*CI*, 81–2). Although he singles this sentence out from the other 'déclarations passionnées',[3] Cellier does not indicate what I would suggest is its principal motivation: Baudelaire, whose childhood letters reveal the precocious despair he felt at his own weaknesses, is seeking someone who can 'rehabilitate' him. Later he became aware that such rehabilitation succeeds only if it stems from the individual himself. Finally, Baudelaire claims of Hugo that 'loin de céder à l'opinion, [il] l'[a] souvent réformée, fièrement et dignement' (*CI*, 82): much of what Baudelaire writes in his own literary criticism shows how much he himself sought to reform and refine public opinion. Moreover, here as in later comments, he insists on Hugo not as rebel or revolutionary, but as a *reformer*.

Although Baudelaire's letters make no further reference to Hugo until 1854, his critical articles reflect a period of youthful rebellion both against Hugo's prestige and against his wide-reaching influence. The *Salon de 1845*, for instance, contains the following deliberately provocative remark: 'voilà les dernières ruines de l'ancien romantisme – voilà ce que c'est que de venir dans un temps où il est reçu de croire que l'inspiration suffit et remplace le reste; – voilà l'abîme où mène la course désordonnée de Mazeppa. – C'est M. Victor Hugo qui a perdu M. Boulanger' (II, 366). Two aspects demand close consideration here. On the one hand, Baudelaire's rejection of inspiration as a sufficient basis for a work of art is to remain constant in his criticism, from the 'Conseils aux jeunes littérateurs' to the review of *Les Martyrs ridicules*. On the other hand, as Cellier points out,[4] the idea that genius can rely on inspiration alone runs counter to Hugo's own convictions. It seems to me that the nub of Baudelaire's attack is twofold: firstly, Boulanger is criticized for using the plastic arts for a purpose better served by literature – he is a 'peintre d'histoire' (II, 366) – and secondly it is not Hugo who is being directly censured in this passage, but those who blindly follow his lead, assuming 'une âme d'emprunt' (II, 3). Can one, therefore, agree with Cellier that the comparison between Hugo and Delacroix in the *Salon de 1846* represents an irritating about-face: 'en 1845 il reprochait à Hugo d'avoir de l'inspiration sans métier, alors qu'en 1846 il lui reproche d'avoir du métier sans inspiration'?[5] In the passage in question, while insisting that he has no desire to diminish the older poet's 'noblesse' and 'majesté', Baudelaire boldly asserts that Hugo, 'naturellement académicien avant que de naître', is less a creator and inventor than an accomplished craftsman. This, of course, is a fairly common contemporary way of attacking a writer the critic disliked, but whose skill and popularity were beyond question. Baudelaire is obviously eager to attract notice by this pugnacious rejection of a widely accepted belief: nevertheless, the criticism is less at odds with his earlier statement than Cellier would have us believe. Firstly, he is not accusing Hugo of lacking inspiration, but of creating his works according to a rigid aesthetic system founded on unrelieved symmetry. Baudelaire himself, of course, called for a blend of symmetry and surprise, although, admittedly, he was not to formulate this conviction until much later. Secondly, he claims Hugo also lacks *creativity*: the essay on laughter, which probably dates from the same year as this *Salon*, sheds some light on this concept by defining it as 'une idéalité artistique' (II, 535). The term *idéalité* is rare, but may well have been suggested by the writings of either Gautier or Poe. Finally, in describing Hugo as an 'académicien avant que de naître' and in admiring the way in which he 'se sert de ses outils avec une dextérité véritablement admirable et curieuse' (II, 431), Baudelaire is voicing an opinion he is to repeat in the preface to Dupont's songs. There he claims that 'le poète me cause moins de colère quand il dit: Moi, je pense . . . moi, je sens . . ., que le musicien ou le barbouilleur infatigable qui a fait un pacte satanique avec son instrument' (II, 27). In both cases a naive exploration of the artist's own temperament is praised to the detriment of technical virtuosity.

Although it is clear that Baudelaire is determined to seize on any opportunity to lay bare what he considers to be false in the aesthetics of Hugo and above all of his followers, it is evident, too, that he is well aware of the great benefits he in particular and French literature in general have drawn from Hugo's example. Thus, in 1851, he emphasizes the value of 'les querelles vives et spirituelles de M. Cousin avec M. Victor Hugo' (II, 30), in the creation of the Academy's dictionary, an allusion Cellier fails to examine. In this antithesis, Hugo's renovatory opinions about rhetoric and grammar fulfil Baudelaire's definition of Romanticism as 'l'expression la plus récente et le plus moderne de la beauté' (II, 419).

A further reference occurs in a letter of 1854, in which Baudelaire comments on a pamphlet Champfleury had sent him. In this pamphlet Champfleury had published a letter Hugo had written him in 1846. Cellier's comment on this letter seems somewhat off-beam.[6] I can find little justification for the belief that Baudelaire was irritated by the substance of Hugo's letter. Surely the point is that it is bad policy for a writer in his early thirties 'exhumer' compliments seven years old, and partly that Hugo's propensity for praising all and sundry severely weakens the value of any such quotation. Baudelaire's concern here is not with literary criticism but with tactics, and represents a constant preoccupation: how can a writer best draw attention to his works?

The following year, Hugo's disparagement of Delacroix provoked the caustic comment that 'M. Victor Hugo est un grand poète sculptural qui a l'œil fermé à la spiritualité' (II, 593): although the remark is very similar to the accusation in the *Salon de 1846* that Hugo lacked creativity, the intensity with which the anthology notice explores Hugo's interest in 'la spiritualité' suggests either that subsequent volumes, such as *Les Contemplations*, altered this evaluation, or that it is more a defence of Delacroix than an attack on Hugo.

Certainly the publication of *Les Contemplations* in 1856 and the appearance of the first series of *La Légende des siècles* in 1859 mark a high point in Baudelaire's admiration for Hugo. In November 1855, shortly before the publication of *Les Contemplations*, Baudelaire wrote to Paul de Saint-Victor begging him to supply 'les deux petites poésies de Victor Hugo' (CI, 324). It seems possible that these poems were from *Les Contemplations*, as J. Crépet suggests (CI, 886); moreover, it may well be that he was eager to review the collection, using these poems as a basis. Certainly the Baudelaire of the late 1850s saw Hugo as a poet who had done a vast amount for French literature, both in his creative writing and in his prefaces, a poet whose success was indeed worthy of emulation: 'je sais que ce volume [*Les Fleurs du mal*], avec ses qualités et ses défauts, fera son chemin dans la mémoire du public lettré, à côté des meilleures poésies de V. Hugo, de Th. Gautier et même de Byron' (CI, 411). It is above all in his essay on Gautier that Baudelaire gives Hugo full credit for the way in which he has 'rajeuni, plus encore [. . .] ressuscité la poésie française, morte depuis Corneille' (II, 110). Once again, he is keenly aware of the debt owed to Hugo and of the need to dissociate political questions from those connected with aesthetics.

Baudelaire's diaries and later letters reflect increasing irritation, mocking the egoism of Hugo's mature works – 'Hugo-Sacerdoce a toujours le front penché; – trop penché pour rien voir, excepté son nombril' (I, 665) – and insisting that 'on peut en même temps posséder un *génie* spécial et être un *sot*. Victor Hugo nous l'a bien prouvé' (CII, 459–60). Yet here, too, hasty comments can lead the unwary astray. The reference to 'Hugo-Sacerdoce' suggests that the anger derives, at least in part, from Hugo's use of literature to teach and moralize. And the second comment is doubtless aimed above all at shocking its recipient, the rather conventional Ancelle, who would have found deeply disturbing the paradoxical but typically Baudelairean bracketing of genius and stupidity. Besides, a letter written in March 1862 suggests that the cause of Baudelaire's later anger is personal as well as literary: 'Hugo va publier ses *Misérables*, roman en dix vol[umes]. Raison de plus pour que mes pauvres volumes, *Eureka*, *Poèmes en prose* et *Réflexions sur mes contemporains* ne soient pas vus' (*C*ii, 238). The hero-worship widely accorded to Hugo,[7] while Baudelaire still struggled for recognition, his increasing didacticism, his unshakeable belief in indefinite progress, and his extraordinary fecundity, particularly contrasted with Baudelaire's relative sparsity in concentrated creation and his growing pessimism about the decadence of society and mankind, have intensified his urgent questioning of the causes of popularity and the link between creativity and destiny.

It is against this background, therefore, that we should consider the article Baudelaire devoted to Hugo in Crépet's anthology. Later critics have approached the review with unease, praising both the percipience of the insights and the beauty of their expression, but also censuring what they consider a lack of sincerity.[8] Although this accusation should not lightly be dismissed, one cannot help feeling alarmed at judgements which do not have sufficient regard for chronology and which give to *boutades*, thrown off in a desire to shock or amuse, the same weight as conclusions reached in the meticulously wrought prose of a notice intended for publication. Of course comments made to friends cannot merely be ignored: Baudelaire himself, in a letter to Fraisse, affirms that the best assessment of Hugo was given by Gautier during an informal dinner (*C*i, 675). Nevertheless, several extra-literary considerations have almost certainly affected Baudelaire's evaluation of Hugo. Firstly, there is the difficulty, familiar to Baudelaireans, of writing on a poet whose work had for so long attracted such frequent and varied commentaries. Secondly, Hugo had written a warmly encouraging preface to the essay on Gautier: common politeness would hardly have allowed Baudelaire openly to denigrate Hugo so soon after such a favour. Thirdly, Hugo epitomized Romanticism, a movement to which Baudelaire himself owed much and whose memory he honoured. Nevertheless, he clearly found it difficult to assess a poet whose temperament differed so much from his own: yet, as well as isolating those qualities which he did share with Hugo or which he considered essential to the artist, Baudelaire also emphasized characteristics he himself lacked. Finally, two different sources of censorship had to be placated. Since Hugo was still in exile, officialdom would prune out political comments not in harmony with government policy. On the other hand, and more immediately powerful, Crépet himself, with his firm belief in Republicanism and progress, would hardly be willing to accept much overtly expressed adverse criticism of Hugo's political thought. Baudelaire justifies his solution to this tricky problem in a letter to Crépet: 'j'esquiverai la question politique: d'ailleurs je ne crois pas possible de parler des satires politiques, *même pour les blâmer*; or, si j'en parlais, bien que je considère l'engueulement politique comme un signe de sottise, je serais plutôt avec Hugo qu'avec le Bonaparte du coup d'Etat. – Donc, impossible' (*C*II, 41). It is significant that it is not the political view as such that Baudelaire opposes, but its means of expression.

In a letter written to Fraisse in 1860, when his own article must have been very much on his mind, Baudelaire comments: 'vous n'avez pas assez distingué *la quantité de beauté éternelle* qui est dans Hugo des *superstitions* comiques introduites en lui par les événements, c'est-à-dire la sottise ou *sagesse* moderne' (*C*I, 675). Has Baudelaire himself been able to surmount the problems facing him sufficiently to make this distinction? To what extent has he distilled from Hugo's poetry 'la quantité de beauté éternelle'? And how far is his distinction valid?

The sort of beauty Baudelaire describes is influenced, I would suggest, by Hugo's most recent publications, *Les Contemplations* (1856) and the first series of *La Légende des siècles*, and it offers numerous parallels with the kind of beauty studied in his own recent articles on Poe and Gautier.

Hugo's celebrity has affected the very structure of Baudelaire's article, rendering unnecessary the traditional historical and biographical survey. After a brief evocation of Hugo's personality, stressing his importance for the poetry of the time, Baudelaire sets out to describe the atmosphere of his works, their universality, and the breadth and depth of the metaphysical questions they debate. Finally he turns to *La Légende des siècles*, indicating the limits of the epic and showing how Hugo has succeeded within that framework, before suggesting how his genius may develop. The review is marked by a continual, highly suggestive, oscillation between response to a certain aspect of Hugo's character and poetry, and meditations both on the attributes of an ideal artist and on general aesthetic questions.

Although less firmly articulated than most of the other studies, the notice is given a sense of unity through the repetition of key words: among terms which appear at least four times each are *conjecture* (five times: II, 138, 139), *force* and *fort* (five times: II, 136), *mystère* and its derivatives (II, 130, 131, 132, 134, 135, 137), *rêveur* or *rêverie* (II, 129, 130, 137, 138, 139, 140) and *universel* and its derivatives (II, 130, 132, 133, 134, 135). On several occasions, too, Baudelaire emphasizes the way in which Hugo's poetry brilliantly evokes colour, sound, movement and shape. Finally, echoing Hugo's own style, the study contains several carefully balanced sentences, frequently using the expression 'non seulement . . . mais aussi', and introducing numerous antitheses, such as that which describes Hugo's poetic nature as 'immense et minutieux' and 'calme et agité' (II, 134).

The article opens by posing a particularly practical problem, that of the author's best approach to creative work. How is Hugo able to harmonize 'les nécessités de son travail assidu avec ce goût sublime, mais dangereux, des promenades et des rêveries?' (II, 129). Both sides of the apparent contradiction are important for Baudelaire himself. On the one hand, his earliest letters, as well as his diaries, show him constantly struggling to work regularly and productively. On the other hand, although many of Hugo's poems do indeed reveal his 'goût [. . .] des promenades et des rêveries', the fact that Baudelaire has chosen to give prominence to this particular characteristic is especially significant since prose poems such as 'Les Foules', the first article on Poe (II, 271) and the study on Guys (II, 687), present as an essential characteristic of the artist the ability to profit both from the 'bain de multitude' (I, 291) and from complete isolation. In a combination of envy at Hugo's ability to harmonize these opposing needs and a tautening of his own resolve to do likewise, Baudelaire concludes that Hugo's success depends on 'une existence bien réglée' and 'une forte constitution spirituelle'. In referring to 'une forte constitution spirituelle', Baudelaire hints that much depends on inherited characteristics, while the 'existence bien réglée' points to will power developed by early training, just as he insists that it was the young Balzac's determination and ambition which established the habit of assiduous application to work.

In Hugo, Baudelaire discerns 'un homme solitaire mais enthousiaste de la vie' (II, 130). An interaction of similar antitheses is described in 'Mon cœur mis à nu', which mentions a 'sentiment de *solitude*, dès mon enfance. Malgré la famille, – et au milieu des camarades, surtout, – sentiment de destinée éternellement solitaire. Cependant, goût très vif de la vie et du plaisir' (I, 680). Since many of the prose poems depict the same dichotomy, Baudelaire is obviously concentrating on those aspects with which he most sympathizes and which most inspire him.

Following tradition, he offers a brief reference to his own memories of Hugo, portraying him as 'toujours maître de lui-même, et appuyé sur une sagesse abrégée, faite de quelques axiomes irréfutables' (II, 130). Although, in his notes to the Pléiade edition, Pichois remarks that 'sans être offensante, la phrase n'est pas élogieuse' (II, 1141), the conviction that a limited, essentially practical form of wisdom can indeed be condensed into a few pithy maxims, is one Baudelaire shared with many contemporaries, notably Delacroix, and it not only underlies his interest in Emerson, but also fits the ideas and formulations of the *Journaux intimes*. Indeed, 'Hygiène' contains the following highly significant note: 'une sagesse abrégée. Toilette, prière, travail' (I, 671). One should not undervalue Baudelaire's belief in the importance of *maxims*, in their expression as practice in distilling thought and in their content as a quintessence of wisdom.

A further characteristic Hugo shares with all great artists is his love for 'le mystérieux et brillant décor de la vie ancienne' (II, 130). Baudelaire's own love of plastic beauty is expressed in many of his earlier critical studies, in prose poems such as 'La Chambre double' and 'Les Projets', and above all in the claim that Gautier introduced into French poetry 'un élément nouveau [. . .] la consolation par les arts, par tous les objets pittoresques qui réjouissent les yeux et amusent l'esprit' (II, 126): here he speaks of 'ce qui fait la joie des yeux et l'amusement de l'imagination'. Throughout this brief evocation of Hugo's personality, therefore, Baudelaire once again throws into sharp relief those elements which find an echo in his own nature or which conform to his vision of the ideal poet.

In stating that Hugo's more recent works continue in the same manner as those of his youth, Baudelaire is certainly side-stepping, as he expressed it in his letter to Crépet, choosing to ignore the increasing didacticism and open polemics of some of Hugo's work, notably *Les Châtiments*. The image which Baudelaire wants to convey, not only, one feels, to his reader, but also to Hugo himself, is that of dreamer and questioner, 'la statue de la Méditation qui marche', as he so solemnly but so aptly expresses it.

The closing paragraph of the article's first section brilliantly mimics Hugo's style: thus, in the expression 'il fait errer ses pieds et ses yeux', the verb, as in many of Hugo's constructions, has a concrete meaning for the first object, and a metaphorical one for the second, while the phrase 'solitudes peuplées par sa pensée' recalls many assertions in Hugo's poetry, and the antithetical 'autrefois' and 'aujourd'hui' are an obvious allusion to the two parts of *Les Contemplations*. Pastiche, in this instance, seems a means of focusing attention – both Baudelaire's and his reader's – on tiny details of style.

In emphasizing Hugo's links with the ocean, Baudelaire echoes a commonplace of contemporary criticism, inspired, of course, not only by Hugo's many poems of the sea, but also by his exile in the Channel Islands. Writing in *Le Siècle*,[9] E. Texier insists that despite his exile Hugo 'vit dans notre pensée comme dans un abri; ses livres sont nos amis, et nous causons chaque jour avec lui par-dessus l'Océan'.[10] And G. Lafenestre's review of *La Légende des siècles* asserts: 'quand la voix de la foule n'a plus grondé sous ses pieds, il a prêté l'oreille aux voix de l'Océan'.[11]

The element of pastiche in Baudelaire's passage does not prevent it from forming a powerful climax to his introductory paragraphs, one which prepares the subsequent discussion on poetry as a legitimate domain for metaphysical questioning by conveying an image of the poet as a personification of productive reverie.

In surveying Hugo's poetic achievements, Baudelaire throws yet again into sharp relief Hugo's success in injecting fresh vitality into French poetry:

> quand on se figure ce qu'était la poésie française avant qu'il apparût, et quel rajeunissement elle a subi depuis qu'il est venu; quand on imagine ce peu qu'elle eût été s'il n'était pas venu [. . .] il est impossible de ne pas le considérer comme un de ces esprits rares et providentiels qui opèrent, dans l'ordre littéraire, le salut de tous (II, 131: cf. II, 110).

Above all, he gives Hugo full justice for teaching the reading public to appreciate 'la bonne poésie, [. . .] la poésie profondément rythmée et vivement colorée'. The emphasis on the evocative rhythms and on the rich imagery is similar to that in the Gautier essay, with its description of 'la pourpre régulière et symétrique d'une rime plus qu'exacte' and a 'couleur plus fine ou plus brillante que les couleurs de la Chine et de l'Inde' (II, 126). Even the 1851 preface to Dupont's songs, which seems to dismiss Romanticism, speaks of 'un livre éclatant comme un mouchoir ou un châle de l'Inde' (II, 27). However apt Baudelaire's descriptions of the visual aspects of a poem, the terms used to evaluate the rhythm are denser and more precise, which suggests that he is more susceptible to sound than to the image evoked.

The passage is central to Baudelaire's evaluation not only of Hugo, but also of French literature in general, an evaluation conveyed with equal force and clarity in the essay on Gautier. As in much of his criticism, he seems to be responding to a particular challenge, which in this case lies in giving full justice to the overall importance and value of a poet who can, in individual works, be intensely irritating to one of Baudelaire's temperament and beliefs.

In underlining Hugo's vital role in French literature, Baudelaire reasserts with particular force his preoccupation with justice, evident in the Dupont preface (II, 33), in the article on Gautier (II, 106), throughout the studies on Poe and in the review of *Madame Bovary*, where it is described as 'ce mot splendide et terrible' (II, 76). Referring to Hugo's importance as guide, Baudelaire insists that 'il ne coûtera à personne d'avouer tout cela, excepté à ceux pour qui la justice n'est pas une volupté' (ii, 131). The intensity of the word 'volupté', given extra prominence by its position at the end of the paragraph, suggests that there is more here than meets the eye. In fact, Baudelaire is almost certainly attacking Barbey d'Aurevilly, who frequently uses the term *la justice* in his criticism, but who, in a highly condemnatory review of *La Légende des siècles*, does not in fact acknowledge the part Hugo has played. Indeed, Barbey roundly castigates all those who have reviewed the work, finding 'nulle Critique vraie, car la Critique vraie, c'est la Justice, et la Justice se compose également de sévérité dans la sympathie et de sympathie dans la sévérité'.[12]

Turning from this general discussion of Hugo's character and importance to an assessment of his poetry, Baudelaire strives to recapture the atmosphere of mystery and grandeur created by 'l'homme le mieux doué, le plus visiblement élu pour exprimer par la poésie ce que j'appellerai le *mystère de la vie*'. In choosing the word 'élu', Baudelaire reflects yet again his constant fascination with the question of whether poets are predestined or created by circumstances and effort. In emphasizing Hugo's power to express this mystery, Baudelaire introduces one of the key phrases of the article, the word *mystère* constantly recurring as he clarifies his vision of the poet. For Baudelaire, it is through the multiplicity of Hugo's gifts that he expresses his sense of mystery and, just as Gautier's poetry, which defines 'l'attitude mystérieuse que les objets de la création tiennent devant le regard de l'homme' (ii, 117), demands a synthetic, rather than an analytical response, so Hugo's poetry enables the three impressions – harmony, shape and colour – 'pén[étrer] simultanément le cerveau du lecteur' (ii, 132). This gift, moreover, combines with his ability 'se mettre en contact avec les forces de la vie universelle' to permit him to suggest 'la *morale des choses*' (ii, 132), and to show how the external world can convey what Baudelaire describes as 'sensations morales'. The expression reflects his continuing interest in the *correspondances* between man and the universe and the need for man to interpret, directly or through art, the messages implicit in nature.

To describe 'le vers de Victor Hugo' (ii, 132), Baudelaire adopts a rhetorical system which is, to say the least, confusing, with its series of superlatives, its clusters of phrases linked by 'non seulement . . . mais aussi' and its rather misleading 'en d'autres termes', which seems to introduce less a summing up, in fresh terms, of what has preceded, than a new direction, as tempting in its promise as it is frustrating in its brevity. The contrast set up between the aspect of the external world, and the latent meaning of that world is further complicated by his defiantly idiosyncratic use of that 'confuse parole', *morales* – 'je dis exprès sensations morales' – and by the opposition he proposes between *figure* and *physionomie*, the former referring to a permanent object and *physionomie* to the transient moods that object expresses. The opposition in the concluding sentence, however, is not so much between the physical and the metaphysical, the permanent and the ephemeral, as between the human and the supernatural: Hugo's poetry reveals 'tout ce qu'il y a d'humain dans n'importe quoi, et aussi tout ce qu'il y a de divin, de sacré et de diabolique'. Here, too, the shading between *divin* and *sacré* is very delicate, *divin* being related specifically to God while *sacré* refers rather to that which has been made holy by man's veneration.

The passage is not easy to follow but Baudelaire's refusal to pander to his reader is implicit in the defiant and familiar cry: 'ceux qui ne sont pas poètes ne comprennent pas ces choses' (cf. *C*ii, 325). To prove his point, he mentions three thinkers, Fourier, Swedenborg and Lavater, who have attempted to reveal, through reasoned argument rather than through imagination and intuition, 'les mystères de l'analogie' or 'le sens spirituel du contour, de la forme, de la dimension' (ii, 133).

Although the discussion is clearly an extension of the passages in 'Notes nouvelles', reproduced in the essay on Gautier, it is also closely linked to Hugo's own preoccupations, as such poems as 'Ce que dit la bouche d'ombre' and 'La Chouette', among many others, clearly show:

> La nature, qui mêle une âme aux rameaux verts,
> Qui remplit tout, et vit, à des degrés divers
> Dans la bête sauvage et la bête de somme,
> Toujours en dialogue avec l'esprit de l'homme,
> Lui donne à déchiffrer les animaux, qui sont
> Ses signes, alphabet formidable et profond.[13]

According to Baudelaire, it is the poet's intuitive rather than reasoned awareness of '*l'universelle analogie*' that enables him to select metaphors, comparisons and epithets which are 'd'une adaptation mathématiquement exacte dans la circonstance actuelle' (cf. ii, 118). This miraculous 'justesse' stands in sharp opposition to the painstaking exactness of Fourier, 'trop épris d'exactitude matérielle pour ne pas commettre d'erreurs et pour atteindre d'emblée la certitude morale de l'intuition' (ii, 132). Furthermore, Fourier's exactness creates too rigid a framework, making insufficient allowance for changes in circumstance: Baudelaire, on the contrary, is careful to stress that the poet's metaphors are admirably suited to 'la circonstance actuelle'. Nevertheless, even at so late a date, Baudelaire admits the value of at least some of Fourier's 'minutieuses découvertes'.

While raising such general questions, Baudelaire ties the discussion firmly to Hugo, highlighting his 'magnifique répertoire d'analogies humaines et divines', and illustrating his vast linguistic knowledge through a strangely physical analogy: he is like the prophet commanded by God to eat a book in order to reproduce the language he would be called on to speak. Admiration for Hugo's extensive vocabulary was shared by many contemporary critics: Planche, for example, despite numerous pungently worded reservations, admitted that Hugo 'trouve pour une idée unique des métamorphoses nombreuses, qui attestent chez lui une connaissance complète du vocabulaire'.[14]

Rejecting a biographical approach, Baudelaire claims that he neither needs, nor is able, to explain 'quelles circonstances historiques, fatalités philosophiques, conjonctions sidérales' have given Hugo to France. This formula, with its concise bracketing of the physical, the intellectual and the metaphysical, not only reflects Baudelaire's preoccupations, but also emphasizes yet again how complex is Hugo's vision of man's existence. Baudelaire suggests simply that 'peut-être est-ce simplement parce que l'Allemagne avait eu Goethe, et l'Angleterre Shakespeare et Byron, que Victor Hugo était légitimement dû à la France' (II, 133). On several occasions, both in his letters and in his articles intended for publication, he draws similar comparisons, remarking in his essay on Gautier, for instance: 'nos voisins disent: Shakespeare et Goethe! nous pouvons leur répondre: Victor Hugo et Théophile Gautier!' (II, 125: cf. CI, 411). Here, he may well be responding to Hugo's assertion in the preface to *Les Orientales*: 'les autres peuples disent: Homère, Dante, Shakespeare. Nous disons: Boileau. Mais passons.'[15] Such comparisons moreover were a commonplace in contemporary criticism.

The analysis of the way in which Hugo's poetry is shaped by his sense of mystery and awe is at once a sensitive pastiche drawing our attention to certain stylistic devices, and a brilliant piece of insight: according to Baudelaire, it is because Hugo's poetry sets out to convey metaphysical fear that it abounds in 'ces turbulences, ces accumulations, ces écroulements de vers, ces masses d'images orageuses, emportées avec la vitesse d'un chaos qui fuit' (II, 134). The emphasis on 'ce sentiment d'effroi' in the face of mystery, together with the reference to 'la terreur catholique' in the essay on Gautier (II, 126), and the general increase in religious imagery, suggest very strongly that Baudelaire himself may be going through a period of metaphysical anxiety.

However general and wide-ranging the discussion may appear, Baudelaire introduces small details which suggest specific poems, a fact which firstly indicates that it is indeed Hugo's work which has inspired the meditation, and, secondly, reveals the extent to which Hugo's poetry has etched itself on his memory. His admiration for much of Hugo's work is evident from the nonchalance and precision of these references.

Choosing a specific example to support his claim, Baudelaire asserts that if Hugo depicts the sea 'aucune *marine* n'égalera les siennes' (II, 135): although the example is fully justified by poems such as 'La Rose de l'Infante' and 'Pleine Mer', it leads to one of the many evocative passages in which Baudelaire is less concerned with criticism than with expressing personal meditations. Here he investigates the intellectual and physical reasons behind the fascination exerted on all men by the sea and the beauty of a ship's movement, a fascination revealed, for example, in poems such as 'La Mer' and prose poems like 'Le *Confiteor* de l'artiste' and 'Le Port'. Indeed, Baudelaire's evocation of Hugo's *marines* seems a preliminary exploration of one of the themes of 'Le Port'. In the article he describes a ship as 'un appareil géométrique et mécanique de bois, de fer, de cordes et de toile; animal monstrueux créé par l'homme, auquel le vent et le flot ajoutent la beauté d'une démarche', while 'Le Port' will speak more succinctly of 'les formes élancées des navires, au gréement compliqué, auxquels la houle imprime des oscillations harmonieuses' (I, 344). Above all, Baudelaire's interest seems to have been seized by the paradoxical way in which ships, for all their abstract geometry and their inanimate mechanism, can nevertheless present 'cette physionomie de lutteurs passionnés' (II, 135). As so often, the exercise of criticism is used to refine ideas and images which are to reappear in the creative writing.

Baudelaire seeks to define not only Hugo's principal sources of inspiration, but also 'l'atmosphère morale qui plane et circule dans ses poèmes' (II, 136). Inspired, like Hugo himself, by antithesis and paradox, he characterizes this atmosphere as reflecting an equal love for the strong and the weak. Hugo's interest in the powerful among men and in nature is of course evident in many poems of *La Légende des siècles*, including, significantly, those Baudelaire praises in a letter written less than a month after the publication of the first series: 'Ratbert', 'Zim-Zizimi', 'Le Mariage de Roland' and 'La Rose de l'Infante' (*C*I, 609). In tracing the source of Hugo's charity to his delight in strength, both physical and spiritual, Baudelaire is following two of his well-established patterns: that of seeking out initial causes and that of inverting common criticisms of the writer under discussion. Emile

Chasles, for example, suggested that 'cette force [. . .] que M. Hugo chante, qu'il affecte de communiquer à ses vers, paraît plus avantageuse au mal qu'elle idéalise qu'au bien qu'elle compromet'.[16] And Montégut, writing for *La Revue des deux mondes*, noted that what he called 'les indifférents' constantly complained: 'la force, toujours la force! L'Esprit se fatigue, au bout de quelques instants, à soulever ces alexandrins robustes, chargés d'épithètes pesantes.'[17] Baudelaire, however, argues that from this very strength derives the more generally admired 'esprit de justice et de charité'. Although they did not connect Hugo's strength with his charity, Laurent-Pichat admired 'la pitié sérieuse du poète' and Claveau threw into sharp relief 'un grand courant de bonté, de philanthropie, un ardent élan de charité'.[18] To some extent, therefore, Baudelaire may be reacting against contemporary opinion as well as expressing deep-seated convictions, particularly in underlining Hugo's 'accents d'amour pour les femmes tombées' (II, 136): as J. Crépet points out (*AR*, 541), the *Salon de 1846* mocks *Marion Delorme* for preaching 'les vertus des assassins et des filles publiques' (II, 477), while his review of *Les Misérables* is more double-edged in its presentation of Hugo's concept of charity and justice (II, 219).

Nevertheless, there is a side of Baudelaire's character that could indeed sympathize with 'les femmes tombées'. As poems like 'Les Petites Vieilles' and prose poems such as 'Mademoiselle Bistouri' reveal, his imagination and insight led to a profound, unsentimental understanding based on both sympathy and horror, which is far removed from Hugo's false glorification and sentimental rehabilitation.

Although, in general, he admires the 'atmosphère morale' of Hugo's poetry, Baudelaire sounds a note of warning, delicate in tone but unmistakable in meaning, when, as in 'Notes nouvelles', he reiterates his opposition to '*l'hérésie de l'enseignement*' (II, 333). What he demands of art is that it contain:

> une morale inspirée qui se glisse, invisible, dans la matière poétique, comme les fluides impondérables dans toute la machine du monde. La morale n'entre pas dans cet art à titre de but; elle s'y mêle et s'y confond comme dans la vie elle-même. Le poète est moraliste sans le vouloir, par abondance et plénitude de nature (II, 137).

Later, in a reference to the questions Hugo poses in his poetry, Baudelaire adds: 'entre les mains d'un autre poëte que Victor Hugo, de pareils thèmes et de pareils sujets auraient pu trop facilement adopter la forme didactique' (II, 139). Hugo's tendency to preach, to use literature as a hammer for altering public opinion rather than as a catalyst for modifying public sensitivity, is obvious even in works published before Baudelaire's article. It seems clear, therefore, that Baudelaire has chosen to suggest his views by ironic intimation rather than explicit attack. In doing so, he is not being insincere, but rather putting into practice his own principles, insinuating instead of pontificating.

When he discusses the metaphysical side of Hugo's poetry, Baudelaire makes frequent use of the key terms *excessif* and *immense*. The study on Gautier also emphasizes these areas as Hugo's natural element: 'chaque écrivain est plus ou moins marqué par sa faculté principale. [. . .] Victor Hugo, grand, terrible, immense comme une création mythique, cyclopéen, pour ainsi dire, représente les forces de la nature et leur lutte harmonieuse' (II, 117). Hugo's desire to explore '*toute la monstruosité*' (II, 137) which lurks in nature makes him appear comparable to 'un Œdipe obsédé par d'innombrables Sphinx'. Janin had drawn the same parallel in reviewing *Les Contemplations* for *Le Journal des débats*, where he insisted that: 'si vous vous plaignez de cette métaphysique ardente et de cet Œdipe questionnant le sphinx, le poète lui-même répondant à cette implacable interrogation, nous vous dirons que vous méconnaissez les droits et les devoirs de la poésie'.[19] But if Busquet, whom Baudelaire had met while working for *Le Corsaire-Satan*, asserted that 'rien ne convient mieux à la poésie moderne que la discussion des redoutables problèmes de l'âme humaine', other critics mocked or decried this 'double cachet du poète et du penseur'.[20] Legendre, writing for *Le Figaro* – whose violent antipathy towards Hugo must be borne in mind – proclaimed heatedly: 'ou la CROYANCE, – ou la SCIENCE! – mais pas de REVES sur ces matières-là' and advised Hugo 'laisser les étoiles et les autres mondes rouler tranquilles, là bas et là haut! – Cela ne nous regarde pas.'[21] And Jouvin, chief editor of *Le Figaro*, wrote condescendingly: 'le poète se croit et se dit un penseur, il se trompe: il n'est qu'un artisan de génie qui *fait* dans la poésie pure'.[22]

Baudelaire presents Hugo's overriding interest in the metaphysical as a recent development, but insists, with remarkable perception, that the tendency was already present in 'La Pente de la rêverie', a poem which appeared in *Les Feuilles d'automne* in 1831. Indeed, he suggests that 'une grande partie de ses œuvres récentes semble le développement aussi régulier qu'énorme de la faculté qui a présidé à la génération de ce poème enivrant' (II, 137). Once again, Baudelaire is seeking out underlying causes and patterns, attempting to discover 'la chaîne de génération'. In Hugo's poem, the narrator sees, in a vision, 'le genre humain complet comme au jour de remords', and compares it to 'un grand édifice / Formé d'entassements de siècles et de lieux':[23] Baudelaire may well have seen a parallel between these lines and the preface to *La Légende des siècles* with its hope that 'cette série d'empreintes, vaguement disposées dans un certain ordre chronologique, pourra former une sorte de galerie de la médaille humaine'.[24] In a more general way, the poet's attempt to penetrate 'cette double mer du temps et de l'espace' in order to 'en rapporter quelque richesse étrange / Et dire si son lit est de roche ou de fange',[25] certainly prefigures the search for order through space and time that marks many of the later poems.

In what H. Tuzet describes as a 'page admirable où le traducteur d'*Eureka* énumère les thèmes les plus féconds de la rêverie cosmique',[26] Baudelaire, like a Catherine wheel spinning off showers of sparks, proposes a long and varied series of the kind of metaphysical questions Hugo explores in his poetry. Above all, he asserts categorically that this is a legitimate area for poetic exploration: 'très légitimement, le poëte laisse errer sa pensée dans un dédale enivrant de conjectures' (II, 138). *Conjecture*, as well as being a key term in this article, is a central concept in Baudelaire's studies on Poe: the preface to 'Bérénice', for example, listed as '*seuls* dignes de l'attention d'un homme *spirituel*: probabilités, maladies de l'esprit, sciences conjecturales, espérances et calculs sur la vie ultérieure' (II, 289). In addition, the famous passage on imagination in the *Salon de 1859* claims that: 'l'imagination est la reine du vrai, et le *possible* est une des provinces du vrai. Elle est positivement apparentée avec l'infini' (II, 621). Hugo himself, mentioning 'l'aspect historique et l'aspect légendaire' of *La Légende des siècles*, insisted in a characteristically paradoxical and balanced sentence that 'le second n'est pas moins vrai que le premier; le premier n'est pas moins conjectural que le second'.[27] In this article, Baudelaire uses *conjecture* to refer to 'le caractère extra-scientifique de toute poésie' (II, 139) and admires Hugo's ability 'traduire, dans un langage magnifique, autre que la prose et la musique, les conjectures éternelles de la curieuse humanité' (II, 139). This he considers a valid use of poetry, provided the poet avoids the pitfalls of didacticism. Developing his thought from the concrete basis of Hugo's poetry, expanding it by a personal meditation on the wonders of the universe and drawing from his reverie a principle which applies to literature in general, Baudelaire reaches the conclusion, concentrated into a characteristically energetic formula, that: 'en décrivant ce qui est, le poète se dégrade et descend au rang de professeur; en racontant le possible, il reste fidèle à sa fonction; il est une âme collective qui interroge, qui pleure, qui espère, et qui devine quelquefois' (II, 139).[28] As in the earlier studies on Poe, therefore, Baudelaire presents as vitally important the poet's role as explorer not merely of what exists but of what might exist, a role which demands imagination, meditation and the deep sense of mystery he admires in Hugo.

Another side of Hugo's writings, illustrated by *La Légende des siècles*, is their fascination with the heroes, events and lessons of history, the order that time imposes on apparent chaos. Typically, Baudelaire chooses to discuss the problems of the genre before embarking on a closer examination of the way in which Hugo exploits it. The problem of the compatibility of poetry and history was suggested partly by such less felicitous works as the epics of the philosopher-poet Quinet, to whose poetry Baudelaire refers in terms of mocking disapproval in his review of *Prométhée délivré*. In Baudelaire's eyes, poetry can no longer draw on history. When a country is young, its poetry can express its identity and its beliefs: more sophisticated nations, however, demand a critical approach to their own history, a sense of judgement and of wisdom – *sagesse* as opposed to *connaissances* – which poetry is unable to convey. Modern poetry, renouncing conventional history, must look at the past through legend and myth. In this discussion, Baudelaire is obviously responding to Hugo's preface, in which he claims that 'c'est l'aspect légendaire qui prévaut dans ces deux volumes' and that 'tous ces poëmes, ceux du moins qui résument le passé, sont de la réalité historique condensée ou de la réalité historique devinée'.[29] Nevertheless, where Hugo emphasizes the legendary and the historical, Baudelaire suggests his own reservations by limiting legitimate poetic exploration firmly to the legendary, to the possible in contrast with the 'real'. He illustrates this idea by a concise evaluation of the treatment of Napoleon in Hugo's work: 'il évoque la légende *possible* de l'avenir; il ne la réduit pas d'autorité à l'état de passé' (II, 140). Where Quinet is seen 'reculer [. . .] les siècles artificiellement', Hugo remains in the domain of conjecture, basing his poem not on cool reason, as Quinet does, but on emotion and imagination: 'quand Victor Hugo, dans ses premières poésies, essaye de nous montrer Napoléon comme un personnage légendaire, il est encore un Parisien qui parle, un contemporain ému et rêveur' (II, 140). The conviction that the modern world is rich in subjects worthy of epic treatment is of course one Baudelaire expressed as early as the *Salon de 1845*. Yet, to discover and depict this 'côté épique' demands both 'une grâce ancienne' and 'longues études', both inherent gifts and consciously accumulated experience.

Baudelaire sounds a note of warning to the loquacious Hugo when he takes up Poe's view, emphasized in 'Notes nouvelles' (II, 332), that modern poetry must avoid 'la longueur insupportable' (II, 139) of the traditional epic: 'les poèmes qui constituent l'ouvrage sont générale-ment courts, et même la brièveté de quelques-uns n'est pas moins extraordinaire que leur énergie. Ceci est déjà une considération importante, qui témoigne d'une connaissance absolue de tout le possible de la poésie moderne' (II, 140). In 'Notes nouvelles', Baudelaire, following Poe, condemns *le poème épique* and points out that 'il est possible que les anciens âges aient produit des séries de poèmes lyriques, reliées postérieurement par les compilateurs en poèmes épiques' (II, 332).[30]

For Baudelaire, Hugo's *La Légende des siècles* reveals him, like Gautier, as a 'prestidigitateur', a 'magicien' capable of revealing 'l'effet magique' of poetry (II, 141). Similarly, Laurent-Pichat claimed of Hugo that 'les mots ont des formes familières pour lui; les consonances ont des mystères; c'est un poète magicien: il évoque, il transfigure, il anime', and Emile Chasles admired in the work 'cette magie [. . .] d'un esprit supérieur qui se joue librement à travers les idées les plus insaisissables'.[31]

Baudelaire's description of *La Légende des siècles*, although brief and very general, suggests, concisely and eloquently, the variety and flavour of Hugo's work. Strangely enough, in praising the 'majesté' with which Hugo 'a fait défiler les siècles devant nous, comme des fantômes qui sortiraient d'un mur' (II, 140) he echoes a poem not published until 1877, although the manuscript is dated 12 August 1859: 'La vision d'où est sorti ce livre' opens with the line: 'j'eus un rêve: le mur des siècles m'apparut'.[32] The coincidence, if it is no more than that, reveals just how much Baudelaire was in tune with Hugo's repertory of images.

The article's concluding paragraph meditates on what Hugo's next volumes might contain, using the opportunity not only to summarize the diversity of Hugo's gifts, but also, one feels, to indicate to Hugo the modes Baudelaire considers most suited to his talent. The language of this final paragraph is highly rhetorical, particularly in the following sentence: 'du fond de son exil, vers lequel nos regards et nos oreilles sont tendus, le poète chéri et vénéré nous annonce de nouveaux poèmes' (II, 141). Possibly Baudelaire is parodying the tones of worship found in such critics as Texier, who wrote: 'o poëte! nous recueillerons pieusement cette gerbe odorante qui nous vient de l'exil'.[33] The modes Baudelaire suggests that Hugo exploit are, on the one hand, 'la bouffonnerie', 'la gaïeté immortelle', 'la joie', and on the other, the 'surnaturel', the 'féerique' and the 'merveilleux'. In his essay on Gautier, Baudelaire had emphasized Hugo's gifts for laughter and the 'sentiment du grotesque' (II, 110), while his preface to Dupont's songs underlined 'cette joie qui respire et domine dans les œuvres de quelques écrivains célèbres' (II, 34). Certainly such a description is particularly apt for *Les Chansons des rues et des bois*. In that volume, most of the poems in which had been completed at least in a preliminary form by 1859, Hugo acknowledges that:

> C'est vrai, pour un instant je laisse
> Tous nos grands problèmes profonds;
> Je menais des monstres en laisse,
> J'errais sur le char des griffons,
>
> J'en descend, je mets pied à terre.[34]

The accuracy of Baudelaire's prediction leads one to speculate on whether he had some knowledge of the atmosphere and content of *Les Chansons des rues et des bois*.

In this notice, then, Baudelaire has not only emphasized those aspects of Hugo's character which serve to elucidate his poetry, and examined those qualities he most admires or which most reward exploration, but he has also used these conclusions as a basis for more general conjecture. Besides, the article contains much that one would hope to find in the very best kind of journalistic criticism: sensitive appreciations and thought-provoking meditations expressed in a style Baudelaire has chosen to vary through such means as pastiche, series of questions, and unexpected metaphors. By leaving aside Hugo's preoccupation with progress, he has indeed been able to isolate the 'quantité de beauté éternelle' in Hugo's poetry. The article both demands and repays careful reading, and, if placed in the context of the age, and provided sufficient attention is given to irony, it seems a remarkably apt assessment of Hugo's gifts. Given the insights it provides into Hugo in particular and poetry in general, one is tempted to suggest that the charges of insincerity are irrelevant.

Baudelaire's review of the first volume of *Les Misérables*, which he published in *Le Boulevard* in April 1862, has aroused in his critics even more unease than the anthology article. Margaret Gilman is typical of many in asserting that this article is 'even more disquieting, in its sense of all that is left unsaid, all its half-truths than the previous one. And Baudelaire's correspondence confirms this impression.'[35] Not only is one led to suspect that the correspondence has determined rather than confirmed this impression, but the letters to which she refers were written some time after the review and inevitably reveal the influence both of the subsequent volumes of the novel and of Hugo's reaction to Baudelaire's review. In writing to his mother in August 1862, Baudelaire angrily described *Les Misérables* as 'immonde et inepte' and added: 'j'ai montré, à ce sujet, que je possédais l'art de mentir. Il m'a écrit, pour me remercier, une lettre absolument ridicule' (*C*II, 254). There can be little doubt that what has aroused his antagonism here is the letter Hugo wrote to thank him for the article; ignoring Baudelaire's reservations, it pompously insists on the fraternity between the two writers. It was not until three years later, when he was ill and extremely depressed, that Baudelaire was to describe the completed novel as 'le déshonneur de Hugo' (*C*II, 460). In contrast to Margaret Gilman, J. Pommier asserts that since Baudelaire 'ne cache pas (sans vouloir en discuter) le point de divergence qui apparaît entre Hugo et lui', the review does not in fact constitute 'un article de complaisance'.[36] Similarly, Lois Boe Hyslop concludes that it reveals 'casuistry perhaps, but certainly not the lies of which he had boasted to his mother'.[37]

This article, too, needs to be seen in the context of its time, as Baudelaire's response to a particularly thorny problem: he had to bear in mind official disapproval of Hugo, *Le Boulevard*'s own support for the poet, Hugo's power and influence in contemporary circles, and his own admiration and respect for the writer who had done most to renew French poetry. It was, after all, a challenge met neither by Sainte-Beuve nor by Gautier.

As is so often the case, Baudelaire's review is firmly structured around a series of key words, all of which are introduced in the first section: these terms are *poète*, *vigueur*, *populaire*, *justice* and *charité*. The opening pages are devoted to a long passage reprinted from the anthology notice. Self-quotation is a device Baudelaire had already used, notably in his assessment of Gautier, and which he was to exploit again in evaluating the life and work of Delacroix: obviously it cannot necessarily be seen as an indication of embarrassment. On a purely practical level, the device saved both time and energy, equally precious to Baudelaire. On a tactical level it gives his criticism a continuity which sets the individual articles in a broader perspective, suggesting that they are part of a harmonious continuum. The brief second section seeks out the reasons behind Hugo's interest in the poor and oppressed, presenting this preoccupation both as characteristic of all poets and thinkers at a given stage of life, and as a personal tendency whose seeds are present even in Hugo's earliest poetry. It is against this background that Baudelaire turns to examine the novel itself, exploring characters rather than analysing theme or plot. His conclusion assesses the philosophical basis of *Les Misérables* and reveals, with admirable clarity, Baudelaire's opposition both to Hugo's beliefs and to his means of expressing them.

The opening sentence, while less arresting than many of his *entrées en matière*, both sets the tone for the whole review and places Hugo in a particular perspective: he is to be considered above all from the point of view of his popularity and his vigour, two central terms in Baudelaire's critical vocabulary. Moreover, in claiming that his earlier statement was to find in *Les Misérables* 'une application plus évidente encore' (II, 217), Baudelaire insists on the validity of his evaluations and asserts the critic's ability to foretell the future development of those he discusses.

His earlier assessment of the innate morality of Hugo's art is altered only by italicizing phrases which seem particularly appropriate to their new context. Thus, with Cosette clearly very much in mind, Baudelaire underlines the reference to Hugo as '*l'ami attendri de tout ce qui est faible, solitaire, contristé; de tout ce qui est orphelin*' (II, 217), and, no doubt with reference to Fantine and Valjean, he emphasizes his evocation of '*ces accents d'amour pour les femmes tombées, pour les pauvres gens broyés dans les engrenages de nos sociétés*' (II, 218). In addition, he draws the reader's attention to 'l'esprit de justice et de charité' which, while certainly present in the earlier works, receives its most forceful expression in *Les Misérables*. Nevertheless, while the anthology notice is content merely to imply that Hugo could run the danger of becoming overtly didactic, the review quite explicitly states that this has indeed happened: 'dans *Les Misérables* la morale entre directement *à titre de but*' (II, 218). Such an approach goes very much counter to the beliefs Baudelaire has been expressing with such cogency since his first critical articles and he makes his disapproval perfectly plain. Moreover, he supports his accusation by quoting Hugo himself, whose intention is revealed not merely through the content of this quotation but also by its position: this 'aveu' – Baudelaire's choice of word is significant – is 'placé, en manière de préface, à la tête du livre'. There is a second point with which Baudelaire takes issue: the expression Hugo uses – 'tant qu'il y aura sur la terre ignorance et misère, des livres de la nature de celui-ci pourront ne pas être inutiles' (II, 218) – obviously implies a belief in the possibility of indefinite progress, a belief Baudelaire deflates by insisting: 'Hélas! autant dire TOUJOURS!' Nevertheless, he refuses to be led into a discussion of principles, specifically directing his reader's attention to the aesthetic question of how Hugo sets about achieving his particular aims. The approach recalls 'Les Drames et les romans honnêtes' with its insistence that 'la question est [...] de savoir si les écrivains dits vertueux s'y prennent bien pour faire aimer et respecter la vertu' (II, 38).

Three aspects demand particular attention in this calmly expressed declaration of intent. Firstly, Baudelaire introduces a concept vital to his literary criticism, that of justice. Secondly, as in many of his reviews, it is the ability to seize attention which has aroused Baudelaire's curiosity: underlying his acknowledgement of the 'merveilleux talent' with which Hugo commands the public's attention is the agonized question: how has Hugo succeeded where I have not? The dichotomy is rendered even more evident – and this is the third point worthy of note – by the very Baudelairean expression 'gouffres prodigieux' and by the typically concrete image comparing 'l'attention publique' to 'la tête récalcitrante d'un écolier paresseux' (II, 218).

Having revealed the central focus of his review, Baudelaire, who constantly seeks out the 'loi de génération' of ideas and tendencies, turns to an analysis of the reasons determining Hugo's interest in 'les misérables'. On the one hand he defines as a general characteristic, and as a measure of a writer's maturity, the development from depicting 'les pompes de la vie' to showing 'inquiétude et curiosité' in regard to 'les problèmes et les mystères' of man's existence. Not only does this progression tally with Hugo's evolution from a work such as *Les Orientales* to *Les Contemplations*, but it also represents a basic element of Baudelaire's own aesthetics. This is clear both from the fact that 'Spleen et Idéal' traces just such a development, and from the use of vocabulary highly reminiscent of the studies on Poe, with their emphasis on *problèmes et calculs* and on the constant questioning of physical and intellectual phenomena.

In order to bring alive the particular problem at the root of *Les Misérables* Baudelaire selects images based on light and dark in an antithetical construction which is in part a pastiche of Hugo himself but which also has overtones of De Quincey: 'cette tache noire que fait la pauvreté sur le soleil de la richesse, ou, si l'on veut, [. . .] cette tache splendide de la richesse sur les immenses ténèbres de la misère' (II, 219). Through the order in which he offers these alternatives Baudelaire throws into stark relief the more pessimistic view of life, a view, moreover, which denies the existence of progress towards greater enlightenment and equality. Furthermore, the language used suggests an affinity with prose poems such as 'Les Yeux des pauvres', published in 1862. Finally, Baudelaire claims to be examining the effect of such a discrepancy on the poet and the philosopher, these two sides to the *littérateur* that he emphasized in his essay on laughter (II, 525).

The question posed by such a contrast, according to Baudelaire, 'c'est de savoir si l'œuvre d'art doit n'avoir d'autre but que *l'art*, si l'art ne doit exprimer d'adoration que pour *lui-même*, ou si un but, plus noble ou moins noble, [. . .] peut lui être imposé' (II, 219). Baudelaire's answer is implicit in the choice of the participle 'imposé'. His calm way of expressing a basic tenet as if it were beyond dispute recalls yet again the opening paragraph of 'Les Drames et les romans honnêtes', while the very specific question echoes the affirmation in the anthology notice on Barbier that 'il y a beaucoup à parier que si vous voulez, vous poète, vous imposer à l'avance un but moral, vous diminuerez considérablement votre puissance poétique' (II, 143). Such parallels indicate the extent to which even a work about which he had severe reservations could serve to refine Baudelaire's awareness of central aesthetic and philosophical problems.

Although he presents metaphysical searching as a characteristic of all mature poets, Baudelaire also claims that it is a trait Hugo revealed from an early stage of his development. The assertion reinforces a point made in the anthology article, declaring that although it is 'surtout dans ces dernières années [que Hugo] a subi l'influence métaphysique qui s'exhale de toutes ces choses' (II, 137), the tendency was already present in 'La Pente de la rêverie'.

In examining the desire for justice which underlies Hugo's choice of subject, Baudelaire suggests that this idea can also be found in many of the youthful works, his references revealing a wide knowledge of Hugo's poetry and theatre. Nevertheless, he insists that the form in which Hugo's longing to bring justice asserts itself is that of rehabilitation. It might be argued here that Baudelaire side-steps a central point of divergence between himself and the poet whose work he is evaluating, but what is under attack in this argument is less the aim itself than the muddled way in which it is put into effect. However that may be, there can be little doubt that Baudelaire's principal preoccupation here is the way in which a certain tendency can develop the proportions of an obsession: this question is basic not only to his studies of intoxicants but also to such prose poems as 'Mademoiselle Bistouri', with its anguished question: 'O Créateur! peut-il exister des monstres aux yeux de Celui-là seul qui sait pourquoi ils existent, comment ils *se sont faits* et comment ils auraient pu *ne pas se faire*?' (I, 356).

Having established the background against which the novel is to be considered, Baudelaire prefaces his study of the work itself with a very clear statement of his approach: since Hugo enjoys such general favour, he can rely on his reader's familiarity with 'la fable et la contexture' and can concentrate his attention on 'la méthode dont l'auteur s'est servi pour mettre en lumière les vérités dont il s'est fait le serviteur' (II, 220). Once again, this brief mention touches on an issue central to Baudelaire's criticism: as early as the Champfleury review he insisted on the importance of method (II, 22: cf. 247), and a letter written to Feydeau in 1858 serves to underline the value he attached to it: 'j'ai décomposé le livre, je l'ai analysé dans sa construction, jusqu'à ce que j'aie

trouvé ou cru trouver la méthode à l'aide de laquelle vous l'avez créé'
(*CI*, 507).

Since an artist's method can be evaluated only in relation to his
aims, Baudelaire strengthens his previous references to social problems
on the one hand and charity on the other, insisting yet again that Hugo
seeks above all to force his reader into judging the issues for himself.
This Baudelaire suggests Hugo has done by choosing a form closer to
the poem than to the novel. The comparison with poetry, particularly
epic poetry, stems from the way in which Hugo has decided to make
his characters 'abstractions vivantes', chosen to serve the purposes of
his general thesis. In what is obviously a further attempt to present
the writer's development, while revealing the constancy of his central
preoccupations, Baudelaire traces such a device to the preface of *Marie
Tudor*, first published in 1833. There, Hugo depicts Hamlet not merely
as a creature of flesh and blood, but as symbolizing mankind. Baudelaire's rejection of such abstractions dates from his review of *Prométhée
délivré*: 'ne confondez jamais les fantômes de la raison avec les fantômes
de l'imagination; ceux-là sont des équations, et ceux-ci des êtres et des
souvenirs' (11, 11). Moreover, in insisting that 'chaque personnage
n'est *exception* que par la manière hyperbolique dont il représente une
généralité' (11, 220), Baudelaire seems to be contrasting Hugo with
Balzac, whose characters were so charged with 'ardeur vitale' that he
was able 'revêtir à coup sûr, de lumière et de pourpre la pure trivialité'
(11, 120). If Baudelaire refrains from explicit criticism of this approach
it is above all because his main concern is with the way in which Hugo
came to terms with a particular problem, and the degree to which his
solution is native to his own personality.

The interest in the continuity of Hugo's thought is also evident
when Baudelaire discusses the second characteristic which makes the
work more of a poem than a novel: in fusing 'le sens lyrique, le sens
épique, le sens philosophique' (11, 221), Hugo, according to Baudelaire,
'confirme une fois de plus la fatalité qui l'entraîna, plus jeune, à transformer l'ancienne ode et l'ancienne tragédie' (11, 221). He elucidates
this fusion by comparing it with the process which produces Corin-
thian brass through combining gold, silver and copper, an image
revealing yet again his interest in scientific processes and discoveries.
Baudelaire might well have chosen to attack Hugo for this confusion
of genres. His reticence, however, probably stems from the fact that
he himself was currently seeking a new genre, or a combination of
genres, which would allow him to express the 'mouvements lyriques
de l'âme', the 'ondulations de la rêverie' and the 'soubresauts de la
conscience' (1, 275–6).

These general affirmations are refined and expanded by a careful study of the four main characters that appear in the first volume of *Les Misérables*: Bienvenu, Valjean, Javert and Fantine.

In discussing the priest, Bienvenu, Baudelaire chooses hyperbolic adjectives to throw into relief the way in which this is a *figure idéale*: Bienvenu represents 'la charité hyperbolique, [. . .] la foi perpétuelle dans le sacrifice de soi-même, [. . .] la confiance absolue dans la Charité prise comme le plus parfait moyen d'enseignement' (II, 221). Although his prose poem 'Assommons les pauvres' violently rejects such a view of charity, Baudelaire's principal concern here lies partly in Bienvenu's unquestioning acceptance of Christianity and particularly the Church's dogma, and partly in the implications lurking in any comparison between Bienvenu and the average priest. The latter point is amusingly illustrated by an anecdote revealing that 'ce genre d'héroïsme pouvait être considéré comme un blâme indirect de tous les curés trop faibles pour se hausser jusque-là' (II, 221). Although such anecdotes are an integral part of Baudelaire's criticism, the relish with which he narrates this story suggests a certain feeling of relief at the opportunity to set *Les Misérables* at least temporarily aside. A further reference to Bienvenu exploits light and dark imagery to show him 'convaincu que le Pardon et la Charité sont les seules lumières qui puissent dissiper toutes les ténèbres' (II, 222).

Bienvenu was seen in a similar light by Cuvillier-Fleury, whose review appeared just over a week after Baudelaire's: 'en le [i.e. Hugo] voyant réunir tant de perfections sur un seul homme, j'ai douté si l'illustre écrivain adressait à la vertu un hommage ou un défi, s'il voulait nous édifier par un beau portrait ou nous provoquer par une antithèse'.[38] Desmarest, however, responded: 'je ne trouve pour ma part rien d'impossible ni même d'invraisemblable dans cette perfection d' un sage chrétien',[39] while P. de Saint-Victor remarked: 'le poète est amoureux de la beauté surnaturelle de cette âme; il la contemple avec ravissement; il déploie lentement ses trésors d'amour et de mansuétude'.[40]

In describing Valjean as 'la brute naïve', 'le prolétaire ignorant', Baudelaire is casting doubt on Hugo's democratic beliefs: his language here recalls many of his attacks on those who seek democracy without understanding what Baudelaire considers to be the true nature of the working classes. Equally Baudelairean is the description of prison as 'l'école du Mal' and the reference to the 'lourdes méditations de l'esclavage'. Typically, too, he insists on the reasons behind Valjean's development and his subsequent transformation into the rich and successful M. Madeleine, stressing far more than does Hugo himself the logic dictating this evolution.

Like many of his contemporaries, he places particular importance on the chapter entitled 'Tempête sous un crâne' in which Valjean struggles to decide whether or not he should give himself up in order to save a man convicted in his place. Mirecourt, who launched a narrowly religious, anti-democratic attack on the novel, nevertheless described this as 'un superbe chapitre'[41] and Saint-Victor, choosing, like Baudelaire, to exploit images based on light and dark, exclaimed: 'quelle clarté dans le récit de ce combat ténébreux! Pas un pli, pas un repli de ce for intérieur que Bacon appelle "une caverne" n'échappe à la lampe ardente que le penseur y porte et y promène en tous sens.'[42] With considerably less enthusiasm Cuvillier-Fleury dourly remarked: 'ce qui serait pour un criminel ordinaire la délibération naturelle d'une âme touchée de Dieu, est une lutte gigantesque pour le héros de M. Victor Hugo'.[43] Nevertheless, Baudelaire's appreciation of this chapter deliberately twists Hugo's meaning, for where Hugo sought to stress the power of the awakened conscience as a basic, overriding factor, Baudelaire's emphasis falls on casuistry, on man's gift for argument and for justifying even the basest actions. The terms 'l'Homme rationnel' and 'l'Homme universel' form a close link with the quotation from *Marie Tudor*, thus reminding the reader that Valjean is to be seen as an abstract concept, illustrating a particular theory. Finally, the reference to 'le Commencement', particularly the use of the capital letter, prepares the review's conclusion with its proclamation of the irremediable nature of Original Sin.

Where Bienvenu is shown to represent unreflecting Charity, and Valjean, animality slowly awakened to intelligence, the police inspector Javert symbolizes intellect deprived of human emotions. Several other critics commented on this tenacious, embittered character, Saint-Victor, for example, claiming: 'ni le roman, ni le drame n'ont créé de type plus parfait que ce "mouchard" dur et pur, rigide et borné, fanatique de l'autorité, ignorant de l'humanité'.[44] Daudet, whose article was published shortly before Baudelaire's and may perhaps have suggested to him the word 'galerie' described Javert as 'assurément le plus original des portraits de cette galerie' while Cuvillier-Fleury, who insisted that Hugo's characters 'sont plutôt des arguments pour une thèse brillante que des ressorts pour un drame vigoureusement conçu', described Javert as 'cette personnification de l'autorité publique dans l'espion' and judged it 'un de ces aperçus où le génie d'un poète peut triompher, où notre simple bon sens résiste et se révolte'.[45]

Baudelaire's evocation of Javert contains the peculiarly intense vocabulary that often seems to indicate close personal involvement: in attacking Javert's application of 'la Lettre sans l'Esprit', he may well be pleading that those judging his own case, his failure to achieve the aims he set for himself, take into consideration the numerous 'circonstances atténuantes' (II, 222–3) that he laments throughout his correspondence. The suspicion that this passage contains elements of self-analysis is strengthened by Baudelaire's admission:

> pour moi, je le confesse, au risque de passer pour coupable ('ceux qui tremblent se sentent coupables', disait ce fou de Robespierre), Javert m'apparaît comme un monstre incorrigible, affamé de justice comme la bête féroce l'est de chair sanglante, bref, comme l'Ennemi absolu (II, 223).

It is in regard to Javert, however, that Baudelaire offers a specific criticism, couched in modest but unmistakable terms: how, he asks, could such a person have come into being? Not only is the desire to comprehend underlying reasons vital to Baudelaire's approach to life and art, but, it seems to me, the question throws doubt on the validity of using the novel to convey a theory, and its characters to personify certain concepts: clearly Hugo needs a character embodying inhumane Justice and is interested in Javert only in that light, just as Ménard needed Jupiter to represent 'une certaine somme d'idées' (II, 11). In both these cases, the poet, according to Baudelaire, is not convinced of his character's existence as an autonomous being: he appears as certain in 1862 as he was in 1846 that 'la grande poésie est essentiellement *bête*, elle *croit*' (II, 11).

Finally, Baudelaire refers briefly to Fantine and Cosette, depicting the first as 'la grisette déchue, la femme moderne, placée entre la fatalité du travail improductif et la fatalité de la prostitution' (II, 223); what has fired Baudelaire's imagination is partly the modernity of Fantine's plight, and partly her devoted love for her daughter. For both aspects his choice of language is illuminating, suggesting, once again, through the repetition of 'fatalité', his belief in a predestined order to existence, and indicating, through the animal imagery with which he evokes maternal love, the intensity and animality of woman as Baudelaire sees her. The remark, like those in the review of *Madame Bovary* and the anthology article devoted to Marceline Desbordes-Valmore, is at once deliberately provocative, in its rejection of the over-sentimental heroines of many contemporary works, and a deeply personal record of Baudelaire's own concept of maternity.

The brief fourth section of the review serves to pull together the various threads of the argument and to insist on the novel as a 'rappel à l'ordre', a 'plaidoyer', both terms conflicting sharply with Baudelaire's demands of a work of art, as expressed in the opening paragraphs of his article. Having made it quite clear that he cannot accept Hugo's use of art for the purposes of explicit didacticism, Baudelaire nevertheless judges the novel both from the point of view of the philosophy it conveys and from that of the extent to which the initial aim has been achieved. Thus, although he underlines the manipulation needed to make a novel a vehicle for philosophical argument, a problem touched on in the analysis of Javert, he concludes, ostensibly in agreement with Hugo, that '*des livres de cette nature ne sont jamais inutiles*' (11, 224). Yet, in insisting that to this extent he thinks 'exactement comme l'auteur', Baudelaire invites his reader to return to the original quotation and thus to become aware of a significant difference between his expression and Hugo's. Indeed, the belief in progress implicit in the expression 'tant qu'il y aura sur la terre ignorance et misère' is once again unhesitatingly rejected by Baudelaire's use of 'jamais'. Moreover, Baudelaire has constantly asserted that art possesses its own, inherent usefulness: 'l'art est-il utile? Oui. Pourquoi? Parce qu'il est art' (11, 41). The irony of Baudelaire's statement would not have been lost on a thoughtful contemporary.

Baudelaire then turns to a summary of Hugo's beliefs, expressed in a style which is a brilliant pastiche of Hugo's brief, antithetical sentence structure. In commenting on Baudelaire's summary, Cellier remarks: 'on ne peut pas souhaiter définition plus exacte de la position hugolienne'.[46] Yet the very exactness allows him to reveal ambiguities and discrepancies which threaten the whole fabric of Hugo's beliefs. *Les Misérables*, Baudelaire reminds his reader, presents a society which is basically evil: yet Hugo has still retained his belief in man's innate goodness as well as his faith in a benevolent God, without making any attempt to deal with the problems such a contradiction poses. Baudelaire's own response is, perhaps, encapsulated in 'L'Irrémédiable':

> — Emblèmes nets, tableau parfait
> D'une fortune irrémédiable,
> Qui donne à penser que le Diable
> Fait toujours bien tout ce qu'il fait! (1, 80).

Also ambiguous is the following remark: 'il repousse le délire de l'Athéisme en révolte, et cependant il n'approuve pas les gloutonneries sanguinaires des Molochs et des Teutatès' (11, 224). Possibly the reference to these pagan gods was suggested to Baudelaire by the way in which society hunts down Valjean as it would a ritual victim, using, moreover, Javert, 'un monstre [...] affamé de justice comme la bête féroce l'est de chair sanglante'. If, in his review of *Prométhée délivré*, Baudelaire has already rejected the atheism that springs from revolt

(II, II), his reaction to the 'gloutonneries sanguinaires' is more ambivalent. In evaluating the life and work of Delacroix in an essay published in 1863, Baudelaire emphasizes that: 'la moralité de ses œuvres, si toutefois il est permis de parler de la morale en peinture, porte [...] un caractère molochiste visible. Tout, dans son œuvre, n'est que désolation, massacres, incendies; tout porte témoignage contre l'éternelle et incorrigible barbarie de l'homme' (II, 760). One could hardly be further from Hugo's convictions. And in 'Notes nouvelles' he affirmed his interest in other religions, asserting 'sans honte' that he prefers the cult of Teutatès to that of Mammon: 'le prêtre qui offre au cruel extorqueur d'hosties humaines des victimes qui meurent *honorablement*, des victimes qui *veulent* mourir, me paraît un être tout à fait doux et humain, comparé au financier qui n'immole les populations qu'à son intérêt propre' (II, 326). Moreover, Baudelaire has no hesitation at all in exploding the theory that 'l'Homme est né bon', declaring, with an ironic repetition of the word 'utile': 'n'est-il pas utile que de temps à autre le poète, le philosophe, prennent un peu le Bonheur égoïste aux cheveux, et lui disent, en lui secouant le mufle dans le sang et l'ordure: "Vois ton œuvre et bois ton œuvre"?' (II, 224). This extraordinarily intense image not only recalls the earlier reference to the poet seizing public attention and forcing it towards 'les gouffres prodigieux de la misère sociale' (II, 218), but it is also highly reminiscent of the tone and content of such prose poems as 'La Femme sauvage et la petite-maîtresse' where the 'bonheur égoïste' of the poet's pampered but plaintive mistress is brought into sudden conflict with 'les enfers dont le monde est peuplé' (I, 290). Finally, Baudelaire's concluding sentence firmly and with no ambiguity at all rejects the belief in progress and asserts 'l'immémoriale réalité' of Original Sin, in a passage entirely contrary to Hugo's convictions.

In this brief review, therefore, he has been able to suggest the perspective in which Hugo's novel is to be considered, to analyse with cogency and insight its central characters, and to reveal to a careful reader his disagreement both with Hugo's beliefs and with his concept of art.

The degree to which Hugo's works and their popularity posed Baudelaire a continuing challenge is reflected in the fact that almost the last lines he was to write were notes jotted down for an assessment of *Les Travailleurs de la mer*. As Cellier has examined them in some detail in his *Baudelaire et Hugo*[47] and as their brevity renders them somewhat cryptic, only four points will be examined here.

Firstly, three allusions suggest that Baudelaire planned an examination of Hugo's use of language: he mentions the 'patois composite' of

Quebec, probably planning to draw comparisons between this and the language of Guernsey; he alludes to the chapter in the second book of Part One entitled 'la vieille langue de Mer' with its typically Hugolian digression on marine vocabulary; and he notes the 'mots suggestifs dans le portrait de Déruchette', this portrait being found in 'Babil et Fumée' in the third book of Part One. This would seem to indicate that Baudelaire was considering a more detailed stylistic analysis than is to be found in his other critical articles.

Secondly, he singles out three elements which are particularly important to his own view of life. Referring, doubtless, to Gilliatt's love for Déruchette, he comments, laconically: 'l'amour fécond en sottises et en grandeurs', a formula which not only recalls much of the personal diaries, but resembles in its dichotomy his description of Hugo as both 'un grand homme' and 'un sot' (CII, 254). This leads naturally to a comment on Gilliatt's suicide, and it is likely that Baudelaire's discussion of that episode would have provided him with the opportunity to explore once again the complex question of self-destruction. A further brief remark which suggests similarities between Hugo's interests and Baudelaire's is 'glorification de la Volonté', a theme very much present throughout Hugo's evocations of Gilliatt's exploits as a sailor.

The third point worthy of particular note here is the comment: 'idylle, petit poème'. Whether Cellier is right in asserting that this is 'une réflexion suggérée par Déruchette et sans doute par l'épisode du nom écrit dans la neige'[48] seems to me rather dubious: what is of particular interest is the use of the term 'petit poème' to depict an episode in prose.

Finally, the jottings do seem to suggest that, contrary to his usual practice but like his review of *Les Misérables*, this analysis would not have set the novel in its contemporary context: no doubt he considered Hugo sufficiently well-known to make such treatment unnecessary, and certainly he was sufficiently in control of the medium to reveal considerable flexibility in exploiting it.

Baudelaire's appreciation of Hugo is certainly one of great complexity, subject to fluctuations caused by external events and changes of mood. More than any other contemporary poet he posed Baudelaire a challenge with which he struggled to come to terms. That struggle may not always have produced his most illuminating critical insights on another poet, but it does reveal much about the development of his own aesthetics and it does have a constant focus: the urgent desire to understand the underlying causes of popularity. And for those interested above all in Baudelaire's creative writing it contains many of the meditations which reappear, transformed but recognizable, in *Le Spleen de Paris*. Hugo, therefore, set an example which aroused in Baudelaire strong feelings both of irritation and of admiration and perhaps it was the very conflict between these reactions that made them so compulsive a source of creative inspiration to him.

6

❧ *The Demands of an Editor*

Between 1859 and 1861 Baudelaire wrote ten notices for Eugène Crépet's anthology, *Les Poètes français*. Of these, Crépet rejected the articles on Barbier, Borel and Moreau: all, except that on Moreau, first appeared in *La Revue fantaisiste* between June and August 1861. Pichois's meticulous edition of Baudelaire's complete works retraces the history of the venture and sketches Crépet's character (II, 1071–8), listing, where appropriate, the poems which illustrate each notice and suggesting the extent to which Baudelaire himself selected the writers and the poems included in the anthology. In this chapter, I have not sought to duplicate Pichois's information, but rather to examine the articles closely, bearing constantly in mind the influence that Crépet may have exerted, but attempting above all to show firstly how Baudelaire, through irony, parody, suggestion and repetition, responds to the challenge posed by a particular writer, and secondly, how he uses the notices as a springboard for wider aesthetic exploration.

Marceline Desbordes-Valmore (*La Revue fantaisiste*, 1 July 1861)

Given Baudelaire's attacks on women writers,[1] his mockery of *le style coulant* (I, 686; II, 105) and his condemnation of those who neglect 'le travail par lequel une rêverie devient un objet d'art' (*C*I, 675), it may seem astonishing that he should have chosen to review for the Crépet anthology the work of Marceline Desbordes-Valmore, a woman whose poetry seems a spontaneous expression of emotion. Yet, his first instinct, in a letter to her son, was to write: 'c'est moi qui me suis chargé de rendre justice à votre admirable mère, et je crois que je l'ai fait dans de bons termes' (*C*I, 621 and variant *C*I, 1053). Clearly, the article set problems he wanted to solve; equally clearly, he was pleased with his response to the challenge.

The date of this letter, 30 November 1859, together with a receipt dated 21 July 1859 and a letter to Crépet in August, in which Baudelaire claims to have finished the seven notices (*C*I, 590), helps to solve a question raised by E. Jasenas. She suggests that the article, although not published until July 1861, was written in the first half of the preceding year, since it refers to *Poésies inédites*, published in August 1860, as being still in the course of preparation.[2] The letters make it likely, however, that the article dates from the middle of 1859; that year, moreover, saw the publication of Baudelaire's essay on Gautier, several assertions in which closely resemble statements in the Desbordes-Valmore notice. Nevertheless, Baudelaire does seem to have revised his original text to some extent: both the quotation from 'Tristesse',[3] and the paragraph which mentions Desbordes-Valmore's death and briefly analyses the posthumous *Poésies inédites*, may well be interpolations.

The notice has once again called into doubt Baudelaire's sincerity. Margaret Gilman interestingly suggests that 'on actually reading the article one feels that Baudelaire, undertaking the article almost as a wager, has in spite of himself been impressed by this poetry, notwithstanding its flaws, its carelessness'. She concludes that his praise is 'certainly sincere in part'.[4] E. Jasenas claims that 'il est certain que Baudelaire dans cet article avait plus d'une fin en vue. Il faisait plaisir à Sainte-Beuve.'[5] Yet Marceline Desbordes-Valmore received qualified praise from that most demanding of contemporary critics, Barbey d'Aurevilly, earned the admiration and affection of Balzac and Sainte-Beuve, and inspired tributes from poets such as Lamartine, Banville, Mallarmé, Verlaine and Aragon.[6] As early as 1860, Montégut was aware that 'son vrai public, chose curieuse à dire, était celui des poètes'.[7] Above all, the tone and imagery of this notice suggest very strongly that Baudelaire is attempting something quite new: if, in his literary criticism, he debates the theoretical questions behind the creation of the prose poems, and experiments with images, situations or themes which achieve a more polished form in *Le Spleen de Paris*, his notice on Marceline Desbordes-Valmore seems to me to be a prose poem in its own right, concentrating less on conventional analysis than on distilling the essence and evoking the atmosphere of her poetry.

Like many of the prose poems, the article begins by posing in immediate personal terms a question of general validity: how can one explain an enthusiasm which apparently contradicts both one's normal reactions and one's cherished theories? Such is Baudelaire's response to Desbordes-Valmore, whose poetry seizes his attention despite himself. This leads to a more general point, that of the role and domain of women writers; this debate prepares the claim that Desbordes-Valmore's poetry, far from aping masculine pretensions, is essentially feminine. Baudelaire then isolates her particular gifts, evoking the atmosphere of her poetry through a peculiarly appropriate series of metaphors. Once again, the supple structure is strengthened by the repetition of central words and motifs, in particular the dichotomy of the artificial and the natural, and the affirmation that what is beautiful in Desbordes-Valmore's poetry is irresistible because of its unexpectedness, its explosive suddenness. Although there is less variety in technique and tone than in some of Baudelaire's other reviews, it does establish from the outset an extremely close relationship between the poet, the reader and the reviewer. Here, too, the article resembles the prose poems in its direct appeal to a reader whom Baudelaire takes into his confidence only then to ridicule or shock, but whom he always keeps closely in mind.

This relationship is established from the opening paragraph, probably the most provocative in Baudelaire's literary criticism. Apparently answering Poe's call for 'a few vivid sentences *imprimis*'[8] he calmly admits that his response to Desbordes-Valmore contradicts not only his spontaneous enthusiasms, but also his maturely considered theories. Yet, urbanely posing the reader a direct question and using the phrase 'plus d'une fois', he disarms cynics by implying that such paradoxes are a common, if inexplicable, phenomenon of human experience. Nevertheless, he attempts, as always, to isolate the causes of his reaction, explaining it partly in terms of the pleasure derived from sharp contrasts. As early as 1846, he saw in 'la loi des contrastes' a principle governing 'l'ordre moral et l'ordre physique' (ii, 19), while one of his planned prefaces to *Les Fleurs du mal* mentions 'un goût supérieur' which teaches us 'à ne pas craindre de nous contredire un peu nous-mêmes' (i, 186). Similarly, Asselineau's notebook includes as a 'phrase admirée par Bodler' Custine's aphorism that 'apprendre c'est se contredire' (i, 710). Finally, his account of the 1855 Exposition universelle concludes ruefully with the famous passage: 'j'ai essayé plus d'une fois [. . .] de m'enfermer dans un système pour y prêcher à mon aise. Mais un système est une espèce de damnation qui nous pousse à une abjuration perpétuelle' (ii, 577).

Despite differences in mood and form, the article's opening paragraph recalls the first lines of 'Le Rêve d'un curieux', first published in March 1860:

> Connais-tu, comme moi, la douleur savoureuse,
> Et de toi fais-tu dire: 'Oh! l'homme singulier!' (i, 128).

Besides, the problem posed is similar to that in Desbordes-Valmore's 'La Prière perdue':

> Inexplicable cœur, énigme de toi-même,
> Tyran de ma raison, de la vertu que j'aime.[9]

Finally, despite differences in expression, there are strong parallels with the opening lines of Sainte-Beuve's important review:

> c'est une chose remarquable, comme, en avançant dans la vie et en se laissant faire avec simplicité, on apprécie à mesure davantage un plus grand nombre d'êtres et d'objets, d'individus et d'œuvres, qui nous avaient semblé d'abord manquer à certaines conditions, proclamées par nous indispensables, dans la ferveur des premiers systèmes.[10]

Struck by these lines, Baudelaire may well have decided to expand the idea in his own way: such a proposition would certainly have appealed to him not only as a challenge but also as an opportunity to please Sainte-Beuve while at the same time gently mocking him.

It is, of course, not merely the contrast between his own ideas and Desbordes-Valmore's which appeals so strongly to Baudelaire: in recreating the atmosphere of the work, therefore, he indicates those elements which exert so strong and so unexpected an attraction. This he does by means of the triple movement so frequent in his literary criticism, singling out those qualities which Desbordes-Valmore possesses in abundance, expressing his reservations, and then showing how it is precisely the blend of qualities and flaws that arouses his enthusiasm.

Among Desbordes-Valmore's dominant characteristics is the ability to give direct expression to the natural expression of her emotions, 'le cri', 'le soupir naturel' (11, 146). Baudelaire's admittedly qualified admiration for gifts alien to his own nature accords with his praise for Gautier's ability 'britanniser son génie' (11, 123) and with a note in the diaries declaring that one should never 'méprise[r] la sensibilité de personne. La sensibilité de chacun, c'est son génie' (1, 661). Not only does his notice on Gautier reveal his sensitivity to 'le cri du sentiment' which, though absurd, is sublime (11, 149), but his very first item of literary criticism showed him receptive to the kind of writing which conveys 'une naïveté d'impressions toute fraîche' (11, 3). And just as the review of Chennevières admires the originality which results from a complete lack of artifice, so the Desbordes-Valmore notice asserts that 'jamais aucun poète ne fut plus naturel; aucun ne fut jamais moins artificiel' (11, 146). Barbey d'Aurevilly also stressed Desbordes-Valmore's lack of artificiality, although his compliment is typically backhanded: 'ce qui enchante plus que le talent de ses vers, quand elle en a, c'est la plus complète absence de pose'.[11] The problem of the artificial versus the natural has been discussed in relation to the studies on Poe: here it is intertwined with another familiar theme, predestination, since Desbordes-Valmore, 'une âme d'élite',[12] expresses with inborn charm 'tout ce qui est gratuit et vient de Dieu' (11, 146). The epithet 'gratuit' is not without ambiguity, suggesting that the poetry comes without effort, inspired but not polished. Although able to admire spontaneity, Baudelaire is sharply aware of all that work can add to inspiration. In concluding that if the qualities connected with spontaneity are those which make 'le grand poète', then 'Marceline Valmore est et sera toujours un grand poëte', Baudelaire is not, of course, claiming that they necessarily do or that she necessarily is. Indeed, this skilfully constructed sentence throws considerable doubt on the statement, partly by the hammerblows of the repeated 'si's, partly by the juxtaposition of terms such as 'ambition' and 'désespérée', 'facultés' and 'irréfléchies', and partly by the somewhat sardonic phrase 'le grand poète' where 'un grand poète' might be more natural. Finally, the irony implicit here becomes more obvious when Baudelaire mentions Desbordes-Valmore's fame, 'que nous croyons aussi solide que celle des artistes parfaits' (II, 147).

Against Desbordes-Valmore's gifts, Baudelaire sets her general weaknesses: negligence, breaks in the rhythm of her verse, a lack of clarity. These, the natural outcome of unbridled spontaneity, are faults of which she herself was aware: 'tout ce que j'écris doit être [. . .] monstrueux d'incohérence, de mots impropres et mal placés'.[13] Baudelaire points them out with apparent reluctance, ironically implying that such fault-finding is the mere cavilling – 'si vous prenez le temps de remarquer tout ce qui lui manque' – of the reader himself, mockingly invoked as 'vous, homme réfléchi et toujours responsable'. Yet he manages to suggest, at one remove, that these flaws are 'un parti pris de paresse', the same 'indolence naturelle des inspirés' which vitiates the poetry of Barbier (II, 144) and Moreau (II, 157).

If these flaws were to be removed, Baudelaire insinuates, one would also lose the 'beauté soudaine, inattendue, non égalable': similarly, he described Balzac as having 'tant de qualités et tant de travers que l'on hésite à retrancher les uns de peur de perdre les autres' (II, 6). Besides, the unexpected beauty, despite the dross in which it may be embedded, nevertheless has the power to transport the reader 'irrésistiblement au fond du ciel poétique': the terms in which the emotion is expressed reveal yet again the physiological intensity of Baudelaire's reaction to art.[14]

Desbordes-Valmore's poetry not only poses the problem of an unpolished outburst which nevertheless contains lines of powerful beauty, but also suggests many questions connected with women and art. According to Margaret Gilman,

> unquestionably there is a less worthy motive in the following paragraphs, which emphasize the characteristically feminine quality of this poetry;

Baudelaire avails himself of the opportunity to compare the poet with other female authors [...] in a vehement passage where only the name of George Sand (which many a passage of the *Journaux intimes* supplies) is lacking.[15]

This comment is quoted at length because it typifies the distortions which can arise if insufficient attention is paid to contemporary critical practice. Like his contemporaries, Baudelaire considered criticism a legitimate opportunity for raising wide-ranging questions of theory and practice; that of women poets would have seemed neither an unwarranted digression nor to have a 'less worthy motive'. On the contrary, few contemporary critics mentioned her poetry without referring, often at considerable length, to her sex. The soldier-novelist Paul de Molènes concludes that 'les femmes sont nées pour mettre au monde autre chose que des volumes de vers';[16] Barbey d'Aurevilly declares crustily that 'elle n'est pas plus poète que les autres femmes qui ont péri dans leurs luttes avec le Vers ou que le Vers, incoercible à leurs pauvres efforts, a dédaignées'.[17] Mallarmé himself will speak of 'l'admirable femme, qui le fut – femme – admirable – dans un art traître au sexe'.[18] Even present-day women critics like Jeannine Moulin fall into such indefensible generalizations as the following: 'femme, elle a simplement témoigné d'une qualité sans laquelle une femme perd sa principale raison d'être: l'indulgence'.[19] It is, therefore, hardly surprising that Baudelaire also seized on the opportunity to raise this question, particularly as his article is as much an exploration and justification of his reaction to her as an analysis of her poetry. Furthermore, his irritation with women who ape the follies of men has become a stock theme of his writing: as early as 1846 his 'Conseils aux jeunes littérateurs' describe the *bas-bleu* as an 'homme manqué' (II, 19), his notes on *Les Liaisons dangereuses* deplore 'la femme qui veut toujours faire l'homme, signe de grande dépravation' (II, 74), and in 'Fusées' he explains: 'nous aimons les femmes à proportion qu'elles nous sont plus étrangères. Aimer les femmes intelligentes est un plaisir de pédéraste' (I, 653). Nor is the passage in the Desbordes-Valmore notice inaccurate, despite its predictable bias, and the force of its language: that the majority of women whose works were being published in France in the mid nineteenth century were not writers of calibre or originality is simply a truism. If Baudelaire perceives in them a lack of *pudeur* it is principally because of the indiscretions of those who, like George Sand and Louise Colet, take revenge on former lovers by publicly exposing their weaknesses.

His argument is quite logical. Firstly, he wonders if any man would want his wife or daughter to have what he terms 'les dons et les honneurs de la Muse' (II, 146). Secondly, he insists that if women do choose to write they should certainly not copy masculine faults which their femininity can only distort and magnify. A woman, he implies, must explore her own personality in her writing. In attacking those who have mimicked masculine pretensions, becoming philanthropists, Republicans or utopians,[20] Baudelaire is probably not mocking a particular woman or women but rather, common contemporary follies which irritate him in either sex. The three follies Baudelaire singles out do, however, reflect his continuing antagonism to those who believe in man's inherent good and who are convinced that equality and indefinite progress are possible.

Baudelaire may have other reasons for suggesting that literature is a male prerogative: his doubts may be based on the conventional Christian concept of woman's role. Not only does the article date from a time when he seems increasingly disturbed by religious questions, but this passage in particular is notable for its religious terminology: 'prêtresse', 'impie', 'impiété', 'sacrilèges'. Alternatively, the profusion of such images could reflect his reading of the poet herself, the critic Vinet pointing out that 'dans aucun recueil de vers modernes nous n'avons si souvent rencontré des mots sacrés; mais aussi nous ne les avons vus profanés d'une manière si affligeante'.[21]

Here, too, Baudelaire's admiration for Desbordes-Valmore's poetry conflicts rather less with either his theories or his passions than might seem likely: far from perpetuating the 'sacrilèges pastiches de l'esprit mâle', her poetry evokes the 'beautés naturelles de la femme' (II, 147), the 'accent délicieux de la femme', nothing but '*l'éternel féminin*'.[22] Although Goethe's phrase was frequently quoted by Baudelaire's contemporaries,[23] his use of it reflects more than the simple desire to suggest culture through cliché. The power that this quality in both Goethe and Desbordes-Valmore exerted over Baudelaire stems from the 'délicieux souvenir' of early childhood, memories stamped and shaped by the '*monde* féminin [. . .] tout cet appareil ondoyant, scintillant et parfumé'.[24] Nevertheless, as so often in Baudelaire's criticism, the passage has a double edge. The 'beautés naturelles de la femme' have frequently aroused Baudelaire's irritation, distrust and scorn.

For Baudelaire, as later for Verlaine, Desbordes-Valmore's poetry reflects three faces of womanhood. According to Verlaine's sonnet:

> Tes premières chansons furent pour l'amitié
> Où ta jeune âme offrait sa meilleure moitié.
> Le délire des sens, dont toute chair rabâche,
> T'inspira des accents que nul n'égalera.
> Et ton œuvre de mère à jamais survivra![25]

Baudelaire's terms for the early poems are at once decidedly less conventional and more appropriate: he speaks of 'les langueurs du désir dans la jeune fille'. His notes on *Les Liaisons dangereuses* describe Cécile as 'niaise, stupide et sensuelle' (II, 71): if Desbordes-Valmore's young girl does not arouse such antagonism, it is perhaps because she is spontaneous and sincere whereas Cécile's education, while leaving her ignorant, has blunted her *naïveté*. Secondly, he mentions the 'désolation morne d'une Ariane abandonnée'. This grief finds voice in poems such as 'Le Miroir', 'Le Ruban', several of the elegies, especially that beginning: 'Ma sœur il est parti! ma sœur il m'abandonne' and in 'L'Imprudence' with its cry: 'tu m'as rendu mon cœur / Et tu me l'as rendu brûlant de ton image'.[26] But it is above all her portrayal of motherhood that has aroused Baudelaire's apparently paradoxical enthusiasm: certainly 'la charité maternelle' colours much of her work, whether she welcomes her son with the words: 'Enfant né de ma vie où je reste pour toi', or finds the courage to go on living through the presence of her surviving children: 'J'ai des enfants! leurs voix, leurs haleines, leurs jeux / Soufflent sur moi l'amour qui m'alimente encore.'[27] Surely it is above all this flame which suddenly illuminates Baudelaire's 'plus intime souvenir' (II, 147). The abrupt intrusion of the personal is introduced here in a strangely impersonal way – 'quelques-uns, parmi les fils de la femme' (cf. II, 85) – no doubt to form a barrier against an emotion painful in its intensity. The expression 'notre plus intime souvenir, amoureux ou filial', the bracketing together of the love of a man for his mistress and the love a child can feel for its mother, is essentially Baudelairean (cf. I, 24 and 661 and CII, 153). It is certainly the intensity of Baudelaire's childhood memories that has enabled him to present, not the conventional, insipid picture of bourgeois sweetness, but an image which suggests a maternal love so passionate as to be animal-like in its intensity. He conveys the ardour of maternal love not merely through the perhaps more conventional terms suggesting light and warmth – the poetry of 'l'ardente Marceline' is like a torch which illuminates the heart – but also through the earthy realism of 'chaleur de couvée', the use of the word 'petit' to refer to human young and the unexpected combination of 'grâce', 'souplesse' and 'violence' (II, 147). In reviewing *Madame Bovary* Baudelaire wrote that 'toutes les femmes *intellectuelles* lui [i.e. à Flaubert] sauront gré d'avoir élevé la femelle à une si haute puissance, si loin de l'animal pur et si près de l'homme idéal' (II, 83). Marceline Desbordes-Valmore, far removed from Flaubert's androgynous heroine, is presented in the anthology notice – with a degree of manipulation – as equally remote from 'les femmes *intellectuelles*' and very close, in her unashamed femininity, to 'l'animal pur'.

Denying Janin's claim that Desbordes-Valmore is already forgotten,[28] Baudelaire highlights the gifts for which she will be remembered: 'elle a les grandes et vigoureuses qualités qui s'imposent à la mémoire, les trouées faites à l'improviste dans le cœur, les explosions magiques de la passion' (II, 147: cf. II, 175). Perhaps the reference to memory reflects, in part, Sainte-Beuve's review: 'quiconque, à une heure triste, recueille, en passant sur la grève, ces accents éperdus, ces notes errantes et plaintives, se surprend bien des fois, longtemps après, à les répéter involontairement'.[29] The expressions 'trouées profondes' and 'explosions magiques', moreover, not only heighten earlier references to her 'facultés soudaines' but also, like many phrases in the criticism and the correspondence, reveal Baudelaire's vision of art as an abrupt outburst of emotion or insight: in Cruikshank's caricatures, for example, Baudelaire admires 'l'explosion dans l'expression' (II, 566) and Moreau earns grudging praise for 'l'accent de vérité jaillissant, l'accent soudain' (II, 161).

Baudelaire throws into high relief the ease with which Desbordes-Valmore seizes on the perfect expression to convey an atmosphere or emotion. Nevertheless, he stresses once again that this ability results from natural gifts rather than conscious effort: it is 'le sublime qui s'ignore'. Although Baudelaire undoubtedly envies her fluency, his expression 'perpétuelle trouvaille' insinuates that she writes too much, a complaint he frequently made of women writers (cf. II, 81), and subtly suggests the other side of art, the 'laborieuse recherche'. Nevertheless, Baudelaire shows his perplexity: why should she have the right 'trace[r] des merveilles' in spite of her negligence? And he introduces a further ambiguity when he describes her works as being created with the 'insouciance qui préside aux billets destinés à la boîte aux lettres': in *La Double Vie* Baudelaire may well have enjoyed the 'négligé de bonne compagnie' which resembled 'la lettre intime confiée à la boîte pour les contrées lointaines' (II, 87), but he lamented of George Sand that she knew neither 'l'art, ni la mesure', adding that 'elle jette ses chefs-d'œuvre à la poste comme des lettres' (II, 283). Although admiration is tempered by envy and exasperation, it seems that Baudelaire's initial response is one of delight, and that his reservations come only after reflection.

Three quotations define Desbordes-Valmore's character and poetry as Baudelaire sees them.

Her passionate, charitable nature is typified by a line from the first poem of *Bouquets et Prières*, 'A celles qui pleurent':

Tant que l'on peut donner, on ne peut pas mourir![30]

Baudelaire's interesting substitution of 'peut' for 'veut', together with a more substantial alteration to a verse quoted later in the article, indicates that he is relying on memory, a point which both reveals the extent to which he has assimilated her poetry and confirms that he is not merely producing a commissioned article on a writer who means little to him. Even in introducing this line, Baudelaire stresses the spontaneous, unconscious nature of her art; after the words 'cueille', 'fougueuse', 'inconscient', 'trouvaille' in the preceding sentences, he twists the screw yet further by adding that Desbordes-Valmore defines her own nature 'bien, mais toujours involontairement'.

Her sensitivity to the harshness of life is reflected in a second couplet, thematically if not stylistically reminiscent of some of *Les Fleurs du mal*:

> Mais si de la mémoire on ne doit pas guérir,
> A quoi sert, ô mon âme, à quoi sert de mourir?[31]

The yearning to escape both memory and suffering finds much harsher expression in Baudelaire's 'De profundis clamavi':

> Je jalouse le sort des plus vils animaux
> Qui peuvent se plonger dans un sommeil stupide (I, 33).

'A Celles qui pleurent' provides a third quotation revealing that her poetry directly expresses her character:

> Prisonnière en ce livre une âme est renfermée![32]

In substituting 'renfermée' for 'contenue', Baudelaire may have been influenced by the last poem from which he quoted, 'Tristesse', with its line:

> Renfermée à jamais dans mon âme abattue.[33]

Certainly the substitution lays bare much of Baudelaire's own disposition, by intensifying the sense of claustrophobia.

Death, according to Baudelaire, took Desbordes-Valmore from a world in which she 'savait si bien souffrir'. Suffering, for Baudelaire, has a positive side: in introducing *Un Mangeur d'opium* he refers to 'la fertilisante douleur' (*MO*, 104) and claims in his dedication to *Les Paradis artificiels* that 'l'être humain jouit de ce privilège de pouvoir tirer des jouissances nouvelles et subtiles même de la douleur' (I, 400). Similarly, in 'Bénédiction' the poet describes 'la douleur' as 'la noblesse unique / Où ne mordront jamais la terre et les enfers' (I, 9). Nevertheless, to my ears there is a suggestion of irony in the statement that Desbordes-Valmore 'savait si bien souffrir', a hint that she knew the poetic worth of her grief and cultivated it as substance for her verses.

Certainly there are times when the constant repetition of the theme, the image of Marceline weeping to her reflection in river or lake, savours of complacency.

The article's concluding paragraph is the kind of *tour de force* in which Baudelaire obviously revels, opening on a quietly confiding note, building up through an elaborate metaphor and closing with a resounding affirmation of the permanent youthfulness of Desbordes-Valmore's poetry. The metaphor, in which the atmosphere of the poetry is evoked through comparison with external nature, could serve to illustrate the theoretical discussion of 'la *correspondance* et [le] symbolisme universels' (II, 117), which recurs in the studies on Poe, Gautier and Hugo.

As E. Jasenas has pointed out,[34] the comparison between Desbordes-Valmore's work and an English garden may well have been suggested by Sainte-Beuve, who found in her descriptions of countrysides 'un certain goût anglais', noting that her shrubberies often contained allegorical and mythological figures, and emphasizing the constant presence of 'un nuage sentimental, souvent confus et insaisissable, mais par endroits sillonné de vives flammes et avec l'éclair de la passion'.[35] Despite the outward similarities, it should be stressed that the two critics have very different aims. Sainte-Beuve is merely describing, in a fairly conventional manner, the rural scenes Desbordes-Valmore depicts: Baudelaire is drawing a close analogy between the English garden and the *atmosphere* of her poetry. Such parallels, moreover, were not uncommon. Vinet's review of *Les Pleurs*, for example, also links Desbordes-Valmore's poetry and external nature: 'les teintes de sa poésie sont comme les teintes les plus chaudes d'un couchant d'été; son harmonie est pleine de vibration; son vers tremble comme les feuilles sous l'orage, retentit comme la cloche d'argent dont la tempête emporte, disperse et fait ondoyer les sons'.[36] Lacaussade's analysis of *Poésies inédites* makes a similar comparison: 'je ne saurais mieux comparer ces éclats déchirants de la lyre qu'à des éclairs au milieu d'une opaque nuit d'orage dans les hautes montagnes; ils illuminent et fendent les ténèbres, et permettent au regards de pénétrer à une immense profondeur'.[37] Indeed, however appropriate to the flower-loving Marceline the image may be, the way in which Baudelaire builds upon it, declaring that the garden he has in mind is not that of Versailles nor yet those of Italy, makes his reader suspect that, as so often, he may be playing with a cliché of the time. He certainly seems to be indulging in parody in the somewhat pompous phrase: 'ce n'est pas non plus le pittoresque vaste et théâtral de la savante Italie, qui connaît si bien l'art d'*édifier des jardins*' with the school-book Latin tag added in parentheses: *aedificat hortos*. Sainte-Beuve's review contains an equally unnecessary quotation.[38]

However much of a pastiche the passage may be, it is certainly not gratuitous but serves to highlight certain themes and devices. Baudelaire's reference to flower-beds which 'représentent les abondantes expressions du sentiment' (II, 149) recalls those poems in which flowers are emblems of past happiness or the swift passage of time. Similarly, in mentioning the lakes which 'figurent la profonde résignation toute parsemée de souvenirs', Baudelaire evokes such works as 'Sol natal':

> Mémoire! étang profond couvert de fleurs légères.[39]

Although his description of the 'mausolée inconnu qui, au détour d'une allée surprend notre âme et lui recommande de penser à l'éternité' may have its source in Sainte-Beuve's reference to 'personnifications allégoriques', among them Death, which 'apparaissent au sein de ces bocages',[40] its inspiration may also be the many poems in which Desbordes-Valmore mourns the loss of a friend or child. In addition, it has a close parallel in the *Salon de 1859*:

> un fantôme décharné et magnifique, qui soulève discrètement l'énorme couvercle de son sépulcre pour vous supplier, créature passagère, de penser à l'éternité! Et au coin de cette allée fleurie qui mène à la sépulture de ceux qui vous sont encore chers, la figure prodigieuse du Deuil [. . .] vous enseigne que richesse, gloire, patrie même, sont de pures frivolités (II, 669).

The similarities between the two passages suggest firstly that they date from within a short space of time, thus confirming 1859 as the year in which the notice was written, secondly that Baudelaire's reaction to the plastic arts and to poetry were in many ways analogous, and thirdly that he is at this time particularly susceptible to works of art portraying mourning and the ephemeral nature of human existence.

Over the garden corresponding to Desbordes-Valmore's poetry Baudelaire indicates the constant threat of gathering storms, clouds menacing bereavement. However elaborate the metaphor, its validity is beyond dispute: Desbordes-Valmore continually gives her reader the impression that joy, however profound, is temporary, and grief inescapable. This leads, according to Baudelaire, to an outburst of 'hysterical tears', tears which nonetheless give to suffering and despair 'la fraîcheur et la solidité d'une nouvelle jeunesse'. The Pléiade note on the expression 'hysterical tears' is misleading in claiming that 'le mot "hystérie" n'a ici aucun sens clinique' (II, 1148). As I have already indicated in reference to the review of *Madame Bovary*, Baudelaire, his readers and, indeed, medical experts of the time, would have considered these tears 'hysterical' in the contemporary medical sense of the term. These tears, moreover, are those whose cause Baudelaire examines both in 'Le *Confiteor* de l'artiste' and in his 'Notes nouvelles':

> quand un poème exquis amène les larmes au bord des yeux, ces larmes ne sont pas la preuve d'un excès de jouissance, elles sont bien plutôt le témoignage d'une mélancolie irritée, d'une postulation des nerfs, d'une nature exilée dans l'imparfait et qui voudrait s'emparer immédiatement, sur cette terre même, d'un paradis révélé (II, 334).

What then has Baudelaire been able to achieve in this brief notice? There are certainly aspects of Desbordes-Valmore's work which are completely ignored: Baudelaire has probably chosen not to mention, rather than to condemn, the highly moralistic poems on children, and his silence on those poems in which she expresses her deep compassion with the poor, the imprisoned and the suffering, was no doubt determined by his response to the challenge posed by her love poetry. Despite such omissions, he has been able to isolate the qualities which make her poetry both rewarding and unique, and, by disregarding the conventional image of woman, has revealed a remarkable degree of insight into her femininity. Through insinuation and irony he points to her weaknesses and limitations and, although the article aims at evocation rather than analysis, when he does refer to her poetry he does so in a way which suggests he knows it well. I find the review more rewarding if seen as a prose poem or as an experiment in blending criticism with creative writing, than as conventional journalism. Certainly there is a degree of bravado in it, but if Baudelaire is responding to a wager, either on the level of content or on that of form, it must surely be acknowledged that he has won.

Auguste Barbier
(*La Revue fantaisiste*, 15 July 1861)

Evaluating Barbier's *Chansons et Odelettes* the critic Rollin bemoaned: 'l'aigle aux cris terribles s'est changé en fauvette de salon'.[41] It was a familiar lament in the 1840s and 1850s: most critics, remembering the enthusiasm aroused by the powerful satire of the *Iambes*, accepted more cautiously *Il Pianto* and *Lazare*, and watched in disappointment as successive volumes belied Barbier's early promise. Planche asserted that it was precisely because he admired 'l'élégance virgilienne du *Pianto*' and the 'gravité philosophique de *Lazare*' that he condemned

Pot-de-vin 'avec une sévérité absolue'.[42] Similarly, the critic of the *Revue de Paris* considered that 'M. A. Barbier dans *Erostrate* et dans *Pot-de-vin* n'a point heureusement appliqué ses efforts', and Labitte, ranking Barbier among the *poetae minores*, judged that 'la source de l'inspiration semble complètement tarie chez l'auteur des *Rimes héroïques*'.[43] H. Manet summarized general critical opinion in declaring that '*Il Pianto* et *Lazare* furent les deux degrés par lesquels passa l'œuvre de Barbier avant d'arriver aux *Rimes héroïques* et aux *Odelettes*, des riens'.[44] Baudelaire, whose creative writing suggests the influence of a careful and sympathetic reading of *Iambes* and *Il Pianto*,[45] uses the notice he prepared for Crépet's anthology to make two important points: he seeks firstly to show how the success of a work of literature may result from non-literary factors, and secondly to suggest why a gifted poet can nevertheless produce works unworthy of him.

For various reasons, the article was one Baudelaire did not find easy to write. Towards the end of July 1859 he mentions it as finished but expresses dissatisfaction with it (*CI*, 589) and, in writing to Crépet in April 1860, he complains:

> vous me tourmentez horriblement et inutilement. J'ai mis, à cause de vous autant qu'à cause de moi, une application énorme dans ces notices. *Ce que j'écris est bon et irréfutable.* Cependant je vous ai déjà promis, par complaisance et par déférence, de remanier plusieurs passages. Je *l'ai déjà fait*, dans le *Barbier* par exemple (*CII*, 21: cf. *LAB*, 104).

Despite these alterations, which seem to have included the removal of a passage castigating Laprade (*CII*, 650), Crépet rejected the article, replacing it with Léon de Wailly's barely more laudatory notice.

For several critics, the notice represents an abrupt about-face, a complete rejection of Baudelaire's earlier assessment of Barbier. The Pléiade edition, for example, contrasts the 'allusion élogieuse' of Baudelaire's Dupont preface (11, 1144) with the 'sentiments hostiles qu'il exprimera plus tard' (11, 1353).[46] This seems to me neither exact nor fruitful. On the one hand, Barbier's early works certainly seem to have stamped themselves indelibly on Baudelaire's mind: the *Salon de 1845* quotes from memory a phrase from Barbier's 'Michel-Ange' (11, 376) and several lines from the tenth *Iambe* are introduced into 'Quelques caricaturistes français' (11, 548). In splicing them into his sentence, however, Baudelaire removes their hint of sentimentality, strengthening their sinews much as he did to Dupont's 'Chant des ouvriers' (11, 31). Thus the 'pâle voyou' is no longer 'au corps chétif' (see 11, 1353), but 'à la voix rauque' (11, 548), with all that the adjective evokes in terms of a search for escape through alcohol. Furthermore, as J. Crépet has pointed out, the description of Popularity as 'la seule des impudiques qui demande à être violée' (II, 79) is almost certainly an allusion to Barbier's fifth *Iambe* (*AR*, 566). And the essay on Gautier, while lamenting that the public are interested only in those of Barbier's works which are '*illustrées* [. . .] par une espèce de vignette politique' (II, 106), nevertheless implies that at least *Il Pianto* and *Lazare* deserve attention. Moreover, as late as 1862, Baudelaire wrote to Flaubert: 'comment n'avez-vous pas deviné que Baudelaire, ça voulait dire: Auguste Barbier, Th. Gautier, Banville, Flaubert, Leconte de Lisle, c'est-à-dire *littérature pure*?' (*C*II, 225). On the other hand, the remarks on Barbier in the Dupont preface, far from being an un-adulterated eulogy, make perfectly plain Baudelaire's reservations about Barbier's talent and the use to which he puts it: according to Baudelaire, when

> un poète, maladroit quelquefois, mais presque toujours grand, vint dans un langage enflammé proclamer la sainteté de l'insurrection de 1830 et chanter les misères de l'Angleterre et de l'Irlande, malgré ses rimes insuffisantes, malgré ses pléonasmes, malgré ses périodes non finies, la question fut vidée, et l'art fut désormais inséparable de la morale et de l'utilité (II, 27).[47]

The attack on those 'rimes insuffisantes', 'pléonasmes' and 'périodes non finies' recurs in the notice, like the counterbalancing assertion that Barbier is 'presque toujours grand'. If the anthology notice high-lights his misuse of his talent, it is surely because, in an article devoted entirely to Barbier, Baudelaire can state his position unequivocally, emphasizing his admiration before pursuing the aesthetic problems involved in intertwining the 'Beau' with the 'Bien'. The vehemence of the tone stems, partly, from his disappointment at Barbier's failure to realize his early promise, and, more generally, from the necessity of repeating yet again his rejection of explicit didacticism in poetry.

Although there is the same movement between the particular and the general as in the study of Hugo, the brevity of this notice has en-forced a simpler structure. After a short introduction, setting the tone and epitomizing Barbier's poetry, Baudelaire poses 'cette fastidieuse question de l'alliance du Bien avec le Beau' (II, 142). It is the resolution of this question that sets Barbier's work in perspective: the second half of the study, therefore, applies these generalizations to his poetry, following his development from the *Iambes* to *Rimes héroïques* and *Chansons et Odelettes*. The article offers many parallels with Baudelaire's essay on Gautier, in particular with the self-quotations from 'Notes nouvelles' and 'Les Drames et les romans honnêtes'. Indeed, the word *honnête*, or its derivatives, appears no less than eight times. Other central words whose repetition strengthens the article's structure are *naturel*, *gloire* and *indignation*.

The notice opens with a striking example of Baudelaire's skill in seizing his reader's attention from the outset: 'si je disais que le but d'Auguste Barbier a été la recherche du beau, sa recherche exclusive et primordiale, je crois qu'il se fâcherait, et visiblement il en aurait le droit' (II, 141). Not only does this statement define Barbier by contrast with Gautier, whose *idée fixe* Baudelaire presents as 'l'amour exclusif du Beau' (II, 111), but it also inverts the familiar cliché of Barbier as satirist pure and simple: Planche, for example, claimed that the *Iambes* 'ont résolu [. . .] d'une façon définitive la question relative à la dignité poétique de la satire';[48] for Nettement, Barbier handled 'l'hyperbole de Juvénal avec une sincérité de colère que n'a pas le rhéteur romain';[49] and Wailly proclaimed: 'la satire, c'est la vocation d'Auguste Barbier'.[50] Only the critic of the *Revue de Paris* suggested that 'Barbier est avant tout un poète épris de son art, né bien moins pour flétrir la laideur que pour comprendre et pour reproduire la beauté'.[51] Not only does Baudelaire provocatively reject the stereotype, but he suggests from the outset the paradox that Barbier's decline has resulted from the very beliefs which caused his early success. Barbier stands in sharp opposition to Baudelaire's idealized artist, for whom poetry has no aim but itself (II, 113); for Barbier, poetry is only a means to an end. Since this idea of poetry raises yet again the question of the relationship between morality and literature, Baudelaire seizes on the opportunity not only of debating it once more, but also of mocking those who believe in indefinite progress: were their theories correct, could there be any 'affaiblissement des esprits', a decadence to which Baudelaire attributes the general failure to comprehend so simple a concept?

Defining his position much as he did in the Flaubert and Gautier reviews, Baudelaire insists that it is possible for him to concentrate on this general problem, precisely because Barbier needs no critical introduction. The twentieth century may see him differently, but Barbier was indeed among the four or five most renowned contemporary poets, and although some readers may have disagreed with the position Castille gave him, few would have considered preposterous his description of Barbier as 'le plus grand poète du XIXe siècle'.[52]

Baudelaire's own 'admiration immense et de vieille date' (II, 142) is evident both in *Les Fleurs du mal* and other early works, and in his ability to convey succinctly and exactly what is admirable in Barbier's poetry: his eloquence, his power of carrying the reader with him, the vigour of his style and his sudden bursts of insight. Much the same

qualities attract Gautier, whose general opinion of Barbier is close to
Baudelaire's: 'avec ce parti pris de style hardiment mené jusqu'au bout,
M. Barbier a produit des effets nouveaux dans la langue et d'une
énergie extraordinaire; sa phrase est large, ample, éloquente, d'une
trivialité robuste, d'un mouvement soudain, la prêtant à tous les
emportements de l'indignation et de la satire'.[53] Even in his praise,
however, Baudelaire suggests certain reservations: he is careful to
say no more than that Barbier's style 'a presque le charme du latin' –
this comparison was a commonplace of contemporary criticism – and
he insists that it is the 'premières chansons' which are engraved 'dans
toutes les mémoires'.

Baudelaire claims, moreover, that the origin of Barbier's celebrity
is not pure, springing not from the unsullied 'mouvement lyrique' but
from the ideas the verse was made to express and from the circumstances which inspired it. The language here, with its stress on literary
purity, on poetry expressing eternal beauty rather than such extra-
literary matters as a belief in progress and in Republican ideals, recalls
a passage in Baudelaire's essay on Gautier: 'le public n'a glané avec
soin [. . .] que les parties *illustrées* (ou souillées) par une espèce de
vignette politique' (II, 106), the word 'souillées' having both physical
and moral connotations.

Introducing the stock line from Juvenal, '*facit indignatio versum*',
Baudelaire, while agreeing that indignation can indeed inspire, points
out with studied simplicity, as though wearily explaining after many
perhaps more eloquent but vain attempts, that 'le monde est plein
de gens très indignés qui cependant ne feront jamais de beaux vers'.
Gautier's review also insists that 'tout le monde a des idées poétiques,
mais les poètes ont seuls les moules où se jettent les idées – le penseur
ne peut pas se passer de l'artiste'.[54] Moreover, Gautier, like Baudelaire,
condemns Barbier's use of poetry as social criticism: 'M. Auguste
Barbier est avant tout moraliste et rhéteur; chez lui l'indignation fait
le vers aussi souvent que chez Juvénal ou Perse: tout a un but visible,
un dessein transparent', and he adds trenchantly, in one of his clearest
formulations concerning the problem: 'la moralité de l'art ne consiste
pas, on ne saurait trop le répéter, en sentences religieuses ou sociales,
mais à élever l'homme par l'admiration du beau et l'attrait des jouissances intellectuelles les plus nobles et les plus pures de toutes'.[55]

Just as, in the article on Hugo, Baudelaire claimed that 'en décrivant
ce qui est, le poète se dégrade et descend au rang de professeur' (II,
139), so here he condemns those who seek to make poetry impart 'des
idées tirées d'un monde étranger à l'art' (II, 143). This may well be a
reaction against Du Camp, according to whom 'l'inutile exagération

des derniers jours de la période romantique a envahi les esprits les meilleurs. La pensée ne se formule plus; la forme seule se contourne et se tourmente pour voiler le squelette qu'elle habille.'[56] Nevertheless, Baudelaire's position has not changed since his review of *Prométhée délivré* (II, 9). Far from being purely theoretical, the debate has practical implications, since those who place more importance on the idea than on the form come to neglect the form altogether: 'le résultat est l'anéantissement de la poésie' (II, 143). This, therefore, is the obverse of the excess deplored in 'L'Ecole païenne': 'le goût immodéré de la forme pousse à des désordres monstrueux et inconnus. [. . .] Comme l'absence nette du juste et du vrai dans l'art équivaut à l'absence d'art, l'homme entier s'évanouit; la spécialisation excessive d'une faculté aboutit au néant' (II, 48–9). Furthermore, Baudelaire insists with greater clarity than elsewhere that the distinction between content and expression is false, stating categorically that 'l'idée et la forme sont deux êtres en un' (II, 143).

In a sentence revealing his gift for the art of transition, Baudelaire applies these ideas to Barbier, emphasizing that his literary decline stems directly from the attempt to make poetry useful or moral. This further sharpens the contrast between Gautier and Barbier: in the former Baudelaire admired 'ce souci permanent, involontaire à force d'être naturel, de la beauté et du pittoresque' (II, 119), while Barbier, although he is 'naturellement poète', is dominated by 'le souci perpétuel et exclusif d'exprimer des pensées honnêtes ou utiles' (II, 143).

Baudelaire illustrates the decline of Barbier's gifts with a brief reference to the spare, vigorous poem 'La Tentation'.[57] Baudelaire who, as the Pléiade notes point out, suggest d unsuccessfully that this poem be included in the anthology (*C*I, 593),[58] emphasizes its 'grandeur' and 'majesté', qualities also singled out in the later works. Nevertheless, he indicates that in subsequent poems the dominant voice is not that of the poet but that of the moralist, a substitution leading inevitably to the neglect of grammar and rhetoric. Where Gautier, guided by beauty alone, never infringed the 'règles les plus sévères de la langue' (II, 152), Barbier's poetry provokes several very precise stylistic criticisms. Indeed, compared with Baudelaire's concise accuracy, other critics making the same reproach seem verbose or vague: Planche described Barbier's style as 'prosaïque jusqu'à la trivialité' and complained that 'il viole jusqu'aux lois de notre langue'; Labitte said of *Rimes héroïques* that 'jamais le style de M. Auguste Barbier n'avait été aussi insuffisant, jamais l'auteur n'avait tant accordé à la périphrase vulgaire, aux épithètes parasites, et, pour parler franc, aux chevilles de toute sort'; and Barthélemy-Lanta wrote: 'il est dommage que des passages d'une grande faiblesse poétique viennent quelquefois déparer les scènes les plus belles, que la loi rigoureuse de la rime ne soit pas toujours respectée, et que des mots bannis par l'usage obtiennent trop aisément droit de bourgeoisie'.[59]

Baudelaire not only rejects Barbier's introduction into poetry of 'l'utile' and 'l'honnête' but he also criticizes 'une nouvelle affectation' (II, 144) which consists in introducing 'une certaine platitude solennelle' as though it were 'une majestueuse et pénétrante simplicité'. While the emphasis placed on Barbier's stylistic errors seems, if not unjust, a little harsh, this criticism is quite fair: although capable of startlingly original metaphors, Barbier does tend, in his striving after sparse simplicity, to fall into platitude.[60] Yet Baudelaire's reason for highlighting this tendency is less to attack Barbier himself than to indicate a more general trend: he mentions as characteristic exponents of the fashion the poets Antony Deschamps and Brizeux. Deschamps had dedicated 'La Jeune Italie' to Barbier and translated Dante, a fact which helps to elucidate Baudelaire's reference to 'cette grimace dantesque' (II, 144). For his part, Barbier's friend Brizeux wrote poetry that was specifically didactic, addressing an idealized young poet, for example, in the following terms: 'va partout relever la morale publique, / Et punir les forfaits, et venger les douleurs'.[61]

Dismissing *Pot-de-vin, Erostrate* and *Chants civils et religieux* as 'œuvres dont chacune a un but moral' (II, 145), and *Chansons et Odelettes* as 'un affligeant effort vers la grâce antique',[62] Baudelaire turns to *Rimes héroïques*, a collection which Barbier describes as 'toutes les pièces de vers que, dans mes lectures ou mes voyages, l'émotion d'un pieux souvenir, un grand acte de vertu ou de patriotisme, avaient pu me suggérer'.[63] With its evocations of Le Cid, Roland, Héloïse and Laura it has far greater breadth and complexity than Baudelaire's reference to it might lead an unsuspecting reader to believe. What he has chosen to emphasize are those poems in which, 'sous prétexte de faire des sonnets en l'honneur des grands hommes, le poète a chanté le paratonnerre et la machine à tisser' (II, 145). Here Baudelaire seeks to drive home a point of general importance by introducing the amusing anecdote of his cynical friend who 'a travaillé à un poème anonyme sur l'invention d'un dentiste' (II, 145). Yet, given his insistence in the review of *Madame Bovary* that 'tous les sujets sont indifféremment bons ou mauvais, selon la manière dont ils sont traités' (II, 81), and his frequently voiced plea for artists to express 'l'héroïsme de la vie moderne' (II, 493: cf. II, 374), one cannot help feeling that the attack is somewhat illogical. Perhaps he is once more reacting against Du Camp's belli-

gerent preface to *Les Chants modernes*, with its call for a very obvious
kind of modernism:

> quoi, nous sommes le siècle où l'on a découvert des planètes et des mondes,
> où l'on a trouvé les applications de la vapeur, l'électricité, le gaz, le chloro-
> forme, l'hélice, la photographie, la galvanoplastie [. . .] nous touchons à la
> navigation aérienne, et il faut s'occuper de la guerre de Troie et des
> panathénées![64]

Moreover, Baudelaire discovers in contemporary literature 'de nombreux symptômes' which imply a belief that: '*le but de la poésie est de
répandre les lumières parmi le peuple, et, à l'aide de la rime et du nombre, de
fixer plus facilement les découvertes scientifiques dans la mémoire des hommes*'
(II, 145). His criticism frequently rejects this use of poetry, and here
he seems to have seized on the opportunity to attack it rather in spite
of Barbier's poetry than in direct response to it.

The review closes with the familiar triple movement, insisting that
Barbier's gifts, although misused, are nevertheless those of 'un grand
poète'. In many ways, the passages which actually assess Barbier's
work seem fair and reasoned, and tend to prove this final judgement,
reaching particularly memorable expression in the following pithy
sentence: 'tout a l'air soudain, spontané; le trait vigoureux, à la manière
latine, jaillit sans cesse à travers les défaillances et les maladresses' (II,
144).

Yet is this notice as a whole 'poised and just criticism'?[65] Not only
does it repeat general principles expressed elsewhere, but, apart from
'La Tentation', it makes little mention of those works which are not
'*illustrées* [. . .] par une espèce de vignette politique' (II, 106). Several
poems or passages in the *Iambes*, *Il Pianto* and *Lazare* depict human
suffering, the glories of art and the beauty of the external world, themes
which Baudelaire might have explored more fully. Moreover, although
Barbier's renown was well established, there had been no general
evaluation of his talent for over twenty years, the reviews written in
the 1840s and 1850s analysing specific volumes. Baudelaire could,
therefore, have side-stepped the political and the didactic in Barbier's
poetry, concentrating on motifs more in harmony with his own
aesthetics, much as he did in Hugo's case. Why, then, did he choose
to throw into such sharp relief aspects which he could only condemn?
I think part of the answer lies in the fact that he could thus attack such
believers in 'l'éternel progrès'[66] as Hugo and Du Camp. Barbier represents many of the tendencies evident in Hugo, but while Hugo's
gifts enable him to escape the fate that befell the less talented Barbier,
his example in this regard is clearly pernicious. Finally, Baudelaire is

obviously irritated at the way in which Barbier's first poems, despite their misuse of poetry, have achieved such apparently unshakeable celebrity. Yet, whatever reservations one may have about the article, it does pose with particular cogency the paradox that the force of circumstance and didactic intention can bring a less gifted poet lasting and undisputed glory, while those like Gautier, who remain faithful to the ideal of pure poetry, are rewarded with oblivion.

Pétrus Borel
(*La Revue fantaisiste*, 15 July 1861)

'*Le Beau*', insisted Baudelaire in 1855, '*est toujours bizarre*', adding: 'renversez la proposition, et tâchez de concevoir un *beau banal*!' (11, 578). In Pétrus Borel, however, one finds a writer who not only takes the idea to extremes but turns it inside out, seeming to find beauty nowhere but in the bizarre. Twenty years after the publication of *Madame Putiphar*, he was largely forgotten, or denoted a 'génie manqué', his only fame the dubious celebrity of having his name invoked as a cliché for censure. Yet Baudelaire, at a time when a barrage of projects demanded his attention, chose to write a notice on Borel for the anthology, a notice Crépet himself neither solicited nor approved, witness the 'détail comique' Baudelaire confided to Boyer: 'il croit que je lui ai joué une farce en faisant un Pétrus Borel. Il croit que *Borel* est un bouffon indigne de figurer dans la collection *Crépet*. Quant à la valeur de circonstance, chose à lui inconnue' (*C*11, 46). A year later Crépet was still expressing reservations and in a note written in mid June 1861 Baudelaire remarks with suppressed irritation: 'il me paraît inutile de faire composer Pierre Dupont, Le Vavasseur et Petrus Borel [sic], puisque dans chacune de ces notices il y a des choses choquantes pour vous' (*C*11, 172). A further letter reveals more obvious vexation, with Baudelaire refusing to alter his article, which he insists is excellent (*C*11, 172). Indeed, although it was published in *La Revue fantaisiste* in July 1861, the article did not appear in the anthology, for reasons which J. Crépet admits to be obscure (*AR*, 547).

The motivation for Baudelaire's initial choice and continuing perseverance is complex. In part, as Margaret Gilman suggests, 'it is the particular individual quality, so well defined in this brief article, that attracts Baudelaire':[67] certainly Borel's individuality comes through in his works and in Baudelaire's notice with a pride, intensity and energy not unlike that of Rimbaud. If Baudelaire is able to distil the essence of Borel's character with such assurance, it is partly as a result of personal knowledge. One of his 'premières liaisons littéraires' (1, 784), Ourliac, first introduced him to Borel and J. Crépet points out that the two men could have furthered their acquaintance at the offices of *L'Artiste* in 1844 (*AR*, 548; II, 129). Although Borel seems to have exercised a significant influence over Baudelaire (*AR*, 548),[68] and despite the community of interests and outlook, their relationship appears never to have developed into a close friendship. Nevertheless, Borel is clearly linked in Baudelaire's mind with the 'temps heureux où les littérateurs étaient, les uns pour les autres, une société que les survivants regrettent' (II, 131): he was the acknowledged leader of the *Bousingots*.[69] Baudelaire's literary criticism reveals that since his apparent denunciation in 1851 (II, 34), he had become increasingly interested not only in the mainstream of Romanticism, but also in its offshoots. More importantly, his letter to Boyer shows his awareness of the 'valeur de circonstance': Borel's death, in July 1859, gave the article a topical interest which the publicity-conscious Baudelaire was eager to exploit.

The intensity of the notice also suggests that Baudelaire saw Borel as more than an interesting character and a figure of historical importance: so many of his own principles and preoccupations stud the article that Borel seems cast as an exaggerated image of Baudelaire himself, who must have wondered, at this moment of increasing renown, whether he himself would come to be classed 'un génie manqué'.

External evidence reinforces this interpretation. Baudelaire's review begins with the sardonic remark:

il y a des noms qui deviennent proverbes et adjectifs. Quand un petit journal veut, en 1859, exprimer tout le dégoût et le mépris que lui inspire une poésie ou un roman d'un caractère sombre et outré, il lance le mot: *Pétrus Borel!* et tout est dit. Le jugement est prononcé, l'auteur est foudroyé (II, 153).

The 'petit journal' in question was, I submit, *La Revue anecdotique* – Baudelaire describes it as such in a letter dated 6 May 1857 (*C*I, 399: see note *C*I, 928) – and the writer thus devastated, Baudelaire himself. In the review, his poems are granted 'au moins le mérite de leur bizarrerie' but are dismissed as 'ragoûts romantiques à la Pétrus Borel'.[70] His notice, therefore, is at once self-analysis in the light of this accusation, and a justification both of Borel and of himself. Finally, the article set Baudelaire a particularly stimulating challenge: where the Desbordes-Valmore notice shows him attempting to understand why Sainte-Beuve and other notable critics and poets should so admire a writer about whom he himself had considerable reservations, in this review he supports, against the opposition both of Crépet and of the general public, a writer whose faults he acknowledges but who never-theless moves him deeply. It is, in part, the need to defend Borel and, in part, the regret that he did not fully harness his gift that makes Baudelaire's notice so intense.

Despite the 'conditions si terribles' which Crépet imposed (*C*II, 40) and which seem to have included a severe restriction on length (*C*II, 41), the article is smoothly and logically articulated. After defending his decision to discuss Borel's works despite their reputation among the general public, Baudelaire turns to an examination of Borel's nature and talent, establishes his importance for the development of con-temporary literature, and explains his art as a reflection of historical circumstances, concluding that, despite his failure fully to realize his promise, Borel commands respect not only because of his originality and his will power, but also because of his uncompromising love of literature.

Borel may well be 'une étoile oubliée ou éteinte' (II, 153), but Baudelaire asserts that he at least knows him well enough to speak of him with authority: as so often, in introducing a well-known quotation, he twists the line from *Médée* sufficiently to rejuvenate it. Although the critics who mentioned Borel in the late 1850s were indeed few, Mon-selet's *Lorgnette* claimed that 'il y avait dans les écrits de M. Pétrus Borel mieux et autre chose que ce qu'on a voulu y voir'[71] and *La Revue anecdotique* devoted to him a typically anecdotal but not entirely un-favourable article. Baudelaire's own familiarity with Borel's writing is amply demonstrated by the ease with which he quotes from his works in several articles. Thus, a reference to adultery in the review of *Madame Bovary* provokes a quotation from 'le Lycanthrope d'insurrec-tionnelle mémoire' (II, 54: cf. *AR*, 566 and II, 1123); Dupont's war poems are contrasted with the more stridently bellicose verse of the preface to *Madame Putiphar* (II, 172);[72] and some vitriolic passages denouncing the Belgians are accompanied by a further quotation from the preface (II, 954). It also seems to me that the *Salon de 1859* alludes fleetingly to this passage when the 'Ame de la bourgeoisie' is addressed as a 'brute hyperboréenne des anciens jours' (II, 655: cf. II, 829). This easy familiarity is evident, too, in the anthology notice, where, in a few concise and arresting phrases, Baudelaire succeeds in evoking the atmosphere and tone of Borel's rather verbose studies of evil and misfortune.

Even while defending his decision to discuss Borel, Baudelaire makes known his reservations, partly through the protests of others, partly by referring to the 'bizarres élucubrations du Lycanthrope' and his excessive love of art, an excess the dangers of which are examined in 'L'Ecole païenne'. Here, too, Borel seems to have taken to its extreme limit an ideal Baudelaire both admired and shared.

Borel's reputation among the general public seems to Baudelaire to be based not only on his strangeness and intensity but also on his 'caractère sombre'. When he tries to understand this characteristic, Baudelaire's general preoccupation with initial causes and predestination seems to have been intensified by the opening passages of *Madame Putiphar*.[73] In terms which recall German and English, rather than French, Romanticism, but which are also reminiscent of 'Les Dons des fées', he asks: 'quel méchant esprit se pencha sur son berceau et lui dit: *Je te défends de plaire*?' (II, 153). If Baudelaire's prose poem isolates as the dominant and eternal characteristic of his fairy godmothers 'le caprice' (I, 306), Borel himself asks, with an intensity bordering on hysteria: 'quel caprice a donné à l'un la bosse du meurtre, et à l'autre la bosse de la mansuétude? Si dès la procréation, ce caprice a départi les bonnes et les mauvaises qualités des êtres, il a départi leurs destinées: les déstinées sont donc écrites.'[74] Later in the article Baudelaire describes more precisely the melancholy which appears to have been Borel's share of 'les Dons, les Facultés, les bons Hasards, les Circonstances invincibles' (I, 305). As in his essay on Gautier (II, 125), he distinguishes between 'le ton mélodieux et attendri des regrets' of early Romanticism, and a second phase in which 'la mélancolie prit un accent plus décidé, plus sauvage et plus terrestre' (II, 155).

In his dedication to *Les Paradis artificiels*, Baudelaire refers to the privilege which allows man 'tirer des jouissances nouvelles et subtiles même de la douleur, de la catastrophe et de la fatalité' (I, 400). In *Madame Putiphar* Borel has, on the narrative level, exploited this privilege; from other points of view, however, he has fallen victim to innumerable *guignons* and his talent has frequently been vitiated by 'maladresse', 'heurts' and 'cahots' (II, 154: cf. II, 146).

In a passage reflecting yet again his delight in the *tour de force*, Baudelaire, who concisely and tellingly evokes lengthy and complex scenes, isolates the flashes of genius against which these flaws stand in such sharp contrast. Firstly, he emphasizes the 'talent véritablement épique' of many scenes in *Madame Putiphar*, that tense, extravagant novel in which Borel reinforces, through his political conviction, the gothic themes of sexual frustration, physical and mental cruelty, and inescapable doom. Although the publication of *La Légende des siècles* has perhaps played a part in determining the perspective in which Baudelaire presents *Madame Putiphar*, the epithet 'épique' is fully justified both by the heroic proportions Borel gives to characters and scenes, and by the way in which the protagonists appear as symbols of abstract concepts, incarnations of cruelty, revenge, oppression, devotion or resignation. The reasons dictating Baudelaire's choice of scenes to illustrate Borel's epic gift seem highly personal: thus, his interest in alcoholism and the relation between the alcoholic and the criminal, an interest revealed in poems such as 'Le Vin de l'assassin' and his proposed play *L'Ivrogne*, has no doubt sharpened his reception of 'l'ivrognerie sauvage et septentrionale' of Déborah's father. As with Desbordes-Valmore's poetry, childhood memories would certainly have been reawakened in him by the affectionate relationship between Déborah and her son. Finally, the extent to which Baudelaire admired Borel's depiction of the 'hideurs et [. . .] tortures du cachot' (II, 154) is obvious from the comparison he draws with Maturin's *Melmoth the Wanderer*. The reference may be to Stanhope's imprisonment in the madhouse, but it is more likely to refer to those passages where the monk Monçada describes his torments at the hands of the Spanish Inquisition:[75] Borel's account closely resembles these scenes both in the horror of the details and in the frequent frustration of any hope of escape. The full weight of the comparison can be assessed only when one realizes the esteem in which Baudelaire held Maturin. In particular, Maturin has left his mark on Baudelaire's essay on laughter, which not only contains specific and detailed references to Melmoth (II, 531, 532, 534), but in which the concept of the interrelationship of laughter and evil seems to me to reflect a close and perceptive reading of Maturin's novel. Besides, Baudelaire described *Melmoth* as 'le code du Romantisme' (CII, 461)[76] and he linked Maturin with Poe and Byron as writers who 'ont projeté des rayons splendides, éblouissants, sur le Lucifer latent qui est installé dans tout cœur humain' (II, 168). With equal conviction, Borel has stripped bare the veneer of civilization to reveal man's inherent evil.

Although he does not discuss Borel's collection of verse, *Les Rhapsodies*, Baudelaire chose for inclusion in the anthology the preface in verse to *Madame Putiphar*,[77] in which Borel depicts with singular intensity the battle waged for his soul by the world, the church and death, each concept being personified and described in minute and memorable detail. If this poem, reminiscent in many ways of 'Les Tentations, ou, Eros, Plutus et la Gloire', arouses Baudelaire's enthusiasm, it is because of its 'sonorité éclatante' and its 'couleur presque primitive à force d'intensité'. The strangely contrasting features in Borel's nature, the way in which the intensity of some of the passages in his work is counterbalanced by stylistic awkwardness, and his inability to overcome misfortune, are all related in Baudelaire's eyes to his morbidity, to his love of contradiction merely for the sake of contradiction, and his readiness 'remonter tous les courants' without being fully aware of what such opposition demands. This predilection could be illustrated by Passereau's abrupt change of character from naive, gentle lover to sardonic, violent murderer, while Borel's eagerness to oppose convention is clear from his study of prejudice and bigotry in 'Dina la belle juive'. Once again, Borel appears as an exaggerated image of Baudelaire's own tendencies: accused in the contemporary press of morbidity, Baudelaire too drew considerable stimulation from shock effects and contrasts.

Since, like his contemporaries, Baudelaire enjoys revealing the human side of a writer, he illustrates Borel's rebellious nature through his handwriting. The attention he paid to such material details is evident from his references to Balzac's galley proofs (II, 17) and to the beauty of Gautier's scripts (II, 118), but it is also possible that his interest was heightened by Poe's amusing articles on autography. Poe, indeed, insists that the assertion that 'a strong analogy *does* generally and naturally exist between every man's chirography and character will be denied by none but the unreflecting'.[78] Not only does the Borel manuscript in the Nadar collection held by the Bibliothèque nationale confirm Baudelaire's description, but the deliberately startling comparison between his letters and soldiers toppling under grapeshot is singularly appropriate to the violent and bloody universe of *Champavert* and *Madame Putiphar*.

In referring to Borel's 'travail si douloureux', to his *ratures* and *repentirs*, Baudelaire tightens the comparison between writer and reviewer, since in January 1859 he described himself as 'un cerveau qui n'accouche qu'avec le forceps' (*C*I, 537), a lament frequently voiced in his correspondence. Moreover, Borel's attempts to recall a word's derivation through its spelling,[79] and the wearisome battles with his printer that must have ensued, arouse a 'sympathique douleur' in Baudelaire, who plays on resonances made possible by suggesting both the contemporary and the etymological meanings of a word and who suffered much from the carelessness and stupidity of proof-readers and printers whose standards fell far short of his own.

Baudelaire asserts that although Borel is a secondary figure he nevertheless deserves close attention not only because his work, despite its flaws, does occasionally strike 'une note éclatante et juste' (II, 155), but also because he has played an important role in literary history. For him, Borel represents the most strident expression of the alliance between Romanticism and 'un républicanisme misanthropique'. Asselineau sees Borel in a similar light: 'Pétrus Borel marque une phase ou plutôt une déviation du romantisme, produite par l'invasion de la politique dans la littérature, après la révolution de Juillet. [...] Le bousingot transporta dans la vie politique le style et les allures de l'école romantique.'[80] Borel himself underlined the almost anti-human nature of his Republicanism in the preface to *Les Rhapsodies*: 'je suis républicain comme l'entendrait un loup-cervier: mon républicanisme, c'est de la lycanthropie!'[81]

The exaggerated rebellion of Borel's work illustrates that aspect that Crépet discounted: the shaping influence of such ephemeral matters as circumstance and prevailing modes of thought.[82] *Madame Putiphar*, with its exaggerated language and over-rich colours, represents an explosive revolt against the repressively respectable ethos of the *juste milieu* that the July Monarchy promoted, an ethos Balzac brings brilliantly alive in *Les Parents pauvres* and particularly in his character Crevel. Typical exponents of this ethos, in Baudelaire's eyes, are Delacroix's *bête noire* Delaroche, whose work he condemns in the *Salon de 1859* as 'un travail purement manuel' (II, 626), and the sentimental but highly popular poet Casimir Delavigne, whom Baudelaire satirized in a poem written in collaboration with Le Vavasseur (I, 213; I, 1242–3). In stark contrast with the sentimental, carefully controlled emotionalism of poets and artists such as these, Borel's work is the turbulent lava of a volcanic outburst against kings and bourgeois alike. Yet the revolt, Baudelaire contends, is not purely negative: it also reflects a very positive sympathy with 'tout ce qui en art représentait l'excès dans la couleur et dans la forme, pour tout ce qui était à la fois intense, pessimiste et byronien' (II, 155). The same hatred of the bourgeois majority colours Borel's Republicanism in which Baudelaire, in a phrase more ironic than paradoxical, perceives 'une haine aristocratique sans limites'. This brief passage is yet another example of how Baudelaire can characterize with startling brevity and preciseness the atmosphere of a particular period.

Baudelaire's forceful assertion of the 'valeur de circonstance' is followed by his truculent admission, doubtless made with Crépet's strictures in mind, that he may well appear ridiculous in expressing sympathy with a novelist in whom he detects genius nipped in the bud and ambition foiled by clumsiness and misfortune. For Baudelaire, Borel's work is illuminated by flares of real genius but overshadowed by an excessive love of the bizarre, and an inability to develop his 'ébauches minutieuses' into a consistently successful work of art.[83] Yet, characteristically, Baudelaire follows these reservations with praise. On the one hand he claims that Borel possesses that rare gift, 'une couleur à lui, une saveur *sui generis*'. This is certainly true, for Borel's best work is instantly identifiable and despite its thematic similarity to other examples of the darker side of Romanticism, its occasional flashes of sardonic humour and self-parody assure it of originality. Furthermore, his work reveals a quality which Baudelaire greatly values and which he highlights in those writers he most admires: 'le charme de la volonté' (II, 156). On the other hand, Borel's uncompromising love of beauty and art contrasts sharply with the attitude of the 'jolis et souples écrivains tout prêts à vendre la Muse pour le champ du potier' (II, 156). The intensity of Baudelaire's feelings, the explosive mixture of admiration and reservation, is suggested not only by the biblical allusion but also by the violence of his language: Borel, he claims, 'aimait férocement les lettres'. In his essay on Wagner, which dates from this same prolific period, Baudelaire singled out as 'les principales caractéristiques' of genius 'tout ce qu'impliquent les mots: *volonté, désir, concentration, intensité nerveuse, explosion*' (II, 807): all these are qualities Baudelaire perceives in Borel, yet, the notice implies, it is the very ferocity with which they manifest themselves that prevents them from achieving perfection.

In reviewing the poetry of Desbordes-Valmore, Baudelaire seems to have felt the need to justify his deeply personal response to her: with Borel, he is concerned above all with defending his reaction against the scepticism of the public. The notice underlines the many characteristics Baudelaire shares with Borel: their uncompromising love of art, their revolt against the current intellectual climate, the intensity of their works. Indeed, one cannot help admiring how much of Borel's nature and art Baudelaire manages to express and convey in this brief review, how energetically he recreates Borel's style, and how wide-ranging are the elements on which he touches, his mind springing from tiny points of detail to questions dealing with the effect on literature of the political climate. Finally, he has clearly fulfilled the task he set himself in the review of the Exposition universelle de 1855: 'la critique doit chercher plutôt à pénétrer intimement le tempérament de chaque artiste et les mobiles qui le font agir qu'à analyser, à raconter chaque œuvre minutieusement' (II, 583).

Théodore de Banville
(La Revue fantaisiste, 1 August 1861)

While Borel epitomized the artist oppressed by bad luck whose work explores and intensifies the darker side of existence, Banville leapt into fame with apparently little effort, seizing the public's attention by a combination of technical virtuosity and fundamental optimism. Baudelaire's response to both is immediate, but not unalloyed. Banville posed the challenge of a particularly skilful writer whose fame depended on presenting subjects which, unlike those that kindle Baudelaire's own creativity, are rarely disturbing or complex. That Baudelaire had for some time been eager to meet this challenge is suggested by his notes for *Le Hibou philosophe*, where Banville's name is bracketed with 'l'école païenne' (II, 51). Nevertheless, as early as 1845 a sonnet inspired by him, with its line:

Et cet air de maîtrise et ce beau nonchaloir (I, 208)

anticipates the notice in conveying an ambivalent blend of admiration, envy and reservations, and in underlining the same combination of temperament held in check by technical skill. A letter written in 1853 designates him with similar ambiguity as 'le poète le plus habile de la jeune école nouvelle, à ce point qu'il réduit l'art de la poésie à de purs procédés mécaniques, et qu'il peut enseigner à devenir poète en vingt-cinq leçons' (*CI*, 209: cf. I, 183). A letter to Poulet-Malassis further illustrates the envy aroused in Baudelaire by Banville's expressive resources: 'je m'escrime contre une trentaine de vers insuffisants, désagréables, mal faits, mal rimants. Croyez-vous donc que j'aie la souplesse de Banville?' (*CI*, 399). An unfinished study casts a different light on Banville, to whom Baudelaire planned to refer in undermining Champfleury's concept of Realism: 'tout bon poète fut toujours *réaliste*', he asserts, adding: 'équation entre l'impression et l'expression. Sincérité. Prendre Banville pour exemple' (II, 58).

Close friends from 1842 to 1846, separated to some extent by their rivalry for Marie Daubrun, Baudelaire and Banville seem to have remained on friendly terms throughout most of their adult lives, with one of Baudelaire's last letters emphatically excepting Banville from the 'racaille moderne' (*CII*, 611).[84] It is hardly surprising, therefore, that Baudelaire should choose to review Banville's poetry, although it is possible that the article was not commissioned by Crépet (*AR*, 552). The idea may have crystallized as a result of Asselineau's assessment of *Odelettes* in 1856: this article contains so many ideas held by Baudelaire and expresses them in images so like his own, that one suspects he may have collaborated on it, just as he worked on the preface to *La Double Vie*. The ideas and language of the anthology notice, however, are very much those of the fruitful period between 1858 and 1860.

One of his most carefully constructed, Baudelaire's notice reflects not only a desire for orderly exposition, but also an ability to flesh out the bones of an outline, so that each topic arises smoothly and naturally from the preceding one, neither unprepared nor laboured. It opens with a survey of Banville's development, analysing characteristics

which mark the collections both of youth and of maturity, and highlighting those aspects which reveal originality and set the poet apart
from his contemporaries. Baudelaire then turns to an analysis of what
is *sui generis* in Banville's poetry, carefully explaining and justifying his
critical approach. Following the example of Sainte-Beuve, he suggests
that a writer's obsession can be discovered by studying those words
he uses most frequently. For Banville, Baudelaire picks the word *lyre*.
The assumption that his poetry is essentially lyrical leads to a discussion
of the language best suited to conveying that mode, and of the ways
in which Banville observes and recreates the world. There follows a
concise and evocative survey of contemporary literature, its mood and
its forms of expression, highlighting the sharp contrast between the
art of most writers and that of Banville. Baudelaire, neither openly
approving nor unequivocally condemning, simply claims that Banville,
unlike those who have drawn their inspiration from a Romantic or a
Satanic view of existence, has attained a noble form of Classicism.

From the outset, Baudelaire seizes his readers' attention with an
arresting, deceptively simple opening sentence: 'Théodore de Banville
fut célèbre tout jeune' (II, 162). Not only does the stress placed on this
'étonnante précocité' strike a note of envy which continues to resound
throughout the article, but it also shows Baudelaire seeking out yet
again the reasons behind a poet's fame.[85] Banville's early success was
thrown into sharp relief by other critics: Labitte remarked that 'un
pareil début indique une singulière précocité de facture', Champfleury
described *Les Cariatides* as 'un volume plein de jeunesse et de sève, qui,
malgré des pastiches ingénieux, était bien osé par certain côté' while
Prarond writes less generously that 'la jeunesse perce partout dans ce
volume [. . .] depuis le style aventureux, brave, ne doutant de rien,
mais encore divers et mal arrêté, jusqu'à la mêlée confuse des idées qui
crient, qui se combattent et qui se nuisent'.[86] Yet Baudelaire alone
found a means of condensing his surprise and envy into so pithy an
opening sentence.

The reasons for Banville's early celebrity, Baudelaire hints, are
partly extra-literary, depending on the astonishment caused by such
precocity, and partly circumstantial, since his leap to fame was assisted
by the existence, at that time, of an 'élite d'hommes chargés de façonner
l'opinion des autres' (II, 162). Although the *jadis/aujourd'hui* antithesis
was a contemporary cliché, Baudelaire does seem to have been particularly sensitive to the contrast, for his critical articles are peppered
with such references and reflect an intense personal regret for the
irretrievable past.[87]

The language of this attack on present-day conditions recalls several of the prose poems: Paris is a 'tohu-bohu, un capharnaüm,[88] une Babel' inhabited by people who are 'peu délicats sur les manières de tuer le temps' (II, 162), while in 'Un Plaisant' it is 'ce tohu-bohu et [. . .] ce vacarme' and the prose poem portrays in tones of bitter cynicism a 'magnifique imbécile' (I, 279) and one of the ways in which he attempts 'tuer le temps'. There are parallels, too, with the tone and imagery of 'A une heure du matin' and 'Le Galant Tireur', just as the description of Parisian society, as it was in the days when a well-informed élite moulded public opinion, echoes the lament expressed in the article on Hugo (II, 131).

Finally, Baudelaire suggests a third reason for Banville's success: he appears as 'un de ces esprits marqués, pour qui la poésie est la langue la plus facile à parler' (II, 162). This assertion not only introduces Banville's facility, a theme repeated throughout the notice, but also presents him in sharp opposition to the ill-starred Poe and Borel. It is impossible not to see behind this description, moreover, a Baudelaire who waited until he had attained a high degree of maturity before he published his work, and for whom poetry was not a question of facility but of dogged will power, a Baudelaire faced with an audience bereft even of literary interest, let alone of poetic insight.

In seeking to distinguish, against a constantly suggested background of youthful imitation, that which is *sui generis* in *Les Cariatides*, Baudelaire emphasizes the obvious qualities of *éclat, abondance* and *variété*, but stresses above all the characteristic which marks the later work, 'la certitude dans l'expression lyrique', this emphasis preparing the subsequent evocation of Banville's lyricism. Many other critics admired the variety and brilliance of the early poems, Paul de Mantz, for example, writing: '[lorsqu'on] ferme les *Cariatides* et les *Stalactites* on reste en proie à un long éblouissement, tourbillonnantes visions où s'emmêlent toutes les couleurs et toutes les formes, musiques confuses où l'on croit entendre chanter, avec tous les rythmes, toutes les idées'.[89]

Banville's second volume, *Les Stalactites*, seems to Baudelaire to have achieved greater clarity by imposing stricter control over the natural explosion of lyrical inspiration. As in the essay on Gautier (II, 118), he admires the virtuoso use of colour and contour, but tempers his praise, presenting *Les Stalactites* less as intrinsically valuable than as a necessary phase in Banville's poetic development, a conscious effort to restrain his 'primitive faculté d'expansion' (II, 163).

Just as *Les Stalactites* has more importance for the poet's development than for its intrinsic value, so the plays and verse published before *Le Sang de la coupe* are described merely as providing 'mille gymnastiques que les vrais amoureux de la Muse peuvent seuls apprécier à leur juste valeur' (II, 163): probably Baudelaire is thinking above all of *Odelettes* and *Odes funambulesques*, with their daring experiments in form and rhythm. On several occasions, he applies the word *gymnastique* to art and literature, and, although its metaphorical use was fairly common, he no doubt delighted in the simultaneous evocation of both the physical and the intellectual meanings.[90] Other contemporary critics also saw Banville's poetry as a series of *tours de force*. Thierry's review of *Odelettes*, for example, spoke of it as 'le jeu d'un poète qui sait admirablement son art, qui en recherche les curiosités, qui en complique les difficultés à dessein et qui s'en tire d'une façon supérieure'.[91] For Jules Bernard, Banville was 'un maître ès-langue française, délicat, un peu chat, qui badine et jongle avec cette admirable prosodie où les initiés seuls ont vu clair'.[92] The antagonistic Francisque Sarcey twisted this judgement, demoting Banville to a mere 'jongleur de la poésie française', while Janin – inconsistently, given his own tendencies – lamented that 'un si bel esprit sacrifie à chaque instant au tour de force'.[93] It was, perhaps, attitudes such as these that lead Baudelaire to insist that 'les vrais amoureux de la Muse' alone can appreciate the importance of these technical exercises.

Baudelaire finds in Banville's mature style a perfect balance between 'l'exubérance de sa nature primitive et l'expérience de sa maturité' (II, 163). In comparing with Ronsard's verse the boldness, elasticity and breadth of poems such as 'Vous en qui je salue une nouvelle aurore' Baudelaire is once again following common practice; Sainte-Beuve, Desnoyers, Janin, and later Des Essarts are among many who responded to Banville's own claim in this poem:

> Comme aujourd'hui rêveur près de quelque fontaine
> Je redemande en vain
> Le secret des amours de Marie et d'Hélène
> A mon maître divin,
>
> Vous redirez aussi les grâces d'Aurélie
> Aux oiseaux de Cypris,
> Au rossignol des bois, à la rose pâlie,
> Au bleu myosotis![94]

The lines seem to attract Baudelaire's attention both for their joy and pride – these are qualities to which he returns in the second half of the article – and for their confident claim to lasting celebrity, a claim he himself makes implicitly in many poems and explicitly in 'Je te donne ces vers'. In addition, the vision evoked, combined with the phrases 'une nouvelle aurore' and 'bataillons sacrés' may well have recalled the days when utopian dreams of a reformed and glorious society seemed within reach.

Having suggested the way in which Banville's talent developed, Baudelaire turns to the unifying thread, the 'charme mystérieux' which Banville, according to Baudelaire, is fully conscious of possessing and which he has, through an effort of will, made an essential element of his poetry. As so often, Baudelaire states with clarity and modesty the aims of his critical approach: not only does he propose to describe this charm in so far as a critic can pin down so elusive a quality, but he also wants to seek out its origins.

Two statements serve to orient the analysis. The first, a self-quotation, claims that Banville's poetry represents those hours when life is radiant with happiness, when one enjoys the sensation of existing and is capable of a heightened comprehension of that existence. Similarly, Baudelaire underlined the joy which characterizes the work of two other writers who seized popularity, Balzac and Dupont (11, 34), and, in searching for 'quelque formule qui exprime la *spécialité* d'Eugène Delacroix' (11, 636), he concluded that Delacroix 'peint surtout l'*âme* dans ses belles heures' (11, 637). Prarond, too, wrote of *Les Stalactites* that Banville 'a trouvé son livre plein d'images grasses de volupté et débordant à toutes les pages de joie, de bien-être et de santé, et il en fait, dans la préface, quelque chose comme le tableau prophétique de M. Papety, le peintre phalenstérien, [...] *Un rêve de bonheur*'.[95] And Lecomte, reviewing *Les Odelettes*, exclaimed: 'bénissons donc la poésie, qui, en ces temps éperdus, dévorés, frénétiques, avides, permet à quelques bons jeunes gens [...] de rêver et d'être heureux, dans le dédain ou l'oubli de tout ce qui passionne cette société industrielle et financière, en marge de laquelle ils savent et peuvent insouciamment vivre!'[96] Secondly, Baudelaire paraphrases Sainte-Beuve's adage that the word which keeps recurring in a poet's work reflects his principal preoccupation:[97] in accepting the challenge, Baudelaire stresses that this word should reflect both natural tendencies and a conscious decision, a combination reinforcing his earlier reference to temperament and experience, and recalling his frequent demands for art to unite the expression of the artist's individuality with will power and the fruits of experience. The word Baudelaire selects is one which conveys a multitude of meanings, while suggesting a degree of conventionality: *lyre*. Similarly, Mallarmé was to write: 'Banville [...] n'est pas quelqu'un, mais le son même de la lyre'.[98] In 1857, however, Habans had claimed of Banville that 'il a confondu le son avec l'idée, le vêtement avec le corps, la fantaisie outrée avec la richesse. Aussi est-il resté non pas lyrique mais descriptif sans trêve ni merci.'[99]

Perhaps Baudelaire has been guilty of manipulation, for although *lyre* appears frequently in Banville's poetry, *étoile*, *rose* and *aimer* are also common: none, however, offers so rich a field for conjecture.[100] *Lyre*, after all, has the advantage of suggesting neither an action, nor a concrete object, but a state of mind, one in which Baudelaire was particularly interested: 'cet état presque surnaturel, cette intensité de vie ou l'âme *chante*, où elle est *contrainte de chanter*' (II, 164). The sensation of expansion, of upward movement to a sphere in which the whole being is filled with light and capable of understanding all that surrounds it, is frequently described in poems and prose passages where Baudelaire attempts to recapture the ecstasy of the 'beaux jours de l'esprit': in 'Elévation' he considers 'heureux celui qui peut d'une aile vigoureuse / S'élancer vers les champs lumineux et sereins' (I, 10); in listening to Wagner's music he conceives 'pleinement l'idée d'une âme se mouvant dans un milieu lumineux, d'une extase *faite de volupté et de connaissance*, et planant au-dessus et bien loin du monde naturel' (II, 785); and in the opening paragraph of the 'Poème du hachisch', he describes those rare days when 'le monde extérieur s'offre à [l'homme] avec un relief puissant, une netteté de contours, une richesse de couleurs admirables' (I, 401). Finally, in 'Fusées', he refers to states of mind in which 'la profondeur de la vie se révèle tout entière dans le spectacle, si ordinaire qu'il soit, qu'on a sous les yeux. Il en devient le symbole' (I, 659). In all these cases, the emotion combines an intense delight in life with a deep comprehension of existence, recalling the earlier dichotomy of *penser* and *vivre* (II, 163).

Yet, even in his description of the 'manière lyrique de sentir', Baudelaire introduces the darker side of experience, intensifying the impression of happiness but also underlining its fragility: 'les hommes les plus disgraciés de la nature, ceux à qui la fortune donne le moins de loisir, ont connu quelquefois ces sortes d'impressions, si riches que l'âme en est comme illuminée, si vives qu'elle en est comme soulevée' (II, 164).

To recapture such moments through poetry the poet must create a 'monde lyrique', a world best conveyed by a language of great vitality, a language of hyperbole and apostrophe. These devices abound in Banville's work; the poem Baudelaire quotes, for example, contains such apostrophes as 'vous, poëtes' and 'vous [. . .] mes fils' and hyperbole such as 'elle ravit d'amour l'azur de la fontaine / Et l'escarboucle des cieux'.[101] In recreating the moments of joy and understanding the lyric mode must seek not analysis but synthesis, the sudden, immediate response. The possibility of a synthetic approach to art has clearly grown increasingly important to Baudelaire, since his essay on Gautier (II, 124). His review of *Tannhäuser*, moreover, portrays Wagner as considering 'l'art dramatique [. . .] comme l'art par excellence, le plus synthétique et le plus parfait' (II, 782). Indeed, it is precisely the synthetic qualities of lyric poetry which encourage the use of myth and allegory, symbols which are instantly recognizable: unlike the attack on 'L'Ecole païenne', therefore, the anthology notice attempts to understand and justify, rather than condemn, the introduction of mythological figures into modern lyric poetry.[102] Perhaps Hugo's *Légende des siècles* encouraged this change in Baudelaire's attitude to myth: in his study on Hugo he likened legend, myth and fable to 'des concentrations de vie nationale, [. . .] des réservoirs profonds où dorment le sang et les larmes des peuples' (II, 140). On many occasions and notably in 'Le Cygne' (1860), which Baudelaire dedicates to Hugo, he himself draws on mythology as a 'dictionnaire d'hiéroglyphes vivants, hiéroglyphes connus de tout le monde' (II, 165). Finally, the use of myth, by giving a sense of comparison across space and time, suggests the possibility of a harmonious pattern to existence, a sense of order perceptible in moments of joyous insight.

To linguistic hyperbole and the concentration of human experience in myth, the lyric mode adds an intensification of earthly beauty and joy: in Banville's poetry, woman is granted 'un genre de beauté tel que l'esprit ne peut le concevoir que comme existant dans un monde supérieur' (II, 165). Banville is seen as achieving this hyperbolic beauty partly by comparing his heroines to famous women whose beauty has been universally celebrated, partly by speaking of their eyes as precious stones and partly by describing them as having '*têtes d'enfants*', an analogy drawn in 'Vous en qui je salue une nouvelle aurore':

> Cette tête ingénue et ce corps de Déesse,
>   Ensemble harmonieux,
> Lui donnent l'éternelle et sereine jeunesse
>   Des enfants et des Dieux.[103]

There can be little doubt that what has drawn Baudelaire's attention to these elements is not so much the frequency with which Banville returns to them, as their affinity with his own ideals. Yet, when Baudelaire himself uses such devices, it is to highlight the ambiguity of happiness and of woman: thus his poem 'Le Serpent qui danse', which uses the expression 'ta tête d'enfant', contains the stanza:

> Tes yeux, où rien ne se révèle
>   De doux ni d'amer,
> Sont deux bijoux froids où se mêle
>   L'or avec le fer (I, 30),

while in the preceding sonnet Baudelaire writes:

> Ses yeux polis sont faits de minéraux charmants,
> Et dans cette nature étrange et symbolique
> Où l'ange inviolé se mêle au sphinx antique,
>
> Où tout n'est qu'or, acier, lumière et diamants,
> Resplendit à jamais, comme un astre inutile,
> La froide majesté de la femme stérile (1, 29).

Similarly, not only do such prose poems as 'Les Veuves' throw into sharp relief the egotism of children (1, 294), but the anthology notice itself quietly casts doubt on Banville's belief that 'le plus beau des visages humains est celui dont l'usage de la vie, passion, colère, péché, angoisse, souci, n'a jamais terni la clarté ni ridé la surface' (11, 165: cf. 1, 657). Although there is a side of Baudelaire's character which can respond to such impassivity – beauty in *Les Fleurs du mal* neither laughs nor cries – his description in 'Fusées' of 'une belle tête d'homme' combines 'quelque chose d'ardent et de triste, – des besoins spirituels, des ambitions ténébreusement refoulées, – l'idée d'une puissance grondante, et sans emploi [...] et enfin (pour que j'aie le courage d'avouer jusqu'à quel point je me sens moderne en esthétique), *le Malheur*' (1, 657). In addition, Baudelaire introduces Banville's image of himself 'vêtu de pourpre en d'éternelles fêtes' by revealing the other side of the coin, emphasizing the poet's struggle to attain perfection in a world that mocks his ideals. As in earlier articles, the concentration of tiny details, such as the description of the poet 'barbouillant une page blanche d'horribles petits signes noirs' (11, 166), strikes an intensely personal note, while the expression 'se battant contre la phrase rebelle' contrasts starkly with Banville's apparent joyous facility. Finally, when Baudelaire points out that Banville avoids mentioning the poet's 'chambre pauvre, triste ou en désordre' (11, 166), one thinks of his own prose poem, 'La Chambre double', with its harsh discordant description of 'ce taudis, ce séjour de l'éternel ennui' (1, 281), in which the poet is condemned to survive. Yet, although he himself is intensely aware of both sides, Baudelaire does not reject Banville's vision. Banville's poetry, after all, represents 'la vraie *réalité*, c'est-à-dire sa propre nature'. This tolerant acceptance of the temperament and sensitivity of other poets sets Baudelaire far apart from the great majority of contemporary critics.

Despite the differences between the two poets, Banville's '*déclaration des droits* du poète' finds a parallel in Baudelaire's 'Bénédiction':

> 'Je sais que vous gardez une place au Poète
> Dans les rangs bienheureux des saintes Légions,

> Et que vous l'invitez à l'éternelle fête
> Des Trônes, des Vertus, des Dominations' (I, 9).

However, whereas Baudelaire can conceive of this state as being reached only after purification through grief and suffering, Banville's poet seems to achieve bliss after a life of joyful serenity.

But can the lyric poet never evoke 'le courant de la vie ambiante' (II, 166), can he never lay bare 'la grotesquerie perpétuelle de la bête humaine, la nauséabonde niaiserie de la femme' (II, 167)? Baudelaire insists not only that he can, but that 'de la laideur et de la sottise il fera naître un nouveau genre d'enchantements' (II, 167). Similarly, he asserts of Gautier that 'quand un objet grotesque ou hideux s'est offert à ses yeux, il a su encore en extraire une mystérieuse et symbolique beauté!' (II, 152). There is, of course, a further parallel with Baudelaire's own desire 'extraire la *beauté* du Mal' (I, 181). Yet, unlike Barbier's satire, which, when it points out the folly and stupidity of contemporary man, 'ressemble [. . .] à une grimace' (II, 144), the *bouffonnerie* of the lyric poet is an 'explosion de gaieté, innocente à force d'être carnavalesque'.[104] In a preface to *Odes funambulesques*, a second edition of which was published in 1859, Banville claimed that what the public sought was:

> la chanson bouffonne et la chanson lyrique. Lyrique parce qu'on mourra de dégoût si l'on ne prend pas, de ci de là, un grand bain d'azur, et si l'on ne peut quelquefois pour se consoler de tant de médiocrités 'rouler échevelés dans les étoiles', bouffonne . . . tout simplement, mon Dieu! parce qu'il se passe autour de nous des choses très-drôles.[105]

Obviously Banville's idea of buffoonery offers far less a contrast to the lyrical than might have been expected. It remains firmly rooted within safe limits, avoiding the bitter edge and chilling irony of Baudelaire's own contrasts. That Baudelaire was sharply aware of this is revealed in the bantering tone of the paragraph in which he claims that 'même dans la poésie idéale, la Muse peut, sans déroger frayer avec les vivants' (II, 167), an allusion to 'La Malédiction de Cypris'. The sardonic note Baudelaire strikes in this passage depends on the introduction of such phrases as 'un piquant, comme on disait autrefois' with its suggestion of the old-fashioned and the frivolous. Clearly ironic in intent is the sentence: 'Phèdre en paniers a ravi les esprits les plus délicats de l'Europe' where the words 'ravi' and 'délicats' suggest once again a degree of superficiality, a pleasure which is far from intellectual. Finally, Baudelaire poses two questions which, without being dogmatic, nevertheless raise doubts: 'D'où tirez-vous le soupçon que cet *anachronisme* est une infraction aux règles que le poète s'est imposées, à ce que nous pouvons appeler ses *convictions* lyriques? Car peut-on commettre un anachronisme dans l'éternel?' (ii, 167).[106]

Despite his reservations, Baudelaire insists that Banville is 'un original de l'espèce la plus élevée' who stands out against contemporary tendencies in two essential ways. Firstly, whereas he is 'naturellement et volontairement lyrique' – Baudelaire stresses once again that this is a result both of inclination and of determination – the best examples of modern poetry combine 'le génie plastique, le sens philosophique, l'enthousiasme lyrique, l'esprit humoristique'. Nonetheless there is a certain ambiguity when Banville is described as using the time-worn means of poetic expression, 'les trouvant sans doute tout à fait suffisants et parfaitement adaptés à son but' (ii, 168): the 'sans doute' immediately makes the reader both wonder if they are sufficient and question the validity of Banville's aims in a modern world. As so often, therefore, Baudelaire indicates his doubts in subtle but unmistakable undertones.

Banville is seen, too, as standing out against his contemporaries in his choice of theme, since he uses poetry, as did poets before the Romantics, to impart dreams of happiness and light to a world sunk in misery and darkness. The potential irony here is more overt, since those who, in music, prose and poetry, have best succeeded in evoking the 'mondes de mélancolie et de désespoir incurable' and who have 'projeté des rayons splendides, éblouissants, sur le Lucifer latent qui est installé dans tout cœur humain' (ii, 168) are major stars in Baudelaire's constellation of genius: Beethoven, Maturin, Byron and Poe. Moreover, the 'tendance essentiellement démoniaque' that Baudelaire detects in modern art is very obviously present in his own work. A particularly physical image further indicates the intensity of his reaction: the picture of 'le genre humain' artificially fattened in the devil's farm-yard to produce 'une nourriture plus succulente' was also sketched in his diary (i, 698), suggesting that he may have seized on the Banville notice as an opportunity to develop an apt image which brought him sardonic delight. In insisting that Banville 'refuse de se pencher sur ces marécages de sang' (ii, 168), Baudelaire recalls, perhaps unconsciously, 'Les Phares', for, if Delacroix's art represents 'l'*âme* dans ses belles heures' (ii, 637), it also evokes a 'lac de sang hanté des mauvais anges' (i, 14). Indeed, all the artists Baudelaire mentions are sensitive to both sides, presenting dreams of delight as well as visions of evil: Beethoven in, for example, his sixth and ninth symphonies, Poe in such tales of fragile joy as 'Eléonora', Maturin in the scenes where Immalee lives alone on her tropical island, Byron in his poems of reciprocated love. Their duality, then, serves to throw into sharper relief Banville's one-sidedness.[107]

Since it is a 'retour très volontaire vers l'état paradisiaque',[108] Banville's verse avoids not only 'les dissonances', 'les discordances des musiques du sabbat' – a reference, perhaps, to the *Symphonie fantastique* of Berlioz, whose reaction to Wagner Baudelaire discusses in his review of *Tannhäuser* – but also 'les glapissements de l'ironie, cette vengeance du vaincu', an expression which returns to the animal imagery of the preceding paragraph and recalls 'L'Héautontimorouménos':

> Ne suis-je pas un faux accord
> Dans la divine symphonie,
> Grâce à la vorace Ironie
> Qui me secoue et qui me mord? (I, 78).

Nevertheless, Baudelaire is being only partly ironic when he praises the boldness and courage with which Banville has sung 'la bonté des dieux' (II, 168–9) in counterpoint to the general 'concert d'imprécations' (see *AR*, 554): in the same way he admires in the *Salon de 1859* Baron's 'Hôtellerie de Saint-Luc': 'quand, au sortir d'un taudis, sale et mal éclairé, un homme se trouve tout d'un coup transporté dans un appartement propre, orné de meubles ingénieux et revêtu de couleurs caressantes, il sent son esprit s'illuminer et ses fibres s'apprêter aux choses du bonheur' (II, 646). Nevertheless he prefaces this evocation with the warning: 'il y a une fatalité dans les enfants de cette école victorieuse. Le romantisme est une grâce, céleste ou infernale, à qui nous devons des stigmates éternels' (II, 645). Baudelaire's attitude towards such dreams of happiness remained ambivalent.

To what extent, one wonders, are the terms *satanique*, *romantique* and *classique* simply being used in this notice as weapons in the contemporary argument? Does Baudelaire really see Banville as 'un parfait *classique*'? To some extent, no doubt, the description is introduced to shock his readers, since Banville was generally presented as a *petit romantique*,[109] but Baudelaire may also have been responding to Sainte-Beuve's claim that 'c'est par une sorte d'abus, mais qui avait sa raison, que l'on a compris encore sous le nom de romantiques les poëtes [. . .] qui sont amateurs de la beauté presque grecque et qui, par là même, sembleraient plutôt classiques'.[110]

Baudelaire's article is not only an interesting early example of thematic criticism, but a masterly proof of the way in which, by revealing qualities, he can also suggest shortcomings: through the subtle use of undertones he can both explain Banville's techniques and highlight his successes, and still raise in the reader's mind doubts which that reader must resolve for himself. Clearly he appreciates Banville's technical skill, envies his fluency and enjoys his visions of an ideal world: nevertheless, although he gives Banville full – perhaps even excessive – praise for these qualities, he subtly suggests that this vision is incomplete and over-simple, since it omits the suffering essential to a mature comprehension of the ideal. While Borel evoked only 'l'horreur de la vie', Banville ignored all but 'l'extase de la vie': for Baudelaire, of course, art must reflect both the ecstasy and the horror.

Leconte de Lisle
(*La Revue fantaisiste*, 15 August 1861)

On 23 February 1860 Baudelaire wrote to encourage the poet Soulary: 'Nous ne sommes, ni vous ni moi, assez *bêtes* pour mériter le suffrage universel. Il y a deux autres hommes, admirablement doués, qui sont dans ce cas: M. Théophile Gautier et M. Leconte de Lisle' (*C*i, 680). Baudelaire's letters contain two further admiring references to Leconte de Lisle:[111] he described him as a creator of '*littérature pure*' (*C*ii, 225), and included him in the select band of those who were not to be confused with the 'racaille moderne' (*C*ii, 611). The challenge he faced in this review, therefore, was once again to account for the discrepancy between his own admiration for much of Leconte de Lisle's work, and the general public's antipathy or indifference.

Baudelaire appears to have completed his notice on Leconte de Lisle by 15 December 1859 (*C*i, 635): certainly its style and imagery recall that exceptionally fruitful year. By that time he could have read *Poèmes antiques* (1852), *Poèmes et Poésies* (1855) and the volume entitled *Poésies complètes* (1858) which combined the previous collections with his 'Poésies nouvelles'. Many of the latter were to reappear in *Poésies barbares* (1862). Moreover, most of the additional *Poésies barbares* had been published in the *Revue contemporaine* or the *Revue européenne* before the end of 1859.[112] Nevertheless, it seems likely that the work Baudelaire had specifically in mind was *Poésies complètes*, since he tempers one of his conclusions with the remark: 'autant qu'on en peut juger par son recueil le plus complet' (ii, 178).

As so often, Baudelaire's central focus here is the qualities which distinguish Leconte de Lisle from other artists and explain his reception by the public. For Baudelaire, the element that is *sui generis* in Leconte de Lisle's verse is determined by 'un sentiment d'aristocratie intellectuelle' (ii, 177). His search for beauty provides a second focus, which Baudelaire examines firstly through comparison and contrast with other writers, and secondly through a study of Leconte de Lisle's poetic development. Simple and lucid, the article's structure is strengthened by the repetition of terms connected with strength, tranquillity, meditation and beauty.

Like those on Desbordes-Valmore, Borel and Moreau, the notice opens on a conversational note of general inquiry, Leconte de Lisle serving as a counter-example to the supposition that Creoles bring to literature nothing of originality and force. Although the charge had become a contemporary cliché,[113] Baudelaire's reasons for introducing it may well be more complex, combining personal with aesthetic or philosophical motives. Firstly, Leconte de Lisle's originality is established from the outset, since he offers so astonishing a contrast with his compatriots. Secondly, the reference to Creoles could be an attack on the most renowned of contemporary Creole poets, Lacaussade, whose rivalry with Leconte de Lisle had led him to write a venomous review of 'La Passion' in 1857.[114] In the same year Baudelaire had suggested that Lacaussade be asked to assess *Les Fleurs du mal* for the *Revue contemporaine* (*C*I, 407): although it was, in fact, the pro-government J. J. Weiss who devoted a damning article to the collection, Baudelaire may well have suspected Lacaussade of complicity and have taken the opportunity of his anthology notice to wreak revenge both for himself and for Leconte de Lisle. Thirdly, the expressions 'îles volcaniques et parfumées' and 'les voluptés de l'atmosphère' (II, 176), suggest that Leconte de Lisle's poetry awoke in Baudelaire memories of his voyage to La Réunion. Indeed, the letter which first refers to this notice also mentions plans for a poem entitled 'Dorothée', described as a 'souvenir de l'Ile Bourbon' (*C*I, 635). This became the prose poem 'La Belle Dorothée', an evocation of tropical life and the beauty of native women which Baudelaire's recent reading of Leconte de Lisle may well have played a part in inspiring. Baudelaire obviously delights in portraying, both here and in his creative writing, the 'pays parfumé que le soleil caresse' (I, 62), the langorous charm of its people and the sensuous if dangerous pleasures of its thought-numbing climate. Finally, on a more intellectual level, such an opening allows Baudelaire to emphasize the importance of 'pensée', 'force de conception' as well as 'travail', 'force d'expression' (II, 176), and to suggest a relationship – both direct and inverse – between physical features and intellectual faculties. His interest in this question, aroused or increased by his reading of Lavater's exploration of 'le sens spirituel du contour, de la forme, de la dimension' of the human face (II, 133), is evident in his first study of Poe where, although he follows his critical sources closely, he draws sufficient parallels with French writers in terms precise and forceful enough to prove his own interest (II, 267).

In underlining Leconte de Lisle's energy, Baudelaire aligns himself with several of his contemporaries, although few stressed the contrast with the stereotype Creole. E. Chasles's review of *Poèmes antiques* remarks on 'un talent que nous croyons énergique et original', while Cherbuliez finds in *Poésies complètes* un 'talent plein de vigueur et d'originalité'.[115] Levallois's article of 1859, however, sees a close link between the poet's strength and his origins: he compares Lacaussade and Leconte de Lisle, insisting: 'vivre dans une île, sous un magnifique climat, au milieu d'une végétation splendide, avec la solitude pour confidente et l'Océan pour maître, c'est une belle préparation à une vaillante carrière, à une militante poésie'.[116]

Returning to the themes of work and thought introduced in the article's opening lines, Baudelaire asserts that Leconte de Lisle is both scholarly and intellectual. It was the former of these characteristics that most other critics emphasized. Terraus, for example, in an article which also attacks Baudelaire, claims that: 'M. Leconte de Lisle ignore que l'érudition a besoin d'aises, et son âme froide imagine trouver l'émotion dans de vieux livres grecs en écoutant l'histoire des dieux', and Planche, while praising Leconte de Lisle's 'sentiment très vrai de l'antiquité' accuses the *Poèmes antiques* of 'des velléités d'érudition'.[117] The classical leanings of Cuvillier-Fleury, however, led him to admire in Leconte de Lisle 'un érudit élégant et vif qui a étudié avec beaucoup de goût, de curiosité, de patience et de prédilection passionnée une époque de l'âge mythologique de l'ancienne Grèce'.[118] Baudelaire neither praises nor condemns Leconte de Lisle's scholarly approach to poetry, but his notice on Hugo indicates that he would certainly have delighted in the importance the poet attached to meditation.[119] This ability enables him, like Gautier (II, 123) and Banville (II, 167), 'extraire le caractère poétique de toutes choses' (II, 176), a gift emphasized again later in the notice. Finally, he possesses 'de l'esprit dans le sens populaire et dans le sens le plus élevé du mot'. This observation seems unique to Baudelaire, for even Flaubert claimed, in a judgement based on some of the poems and on second-hand personal knowledge: 'une chose lui manque: *le sens comique*. Je défie ce garçon de me faire rire, et c'est quelque chose, le rire: c'est le dédain et la compréhension mêlés.'[120] Baudelaire's assertion that this faculty does not appear in Leconte de Lisle's 'ouvrages poétiques' is included above all, I suggest, to allow him to reject the combination of wit and poetry: this may well be a covert allusion to *Odes funambulesques* which the notice on Banville avoids mentioning.

While irony is the vengeance of the vanquished, wit is the resource of those content with easy victory.

In a sentence demonstrating yet again Baudelaire's mastery of the art of transition, he consolidates his description of Leconte de Lisle by repeating the adjectives 'tranquille' and 'vigoureux' and indicates his own appreciation of a poet whom he considers 'l'un de nos plus chers et de nos plus précieux' (II, 177): once again, Baudelaire is definitely reversing widely accepted judgements, provoking his reader, through shock techniques, to reconsider evaluations he may have taken for granted. For several reasons, Leconte de Lisle had not in fact achieved anything like universal popularity. Firstly, his 'sentiment d'aristocratie intellectuelle' kept him far removed from the populace: Pontmartin, in his review of *Poèmes antiques*, asked: 'Savez-vous quelle sera la première condition, j'allais dire le premier châtiment, de votre tentative? L'isolement.'[121] Leconte de Lisle's unpopularity is also seen to derive from the public's unease in the face of perfection (cf. II, 150). Sainte-Beuve, in describing *Poèmes antiques* as 'une poésie amante de l'idéal', admits that Leconte de Lisle 'n'est encore apprécié que de quelques-uns', and Melvil-Bloncourt, whose article plagiarizes Baudelaire's, takes up the point again: 'l'œuvre de M. Leconte de Lisle ne s'adressait qu'à un petit nombre de lecteurs, à ceux surtout qui, tout en aimant la poésie de toute leur âme, savent respecter la Philosophie et ne dédaignent point l'érudition'.[122] Finally, Baudelaire emphasizes the distance separating Leconte de Lisle's poetry from the works the public are accustomed to receiving, the albums and keepsakes 'où tout, philosophie et poésie, est ajusté au sentiment des demoiselles' (II, 177).[123]

According to Baudelaire, the contrast between Leconte de Lisle and the 'fabricants d'album' is as great as that between Cornélius, a painter whose work Baudelaire admired in his early *Salons* (II, 374, 471 but cf. II, 599) and Ary Scheffer, whose sentimentalism is lampooned in the *Salon caricatural*, and condemned in the 'Musée du Bazar Bonne-Nouvelle' (II, 413) and in the *Salon de 1846* (II, 474–5), while his lack of vigour incites Baudelaire's mockery in the *Salon de 1859* (II, 649). Scheffer's name no doubt sprang to mind because of his recent death and the memorial exhibition of his works, visited, according to contemporary reports, by over 2000 every day.[124]

The comparison with pictorial art leads to a more thorough analysis of the ways in which Leconte de Lisle, while still retaining his originality, resembles Gautier on the one hand and Renan on the other. Margaret Gilman rightly considers this passage 'one of the best in all Baudelaire's literary criticism, with its sure choice of parallels, its careful discriminations and its precise and balanced phrases'.[125] Certainly the crisp, concise analysis with its burst of detail contrasts sharply with the style and technique of the great majority of contemporary critics.

Baudelaire draws four main parallels between Gautier and Leconte de Lisle, meticulously indicating differences as well as similarities. Firstly, both are cosmopolitan in outlook, finding delight in clothing 'leur pensée des modes variables que le temps éparpille dans l'éternité' (II, 177), but whereas Gautier takes more pleasure in colourful details, Leconte de Lisle studies 'l'armature philosophique'. Although Baudelaire frequently emphasizes the value of a cosmopolitan outlook, other journalists were highly critical, Levallois, for instance, asking petulantly: 'pourquoi traiter notre âme à la manière d'un caméléon, et supposer qu'elle se teindra docilement des couleurs et des passions de chaque contrée? Elle n'est pas encore si changeante.'[126] Baudelaire, however, is clearly interested in their search for a harmonious pattern to existence linking both ages and countries. Secondly, Baudelaire suggests, the admiration both Leconte de Lisle and Gautier feel for repose as a 'principe de beauté' has led to their love of the East and of the desert: once again, therefore, he attempts to reveal the reasons for a certain tendency in a poet's work. Gautier's predilection for the desert and the East, evident in his travel diaries, is also present in such poems as 'L'Obélisque de Luxor', while that of Leconte de Lisle is given full rein in such *poèmes barbares* as 'Les Eléphants' and 'L'Oasis'. The importance of repose is expressed with particular force in 'Khîron', with its evocation of the 'dieux inconnus' who 'règnent calmes, heureux, immobiles'.[127] Similarly, the 'Vénus de Milo' is invoked as

> Du bonheur impassible ô symbole adorable,
> Calme comme la Mer en sa sérénité,
> Nul sanglot n'a brisé ton sein inaltérable,
> Jamais les pleurs humains n'ont terni ta beauté.[128]

Just as Baudelaire emphasizes cosmopolitanism because it is a quality he admires, so his own preoccupation with the immensity of space and the value of repose plays a part in his selection of this aspect in Gautier and Leconte de Lisle. In both Leconte de Lisle and Baudelaire there is a constant struggle between the repose of death and the demands of the life force, 'l'horreur de la vie et l'extase de la vie' (I, 703). The third point of comparison is the 'lumière passionnée' which floods their poetry, a light which Baudelaire describes as 'plus pétillante' in Gautier, 'plus reposée' in Leconte de Lisle. The image of the sun as god in Leconte de Lisle's poems of India, with their description of 'Un Etre pur et beau comme un soleil d'été', the personification of 'Midi', the king of summers, 'tomb[ant] en nappes d'argent des hauteurs du ciel bleu', and the 'ardente lumière / Des étés sans ombrage'[129] of 'Juin' are only a few of the many examples illustrating his frequent, forceful and gifted use of the image of light, one of the more obvious legacies of a childhood spent in the 'îles volcaniques et parfumées' (11, 176). Baudelaire's own poetry, though more sombre and based on different techniques, also recreates light with particular intensity in poems such as 'Parfum exotique', with its evocation of the 'rivages heureux / Qu'éblouissent les feux d'un soleil monotone' (1, 25), and in such prose poems as 'Le Fou et la Vénus', in which 'une lumière toujours croissante fait de plus en plus étinceler les objets' (1, 283). Finally, Baudelaire proposes as a further parallel between the two poets their indifference to 'les piperies humaines'. He frequently underlines the need for an artist to recognize the illusory nature of contemporary enthusiasms: Poe, for example, never fell victim to 'la sagesse moderne' (11, 322). Similarly, the narrator of 'La Femme sauvage et la petite-maîtresse' remarks sardonically: 'tant poète que je sois, je ne suis pas aussi dupe que vous voudriez le croire' (1, 290). Likewise, Baudelaire insists that Gautier rejected 'la grande fatuité du siècle' and 'la folie du progrès' (11, 108). In much the same way Leconte de Lisle's preface to *Poèmes et Poésies* proclaims 'que les esprits amoureux du présent et convaincus des magnificences de l'avenir se réjouissent dans leur foi, je ne les envie ni ne les félicite, car nous n'avons ni les mêmes sympathies ni les mêmes espérances'.[130]

Leconte de Lisle's poetry is more sharply defined not only by this comparison with Gautier, but also through a far-sighted analogy with Renan. According to Baudelaire, Renan and Leconte de Lisle have two qualities in common. On the one hand, they share an 'ardente, mais impartiale curiosité des religions'. Unlike the Ménard of *Prométhée délivré*, therefore, they, like Baudelaire, respect and admire man's search for a more harmonious existence. Baudelaire's use of the term *curiosité* in his analyses of Poe (11, 248, 279, 317) and of Gautier (11, 107), and the way in which he brackets it with the epithet *ardente* (11, 279, 317), suggests that ardent curiosity is an essential attitude of the ideal artist: it is certainly dominant in the voyager willing to penetrate 'au fond de l'Inconnu pour trouver du *nouveau*' (1, 134). The adjective 'impartiale' not only refers back to the theme of cosmopolitanism, but also emphasizes, as R. Chadbourne points out, that it is an 'ardour of the *mind*, of knowledge'.[131] On the other hand, Baudelaire claims that in both writers this curiosity is directed less towards humanity than towards 'les différentes formes dont l'homme a, suivant les âges et les climats, revêtu la beauté et la vérité' (11, 177-8). Baudelaire's ability to see this as a dominant thread in both writers at such an early stage in their careers is both striking and highly original. Furthermore, by presenting Leconte de Lisle in this light, Baudelaire makes him, as he makes Gautier, resemble more closely the ideal poet whose sole aim is the pursuit of beauty and a deeper comprehension of man's existence.

Where the comparison with Gautier leads to a more precise description of the nature of Leconte de Lisle's poetry, that with Renan allows Baudelaire to define his aims, and acts as a smooth transition between general considerations and a closer examination of the poetry. Of course, Baudelaire's evaluation of Renan was to alter sharply after the publication of *La Vie de Jésus* (see I, 694, 706) and Leconte de Lisle's main anti-clerical poems, which might well have affected Baudelaire's judgement of the poet, had not yet been published.

Developing his earlier reference to Leconte de Lisle's cosmopolitanism, Baudelaire recalls that 'son premier pèlerinage fut pour la Grèce' (II, 178), a reference to those poems ostensibly recreating the legends of ancient Greece, many of which were published in the Fourierist press before being collected in *Poèmes antiques*. In fact, Leconte de Lisle's principal motivation is less a reconstruction of Greek beliefs than an examination, in an allegorical mode, of present times. It is probable that Baudelaire leaves this symbolic significance unmentioned both because it is too close to his own earlier belief in the possibility of a better society, and because of Leconte de Lisle's overtly didactic intentions. Tactfully glossing over the poems' failure to arouse public interest, he asserts, like several other critics, that they were 'remarqués par les connaisseurs'.[132] Secondly, he mentions Leconte de Lisle's versions of Horace's odes, intimating his reservations by adding to his description of the Greek poems as an 'écho de la beauté classique' the remark that these are 'imitations'. In preferring the Latin to the Greek poems, Baudelaire admits that his judgement has been affected by his 'prédilection naturelle pour Rome'. Certainly this admiration is reflected in his desire to translate Petronius's *Satyricon* (*C*II, 416), his proposed poem entitled 'Les Derniers Chants de Lucain' (I, 368) and in the reference in his article on Barbier to 'le trait vigoureux à la manière latine' (II, 144). If he pours bitter scorn on Horace himself in the unfinished reply to Janin, his motive is less to attack the poet than to ridicule the critic.[133] More importantly, one notes here that although Baudelaire insists that to separate form from content is to make a false distinction, he very often responds instantaneously to one or the other, coming only on reflection to consider the two as one. In this case his response is obviously dictated by the subject rather than by the way in which it is treated.

Baudelaire is, however, less interested in the 'beauté classique' than in Leconte de Lisle's evocation of the 'mondes de beauté plus mysté-rieux'. Where other contemporary critics mocked or attacked Leconte de Lisle's use of Indian mythology in his *Poèmes antiques*, Baudelaire attempts to understand it, explaining it in terms of the poet's 'sentiment d'aristocratie intellectuelle' and above all of his longing for 'l'immuable, pour l'éternel, pour le *divin Néant*' (II, 178). This claim both reinforces Baudelaire's earlier assertion that Leconte de Lisle admires repose as a principle of beauty, and reflects his reading of such poems as 'Çunacépa': 'Va! le monde est un songe et l'homme n'a qu'un jour, / Et le néant divin ne connaît pas l'amour.'[134] Baudelaire's own disgust with 'les choses transitoires' also leads to such a longing: thus, in 'Le Goût du néant', first published in January 1859, he writes: 'Résigne-toi, mon cœur; dors ton sommeil de brute' (I, 76). Nevertheless, death is more often present in terms of horror, as in 'L'Horloge', or in the search for something new which marks 'Anywhere out of the World' and 'Le Voyage'.

In an image which is not only appropriate to Leconte de Lisle but also suggests Baudelaire's own ambiguous fascination with the coun-tries of the far North, he evokes Leconte de Lisle's Scandinavian poems. The language he uses, with its sharp contrast between the snows and mists of the North and the 'rayonnant enfant de la Judée' recalls above all the Finnish poem 'Le Runoïa':

> [. . .] je vois venir le Roi des derniers temps,
> Faible et rose, couvert de langes éclatants.
> L'étroit cercle de feu qui ceint ses tempes nues
> Comme un rayon d'été perce les noires nues.[135]

Despite the brevity of the allusion to the Scandinavian poems, Baude-laire conveys their atmosphere with an intensity which argues a close knowledge of them: nevertheless, the emphasis he places on the rise of Christianity underlines the extent to which his own preoccupations colour his reading of other poets.

Yet Baudelaire's interest is seized less by the poems which explore the 'formes successives de la pensée humaine' (II, 178) than by those revealing 'un certain filon tout nouveau qui est bien à lui et qui n'est qu'à lui', the poems which present Leconte de Lisle's own vision of beauty. Significantly, the examples chosen to illustrate this unique vein all have a counterpart in Baudelaire's own creative work. Thus, Leconte de Lisle's awareness of 'les forces imposantes, écrasantes de la nature', a quality which, together with the power of his verse, recalls Baudelaire's description of Hugo (II, 117), finds striking expression in such poems as 'Les Hurleurs' with its terse evocation of a 'Monde muet, marqué d'un signe de colère, / Débris d'un globe mort au hasard dispersé':[136] similarly, Baudelaire's own sonnet 'Obsession', completed in February 1860, exclaims:

> Grands bois, vous m'effrayez comme des cathédrales;
> Vous hurlez comme l'orgue; et dans nos cœurs maudits,
> Chambres d'éternel deuil où vibrent de vieux râles,
> Répondent les échos de vos *De profundis* (1, 75).

The 'majesté de l'animal', conveyed with such felicity in 'Les Eléphants' and 'Le Sommeil du condor' also provides images for Baudelaire's poems 'Les Chats' and 'Le Serpent qui danse', although the aim here is strictly anthropocentric:

> Sous le fardeau de ta paresse
> Ta tête d'enfant
> Se balance avec la mollesse
> D'un jeune éléphant (1, 30).

'La grâce de la femme dans les climats favorisés du soleil' is exploited by Baudelaire in poems such as 'A une dame créole' and in prose poems like 'La Belle Dorothée', and Leconte de Lisle gives it its most eloquent expression in 'Le Manchy', described by Baudelaire as 'un chef-d'œuvre hors ligne' (11, 179). In recreating the atmosphere of this poem Baudelaire stresses the mystery, magic and uniqueness of the beauty it evokes, and certainly its sensuous *correspondances*, the way in which the sound echoes the swaying litter, and the bitter emphasis it places on the fragility of happiness and beauty justify the value he places on it. Finally, Baudelaire admires Leconte de Lisle's depiction of 'la sérénité du désert' and the terrible magnificence of the ocean. These themes, too, are not only explored by Leconte de Lisle in such poems as 'Les Hurleurs' and 'Les Eléphants', but also find expression in Baudelaire's own 'L'Homme et la mer', 'Parfum exotique' and 'La Chevelure'. Two further points should be made here: firstly, these aspects of Leconte de Lisle's talent aroused almost no interest among contemporary critics, and, secondly, Baudelaire makes no mention of the fact that these poems all have an allegorical side.

As in many of his articles, Baudelaire leaves his stylistic discussion until last, but whereas his analysis of technical details is sometimes vague and sketchy, here he attempts to describe concisely but evocatively the central aspects of Leconte de Lisle's style, squeezing a wealth of suggestions into an extremely limited space and setting up resonances with earlier reviews and notices. Once again, he emphasizes Leconte de Lisle's strength, nobility and certitude. Unlike such lesser poets as

Desbordes-Valmore, Barbier and Borel, his poetry is free of 'notes criardes' (cf. II, 144, 146, 154): like Gautier's and Hugo's his vocabulary is 'très étendu'. Just as Hugo created a 'poésie profondément rythmée' (II, 131), so Leconte de Lisle 'joue du rythme avec ampleur et certitude'. Influenced, perhaps, by his enthusiasm for Wagner, Baudelaire draws one of his rare comparisons between poetry and music,[137] claiming of Leconte de Lisle that 'son instrument a le ton doux mais large et profond de l'alto' (II, 179). Unlike Gautier, whose *Emaux et Camées* Baudelaire described rather ambiguously as revealing 'la pourpre régulière et symétrique d'une rime plus qu'exacte' (II, 126), Leconte de Lisle fulfils 'cet amour contradictoire et mystérieux de l'esprit humain pour la surprise et la symétrie'. Similarly, one of Baudelaire's projected prefaces remarks that 'le rythme et la rime répondent dans l'homme aux immortels besoins de monotonie, de symétrie et de surprise' (I, 182): one might well draw an analogy here with Mallarmé's experiments in using a liberated verse form against a background of symmetry. Significantly, where the anthology text has 'ses rimes, toujours exactes' (II, 1162), Baudelaire's final version omits 'toujours', no doubt feeling that it weakened the force of 'la surprise et la symétrie'.[138]

Baudelaire's final paragraph, referring once again to Leconte de Lisle's failure to arouse general acclaim, asserts that 'il lui suffit d'être populaire parmi ceux qui sont dignes eux-mêmes de lui plaire', thus removing the sting that his earlier remark might have carried. At the same time the claim is intended to crush those who have rejected Baudelaire's own poetry.

In his notice, Baudelaire has conveyed much in a restricted space. Nevertheless, there are surprising omissions. The poem *'Dies irae'*, with its pessimistic philosophy, based more on contemporary life than on ancient myths, contains many lines which one might have expected Baudelaire to admire and discuss. Similarly, some of the evocations of Greece, especially the often-quoted 'Vénus de Milo', might well have appealed to the author of 'J'aime le souvenir', particularly as these poems are concerned with the evocation of an eternal, universal beauty. Perhaps he preferred to limit his close study to those poems which were included in the anthology.[139] Unlike his contemporaries, Baudelaire makes no mention of the prefaces Leconte de Lisle wrote for *Poèmes antiques* and *Poèmes et Poésies*: if he had read the poems only in reviews or in *Poésies complètes*, it is possible that he had not seen the prefaces, but it is also likely that he deliberately avoided referring to them, because they contain assertions and proposals which he would have either supported with too much enthusiasm or disputed with too much violence. Perhaps, too, he considered such a discussion out of place in a volume devoted to poetry.

Like the poems it assesses, the study is rich in adjectives and descriptive nouns. Most of them, however, cluster around four central themes: beauty, strength, intellect and serenity. The insistence on these qualities, combined with the emphasis on Leconte de Lisle's aristocratic outlook, and the brief evocations of the poetry, provide an illuminating and provocative analysis of Leconte de Lisle, but one in which Baudelaire subtly suggests several reservations. Its precision and aptness make it one of Baudelaire's best critical assessments of a contemporary.

Hégésippe Moreau

The desire to help friends at the outset of their careers, to extend the public's awareness of writers who had achieved fame, and to redress the balance in favour of those unjustly neglected, forms only part of the complex motivation behind Baudelaire's literary criticism: the spark of anger at contemporary blindness, and the explosion of fury when the public extolled the unworthy, produced the ephemeral but searing fireworks of the unfinished articles on Janin and Villemain, and fed the more constant fire that smoulders behind 'Hégésippe Moreau'. While the aberrations of a Janin and the smart of the personal humiliation to which Villemain subjected him could not provide the necessary impetus to develop a complete study, the public's misconception of genius, and their failure to judge poetry on grounds Baudelaire considered valid, were problems sufficiently widespread and tenacious to sustain more constant anger and thus produce the review of Moreau. Moreau died in 1838, and the following years saw a flurry of reviews depicting him, for all his faults, as one of the 'martyrs de l'ambition littéraire',[140] a title Baudelaire reserved for writers such as Poe, Balzac, Nerval, Hoffmann, and, implicitly, himself. Sainte-Beuve's lengthy study, which first appeared in *Le Constitutionnel* in 1851, sparked off several further articles and when Moreau's poems were published in 1860, with Sainte-Beuve's notice as an introduction, attention was focused once again on this star-crossed poet. It is possible that Baudelaire's antagonism towards Moreau was born in the early 1840s, the fruit of such comments as the following: 'Moreau était gai jusque dans la mélancolie, enjoué dans la tristesse, insouciant jusque dans le désespoir. Son génie était fait à son image. [. . .] Il a été simple, et par là il a été grand.'[141] Equally likely to irritate Baudelaire was the anonymous article in *La Semaine* of 1845, which claims of the new poets that 'aucun d'eux n'a su ramasser la lyre d'Hégésippe Moreau, et en tirer ces harmonieux accords qui rappelaient Gilbert et promettait un nouveau Chénier'.[142] It is more likely, however, that memories of 1848 are closely linked in Baudelaire's mind with Moreau's name: as Giraud trenchantly claimed:

> le parti qui considérait Moreau comme un des siens, parce qu'il avait été des vainqueurs de 1830 et qu'il avait chanté un hymne aux vaincus de juin 1832, prit l'humble fosse du poète pour un champ de bataille, et se fit une arme de son cadavre contre la société, qui l'avait ainsi laissé mourir misérablement sur un grabat. D'un autre côté, on récrimine avec amertume. [. . .] Il résulta de cette polémique, de ce choc d'opinions diverses, et toutes empreintes d'exagération, une grande émotion dans le monde littéraire.[143]

There can be little doubt that Baudelaire was infuriated by this further proof of the public's preference for works of art '*illustrées* (ou souillées) par une espèce de vignette politique' (II, 106). Indeed, it was the anti-Republican nature of the notice Baudelaire prepared for Crépet's anthology that led to its rejection (II, 1152).

Nonetheless, the main focus of this review is to be found in the parallels Baudelaire discovered between himself and Moreau. Both were outcasts from a society which seemed – at least during their lifetime – unable and unwilling to understand them, and both used their poetry to explore similar themes. But Moreau, while failing to subject his talent to the iron discipline of an aesthetic ideal, had eventually aroused the public acclaim that constantly eluded Baudelaire.

The article, rich in side-references and allusions, is perhaps the most carefully constructed of all Baudelaire's literary reviews. A filigree of expressions and images, repeated, developed and embellished as the article progresses, serves to tie the central themes together in a structure at once firm and subtle. Words such as *malheur, souffrir, génie, enfant* and *gloire* constantly reappear, often used with ironic overtones made possible by this very repetition and by our memory of earlier uses. Contrasting ideas such as genius and the crowd, joy and melancholy, fame and misfortune, are bracketed together in a sardonic refutation of the link between popularity and ability. And the arrestingly paradoxical opening and closing sentences seek to shake the reader's comfortable faith in established tenets.

In the first paragraphs, Baudelaire puts forward the main theme of the review, by contrasting the lack of popularity granted two writers of genius with the fame that Moreau has acquired despite basic faults, not merely in his poetry but in his very attitude towards art. In an attempt 'expliquer cette merveilleuse fortune' (II, 157), he describes in detail the 'immense échafaudage' of Moreau's popularity, referring to the emphasis the poet placed on his own misfortune and using four lines of Moreau's poetry to justify a many-pronged condemnation. Nevertheless, he devotes a brief passage to revealing Moreau's gifts before drawing his conclusions.

The opening paragraph is designed to shock and perturb, its first sentence as pithy and elliptical as the maxims of Bossuet or Bourdaloue: 'la même raison qui fait une destinée malheureuse en fait une heureuse' (II, 156). While the term 'destinée' recalls Baudelaire's long-standing interest in fate, the presence of the word 'raison' suggests once more his longing to discover a logical law capable of explaining the convolutions of an individual's life. And the contrast between fortune and bad luck prepares the reader for the way in which Baudelaire uses the example of Moreau's fate to elucidate a question of general import.

In terms of quiet sympathy and comprehension, Baudelaire develops his opening sentence with two examples, drawn from the select band of literary martyrs whose fate he has so often examined and lamented. Nerval's suicide, seen as the only possible solution to his persistent melancholy, and Poe's defeat by alcoholism, drew from the public a wrath and refusal to understand at whose roots Baudelaire perceives the specious argument dictated by selfishness: 'pourquoi plaindre ceux qui méritent de souffrir?' (II, 156). As in earlier articles, Baudelaire presents suffering as something the public resents, particularly if those who suffer distinguish themselves by their intellect or sensitivity. Provocatively overturning the customary picture of Nerval as a mind deranged, Baudelaire defiantly describes him as 'doué d'une intelligence brillante, active, lumineuse, prompte à s'instruire' (II, 156), just as he depicted him in 1856 as 'un écrivain d'une honnêteté admirable, d'une haute intelligence et *qui fut toujours lucide*' (II, 306). Poe is denoted 'un vaste génie, profond comme le ciel et comme l'enfer', a dichotomy recalling 'Hymne à la beauté' with its initial question: 'Viens-tu du ciel profond ou sors-tu de l'abîme, O Beauté?' (I, 24).

Baudelaire is brutally direct in explaining why the gifts and methods of Poe and Nerval are generally decried while those of Moreau earn admiration:

> s'il n'y a dans le malheureux ni génie ni savoir, si l'on ne peut trouver en lui rien de supérieur, rien d'impertinent, rien qui empêche la foule de se mettre de niveau avec lui et de le traiter conséquemment de pair à compagnon, dans ce cas-là constatons que le malheur et même le vice peuvent devenir une immense source de gloire (II, 156–7).

This is the embittered realization to which Baudelaire's thoughts were already tending in his preface to Dupont's songs. There, still buoyant with the hopes of the Revolution, he presents the public as addressing the poet in the following terms: 'tu as touché notre cœur! Il faut nous démontrer que tu n'es qu'un homme, et que les mêmes éléments de perfectionnement existent pour nous tous' (II, 28).

Moreau, according to Baudelaire, resembled Poe and Nerval only in so far as he was an outcast in the France of Louis-Philippe, 'un Arabe nomade dans un monde civilisé' (II, 157). There is an interesting parallel between this expression and a comment Baudelaire made in his version of De Quincey's *Confessions*:

> Pour sentir de cette façon, il faut avoir souffert beaucoup, il faut être un de ces cœurs que le malheur ouvre et amollit, au contraire de ceux qu'il ferme et durcit. Le Bédouin de la civilisation apprend dans le Saharah des grandes villes bien des motifs d'attendrissement qu'ignore l'homme dont la sensibilité est bornée par le *home* et la famille (*MO*, 132).

Yet, whereas Nerval and Poe were prolific writers whose works were 'tous marqués par le goût' or written in a style 'prodigieusement original et parfaitement correct', not only did Moreau write little, but the derivative nature of his style, 'moitié classique, moitié romantique', made his songs all the easier for the public to accept and remember. This is certainly one of the points where the reader feels Baudelaire's astonishment at both the similarities and the differences between himself and Moreau, for whereas his own output was also relatively small, he himself struggled to achieve a style distinct both from Romanticism and from Classicism.

It is because the public found Moreau's songs so easy to accept, that they were led to interpret 'le désordre' of Moreau's life as 'génie incompris'. The notes to the Pléiade edition point out that this formulation recalls Dumas's play *Kean: ou désordre et génie* (II, 1153), a work whose influence Baudelaire lamented as early as 1846 (II, 19). Nevertheless, it seems to me extremely likely that Baudelaire is also suggesting links with Chatterton, particularly since Vigny's play was produced amid such enthusiasm only three years before Moreau's death. This was, after all, a time when public emotions could be aroused by even the slightest allusion to that trio of 'poètes maudits' or 'poètes victimes': Chatterton, Gilbert and Malfillatre.

As so often, Baudelaire seizes on this opportunity to attack those theories, 'fautrices de paresse', which present poetry as the unchecked outpourings of disordered emotion, rather than a complex blend of inspiration and work, dominated by reason. This view of Moreau's talent is justified by the poet himself, who claims:

Et le vers pousse bien comme la giroflée,
Aux crevasses d'un mur, au pied d'un mausolée.[144]

The image Baudelaire uses not only shows him turning to external nature to symbolize 'les impressions d'un ordre spirituel' (II, 148), but also, I suggest, recalling a scene from that 'catéchisme de haute esthétique', Hoffmann's *Prinzessin Brambilla* (II, 542): just as Giglio Fava finds himself turned into a multicoloured bird because of his refusal to accept the demands of true art, so Moreau is like 'un oiseau bavard, léger, irresponsable, insaisissable, et transportant son domicile d'une branche à l'autre' (II, 157).

Having briefly contrasted Moreau's talent and fate with those of truly gifted poets, Baudelaire reveals what he considers to be his task as a critic and prepares the reader for the line his investigation is to pursue: 'mais il faut expliquer cette merveilleuse fortune, et avant de parler des facultés séduisantes qui ont permis de croire un instant qu'il deviendrait un véritable poète, je tiens à montrer le fragile, mais immense échafaudage de sa trop grande popularité' (II, 157). Once again, the accent is on explanation as well as on evaluation. The word 'échafaudage' not only shows Baudelaire drawing images from the experience of the city-dweller in Haussmann's Paris, but also twists the phrase *l'échafaudage de sa fortune*, by concentrating attention, not on the progressive construction of fame, but on the fragility and structural weaknesses of Moreau's reputation. Baudelaire attributes this sudden leap into the limelight to a 'conspiration': his thought here is echoed by a passage in the anthology notice on Dupont, which, recalling the equally sudden rise to favour of the neo-classicists, comments: 'c'est toujours une belle histoire à raconter que la conspiration de toutes les sottises en faveur d'une médiocrité' (II, 169). The fact that assertions in one notice set up resonances with those in another emphasizes the way in which Baudelaire used the opportunity afforded by the anthology to strengthen and justify, as much in his own mind as for that of his reader, central problems concerning literature and the public's acceptance of it.

Taking up the expression 'vanité de malheur' (II, 158), which for him characterizes much of Moreau's poetry, and therefore affects his popularity, Baudelaire poses the question of the degree to which poetry can or should represent the individual's physical sufferings. In contrast with the time when poets sang of 'douleurs mystérieuses, vagues, difficiles à définir, espèce de maladie congéniale de la poésie' – an allusion perhaps to Chateaubriand and certainly to Sainte-Beuve and other early Romantics – Baudelaire refers to the vogue for depicting 'de belles et bonnes souffrances bien déterminées'. His attack on those poets who, simply because it is 'à la mode' (11, 158), complain in their writing of hunger and cold, of extreme personal and physical suffering, is developed in his article on Banville, who, according to his critic, would never describe himself as dragging out a meagre existence in 'une chambre pauvre, triste ou en désordre' (11, 166). What is important, whether the poet depicts 'l'horreur de la vie' or 'l'extase de la vie', is that in doing so he must reflect his own nature and not adopt 'une âme d'emprunt' (11, 3). Baudelaire clearly had not just Banville but also Delacroix and Gautier in mind as a counter-example to Moreau: the poet, he contends, in terms reminiscent of Gautier's *Fortunio*, should present himself as 'un homme enivré d'une richesse asiatique et vivant dans un monde de luxe et de beauté' (11, 158).

It is according to these standards, therefore, that Baudelaire judges Moreau, whom he rather disdainfully calls 'Hégésippe'. He softened his blows in the corrected copy of the manuscript, removing the two uses of 'trop' from the accusation that Moreau 'parla de lui-même beaucoup trop, et pleura beaucoup trop sur lui-même'. This criticism stands in sharp contrast to Baudelaire's acceptance of Poe's 'abus du *je*' (see 11, 282), and to his justification, in the review of *Tannhäuser*, of his intention 'parler souvent en [son] nom personnel. Ce *Je*, accusé juste-ment d'impertinence dans beaucoup de cas, implique cependant une grande modestie; il enferme l'écrivain dans les limites les plus strictes de la sincérité' (11, 779). Almost certainly, Baudelaire considered that Moreau's pillaging of Romantic and Classical techniques and themes classed him amongst those who assumed a certain character and who were not, therefore, sincere in the meaning that Baudelaire gives the word. According to him, Moreau 'singea [. . .] les attitudes fatales des Antony et des Didier' (11, 158). Not only are Antony and Didier familiar Romantic heroes, but the epithet 'fatales' is also a common-place of Romantic vocabulary. As in the Dupont preface, with its dismissal of the 'ombres fallacieuses' which mimic the great Romantic protagonists, and in the numerous castigations of those who are content with 'une âme d'emprunt', the principal focus of Baudelaire's attack is not Romanticism itself but the falseness of Moreau's art, his failure to rely on and develop his own personality. Once again there is an implicit comparison with Baudelaire himself, who realized both the great impetus Romanticism had given French literature, and the need to break free from it.

It is not only in his exploitation of Romanticism that Moreau, according to Baudelaire, reveals both opportunism and illogical think-ing, but also in the fact that he adopted a further mask: 'le regard courroucé et grognon du démocrate'. This is in stark contrast with Borel, for example, whose Republican convictions were founded on an 'haine aristocratique [. . .] contre les rois et contre la bourgeoisie', a hatred far removed from 'la passion démocratique et bourgeoise' (II, 155), which Baudelaire describes as having so 'cruellement opprim[é]' the France of later years. Much has been made of Baudelaire's frequent and often acerbic attacks on democracy. Yet, as with the unthinking acceptance of an aesthetic theory, he reviles only those whose democracy stems from stupidity or basely personal motives. As early as 1849, he recounts the visit of Madier de Montjou, 'un aigle démocratique' (*C*I, 157), who was shocked and horrified when Baudelaire described the 'socialisme des paysans, – socialisme inévitable, féroce, stupide, bestial comme un socialisme de la torche ou de la faulx' (*C*I, 158). For analogous reasons he ridicules Hugo's professed 'tendre et profond amour du peuple' (II, 228). The condemnation of American democracy in the essays on Poe has its roots in the country's failure to accept men of genius who were unable to adapt to the needs and aspirations of the common man. Similarly, 'Le Peintre de la vie moderne' depicts democracy as a 'marée montante', which 'envahit tout et [. . .] nivelle tout' (II, 721). Both factors, the self-interest or stupidity he found in many democrats and the inability of the system to encourage or even admit exception, are present in Baudelaire's reaction to Moreau's democratic convictions.

According to Baudelaire, Moreau believed that he deserved better treatment, both from nature and from society: not only, therefore, is he motivated by self-interest, but, as Baudelaire has already insisted, the fame society has given him stems from the fact that the average reader feels Moreau to be very like himself. Moreau did indeed frequently lament the harshness of his fate, asserting for example:

> [. . .] le sort
> A de sa main de fer encloué mon essor
> Et comme le chevreau captif au pied d'une chêne,
> Pour brouter quelques fleurs je tiraille ma chaîne.[145]

Finally, the reference to Moreau's 'regard courroucé et grognon' recalls a question Baudelaire posed in his article on Barbier: 'se figure-t-on une *Muse* qui *grimace*?' (II, 144) and his justification to Crépet of his approach to Hugo's poetry: 'je considère l'engueulement politique comme un signe de sottise' (*C*II, 41). It is, of course, important to distinguish between Moreau's sulkiness which sees misfortune and unhappiness as undeserved and incomprehensible, and Baudelaire's own preoccupation with 'la fertilisante douleur' (*MO*, 104), which he considers 'la noblesse unique / Où ne mordront jamais la terre et les enfers' (1, 9).

To illustrate Moreau's attitude and lay bare both its exaggeration and its hypocrisy, Baudelaire quotes four lines recalling the poet's school days in the Jesuit seminary at Montrouge.[146] These lines certainly do reveal a ludicrous tendency to overstate. Although the initial cause of Baudelaire's anger seems to lie in the abuse of the Church, he supports his rejection of such poetry through close textual analysis. If close study was fairly rare at the time, Baudelaire's searing mockery is nevertheless reminiscent of the minute examinations prevalent in Poe's criticism. For a variety of reasons, Baudelaire usually avoids word-for-word appraisal but the passage certainly reveals not only that he was capable of this approach but also that he exploited it more in moments of anger, as in the case of Villemain and Ménard, than as a means of justifying enthusiasm.

In analysing the lines from Moreau, Baudelaire mocks with rather heavy irony the hyperbolic use of 'ogre' – 'nous voyons par le vers suivant que le jeune Hégésippe n'a pas été mangé' – and scornfully points out the unacknowledged advantages Moreau has gained from such an education, whose similarities with his own Baudelaire must instantly have recognized. It is thanks to his knowledge of Latin, Baudelaire sardonically asserts, that Moreau can 'écrire sa langue un peu moins mal que tous ceux qui n'ont pas eu le malheur d'être enlevés par *un ogre*' (11, 159). Moreover, he cogently and pertinently suggests that Moreau has deliberately sought to render his case more interesting to a public full of enthusiasm for Romanticism, by referring to the priest in this way, using an expression which is not merely intrinsically emotive, but also recalls Hugo's priest Claude Frollo in *Notre-Dame de Paris* and the defrocked socialist mystic Lamennais. The bitterness of the reference to Lamennais, whose ideas are very close to those of the young Baudelaire, reveals yet again the intense disappointment aroused in him by the failure of the 1848 Revolution.[147]

His criticism is also directed at the expression 'noirs frelons' which, he suggests, reveals the profound hypocrisy of Moreau's proclaimed Republicanism. Addressing his reader directly in tones of grim humour, Baudelaire underlines the difference the image implies between the unproductive hornets – the other pupils – and the hardworking Moreau. The implication is, of course, that despite all his apparent support for Republican and democratic ideals, Moreau envisages himself as being apart from, and better than, his fellows.

The four lines quoted serve not merely to demonstrate Moreau's style but also to exemplify what Baudelaire calls 'la note morale' of his poetry. The meaning of this phrase becomes clearer if one remembers the reference in the Hugo notice to 'l'atmosphère morale qui plane et circule dans ses poèmes' (11, 136), that is, the attitude to life and mankind that the work reveals. Just as Baudelaire depicted Moreau's style as a mosaic of romantic and democratic tendencies, so he describes this 'note morale' as comprising 'un poncif romantique, collé, non pas amalgamé, à un poncif démocratique'.[148] Like Flaubert, Baudelaire was at once repelled and fascinated by banality and cliché (1, 650, 662; 11, 609): his criticism of Moreau, therefore, stems not from a rejection of the *poncif* as such, but from the way in which these clichés are accepted with neither originality nor insight. There is a further criticism implied by the expression 'collé, non pas amalgamé'. Moreau has not only borrowed his basic materials, but he has not even soldered them together with the originality that could create from them something new. As on other occasions in the literary criticism, it is evident that Baudelaire is not interested in novelty for its own sake, but believes rather that the poet can draw on well-worn themes and techniques, forging them anew in the fire of his own personality to create something both fresh and *sui generis*, as he himself has done, for instance, in the poem 'Le Guignon'. In addition, Baudelaire's own preoccupation with the total effect of a work of art clearly cannot accept Moreau's failure to amalgamate his borrowings into the substance of his own creativity. This conviction, together with his predilection for drawing on the contemporary world for comparisons and images, underlies his assertion that 'tout cela ne fait pas une société, c'est-à-dire un tout, mais quelque chose comme une cargaison d'omnibus' (11, 159).

Baudelaire supports his attack on the derivative nature of Moreau's work by suggesting links with Romantic writers such as Hugo and Musset, as well as with the Republican Barbier, and by recalling Sainte-Beuve's comment that Moreau's *Diogène* was similar in function to Barthélemy's *Némésis* (see 11, 1154). Further parallels are drawn with Boileau and Delille as well as with Béranger and Désaugiers, whose influence contemporary critics frequently noted.[149] The charge of plagiarism is backed by yet another precise reference, this time to the poem 'Les Deux Amours', in which, as Baudelaire succinctly reminds his reader, 'un homme se livre à l'amour banal, la mémoire encore pleine d'un amour idéal' (11, 159). Once again, although he has insisted that theme and approach cannot be separated, he is again forced to distinguish between, on the one hand, a subject which, as his own poem 'Une nuit que j'étais' clearly reveals, he considers 'd'une nature profonde et poétique', and on the other hand Moreau's 'manière anti-humaine'. The epithet serves yet again to underline the difference between Moreau and the true democrat. The unalleviated symmetry with which the ideal love and the earthly love alternate is not only derivative, since it offers such obvious parallels with both Virgil's *Bucolics* and the style of Boileau, but it also runs counter to Baudelaire's call for symmetry to be enriched by surprise.

With a carefully prepared play on words, Baudelaire presents Moreau as being not merely 'l'élève de quelqu'un', whatever theme he chooses and however he treats it, but also an 'écolier [. . .] pédant', so that his love poetry, far from revealing 'la volupté de l'épicurien', merely displays 'la sensualité claustrale, échauffée, du cuistre, sensualité de prison et de dortoir' (II, 160). There is surely more to Baudelaire's anger here than is at first apparent. Although Moreau's poetry reveals little originality, it does not really consist of 'lieux communs de morale lubrique', as Baudelaire asserts in Boileau's famous phrase. Two possible reasons for the outburst suggest themselves. Firstly, Moreau's evocation of his school days may well have reminded him of his own treatment of the theme in the poem sent to Sainte-Beuve, with its allusion to 'les soirs malsains, les nuits fiévreuses' (II, 207) and no doubt he felt that Moreau had chosen a richly suggestive theme and failed to exploit its potential. How, therefore, Baudelaire must have wondered, has he become so popular? Secondly, just as he seems to have used Barbier as a scapegoat for his censure of Hugo's political poetry, so Moreau may be a shield for Béranger, still too closely associated with the 1830 Revolution to be directly attacked in any work edited by Crépet, but whose 'bonnes ordures' Baudelaire asked Chaix d'Est-Ange to quote 'avec dégoût et horreur' in his support of *Les Fleurs du mal* (CI, 419).

Taking up the implications of 'élève', 'écolier', 'collégien' and 'gamin', Baudelaire paradoxically uses the word 'enfant' as a focus for what is praiseworthy in Moreau's work. Baudelaire's interest in childhood, its qualities and its appreciation of the outside world, is given forceful and highly original expression in *Un Mangeur d'opium* (II, 497–8) and in 'Le Peintre de la vie moderne' (II, 687–94), as well as throughout his literary criticism. It is, therefore, a measure of his irritation that he does not lead straight into an exploration of this more pleasant avenue, but justifies instead the ferocity of his condemnation: 'action, réaction, faveur, cruauté, se rendent alternativement nécessaires. Il faut bien rétablir l'équilibre. C'est la loi, et la loi est bien faite' (II, 160). The argument is familiar, Baudelaire having already used it in the letter to Hugo which requests an introduction to the Gautier essay: 'en un temps où le monde s'éloigne de l'art avec une telle horreur [. . .] je crois qu'il n'y a pas grand mal à exagérer un peu dans le sens contraire' (*CI*, 597). Certainly one feels throughout his criticism a desire less for a sober, balanced appreciation than for total justice, for redressing the balance and for expressing new points of view rather than calmly weighing up both sides of an argument. And for the Baudelaire smarting under the barrage of attacks on *Les Fleurs du mal* and *Les Paradis artificiels*, the assertion that the need to restore the balance represented a law may not have been essential to his article but it was certainly a vital psychological necessity.

Baudelaire supports his rejection of the title 'le prince des poètes' for Moreau, partly by contrasting him with such truly gifted poets as Ronsard, Hugo and Gautier, and partly by examining his reaction to adversity and suffering.

Moreau, he insists, cannot be regarded as a literary prince because, unlike Soulié and Balzac, he is not 'un homme chargé de grands devoirs, les acceptant humblement et se débattant sans trêve contre le monstre grossissant de l'usure' (II, 160). The comment commands attention both for the remarkable brevity of the powerful metaphor depicting 'l'usure' as an ever-increasing monster, and because the language recalls the earlier description of Poe and Nerval 'se courbant humblement sous la loi inévitable'. Moreover, the expression 'chargé de grands devoirs' suggests the same belief in predestination conveyed in the 1856 study on Poe, with its assertion: 'on dirait que la Nature fait à ceux dont elle veut tirer de grandes choses un tempérament énergique, comme elle donne une puissante vitalité aux arbres qui sont chargés de symboliser le deuil et la douleur' (II, 309). Above all, the image of the 'monstre grossissant de l'usure' carries unmistakable personal overtones which reinforce the many parallels between Moreau and his critic. Clearly he is being held up not only against the gradually sharpening image of an ideal poet, but also against Baudelaire himself, and he is found wanting.

According to Baudelaire, Moreau's attitude to suffering was at distinct variance with that of the great poets. The earlier phrase, 'la vanité du malheur', is intensified by the assertion that Moreau could see suffering neither as a blessing nor as having 'une aristocratique beauté': the epithet here is obviously meant to conflict with Moreau's proclaimed Republican beliefs and Baudelaire draws particular attention to it by its unusual position in the phrase. Moreover, Moreau, so Baudelaire insists, had no real awareness of 'ces enfers-là'. He did not know, as Desbordes-Valmore, Nerval and Baudelaire himself knew, the 'tortures d'un cœur inassouvi, les douloureuses pâmoisons d'une âme aimante et méconnue' (II, 161). Such references recall Baudelaire's famous definition of his image of beauty and his confession that he cannot conceive of 'un type de Beauté où il n'y ait du *Malheur*' (1, 658).

Having made this general point, Baudelaire turns again to his paradoxical belief that the reason for Moreau's artistic failure is also the cause of his success: the 'beauté du diable' which springs from the grace and charm of youth. Once again, despite his avowed intention of finding in Moreau characteristics worthy of praise, Baudelaire does so only after establishing the background of the 'amas de pastiches' and repeating the words 'enfant et écolier', which recall his earlier condemnation of Moreau's love poetry and thus determine the perspective in which the reader sees the successful facets of this deceptive diamond. Like Barbier he possesses 'l'accent de vérité jaillissant, l'accent soudain, natif, qu'on ne peut confondre avec aucun autre accent' (11, 161). The repetition of 'accent', together with the three uses of 'grâce' in the following sentence, suggest that Baudelaire may be forcing himself to make this concession and that his anger is fired anew at the realization that despite all his faults Moreau has unaccountably been granted 'la grâce, le don gratuit': one thinks immediately of the illogical nature of the gifts in 'Les Dons des fées'. Clearly, as with Desbordes-Valmore, Baudelaire resents the apparently inexplicable contrast between the facility of others and his own creative struggle.

In this moment of wrath, he groups together the elements of Moreau's work which most grate on his nerves: Moreau is 'sottement impie', like the poets of 'l'école païenne'; he has become the mindless mouthpiece of a political faction – the word 'perroquet' here tautens the structure by echoing the earlier image of the 'oiseau bavard'; and he is a symbol of unthinking democracy. It is not merely or even primarily because Moreau's attitude to politics and religion runs counter to Baudelaire's own that he is infuriated: it is the unquestioning acceptance of these ideas and the resultant abnegation of intellect and will power that he finds totally unacceptable.

Baudelaire laments this abnegation all the more intensely because the 'merveilles inattendues' of such poems as 'La Voulzie' and 'La Fermière' indicate that had Moreau demanded more of himself he could have become 'un remarquable homme de lettres'. The assertion reveals yet again Baudelaire's firm belief that work and the voluntary recall of 'les heures favorisées' are essential if genius is to come to full fruition. Nevertheless he adds with the sardonic insight culled from personal experience, and from his incessant examination of the fate meted out to other poets, that Moreau would then not be 'l'idole des fainéants et le dieu des cabarets' (11, 161): once again, the phrase 'le dieu des cabarets' suggests that Béranger is hovering in the wings.

The sustained anger underlying this article is kept rigidly under control, breaking out only in such physical images as 'rogatons du dernier siècle' (II, 160) and in the accumulation of terms which describe Moreau's works as 'ce paquet d'emprunts, [...] ce fouillis de plagiats vagues et involontaires, [...] cette pétarade d'esprit bureaucratique ou scolaire' (II, 161). The study's careful structure and the repetition of key words in strategic positions reveal that even when he does appear to deviate from the line he has set himself he does so both consciously and voluntarily. In this he stands in sharp opposition to many of his contemporaries, whose anger found far less articulate and reasoned expression. Moreover, as in the reviews which praise or defend, he has seized on the opportunity to examine broader issues, such as the nature and cause of popularity, and the essential characteristics which differentiate the mediocre from the gifted. And by submitting wrath to reason he subtly exemplifies his increasingly imperious call for inspiration to be refined by labour.

7

❧ *Master and Disciple: Léon Cladel*

The year 1861 was a time of rich and almost frenetic activity on
Baudelaire's part: not only was it in that year that he published the
second edition of *Les Fleurs du mal* and all but one of the *Réflexions sur
quelques-uns de mes contemporains*, but he also wrote his masterly review
of *Tannhäuser*, saw nine prose poems accepted by the *Revue fantaisiste*
and, in the words of Enid Starkie, 'wasted days and weeks of his
precious time preparing Léon Cladel's manuscript for the press'.[1] Yet
Baudelaire's literary criticism in general, and his preface to *Les Martyrs
ridicules* in particular, show how little anything he read or worked on
was wasted, and how successfully he could turn the beliefs, experiments,
successes and failures of other writers into lenses bringing sharply into
focus his own preoccupations. The relationship between Cladel and
the poet he was to describe as 'le docte et puissant rhéteur' and 'le
tenace étymologiste'[2] has been explored, in novelistic form, by Cladel
himself in *Bonshommes*, and, more conventionally, by Cladel's daughter
Judith.[3] Baudelaire's correspondence sheds little extra light on the
matter: indeed, according to Judith Cladel, several of the letters were
lost (*CII*, 636). Of the two that remain one affectionately suggests that
'il serait bon de revoir ensemble une fois pour toutes [les] "Amours
éternelles"' (*CII*, 184), while a second, dated some six months later,
is a far colder 'prière à Cladel de toujours corriger les fautes d'impression sur les exemplaires destinés aux amis' (*CII*, 213).

In agreeing to write a preface for *Les Martyrs ridicules*, and in offering
so much advice, Baudelaire seems to have been motivated by three
main considerations. Firstly, he no doubt wanted to help his friend
and publisher, Poulet-Malassis, to whom Cladel had sent his manuscript. A second, more important reason was that the preface would
enable him to depict contemporary trends in youth and literature, and
direct the public's attention away from the fatuous and false. Finally,
and most vitally, he discovered in the work itself illuminating affinities
with his own beliefs and tendencies, affinities which not only sharpened
his self-awareness but which he could use as a scourge to repress what
he saw as fatal propensities in his own personality.

According to Judith Cladel, and the preface supports both the expression and the meaning of her statement, Baudelaire told Cladel: 'il y a dans votre charabia gascon ou basque une flamme plus ou moins satanique qui m'a séduit, entraîné, brûlé même'.[4] It is this satanic flame that Baudelaire's preface examines, using it with lucidity and courage to explore the recesses of his own psyche.

The preface, like most of Baudelaire's later criticism, is carefully articulated, although in this case the structure depends less on the repetition of key words than on a logical progression from an initial paradox. This opening paradox opposes his contempt for the youth of his time to his pleasure in a contemporary work produced by a young man. The antithesis is developed through an exploration of the four main tendencies he perceives in 'la *gentry* parisienne' (II, 182), a scathing summary which highlights Cladel's originality and thus explains and justifies Baudelaire's reaction to *Les Martyrs ridicules*. Turning to a closer examination of the novel, he reveals the depth of meaning in the title before evoking the general tone and assessing the characters. His conclusion is spare and sardonic, pointing briefly to the work's value as satire, to its morality and to its chances of popular success. Although repetitions of words are less frequent as a structural device than in other articles, the preface does contain two important leitmotifs: a group of terms conveying the laziness and fatuousness of *la jeunesse littéraire*, and the epithet *instructif*, repeated as a proclamation of the novel's power to guide and warn.

As with many of his critical reviews, Baudelaire is obviously reacting here to a particular challenge. Yet even the disarming frankness with which the *gageure* is expressed is clearly part of a careful strategy: in admitting that when he was asked to read *Les Martyrs ridicules* his first reaction was one of 'excessive répugnance' (II, 182), Baudelaire not only arouses the sympathy of his readers – and a feeling of fraternity with those who share that disgust – but also awakens a desire to know how this repulsion was overcome. As on other occasions he gives the expression particular force, partly by placing the adjective before the noun, and partly by the choice of a strongly physical term to convey an intellectual reaction. Moreover, he is sufficiently in control of his medium not to justify his change of mind immediately, but rather to explain and support his initial disgust at a novel written by 'un jeune homme': 'la Jeunesse, dans le temps présent, m'inspire, par ses défauts nouveaux, une défiance déjà bien suffisamment légitimée par ceux qui la distinguèrent en tout temps' (II, 182). As Pichois points out, there is a clear parallel between this embittered attack and the notes jotted down in 'Mon cœur mis à nu' under the heading 'portrait de la canaille littéraire' and ending with the phrase: 'un joli tableau de la jeunesse moderne' (I, 688). In his article on Moreau, Baudelaire had remarked that 'il y a dans la jeunesse littéraire, comme dans la jeunesse physique, une certaine beauté du diable qui fait pardonner bien des imperfections' (II, 161): here he is concerned to show that Cladel's novel has no need to rely on the superficial 'beauté du diable'.

His uneasiness when faced with contemporary youth is brought vividly alive through a brief but amusing parallel with 'la [. . .] sensation de malaise [qu'il éprouve] à la rencontre d'un camarade de collège oublié, devenu boursier, et que les vingt ou trente années intermédiaires n'empêchent pas de me tutoyer ou de me frapper sur le ventre' (II, 182). Both the tone and the element of caricature recall the prose poem 'A une heure du matin':[5] as so often, Baudelaire appears to be perfecting in the literary criticism techniques which he exploits in his creative writing.

Despite this initial repugnance and unease, Baudelaire openly admits that *Les Martyrs ridicules* did indeed bring him considerable pleasure. His delight here stems partly from the work itself and partly from the surprise this delight caused him; the ability to surprise frequently appears among the characteristics of works or writers who have impressed him (II, 248, 578). As with the Marceline Desbordes-Valmore article, Baudelaire amuses his reader by this unashamed admission of a conflict between expectation and reality, but whereas he enjoyed Desbordes-Valmore's poetry because of 'la violente contradiction qu'y trouve tout [son] être' (II, 146), *Les Martyrs ridicules* pleased him not only by differing sharply from what he had feared but also because he found in both the author and the novel so many similarities with his own beliefs and personality.

In order to emphasize the difference between Cladel and the majority of young writers, Baudelaire describes with considerable acerbity the four categories he perceives in contemporary youth. The careful distinction between numbered groups is of course a Classical technique, but it suggests both that Baudelaire has given much thought to the matter and that he is attempting here to evoke in very concise terms the atmosphere of the age, just as, in his preface to Dupont's songs, he suggests the possibility of a work recounting 'les sentiments, les doctrines, la vie extérieure, la vie intime, les modes et les mœurs de la jeunesse sous le règne de Louis-Philippe' (II, 27). The attack, according to an anonymous note in *La Revue anecdotique*, caused considerable consternation:

M. Baudelaire ne consent pas de voir dans la jeunesse française plus de quatre classes, dont on peut qualifier ainsi les membres: 1° les sensuels; 2°

les avares; 3° les mauvais politiques; 4° les mauvais littérateurs. Tous les admirateurs des *Fleurs du mal* âgés de moins de vingt-cinq ans proposent de recourir en grâce. Mais les termes absolus de leur arrêt laissent peu d'espoir.[6]

One wonders whether Baudelaire himself had a hand in this ironic notice as a means of drawing attention to the novel.

The analysis of modern youth opens on a sarcastic note, with the use of the term *gentry*. Although this anglicism was admitted into the language as early as 1688, the fact that Baudelaire italicizes it suggests that he perceives a degree of pretentiousness in this self-appointed aristocracy. The first group is distinguished by being interested only in 'la paillardise et la goinfrerie', base instincts that Baudelaire renders even more vile by evoking them first in extremely physical terms, then in lofty language: to the religious terminology of 'adorant' and 'divinités' he adds the literary concept of the Muses. The paradoxical description of gluttony and debauchery as 'ces muses du vieillard sans honneur' implies that there is something very much wrong with young men enslaved by old men's passions and also recalls the description of Michelet as 'un vieillard sans majesté' (II, 116). Above all, however, it is the animality of such desires that disgusts the dandy who claimed in 'Mon cœur mis à nu': 'la femme a faim et elle veut manger. Soif, et elle veut boire. Elle est en rut et elle veut être foutue. Le beau mérite! La femme est *naturelle*, c'est-à-dire abominable. Aussi est-elle toujours vulgaire, c'est-à-dire le contraire du Dandy' (I, 677).

The second caste, differentiated from the first by being neither rich nor idle, is, according to Baudelaire, equally '*bête*', worshipping that 'troisième divinité du vieillard', money. Once again, Baudelaire emphasizes the paradox inherent in young men seeking that which normally preoccupies only the old, adding further weight by the choice of the term 'divinité' for so materialistic a passion. The assertion that this category is destined 'faire fortune', although ostensibly an angry denial of the value of such success, nevertheless contains a fleeting note of envy and of frustrated incomprehension in the choice of that loaded word 'destinée'.

Baudelaire is obviously more interested in the third group, the utopians and democrats who still hold dear hopes and beliefs that he himself rejected after the *coup d'état*. His self-mockery, disappointed anger and frustration become all the more evident if one compares the italicized expression '*aspirent à faire le bonheur du peuple*' with the opening lines of 'Assommons les pauvres': 'Pendant quinze jours je m'étais confiné dans ma chambre, et je m'étais entouré des livres à la mode dans ce temps-là [. . .]; je veux parler des livres où il est traité de l'art de rendre les peuples heureux, sages et riches, en vingt-quatre heures'

(I, 357). In the Cladel preface, Baudelaire seizes on this splendid opportunity to mock his *bête noire*, *Le Siècle*, a daily paper established in 1836 which had, according to Hatin, an 'immense auditoire parmi le public affairé des trafiquants des villes et des campagnes' and which quickly established itself as the organ of 'la gauche dynastique'.[7] Its frequent attacks on Proudhon, whom Ch. de Mathurel among others called 'ce grand mystificateur',[8] may well have aroused in Baudelaire an antagonism which only increased with time. In his *Salon de 1859*, for example, he ridicules the journal by caricaturing it in typically concrete terms as 'ce vaste monument de la niaiserie, penché vers l'avenir comme la tour de Pise, et où s'élabore le bonheur du genre humain' (II, 653). And in commenting on his famous dream in the letter to Asselineau he remarks: 'il n'y a vraiment dans le monde qu'un seul journal, et c'est *Le Siècle*, qui puisse être assez bête pour ouvrir une maison de prostitution, et pour y mettre en même temps une espèce de musée médical' (*CI*, 339–40).

As in the article on Moreau, Baudelaire attacks above all the shallowness and falsity of the self-styled democrats. The choice of language leaves no doubt as to the focus of his censure: the 'petits avocats', ridiculed in 'Les Drames et les romans honnêtes', 'se *grim*[ent] pour la tribune' and '*sing*[ent] Robespierre' (II, 182: my italics). In his plans for future novels, Baudelaire admired in Robespierre 'ce style sentencieux dont [sa] jeunesse s'est enivrée' (I, 592) and he adds to De Quincey's *Confessions* an extraordinarily complex reference to Robespierre's 'style de glace ardente, recuit et congelé comme l'abstraction' (*MO*, 128), a phrase which, like the description of *Les Liaisons dangereuses*, blends intense heat and bitter cold, but whose culinary comparison is difficult to understand rationally. Here he is content merely to insist that Robespierre's modern imitators could not even equal his purity of style, since grammar and reason have been abandoned (cf. II, 40, 48). This assertion provides him with an excellent excuse to attack the ideals of progress: 'au train dont nous marchons vers les ténèbres, il y a lieu d'espérer qu'en l'an 1900 nous serons plongés dans le noir absolu' (II, 183). His ironic use of 'marchons' and 'espérer' twists contemporary belief in the possibility of advancement towards a more perfect world and recalls the fourth stanza of 'Au lecteur':

> C'est le diable qui tient les fils qui nous remuent!
> Aux objets répugnants nous trouvons des appas;
> Chaque jour vers l'Enfer nous descendons d'un pas,
> Sans horreur, à travers des ténèbres qui puent (I, 5).

Because this slight digression has led him somewhat astray, Baudelaire prepares his reader for the examination of the fourth group by briefly suggesting the initial cause of the first three divisions, asserting that the epicureans and speculators were already present in the July Monarchy, whereas the third category was 'née de l'espérance de voir se renouveler les *miracles* de février'. The use of this religious term, with its sarcastic italics, argues that his irritation may well stem, at least in part, from the abuse of language he had previously discussed in 'Les Drames et les romans honnêtes' and 'L'Ecole païenne'.

The genesis of the fourth group Baudelaire presents as a mystery, merely indicating, in an astonishing image based, it seems to me, on recent scientific discussions,[9] that it was produced by spontaneous generation 'comme les infiniment petits dans une carafe d'eau putride, la grande carafe française' (II, 183). This category consists of *la jeunesse littéraire*, described as 'la jeunesse *réaliste*, se livrant, au sortir de l'enfance, à l'art *réalistique*' (II, 183). His mocking denigration of contemporary vocabulary and of the very idea of Realism recalls many passages in his critical writing. In the unfinished article, 'Puisque Réalisme il y a', for example, Baudelaire insists that 'tout bon poète fut toujours *réaliste*' (II, 58). And he returns to the attack in the review of *Madame Bovary*, where the term is described as an 'injure dégoûtante jetée à la face de tous les analystes, mot vague et élastique qui signifie, non pas une méthode nouvelle de création, mais une description minutieuse des accessoires' (II, 80). Similarly, in the *Salon de 1859*, the Realist painter is depicted as one who seeks to portray 'l'univers sans l'homme' (II, 627), and the essay on the life and work of Delacroix reinforces the earlier conviction that Realism sprang from intellectual as well as physical myopia: 'cette tourbe d'artistes et de littérateurs vulgaires dont l'intelligence myope s'abrite derrière le mot vague et obscur de *réalisme*' (II, 747: cf. 58).

The most obvious characteristic of the Realists, according to Baudelaire, is their rejection of museums and libraries, of the value of past knowledge. The accusation resembles a statement in 'L'Ecole païenne': 'renier les efforts de la société précédente, chrétienne ou philosophique, c'est se suicider, c'est refuser la force et les moyens de perfectionne- ment' (II, 47). Even when the Realists do look to the past for inspira- tion, they are incapable of fully understanding the models they choose. The two 'classiques' Baudelaire isolates are Murger and Musset. The reference to the first of these possesses a certain 'valeur de circonstance' since Murger had died on 28 January 1861, but his *Scènes de la vie de bohème* also offers obvious parallels, as other critics pointed out, with Cladel's novel. Thus, Glatigny's review asserts that Cladel 'vient de faire, lui aussi sa vie de bohème'[10] while Catulle Mendès insists that

'Maurthal, le héros des *Martyrs ridicules*, est victime par les trois choses qui font le charme supposé de la vie de Bohème; l'ambition, l'amitié, l'amour'.[11] What Baudelaire emphasizes in discussing Murger's treatment of the subject is his 'amère gausserie', an expression which characteristically yokes together two contrasting ideas: clearly, Baudelaire, who knew Murger personally, was fully aware of the deeper implications of his novel. The other hero of the Realists, according to Baudelaire, is Musset, a poet he has consistently rejected as 'un paresseux à effusions gracieuses' (11, 110), a 'croquemort langoureux' completely incapable of understanding 'le travail par lequel une rêverie devient un objet d'art' (*C1*, 675). Nevertheless, the 1852 study of Poe suggested that Musset possessed 'étonnantes qualités' (11, 247) and the Cladel preface, despite the predictable reference to fatuousness and laziness, also hints at 'nobles attitudes' which are worthy of emulation. Clearly, Baudelaire is reassessing Musset's potential: clearly, too, he would not express himself so forcefully if he did not think that this emphasis on inspiration was a false and dangerous influence and if he did not feel that such ideas led to the atrophy of gifts which were potentially of great value. As with Moreau, therefore, Baudelaire's anger springs partly from misguided public enthusiasm and partly from a feeling of wasted potential.

Unlike most critics, Baudelaire bases his censure of the Realists less on the subjects they choose or the way in which they treat them, than on the rejection of the need 'se soumettre à aucune gymnastique' (11, 183). On many occasions Baudelaire has insisted that intellectual gymnastics are essential for the poet, his article on Le Vavasseur drawing a particularly neat parallel between physical and aesthetic training. This, however, is his clearest statement of a belief expressed as early as the 'Conseils aux jeunes littérateurs' (11, 18), that genius is only one element – albeit the most vital – in the complex make-up of 'le grand homme':

[la jeunesse réaliste] ignore que le génie (si toutefois on peut appeler ainsi le germe indéfinissable du grand homme) doit, comme le saltimbanque apprenti, risquer de se rompre mille fois les os en secret avant de danser devant le public; que l'inspiration, en un mot, n'est que la récompense de l'exercice quotidien (11, 183).

The choice of image in this obviously personal call to arms, which owes something to Hoffmann's *Prinzessin Brambilla* and to Daumier's *Les Saltimbanques*, adds to Baudelaire's complex portrait of the artist as juggler, snake-charmer and duellist. He seems to have been drawn to the theme as early as 1845, in the poem attributed to him, 'A une jeune saltimbanque', and he turned to it again in a prose poem published, significantly, a mere two weeks after the Cladel preface, 'Le Vieux Saltimbanque'. In the prose poem, moreover, the mountebank is specifically presented as 'l'image du vieil homme de lettres qui a survécu à la génération dont il fut le brillant amuseur' (I, 297).

Not only, therefore, do the Realists base their art on 'inspiration' alone, indulging thereby their self-satisfaction and laziness – the terms *fatuité* and *paresse* are repeated – but they also run counter to Baudelaire's image of the poet in that, rather than exploring their own natures, they base their lives on 'le patron de certains romans' (II, 183). Here he touches on a theme Oscar Wilde was to elaborate: that of life imitating art. Baudelaire illustrates his point by drawing a comparison with the plastic arts: these writers are like the prostitutes who tried to resemble Gavarni's drawings, whereas Gavarni's subjects sprang less from experience than from imagination (II, 560). Gavarni may well have leapt into Baudelaire's mind when he read the title *Les Martyrs ridicules*, since Gavarni's 'Les Martyrs' places the theme in a contemporary bourgeois setting.

From these specific examples of the influence of art on contemporary reality Baudelaire formulates a general rule, expressed in typically crisp and symmetrical terms: 'ainsi l'homme d'esprit moule le peuple, et le visionnaire crée la réalité' (II, 183).[12] The term 'visionnaire', as the Pléiade notes point out, evokes Balzac, described in the essay on Gautier as a 'visionnaire passionné' (II, 120) and it is indeed to Balzac and his short novel *Ferragus XXIII* that Baudelaire turns for a literary example to support his claim.

While Baudelaire presents Cladel as sufficiently distinct from this group to be able to depict it with 'rancuneuse énergie', Janin, perhaps justifiably, sees him very much as a member of the Realist school: 'on dirait que l'auteur a voulu pousser à l'excès l'art réalistique, il y a ce mot-là écrit en toutes lettres et le mot de réalisme est déjà de trop vieille date'.[13] As in his essay on *Madame Bovary*, therefore, Baudelaire has set out to explain why a certain work should have come into being at a certain time, and to protect it from being set aside on the grounds that it belongs to a literary movement antipathetic to most critics.

As with Asselineau's *La Double Vie*, the title *Les Martyrs ridicules*, based of course on Chateaubriand's great prose epic *Les Martyrs*, has aroused Baudelaire's curiosity by its power of suggestion. Glatigny reveals a less explicit admiration of the title when he asserts: 'qu'ils sont malheureux et qu'ils sont ridicules aussi, ces pauvres chercheurs d'art et d'amour'.[14] Baudelaire goes further, indicating the areas in which the novel's characters reveal themselves as 'martyrs ridicules'.

The terms used in this discussion recall his evocation of the 'jeunesse *réaliste*': 'je vis défiler les *martyrs* de la sottise, de la fatuité, de la débauche, de la paresse juchée sur l'espérance, des amourettes prétentieuses, de la sagesse égoïstique, etc.; tous *ridicules*, mais véritablement *martyrs*' (II, 184). Thus, with great clarity but with a degree of manipulation, Baudelaire cuts through Cladel's verbiage to present the novel as an ordered study of morals. Although it is difficult to believe that Cladel himself saw the work in such clear terms, it is possible and profitable to examine it in this light. *Sottise* and *fatuité* are of course to be found in all the characters. Pipabs, with his addiction to absinth, has become a martyr to debauchery: he is described as a 'grande intelligence frappée d'imbécillité'.[15] Maurthal, the protagonist, exemplifies 'la paresse juchée sur l'espérance'. Cladel says of him: 'les découragements continus, les douleurs latentes pétrissent l'homme et le rendent malléable comme de la cire molle; sa volonté se corrompt et s'affaiblit au point qu'il ne parle, n'agit, n'existe que par assimilation'.[16] The tubercular Julie suffers from her 'amourettes prétentieuses', offering significant parallels with Mademoiselle Bistouri in that she has 'la manie [...] de *collectionner des originalités*'.[17] Examples of 'sagesse égoïstique' are to be found in two of Maurthal's companions; Malès is 'dévoré d'une ambition sans bornes, et, pour l'assouvir il s'étay[e] sur un inexorable égoïsme, sur une impiété absolue et de brillants avantages intellectuels et physiques'; of Sapy, Cladel says: 'égoïsme et probité, scepticisme et philanthropie théorique, tels étaient les saillants contrastes que l'on découvrait dans cette robuste individualité'.[18] Baudelaire's hand can indeed be detected in both the choice and the formulation of these themes, with their multiple echoes in his own writing.

Cladel's novel has delighted Baudelaire not merely through its antithetical title and its portrayal of contemporary youth but also because it upholds a central principle of his own essay on laughter: its comic elements are all the more in evidence because of the complete solemnity and emphasis with which they are expressed.

Very often in his literary reviews Baudelaire removes the sting from possible criticism by admitting that a certain accusation is indeed valid, before asserting that it misses the main point. In this case, he forestalls any rejection of the novel on the grounds that its subject-matter is unoriginal by reminding his reader yet again that the topic has already been captured by 'le pinceau si vif de Murger' (II, 184). Nevertheless, he calmly points out, in an allusion to plastic art, 'le même sujet, mis au concours, peut fournir plusieurs tableaux également remarquables à des titres divers'. Baudelaire himself, of course, can often be seen, in his criticism, taking up an idea suggested by another writer and exploring it in his own way. While Murger 'badine en racontant des choses souvent tristes', Cladel 'raconte avec une solennité *artistique* des faits déplorablement comiques' (II, 184). Several critics[19] have suggested similarities between this statement and the passage in 'Fusées': 'raconter pompeusement des choses comiques', and there are many further echoes in the essay on laughter, notably the statement that 'les animaux les plus comiques sont les plus sérieux' (II, 532: cf. 542 and see also 200). A second difference between Cladel and Murger is touched on merely in passing. The use of the italicized epithet '*artistique*' with reference to Cladel implies that Baudelaire sees him as a more conscious artist than Murger. A third and more vital contrast lies in the fact that whereas Murger, rather like Banville, side-steps aspects which would distress his 'tendre esprit', Cladel, like Borel, 'insiste avec fureur'.

The terms used to describe Cladel's technique reveal quite unmistakably the degree to which he is seen as exploiting Baudelaire's own processes and carrying out aims very similar to those which motivated *Les Fleurs du mal*: 'il ouvre la plaie pour la mieux montrer, la referme, en pince les lèvres livides, et en fait jaillir un sang jaune et pâle. Il manie le péché en curieux, le tourne, le retourne, examine complaisamment les circonstances, et déploye dans l'analyse du mal la consciencieuse ardeur d'un casuiste' (II, 184). The image of the wound was pounced on by Mendès, who claims in his review that Cladel is one of those who 'pensent qu'il vaut mieux montrer [les] plaies, non pour en tirer vanité ni pour décourager ceux qui s'exposeraient à en voir saigner un jour de pareilles sur leur poitrine, mais afin de leur indiquer par quelles terribles épreuves ils auraient à passer'.[20] Glatigny, however, while admitting that Cladel laid bare 'ces dégoûts et ces ténèbres avec l'instinct d'un grand artiste' could not refrain from hoping 'qu'il s'en retourne vite vers la clarté des étoiles'.[21]

Having shown Cladel's main purpose, Baudelaire turns to Alpinien Maurthal in order to reveal how intention has been translated into reality. In doing so, he presents Maurthal almost as a double of himself, just as his main focus in the articles on Moreau, Banville and Borel was on those elements that they had in common with him. Maurthal's 'perpétuelle oscillation', which Cladel himself clarifies in *Les Martyrs ridicules* by asserting that 'la conscience de Maurthal [est] envahie par le remords presque aussi vite que par la pensée du crime',[22] recalls Baudelaire's simultaneous 'horreur de la vie' and 'extase de la vie'. Similarly, the 'incurable maladie voilée sous le repentir périodique' (II, 184) is reminiscent of much of *Les Fleurs du mal* and *Les Paradis artificiels*, notably such poems as 'Au lecteur', 'L'Héautontimorouménos' and 'L'Irrémédiable'.

Despite the bitterness of this personal attack, Baudelaire describes Maurthal's case as 'instructif': clearly he believes that Cladel has avoided overt didacticism, that in this case 'la morale n'entre pas dans cet art à titre de but; elle s'y mêle et s'y confond comme dans la vie elle-même' (II, 137). Other critics saw the novel in a similar light, perhaps precisely because of Baudelaire's preface. As we have seen, Mendès considered that it should show young writers 'par quelles terribles épreuves ils auraient à passer',[23] while the critic of *La Revue européenne* referred to it more pompously as 'un livre dont je conseillerais la lecture à toute cette génération de jeunes gens dévoyés qui livrent leur corps et leur âme en pâture à la sensualité'.[24] Baudelaire alone, however, is clear-sighted enough to see that Cladel is holding a mirror not just to the young, but to all his contemporaries: 'j'espère que quelques-uns du siècle sauront s'y reconnaître avec plaisir' (II, 185). Possibly there is once again a punning allusion to *Le Siècle*. Certainly there are parallels with his reaction to *La Double Vie*: 'heureux le lecteur pensif, l'*homo duplex*, qui, sachant reconnaître dans l'auteur son miroir, ne craint pas de s'écrier: *Thou art the man!* Voilà mon confesseur!' (II, 91).

Having revealed Cladel's originality of treatment, Baudelaire examines more closely the 'disproportion du ton avec le sujet' (II, 185) already mentioned in an earlier paragraph (II, 184). There are two purposes behind this study: firstly it attempts to turn potential criticism to Cladel's advantage, thus forestalling those who might argue – with some justification – that the intensity of the prose is exaggerated in relation to the often rather trivial events it conveys; secondly, it offers an opportunity to establish the position of the true critic as a 'sage désintéressé' in terms which run counter to Baudelaire's very early assertion that true criticism is both prejudiced and passionate, and which recall the essay on laughter, with its focus on the reaction of 'le sage'. The essay on laughter is clearly very present in Baudelaire's mind when he insists that 'si grand que soit un être, et si nul qu'il soit relativement à l'infini, le pathos et l'emphase lui sont permis et nécessaires' (II, 185). Probably as a result of his attempt to stress man's relative insignificance Baudelaire illustrates this comment by comparing 'l'Humanité' to 'ces éphémères de l'Hypanis' and by insisting that 'les fourmis elles-mêmes, pour leurs affaires politiques, peuvent emboucher la trompette de Corneille, proportionnée à leur bouche' (II, 185). The allusion is unexpected and it seems unlikely that it is principally Aristotle's work that Baudelaire has in mind. Possibly the parallels he saw between Cladel's technique and his own study on laughter had reminded him of that master of the comic, E. T. A. Hoffmann, and his portrait of the complex political system of the fleas in *Meister Floh* (cf. II, 542). It is also possible that his initial source of inspiration is the plastic arts, perhaps the fantastic drawings of Grandville or the political caricatures of Daumier. Certainly there seems to be an echo of Baudelaire's own comment in the review of *Madame Bovary* that 'les paroles les plus solennelles, les plus décisives, s'échapperont des bouches les plus sottes' (II, 80).

Although he justifies Cladel's insistence on the mediocre and asserts that 'pénétration psychique' is his strongest quality, Baudelaire adds a carefully expressed warning based not on the subject but on the tone and style: 'son art, minutieux et brutal, turbulent et enfiévré, se restreindra plus tard, sans nul doute, dans une forme plus sévère et plus froide, qui mettra ses qualités morales en plus vive lumière, plus à nu' (II, 185). Other critics also attacked Cladel's language. Janin reluctantly admitted that 'il a le pressentiment d'un certain art d'écrire, M. L. Cladel; au milieu de toutes ces violences d'un langage *inénarrable* (c'est son mot) se rencontrent parfois des paroles claires, élégantes, bienséantes'.[25] Mendès, however, aggressively insisted: 'le style de M. Léon Cladel est dans une concordance parfaite avec le sujet de son livre'.[26] And the critic of the *Revue européenne*, inspired perhaps both by Baudelaire's article on Borel and by the fact that the third section of the novel has as its epigraph the poem which prefaces *Madame Putiphar* (see II, 1165), remarked that:

> par ses défauts et par ses mérites, [le roman] rappelle cette fraction de l'école de 1830 dont le chef-d'œuvre fut *Madame Putiphar*. Même recherche de la bizarrerie, mêmes inversions de phrases, mêmes violences de style, même dédain des traditions lexicologiques de notre langue, mais aussi même souffle, même puissance, même naïveté d'impressions.[27]

Baudelaire's criticism differs in that he expresses extremely cogently the advantages of other approaches while nevertheless revealing that he understands why Cladel is as yet incapable of greater sobriety: 'en même temps que sa clairvoyance s'exerce avec volupté, sa sensibilité, furieuse d'avoir été refoulée, fait une subite et indiscrète explosion' (II, 185). The term 'explosion' is of course vital to Baudelaire's concept of art and the human psyche, but all his critical articles and in particular the review of *Tannhäuser* with its emphasis on *volonté*, as well as *explosion*, reveal his constant belief that such outbursts should be firmly controlled by the poet's will power and self-discipline. The word 'indiscrète', moreover, leaves the reader in no doubt about Baudelaire's position.

He illustrates his affirmation by recounting, with typical conciseness and linguistic virtuosity, the episode in which Pipabs is forced, in exchange for the essential glass of absinth, to entertain a group of young men to whom Baudelaire awards the title 'bourreaux'. In describing Pipab's plight, Baudelaire uses the phrase 'la fausse hygiène de l'ivrognerie', the very language of which reveals yet again the extent to which his pleasure in the novel derives from the parallels he detected with his own beliefs. The term 'hygiène', which replaces the original word 'penchant', recalls the personal diaries, while the interest in the mistaken conviction that stimulants further creativity, suggests the articles on Poe, the studies on intoxicants and the plans for a play, *L'Ivrogne*.

However much Baudelaire may have enjoyed the scene itself, he firmly rejects Cladel's authorial intervention, pointing firstly, by the use of the word *'discours'* (II, 186: cf. II, 11), to the falsity that this intervention involves, and then criticizing it on more general, aesthetic grounds. 'Le suprême de l'art eût consisté à rester glacial et fermé, et à laisser au lecteur tout le mérite de l'indignation' (II, 186: cf. II, 80). This statement, of course, strikes a further blow in Baudelaire's constant campaign against specific moralizing in art and goes unashamedly against Sainte-Beuve's accusation that in *Madame Bovary* 'le bien est trop absent; pas un personnage ne le représente'.

This discussion of the links between art and morality leads naturally to an analysis of the way in which the central characters 's'étalent avec une instructive nudité' (II, 186), the choice of epithet reinforcing Baudelaire's conviction that true art is instructive without being overtly didactic. He selects three examples from the novel to illustrate his claim.

Firstly, he reveals the pretentious snobbery of the two working-class women who 'se font des révérences d'un autre monde'. The first of these, whose 'douceur animale' has so enchanted her lover, is probably Maurthal's mistress Claire with whom he fell in love initially and primarily because of 'le culte qu'[elle] affectait d'avoir pour sa mère'.[28] Nevertheless, it is the 'modiste prétentieuse', Madame Salvanole, who recalls a sphinx, since she possesses 'cette profondeur insondable que les poètes donnent aux yeux de leurs maîtresses idéales'.[29] This expression has close parallels in *Les Fleurs du mal*, especially with 'L'Amour du mensonge'. Certainly the way in which she dominates and bullies her husband, on the other hand, may well have provoked Baudelaire's remark, with its unusual image, that she has 'fouaillé son imagination avec toutes les orties de George Sand'.[30]

Baudelaire's second example, given partly to insist on the insincerity typical of contemporary youth and partly to assert 'la puissance sinistre-

ment caricaturale de M. Cladel', is based on a scene in which Claire
and Maurthal adopt the names and personalities of characters in
Murger's *Vie de bohème*. This scene not only justifies Baudelaire's earlier
claim that the Realists misunderstood their idol Murger, since here he
has been 'transformé en truchement', but it also supports his complaint
that *la jeunesse littéraire* base their lives on novels, transforming Murger's
work into a '*Parfait secrétaire des amants* de l'an de *grâce* 1861', that is, a
ready-made source of expressions and reactions. The emphasis placed
on '*grâce*' intensifies the sarcastic tone.

The third example leads to a closer examination of Maurthal and a
tightening of the parallels between this anti-hero and Baudelaire himself. On the one hand, Baudelaire insists on Maurthal's 'mauvaises
mœurs, sa fainéantise et sa rêverie vagabonde' (II, 186), recalling not
only such poems as 'Le Mauvais Moine' with its despairing injunction:

> [. . .] quand saurai-je donc faire
> Du spectacle vivant de ma triste misère
> Le travail de mes mains et l'amour de mes yeux? (I, 16),

but also the puzzled affirmation in the anthology notice that Hugo
could indeed 'concilier les nécessités de son travail assidu avec ce
goût sublime, mais dangereux, des promenades et des rêveries' (II,
129). The expression, moreover, echoes a passage in *Les Martyrs
ridicules*: 'nous sommes d'obstinés rêveurs, et la rêverie prolongée,
c'est l'impuissance'.[31] On the other hand, Baudelaire emphasizes
Maurthal's tendency to elevate love and fame to the status of religions.
While remaining true to Cladel's intention in depicting the tormented,
almost insane, Maurthal visiting the tombs of great writers, Baudelaire's choice of expression nevertheless calls to mind much of his
literary criticism: 'Alpinien court la gloire, et errant dans les cimetières,
il implore les images des grands hommes défunts; il baise leurs bustes,
les suppliant de lui livrer leur secret, le grand secret: "Comment faire
pour devenir aussi grand que vous?"' (II, 186–7).[32] This kind of
question – although, of course, at a deeper level – is present throughout
Baudelaire's criticism and his answer is as typically direct and down-
to-earth as the tone of his very early 'Conseils aux jeunes littérateurs': 'il
faut rester chez toi, méditer et barbouiller beaucoup de papier!' The
emphasis on meditation, however, is of more recent date, the first
important use of the term appearing in the Gautier essay of 1859 (II,
105). In affirming that so simple and obvious a course is beyond the
reach of 'un rêveur hystérique', Baudelaire, without pervertring Cladel's
purpose, is once again emphasizing those elements which offer most
similarities with his own predicament. It is not impossible that he

considered himself, like Maurthal, as one of the 'solitaires oisifs et impuissants': it is quite certain that he regarded himself as a 'rêveur hystérique' in the nineteenth-century use of that epithet (cf. II, 83). At least one contemporary critic took up this reference, remarking on 'les cercles désolés de cet enfer de la sensation, où l'idéal se traduit par la frénésie hystérique'.[33] What would have made the parallel between Baudelaire and Maurthal seem even closer is the fact that the tomb at which Maurthal worships most fervently is that of Balzac, whom Baudelaire himself has so often held up as an example of hard work and determined will power.

Finally, Baudelaire is eager to reveal the full importance of Maurthal's rejection of the counter-religions of love and fame, and his return to the blend of credulous superstition and naive Christianity that marks childhood. The use of the term 'contre-religion' is fully justified by the novel itself, in which Maurthal asserts that 'la volupté, c'est la seule vérité de l'amour comme l'ivresse en est l'apéritif. L'ivresse et la volupté, voilà mes croyances.'[34] In one of the rapid but richly suggestive side-allusions at which he excels, Baudelaire like Flaubert insists that superstitions are worthy of attention since they symbolize 'l'universelle vérité', a remark which recalls his belief that 'rien n'est plus beau que le lieu commun' (I, 670). Among the 'salutaires impressions de l'enfance', moreover, Baudelaire singles out 'le chant fortifiant des cloches' in a phrase reminiscent both of Chateaubriand's *René* and of his own poem 'La Cloche fêlée'.

Above all, it is Maurthal's return to his mother which seems to have filled Baudelaire with 'un délicieux et douloureux attendrissement', just as he was so affected by Mrs Clemm's energetic and determined support for Poe. As the notes to the Pléiade edition point out, it is principally of himself and his own relationship with his mother that Baudelaire is thinking here. Nevertheless, he links his comments firmly to the novel in the choice of the expression 'fruits secs', Cladel himself having evoked the 'fruits secs de l'art, gens aux rancunes incurables, éteignoirs systématiques de toutes les lueurs naissantes'.[35] Characteristically, Baudelaire allows himself no hint of self-pity: the sentimental, nostalgic return to childhood beliefs, he claims, cannot alone save Maurthal. What is essential, he adds, in terms that recall both the self-confident 'Conseils aux jeunes littérateurs' and the despairing *Journaux intimes*, is that Maurthal must become 'un homme d'action, un homme de devoir, au jour le jour' (II, 187). By 1846 Baudelaire was already aware that 'si l'on veut vivre dans une contemplation opiniâtre de l'œuvre de demain, le travail journalier servira l'inspiration' (II, 18), while in 'Hygiène' he desperately tries to convince himself that 'plus on travaille, mieux on travaille, et plus on veut travailler. Plus on produit plus on devient fécond' (I, 668).

The preface closes on a three-pronged conclusion, considering the novel from the point of view of satire, of its morality and of its possible success. Firstly, in a passage which indicates that his notice on Barbier has led him to sharpen his awareness of the role and potential of satire, Baudelaire, as in his essay on the comic, indicates the close proximity of tears and laughter and insists that the ability to laugh at contemporary follies, however much one may, at another level, grieve over them, indicates a state of 'parfaite santé'.

In affirming the non-didactic *moralité* of *Les Martyrs ridicules*, Baudelaire strengthens the structure of the preface by using an image based on scientific discoveries, just as he did in suggesting the way in which the Realists came into being: 'quant à la moralité du livre, elle en jaillit naturellement comme la chaleur de certains mélanges chimiques' (II, 187). Although the image is new to Baudelaire's criticism, the semantic field from which it is borrowed, and the conviction itself, are familiar not only from Balzac's writings but from the anthology notice on Hugo with its reference to 'une morale inspirée qui se glisse, invisible, dans la matière poétique, comme les fluides impondérables dans toute la machine du monde' (II, 137). Moreover, in expanding on this assertion, Baudelaire chooses an illustration which reflects his use of *gentry*: 'il est permis de soûler les ilotes pour guérir de l'ivrognerie les gentilshommes' (II, 187).

This conscious desire to provoke his reader is also very much to the fore when Baudelaire turns to examine the possibility that the novel would achieve success. Here he reveals a new outlook on what has been a central problem throughout his criticism. Whereas before he incessantly sought to understand the rules governing success, here he concludes that it is a 'question sur laquelle on ne peut rien présager' (II, 187) and insists, in terms which are partly a challenge, partly an attempt to convince himself, that public acclaim is desirable only in so far as it provides the author with 'une excitation nouvelle'. His studies of writers such as Dupont and Barbier have revealed only too clearly that success is 'si facile [...] à confondre avec une vogue momentanée'. And he ends his preface with a characteristic twist, a sting in the tail destined to annoy and astonish a complacent reader: if the novel is successful, he calmly declares, that fact 'ne diminuerait en rien tout le bien que le livre me fait conjecturer de l'âme et du talent qui l'ont produit de concert'. In emphasizing the combination of 'âme' and 'talent', moreover, Baudelaire reinforces his earlier call for genius to be combined with aesthetic gymnastics.

Thus, however clearly it sums up contemporary youth, however cogently it supports the innate morality of a work of art and however subtly it indicates not only those areas where Cladel has succeeded but also those where he could have achieved more, the preface to *Les Martyrs ridicules* is above all a penetrating analysis both of Baudelaire's art and of his own personality.

❧ Conclusion

At times pugilistic and provocative, often far-sighted and always sensitive, Baudelaire's literary criticism, although deeply bedded in contemporary debate, theory and practice, still has much to offer present-day readers. What is it, in his ideas about literature and criticism, and in his means of conveying them, that makes Baudelaire's criticism so rewarding?

His opinion of most contemporary critics seems to have been consistently astringent: the *Salon de 1845* deplores 'la critique des journaux, tantôt niaise, tantôt furieuse, jamais indépendante' (II, 351); in 1857 he referred to 'un de ces nombreux réquisitoires dressés par les critiques parisiens contre ceux de nos poètes qui sont le plus amoureux de perfection' (II, 337); in an article on Gautier he attacked the stupidity of 'les badauds de la critique' (II, 150); and a note in *Un Mangeur d'opium* is scornfully ironic: 'il faut pour s'élever jusque là, être doué de l'esprit envieux et quinteux du critique moral' (*MO*, 216). Yet some critics did win his praise, however temporary or guarded it may have been. In 1860 he found in Villemain, Barbey d'Aurevilly and Renan, for example, critical 'clairvoyance' and wisdom (*C*I, 675). Nevertheless, by 1864 Villemain had provoked the angry notes on his 'esprit' and 'style', and Renan was bracketed with 'toutes les stupidités propres à ce dix-neuvième siècle' (II, 229). In this regard, too, he challenges the reader, referring for instance with considerable irony to a major critic, Gustave Planche, as 'un paysan du Danube dont l'éloquence impérative et savante s'est tue au grand regret des sains esprits' (II, 351).

However deeply he may have despised many critics, however quick he was to condemn the few who briefly earned his praise, he was certainly aware, as his letters and notes as well as his articles bear witness, both of their convictions and of their techniques. Indeed, as the preceding chapters demonstrate, his contemporaries frequently acted as a stimulus to Baudelaire's own thought, provoking the explosion of anger or pleasure leading to deeper exploration.

Two critics in particular seem to have influenced both his thinking and his expression: Sainte-Beuve and Gautier. No doubt his interest in their criticism, which, at least for Gautier, dates from Baudelaire's school days, was intensified by his enthusiasm for their poetry and his enjoyment of *Volupté* and *Mademoiselle de Maupin*. While Baudelaire was indeed very familiar with Sainte-Beuve's reviews, he seems not to have been crushed by them, as Pichois believes (II, 1070), but rather to have found the older critic's power and fluency a source both of envy and of irritation, emotions which, in Baudelaire, can be equally productive. Gautier's influence was probably even more important, both in specific instances, such as his study of Balzac, and, more generally, in the thought and imagery of the poetry and of *Mademoiselle de Maupin*. As his reviews constantly reveal, both the novel and its preface have bitten deeply into Baudelaire's memory and there can be little doubt that his first reading of it, like that of *Volupté* (*C*I, 61), was a formative experience in his career.

Although he elaborates no rigid theory of criticism in the manner of a Veuillot, a Planche or a Barbey d'Aurevilly, many of Baudelaire's articles suggest the way in which he envisaged the critic's task. Far from basing his judgements on a preconceived idea of criticism, he responds very much to the individual challenge posed by each writer under consideration.

Those dual keystones of Baudelaire's aesthetic beliefs – the rich and varied imagination, and the power of reflection combined with the ability to modulate from individual examples to general precepts – are also basic to his criticism. The unfinished article on Villemain, for example, contains the following tantalizing note: 'portrait du vrai critique. – Métaphysique. – Imagination' (II, 192). Similarly, in his *Salon de 1846*, he leaves no doubt that the best criticism is that which presents the work of art 'réfléchi par un esprit intelligent et sensible' (II, 418). The emphasis, as so often in Baudelaire's criticism, lies on both an intellectual and an emotional response. These two poles of emotion and intelligence are also present, for example, in the notice on Banville with its evocation of the moments when 'l'on se sent heureux de penser et de vivre' (II, 163), and in the famous expression from the review of *Tannhäuser*: 'transformer ma volupté en connaissance' (II, 786). The critic, therefore, should not merely reproduce the main outline or the basic themes of a work, he should not, for example, be content, as many of Baudelaire's contemporaries were content, merely to offer a synopsis of a novel or a minute description of a painting, but must recreate its atmosphere and use it as a springboard for his own reveries. The best critic, therefore, is 'un rêveur dont l'esprit est tourné à la généralisation aussi bien qu'à l'étude des détails' (II, 575), a thinker who seeks to reveal the wider implications of a writer's character or of his experiments, and who uses an individual artist to support or refine an idea of general application.

This belief, sketched in 1846 and expanded in 1855, received its most telling expression in Baudelaire's last major review: 'les considérations et les rêveries morales qui surgissent des dessins d'un artiste sont, dans beaucoup de cas, la meilleure traduction que le critique en puisse faire; les suggestions font partie d'une idée mère, et, en les montrant successivement, on peut la faire deviner' (II, 712). Like creative art itself, criticism, for Baudelaire, is far removed from didacticism, being above all the art of suggestion, the creation of 'une magie suggestive, contenant à la fois l'objet et le sujet, le monde extérieur à l'artiste et l'artiste lui-même' (II, 598). Just as creative writing explores both the outer world and that of the imagination, so criticism examines both the particular world of the writer discussed and his relationship with art in general. To some extent, Baudelaire is no doubt making a virtue of necessity: by encouraging the reader to respond to suggestion he is not only rendering censorship impotent, but making his public more alive to the suggestive powers of literature itself.

The critics most able to live up to this ideal are those who are also poets: 'il n'y a que les poètes pour bien comprendre les poètes' (*C*II, 325). That poets can understand not only the successes but also the experiments of other poets better than the uninitiated is hardly surprising. Yet Baudelaire also claims that 'tous les grands poètes deviennent naturellement, fatalement, critiques' (II, 793). As Baudelaire's articles reveal, he himself has turned to criticism not merely to live up to his constant ideal of the artist equally gifted in all genres, but also, and perhaps more urgently, because the analysis and exploration of another poet's solution to perennial aesthetic problems offers a rich and stimulating training-ground for his own creative writing.

Armed with this double-bladed sword, imagination and the 'manie philosophique' (II, 248), the critic can cut through pretence and cliché and therefore has no need to shield himself with dogma. In reviewing the Exposition universelle of 1855 Baudelaire ruefully admits in a well-known passage: 'j'ai essayé plus d'une fois, comme tous mes amis, de m'enfermer dans un système pour y prêcher à mon aise. Mais un système est une espèce de damnation qui nous pousse à une abjuration perpétuelle' (II, 577). The true critic, like the poet, is 'ouvert à toutes les beautés' (II, 630) and unafraid of contradicting himself. He must, therefore, refuse to analyse art according to rigid moral precepts (II, 495) or to blind patriotism (II, 610). This was a central problem in an artistic world dominated by critics whose conclusions consistently

derive from such extra-literary considerations. Similarly, just as Baudelaire does not insist that a work of art conform to his own ideas,
neither would he demand of the writer any more – or any less – than
'la naïveté et l'expression sincère de son tempérament' (II, 419). Although he suggests themes or questions in which a writer's gifts might
find fulfilment, Baudelaire avoids appearing to dictate. As early as the
review of Champfleury's tales, he remarked: 'il ne faut forcer la destinée
de personne' (II, 23) and in his study of *La Légende des siècles,* while
proposing various moods Hugo might explore in his next work, he is
careful to add a modest disclaimer: 'Dans quel ordre de choses, par
quels nouveaux moyens renouvellera-t-il sa preuve? [. . .] il n'est pas
permis à la critique de le dire' (II, 141). Yet, as with so many of Baudelaire's convictions, there is a second side to this belief. Without being
dogmatic he often reveals, in deceptively simple side-comments, what
he would prefer, and to what temptations he fears the writer may succumb. Baudelaire does not, however, reduce the role of the critic to
that of interpreter: discerning enough to detect the writer's intentions,
sufficiently imaginative to see how they could be attained and fully
sensitive to all forms of beauty, the critic should show the poet how
and why he has failed to achieve, not the critic's ambitions, but his
own (cf. II, 328).

Although such basic tenets seem to have remained constant, it
would be false to assume that Baudelaire the critic leapt into his first
feuilleton fully fledged and fully armed. He constantly perfects techniques
and experiments with ways of presenting facts and ideas, just as he
gradually arrives at images expressed with such cogency in the articles
and poems of his maturity.

On the one hand, he conveys his central points with increasing conviction and skill. The Poe studies in particular show him rearranging
his material so as to achieve maximum impact, and also reveal his
growing command of the *entrée en matière.* Similarly, his ability to use
detailed references allusively and still explain the general nature of a
work has grown considerably from the rather pedestrian article on
Champfleury to the passing allusions in the anthology notices, the
study on Hugo providing a remarkable illustration: 'c'est surtout dans
ces dernières années qu'il a subi l'influence métaphysique qui s'exhale
de toutes ces choses, curiosité d'un Œdipe obsédé par d'innombrables
Sphinx' (II, 137).

On the other hand, he has learnt to convey his reservations indirectly
but unmistakably, using devices which, like dark lanterns, guide the
wary. Not only is adverse criticism sandwiched between praise, suggesting both the poet's limitations and his gifts or promise, but Baudelaire

also repeats certain words so that, without appearing to stress them, he nevertheless imprints them on his reader's mind. Thus, in the review of Asselineau's *La Double Vie*, the word *petit* appears in the first and last paragraphs, as well as in the middle of the article (ii, 87, 89, 91), and terms such as *morceau* (ii, 88, 90) further enforce the implication that the tales are little more than preliminary sketches. Reservations can also be suggested by introducing a statement with the word *si*, by claiming, for instance, that if certain qualities make a great poet, then the writer under discussion is indeed worthy of that title; this technique is exploited with considerable skill in the notice on Desbordes-Valmore.

As in the art criticism, Baudelaire also raises doubts in the reader's mind by placing an adverse judgement or merely a pertinent question in the mouth of a third person, who is sometimes the imaginary reader himself. In the preface to Dupont's songs, for example, he suggests that 'plusieurs personnes regretteront de ne pas trouver dans ces chants politiques et guerriers tout l'éclat de la guerre' (ii, 32). By 1859 Baudelaire was even more adept at this technique: in discussing the eclectic nature of modern poetry he writes: 'aucuns y pourraient voir peut-être des symptômes de dépravation' (ii, 167), suggesting in this way the possibility of different points of view, but at the same time making his own feelings clear in a subtle way.

In mastering the medium, Baudelaire was not merely responding to a personal challenge. Although his criticism brought him intellectual pleasure and profit, serving to focus his thoughts on schools, genres and general aesthetic questions, and, often, enabling him to draw resolution from the example of other writers, his critical articles are never directed solely or even principally at himself. Certainly there are times when a burst of detail or extreme intensity in expression suggests that he is analysing himself rather than, or at least as much as, the writer ostensibly under discussion. Yet even there he keeps in mind an imaginary reader whom he seeks to inform or persuade, a reader whose protests serve as a shadow against which the outline of Baudelaire's ideal poet is more sharply defined. The same device may be found, of course, in the art criticism (e.g. ii, 654–5) and the prose poems, as well as in other contemporary poets, but whereas Hugo, for example, overdoes the technique in his poetry, rendering it at times prosaic and trivial, Baudelaire's wit and irony strike a balance between the patronizing and the over-familiar.

Baudelaire certainly makes exacting demands on the 'amateurs curieux de la vraie littérature' (ii, 3: cf. ii, 106), the 'vrais amants de la Muse' (ii, 124: cf. ii, 163, 179) to whom he addresses his criticism.

Although it is clear that he expects them to possess the two qualities of sensitivity and intellect that he stresses in his own reactions to art, it is the second of these twin pillars that he emphasizes. His articles address those who are not only intelligent (II, 91), 'clairvoyants' (II, 152) and 'gens d'esprit' (II, 127), but have also turned this intelligence to questions of literary theory and felt the need to 'se créer une esthétique à leur usage' (II, 23). They are expected to recognize allusions and unidentified quotations as well as to react to more definite references, to bring to Baudelaire's criticism, in fact, not the passing glance of the casual newspaper browser but alert and percipient attention. The review of the Museum at the Bazar Bonne-Nouvelle poses the challenge forcibly and succinctly: 'nous rapportons des faits; lecteur, à vous les réflexions' (II, 409).

But the reader is not left to make those reflections unaided: Baudelaire confronts him, mocking him as in the review of Ménard – 'pauvre lecteur, comme vous prenez le mors aux dents, quand on vous met sur une pente!' (II, 9) – cajoling him, as in the notice on Desbordes-Valmore, where he is addressed as 'vous, homme réfléchi et toujours responsable' (II, 146), or simply calling on his experiences to affirm a supposition: 'quel est celui de nous qui [. . .] n'a pas fait forcément connaissance avec le prêtre incompétent?' (II, 85); 'qui parmi nous n'est pas un *homo duplex*?' (II, 87: cf. II, 145). It is also Baudelaire's half-mocking attitude towards his reader, as well as his pleasure in paradox and deliberate provocation, that underlies his obvious delight in reversing habitual clichés and overturning prejudices, forcing his reader to reconsider ideas whose validity he might formerly have thought beyond question.

Baudelaire's constant awareness of his reader, who becomes a sparring partner – albeit a junior partner – in the act of criticism, sets him apart from the great majority of contemporary critics. While Gautier looks on his readers as like-minded companions, Janin as an admiring audience for his pirouettes, and Sainte-Beuve as a sympathetic but uninformed public needing education, Baudelaire alone seems to hold a clear picture of a reader whose intelligence, sensitivity and taste, although not necessarily opinions, resemble his own, a reader who may often be teased, shocked and provoked, but who is always respected, in fact an 'Hypocrite lecteur, – mon semblable, – mon frère!' (I, 6).

This image of his reader profoundly affects the kind of background information Baudelaire provides. The essay on Gautier (II, 104) shows how scornfully he regarded the *compilateurs* who reduced criticism to biography. Certainly the destinies of other writers interest him: he

frequently mentions the apparent capriciousness of the fates of Hoffmann, Balzac and Poe, for example. His interest here is twofold: not
only is it closely connected with his constant exploration of the causes
of popularity, but it also springs from his ambivalent attitude towards
fate, which, however absurd it may appear in individual cases, can
nevertheless be seen as forming a harmonious universal pattern: even
if the angel of expiation is blind, it is not purposeless when it seizes on
individuals and whips them 'pour l'édification des autres' (11, 296).

Although biographical details had come to be expected in literary
criticism (cf. 11, 267), Baudelaire never introduces them merely as a
matter of course: they are used to amuse, to provoke and to enlighten
and, far from finding them the predictably safe means of entertainment
he expected, a bourgeois reader must often have regarded them as
unreliable fireworks, threatening to explode in his face. When he
introduces such information, Baudelaire turns it very much to his own
purposes. Thus he emphasizes, in the case of Dupont, the need for a
sudden outburst of rebellion against the stifling influence of the family,
and his essay on Gautier discounts the value of those conventionally
accepted indicators of future success, school prizes. In both cases there
is a deeply personal side, recalling both his dislike of his stepfather and
the pressure his family exerted on him to win prizes when he was at
school. Even while remaining within traditional frameworks, therefore,
he seizes on any opportunity to deflate bourgeois ideals and values,
but he also brings to his criticism that intensity that springs from
personal involvement.

Baudelaire's studies also reveal the influence of a writer's historical
background, showing for example the regenerative powers of Romanticism, and the way in which Borel's hyperbole stems from a revolt
against the July Monarchy's doctrine of the *juste milieu*, while Dupont's
songs gained popularity partly because their freshness delighted the
jaded palates of those who had grown up under Louis-Philippe. In
this Baudelaire is in harmony with contemporary practice, although he
places more emphasis than is usual on suggesting a logical link between public events and personal characteristics. Indeed, this way of
looking at literature seems to come so naturally to him that it would
be false to consider it an acquired technique. It is certainly in this area
that he reveals one of his greatest gifts as a critic: the considerable
skill with which he recreates, concisely yet with provocative precision,
the atmosphere of an era.

It is also his search for the underlying logic that leads him to throw
into relief, far more than his contemporaries, the importance of childhood, asserting that 'le génie n'est que *l'enfance retrouvée* à volonté'

(II, 690) and concluding that: 'tous les biographes ont compris, d'une manière plus ou moins complète, l'importance des anecdotes se rattachant à l'enfance d'un écrivain ou d'un artiste. Mais je trouve que cette importance n'a jamais été suffisamment affirmée' (*MO*, 222). His sharpest attention, as the articles on Dupont, Banville and Barbier demonstrate, centres on the 'diverses transformations' of a writer's art and on the corresponding 'préoccupations successives de son esprit' (II, 361).

The focus on the poet's mind rather than on his life is closely linked to one of the principal stated aims of Baudelaire's criticism: the discovery and description of what is *sui generis* in a writer's work. Acutely aware of the difficulties of providing an exact definition, he offers not dogmatic assertions but rather suggestive indications, challenging the reader to explore the problem for himself. The ways in which he conveys this essence are very varied, ranging from comparison with other artists, through paraphrase, résumé and quotation, to parody and pastiche.

The earliest of his literary articles show him delighting, like Sainte-Beuve, in suggesting the literary family to which a writer belongs, likening Chennevières to Hoffmann, Champfleury to Balzac. This device is still used in the review of *Madame Bovary*, where he distinguishes contemporary novelists 'tournés à la Dickens' from those 'moulés à la Byron' (II, 79). His later criticism, however, perhaps merely because it tends to deal with established figures, emphasizes individuality rather than similarities. Thus, the way in which Gautier upholds the concept of *poésie pure* is contrasted with Hugo's use of his poetry to convey hopes and beliefs, and Leconte de Lisle's gifts are illuminated by the precise and discriminating comparison with Gautier's art and Renan's thought. Although the writers to whom Baudelaire refers in these comparisons are usually those whose names would be familiar to the general public, the influence of his eclectic reading is often evident, particularly in the later articles. Comparisons between poetry and the plastic arts also become more frequent: *Mademoiselle de Maupin* is described as 'cette rêverie continuée avec l'obstination d'un peintre' (II, 111), Balzac is compared to 'ces aquafortistes qui ne sont jamais contents de la morsure, et qui transforment en ravines les écorchures principales de la planche' (II, 120), and Hugo's poetry combines the gifts of sculptor and painter in its recreation of form and colour (II, 132: cf. II, 135).

Since Baudelaire's criticism is above all an incitement to read the works discussed, paraphrase is less common than comparison, except in the case of some of Poe's works, where it was justified by the lack of translations. In this, too, Baudelaire stands apart from the majority of contemporary critics who often devoted the greater part of their studies to recapitulating the novel or play they were reviewing. He did, however, revel in condensing a poem or tale into an arresting sentence or brief paragraph. The reviews of Champfleury's short stories and Asselineau's *La Double Vie* reflect his increasing control of this technique, while the article on Flaubert and the notice on Leconte de Lisle yield further remarkable examples of his skill. There can be no doubt that Baudelaire very much enjoys conveying the basic details of a work of literature in taut, memorable phrases and that it is for him a valuable stylistic exercise: nevertheless, the very brilliance of these *tours de force* challenges the reader to question their accuracy and thus sharpens his awareness of the work Baudelaire so brilliantly condenses.

Among Baudelaire's contemporaries, the most common method of suggesting the theme and flavour of a work was by quotation. Sainte-Beuve, like other regular columnists, was no doubt glad to devote much space to lengthy quotations, and many journals seized on the pretext of a literary study to gain readers by offering copious extracts from popular writers, the publication of Hugo's *La Légende des siècles* and *Les Misérables* being cases in point. By comparison, Baudelaire's use of quotation is far more sparing, and this holds true for all his criticism, whenever it was written. Although quotations in the reviews of *Prométhée délivré* (11, 10), *La Double Vie* (11, 89), and Banville's poetry (11, 163, 166) suggest by their accuracy that he had the text to hand, slight variations indicate that in quoting from Proudhon (11, 34), Desbordes-Valmore (11, 148) and Borel (11, 172), he is relying on memory. His ability to recall lines and even complete stanzas indicates the impact some works made on him and reveals the extent to which they had become part of the fabric of his mind.

This is further indicated by the fragments of lines embedded in his articles. In referring to Romanticism, for example, Baudelaire quotes, without explanation, Hugo's line: 'O splendeurs éclipsées, ô soleil descendu derrière l'horizon' (11, 110). Similarly, De Quincey's phrase 'touched with pensiveness' has leapt into his mind as he reviewed *La Double Vie* (11, 87).[1] There is a degree of playfulness in the way in which Baudelaire includes these quotations: in like manner, he punningly incorporates titles into his sentences. 'Comment on paie ses dettes' offers several examples (11, 6), while the essay on Gautier insists that the public 'n'a pas, avec [Barbier], versé son *pianto* sur l'Italie désolée, et il ne l'a pas suivi dans son voyage chez le *Lazare* du Nord' (11, 106).

Connected with this element of play and the use of criticism as a valuable stylistic exercise is perhaps the most original and effective of Baudelaire's critical methods: the way he exploits his gift for parody and pastiche. Of these, parody, the mimicking of characteristic turns of phrase for purposes of mockery, is the more rarely employed. In the essay on Gautier, however, an amusing mimicry of bourgeois vocabulary and opinions sharpens Baudelaire's image of a poet radically different from the witty, fluent *feuilletoniste* with whom the name is generally associated (II, 105). More important, and far more subtle, is what Pichois, in another context, terms Baudelaire's 'pastiche d'admiration' (I, 1016). Among the best examples are those in the review of *Madame Bovary*, where Balzac, for instance, is described as 'ce prodigieux météore qui couvrira notre pays d'un nuage de gloire, [. . .] comme une aurore polaire inondant le désert glacé de ses lumières féeriques' (II, 78), while Barbey d'Aurevilly's ardour is admirably captured in a pastiche depicting him 'évoquant la passion pour la vaincre, chantant, pleurant et criant au milieu de l'orage' (II, 78). There are several more examples in this passage, their brilliance heightened by the casual way in which Baudelaire seems to include them merely in passing. Similarly, Gautier's half-humorous, half-melancholy approach to time, and the intricate imagery of his style, are echoed by the lament: 'depuis cette petite fête de ma jeunesse, que d'années au plumage varié ont agité leurs ailes et pris leur vol vers le ciel avide!' (II, 109). Finally, Hugo's love of balanced and antithetical sentences has left its unmistakable imprint on the style of the anthology notice devoted to him: 'comme Démosthène, il converse avec les flots et le vent; autrefois, il rôdait solitaire dans des lieux bouillonnant de vie humaine; aujourd'hui, il marche dans des solitudes peuplées par sa pensée' (II, 130).

In general, Baudelaire's use of pastiche indicates his familiarity with the methods of those he discusses and shows that, as a stylistic exercise or as a proof of his own gymnastic skill, he takes the same pleasure in experimenting with such devices as he does in working out for himself the themes a work develops or the problems it raises.

Although such pastiches show that Baudelaire was keenly aware of the technical aspects of art, he rarely analyses literary styles in detail. Once again, it is necessary to remember that subtle linguistic analysis was neither expected nor, indeed, did it exist. Classical critics certainly indulged in a pedantic form of stylistic evaluation, on the rudimentary level of grammatical correctness. Baudelaire's perception of the inadequacy of such methods, his own self-questioning about what was needed, and the insights he does offer, go far beyond the usual attitude and capabilities of his contemporaries. One of the prefaces he sketched out for *Les Fleurs du mal* shows him torn between a longing to illuminate his reader and thus alter public sensitivity, and the overwhelming, almost physical sense of the uselessness of any such attempt:

> j'avais primitivement l'intention de répondre à de nombreuses critiques et, en même temps, d'expliquer quelques questions très simples [. . .]: qu'est-ce que la Poésie? quel est son but? [. . .]; soudain, une indolence, du poids de vingt atmosphères, s'est abattue sur moi, et je me suis arrêté devant l'épouvantable inutilité d'expliquer quoi que ce soit à qui que ce soit (I, 182).

His general attitude is clearly conveyed in another projected preface where he angrily asserts: 'ceux qui savent me devinent, et pour ceux qui ne peuvent ou ne veulent pas comprendre, j'amoncellerais sans fruit les explications' (I, 182). Baudelaire's awareness that technical analysis was vital and that there was as yet no way in which such an analysis could be made with sufficient precision and subtlety and without alienating the readers he was intending to assist, was not only well ahead of his time but is still a valid argument in contemporary debates.

Nevertheless, Baudelaire's interest in rhetoric and prosody as 'une collection de règles réclamées par l'organisation même de l'être spirituel' (II, 627), made him sensitive from his earliest criticism to what he calls 'toutes les ruses du style' (II, 3). He insists on the necessity for critics, as well as poets, to be alert to such techniques, accusing Janin of not understanding 'l'architecture des mots, [. . .] la plastique de la langue' (II, 239). His attacks on infringements of stylistic laws are cogent and precise: Ménard, for example, is criticized for neglecting both 'les rimes puissamment colorées' and 'les effets qu'on peut tirer d'un certain nombre de mots' (II, 11), while Barbier is accused of suppressing the possessive adjective and of misusing words according to the number of syllables needed. The variants to some of Baudelaire's literary reviews, particularly that on Gautier, as well as the attention he paid to tiny details in *Les Fleurs du mal*, offer more than adequate proof that he could have included illuminating stylistic analysis had this been an accepted part of journalistic criticism and had there existed terms precise enough and techniques sufficiently subtle.

Baudelaire draws attention not only to stylistic flaws, but also, although perhaps with less precision, to the 'magie de langage' (II, 150) he perceives in certain writers. Flaubert's style is aptly described as 'nerveux, pittoresque, subtil, exact' (II, 80), Gautier's has 'une justesse qui ravit, qui étonne' (II, 118) and Leconte de Lisle's language is 'toujours noble, décidée, forte, sans notes criardes, sans fausses pudeurs' (II, 179). Occasionally, Baudelaire suggests the reasons dictating a writer's adoption of a certain style: he asserts, for example, that Hugo's technical devices are 'tous destinés à exprimer des ténèbres captivantes ou l'énigmatique physionomie du mystère' (II, 134). Sometimes, too, his stylistic comments become very precise. Thus, he mentions Gautier's introduction of 'la majesté de l'alexandrin dans le vers octosyllabique' (II, 126). Furthermore, the preface to *Nouvelles Histoires extraordinaires* illustrates the way in which precise technical comments are related to wider issues. Thus, when Baudelaire points to 'un usage heureux des répétitions du même vers ou de plusieurs vers', suggesting that such repetitions 'simulent les obsessions de la mélancolie ou de l'idée fixe' (II, 336), he shows how stylistic devices reflect and enforce the content of the work. The preface also mentions 'un genre de rime qui introduit dans la poésie moderne, mais avec plus de précision et d'intention, les surprises du vers léonin' (II, 336). This comment is linked to Baudelaire's call for art to reflect the processes and needs of the human mind in balancing expectation with surprise.

It seems, therefore, that Baudelaire oscillates between a desire to arouse in the general public an enthusiasm and comprehension similar to his own, and a feeling that this is not only impossible but that attempts to do so may even serve further to isolate the artist from the wider public.

For Baudelaire, however, criticism is not merely an opportunity to convey information, debate ideas and suggest opinions. As early as 1846 he wrote: 'je crois sincèrement que la meilleure critique est celle qui est amusante et poétique' (II, 418). Few would deny that his literary criticism is amusing. There is, for example, the teasing treatment of the reader which opens the review of *Prométhée délivré*, the urbane admission that serves as an introduction to the notice on Desbordes-Valmore, and the conversational tone of the first sentence of the Gautier essay: 'je ne connais pas de sentiment plus embarrassant que l'admiration' (II, 103). The personal reminiscences, the passage recalling the first time he heard Dupont sing 'Le Chant des ouvriers' (II, 31), the reported conversation with Gautier, and the account of the pagan poet weeping over Daumier's cartoons all succeed in making their point all the more forcefully because the reader is amused and therefore more open to new ideas.

The amusement derives, in part, from Baudelaire's many variations of register, switching from straightforward description to conversation, both remembered and imagined, from dramatized narration to the highly poetic evocations in parts of the Hugo and Desbordes-Valmore notices.

As L. J. Austin points out, the poetic nature of Baudelaire's criticism results principally from his 'maîtrise de la métaphore'.[2] The literary criticism bears eloquent witness to Baudelaire's success in finding 'dans la nature extérieure et visible des exemples et des métaphores qui me servissent à caractériser les jouissances et les impressions d'un ordre spirituel' (II, 148). Indeed, many of his comparisons are arresting not merely because of their 'adaptation mathématiquement exacte dans la circonstance actuelle' (II, 133), but above all because they are so intensely visual. In Dupont's songs, for example: 'on voit toujours, on entend toujours, comme au sein des chaînes tourmentées de montagnes orageuses, à côté de la route banale et agitée, bruire doucement et reluire la fraîche source primitive qui filtre des hautes neiges' (II, 32).

Food and its consumption form the basis for many images. Passion for some people, for example, is 'la muscade qui leur sert à assaisonner tout ce qu'elles mangent' (II, 111) and Baudelaire asserts that 'quelque politique que soit le condiment, le Beau amène l'indigestion' (II, 125). Baudelaire, who draws attention in his diaries to 'la prédilection des Français pour les métaphores militaires' (I, 690-1), often uses such images himself, comparing Balzac's characters to 'armes chargées de volonté jusqu'à la gueule' (II, 120), insisting that Poe possesses 'un arsenal d'images' (II, 313) and declaring that Borel's handwriting resembled 'des files de fantassins renversés par la mitraille' (II, 154). His call for artists to draw on themes and images from the modern world is balanced by his own use of metaphors reflecting contemporary life. The résumé of 'Bérénice' provides what is perhaps the most memorable metaphor based on modern technology: when Bérénice smiles at her lover, her teeth remain 'daguerréotypées' in his brain (II, 281).

Scientific discoveries have inspired several metaphors in the literary criticism. In rejecting the possibility of unprepared success, for instance, Baudelaire claims that 'il y a lente agrégation de succès moléculaires; mais de générations miraculeuses et spontanées, jamais' (II, 13). He asks of one of Dupont's songs: 'était-il un de ces atomes volatils qui flottent dans l'air et dont l'agglomération devient orage, tempête, événement?' (II, 171-2). And, in reference to the morality of *Les Martyrs ridicules*, he insists that 'elle en jaillit naturellement comme la chaleur de certains mélanges chimiques' (II, 187).

Although the preoccupations and discoveries of modern life thus form the basis of many amusing and poetic metaphors, art is also frequently compared to nature. The songs of Dupont provide 'un rafraîchissement [...] une oasis' (II, 28), while, in a letter to Fraisse, Baudelaire describes Musset's poetry as a 'torrent bourbeux de fautes de grammaire et de prosodie' (*CI*, 675). Poe's works are 'éblouissantes végétations' (II, 291) and the publication of his first volume of poetry is likened to 'une aurore éclatante' (II, 302), the stress on blinding light being taken up in the following year by the *Madame Bovary* review, in which Balzac is compared both to a 'prodigieux météore' and an 'aurore polaire' (II, 78). Finally, in addition to the complex analogy which closes the Desbordes-Valmore notice, the 1852 study on Poe provides an amusing example of metaphors drawn from nature, when Baudelaire, rejecting the call for Poe to write 'un livre de famille', comments drily: 'il est donc vrai que la sottise humaine sera la même sous tous les climats, et que le critique voudra toujours attacher de lourds légumes à des arbustes de délectation' (II, 269).

The care Baudelaire pays to such details, the aptness of the metaphors and the attention devoted to small stylistic points, add to one's sense that he is using his criticism to work out his own creative enterprise, not only in the area of aesthetic problems, but also in that of themes and images. There can be little doubt that Baudelaire delighted in the stylistic *tours de force* for which his criticism offered such splendid opportunities, and that he used it as a testing ground both for his skill and for his theories. Just as there is a firm, if complex, interrelationship between Baudelaire's criticism and the theory and practice of his contemporaries, so there is a continual flow of ideas and expressions between his literary criticism and his creative writing. In particular, the articles written after the publication of *Les Fleurs du mal*, at a time when Baudelaire was experimenting with new genres, show him examining the nature and role of different modes of expression and the possibility of combining them. In a letter written to his mother in February 1858, he claimed: 'je porte dans ma tête une vingtaine de romans et deux drames. Je ne veux pas d'une réputation honnête et vulgaire; je veux écraser les esprits, les étonner, comme Byron, Balzac ou Chateaubriand' (CI, 451). The theatre tempted him as a swift path to the fame and fortune he craved, but in his essay on Gautier he admitted: 'l'imitation de la passion, avec la recherche du Vrai et un peu celle du Beau (non pas du Bien) constitue l'amalgame dramatique; mais aussi c'est la passion qui recule le drame à un rang secondaire dans la hiérarchie du Beau' (II, 114). His articles on Poe as well as the later criticism show him defining the nature of the novel and the short story, the flexibility of both (II, 119) and the advantages of the short story over the full-length novel (II, 329 and 119), as well as the pitfalls surrounding 'la nouvelle du genre poétique' (II, 121). Throughout his criticism, too, he evaluates the extent to which a writer can profitably draw on the resources of different genres. Within certain limits, his ideas on this subject remained unchanged from his first reviews. As early as 1846, for example, he mocked 'les essais de moyens contradictoires, l'empiètement d'un art sur un autre' (II, 473). Yet, although opposed to the confusion of genres, to the use of poetry, for instance, to convey a moral or scientific lesson or to expound a philosophical argument, Baudelaire is aware of the extra depths that can be reached through certain combinations. Similarly, he insists in his essay on Gautier that 'plus un objet réclame de facultés, moins il est noble et pur, plus il est complexe, plus il contient de bâtardise' (II, 112), yet he would hardly deny that certain faculties can be brought together to increase one's reception of external phenomena, particularly in the case of synaesthesia. I think this is a question over which Baudelaire hesitated and that even in 1859 he had not reached an unequivocal decision about its complex ramifications.

A further question he examined in his criticism without reaching a definite answer is that of the relationship between theme and expression. Although he argues in his notice on Barbier that any distinction between them is false (II, 143), it is clear that he himself often reacts spontaneously to one and is forced to admit that the other is flawed. Barbier's poetry moves him despite its poor expression, Desbordes-Valmore's and Borel's despite their stylistic carelessness, and if he prefers Leconte de Lisle's imitations of Latin odes to his Greek poems he confesses that this is because he feels more drawn to Rome than to Athens. Whereas, on an intellectual level, he considers the distinction to be false, he is aware that emotionally he still separates them.

Such hesitations and changes of mind reveal Baudelaire using his criticism as a means of clarifying theoretical questions that perplex him and indicate that, despite his undeniable precocity, his aesthetic theories, at least as far as literature is concerned, were not entirely and un-alterably formed from the beginning, but developed as a result of circumstance and external influence as well as through long and thoughtful consideration.

It is doubtless as a result of this very personal use of his criticism that Baudelaire is always present in his articles, not as a bland voice, but as an enthusiastic, exasperated, amused or angry guide, eager to make his reader understand, but offering few concessions. Seeking to transform his 'volupté en connaissance', moved by the physical intensity of his immediate response and by the stimulus given to his imagination and intellectual curiosity to discover the underlying causes of a writer's development or his reaction to a certain situation, Baudelaire looks on criticism as providing a series of infinitely varied challenges to his susceptibility and intelligence. He is not the unmoved, Olympian judge dispensing knowledge, formulating rules and passing judgement, but a tactician, attempting to present the writers who interest him in the manner most calculated to reveal their originality and to seize his reader's attention. Indeed, criticism presents him with the kind of *gageure* he detects at the heart of certain works of literature. His image of Poe creating 'The Raven' and his portrait of Flaubert planning *Madame Bovary* or Gautier writing 'Le Roi Candaule' in response to a series of aesthetic and practical questions, seem to offer an accurate reflection, one might say a *mise en abyme*, of Baudelaire's own approach to criticism.

However much his critical articles represent a personal challenge, they also stand as permanently provocative studies of a wide range of contemporary writers. Given the very brief span of time he devoted to them, and the fact that his major preoccupation was, of course, his creative writing, his reviews touch on, or explore at length, almost all the main literary figures or schools of the period, as well as providing invaluable information on lesser writers and minor movements. Apart from Poe and De Quincey, whose work appealed to him for particularly personal reasons, he concentrated on his French contemporaries, focusing attention on works written in the 1830s, 40s and 50s. Provided one bears in mind these restrictions and remembers that, unlike Sainte-Beuve and Gautier, he had no periodical on which he could rely to accept his reviews, and therefore less incentive for writing them, there seems little justification for Margaret Gilman's assertion that the literary criticism 'neglects significant figures and over-emphasizes lesser ones'.[3] True, one might have expected a more detailed study on Balzac, a review of Mérimée, articles on Lamartine or Vigny: but to condemn Baudelaire for not providing them seems to me to reveal a misunderstanding both of contemporary problems and the role of criticism as Baudelaire saw it. After all, what fired his enthusiasm or anger was not so much the individual writer but the problem posed by that writer's work or by his renown.

The blend of mockery and high seriousness in his articles, together with the need to placate the censors, to avoid alienating readers and to side-step issues which might enrage influential critics or poets, results in Baudelaire's beliefs either bursting forth in an explosive reaction to contemporary blindness, or lying, half-hidden, in parody, quotation, and insinuation. His critical reviews can be appreciated neither in isolation nor in haste, but they debate issues and raise questions which continue to be central to aesthetics in general and literature in particular. They are lanterns which not only shed light on the writers discussed, the time in which they lived, and perennial aesthetic and critical problems, but also elucidate the recesses of the mind that created *Les Fleurs du mal* and *Le Spleen de Paris*.

❧ *Notes*

All works in French are published in Paris, all those in English are published in London unless otherwise stated.

In addition to the abbreviations already given on p. x, the following symbols are used:

A	*L'Artiste*
AF	*L'Athenaeum français*
AN	*L'Assemblée nationale*
B	*Le Boulevard*
CF	*La Chronique de France*
Const	*Le Constitutionnel*
Corr	*Le Correspondant*
CS	*Le Corsaire-Satan*
DP	*La Démocratie pacifique*
Echo	*L'Echo de la littérature et des beaux-arts*
F	*Le Figaro*
GP	*La Gazette de Paris*
IB	*L'Indépendance belge*
JD	*Le Journal des débats*
MF	*Le Mercure de France*
MU	*Le Moniteur universel*
N	*Le National*
ON	*L'Opinion nationale*
P	*La Presse*
Ph	*La Phalange*
RA	*La Revue anecdotique*
RC	*La Revue contemporaine*
RCLN	*La Revue critique des livres nouveaux*
RDM	*La Revue des deux mondes*
RE	*La Revue européenne*
REnc	*La Revue encyclopédique nouvelle*
RFr	*La Revue française*
RFt	*La Revue fantaisiste*
RG	*La Revue germanique*
RHLF	*Revue d'histoire littéraire de la France*
RI	*La Revue indépendante*
RP	*La Revue de Paris*
RSH	*La Revue des sciences humaines*
S	*Le Siècle*
U	*L'Univers*

Introduction

1 H. Lemaitre, *Curiosités esthétiques* (Garnier Frères, 1971), lxi.
2 D. Parmée, *Selected Critical Studies* (Cambridge: Cambridge University Press, 1949), xxxii.
3 Lemaitre, *Curiosités esthétiques*, xv.
4 L. B. Hyslop and F. E. Hyslop, *Baudelaire as a Literary Critic* (University Park, Pennsylvania: Pennsylvania State University Press, 1964).
5 G. Poulet, 'Baudelaire précurseur de la critique moderne', *Journées baudelairiennes* (Brussels: Académie royale de langue et de littérature françaises, 1968), 232.
6 *Ibid.*, 237.
7 L. J. Austin (ed.), *L'Art romantique* (Garnier-Flammarion, 1968), 22 and 24.
8 *Ibid.*, 23.
9 C. Pichois (ed.), *Critique littéraire et musicale* (Armand Colin, 1961), 7.
10 M. Gilman, *Baudelaire the Critic* (New York: Octagon Books, 1971), 203.
11 *Ibid.*, 221.
12 *Ibid.*, 222.
13 Henri Peyre, *Connaissance de Baudelaire* (Librairie José Corti), 143.
14 P. Spencer, 'Censorship of Literature under the Second Empire', *The Cambridge Journal*, III, i (October 1949), 49.
15 C. Bellanger (ed.), *Histoire générale de la presse française*, II (Presses universitaires de France, 1969), 249.
16 *Ibid.*, 257.
17 *Ibid.*, 265.
18 L. B. Hyslop, 'Baudelaire on "Les Misérables"', *French Review*, I (October 1967), 24.
19 See, in particular, M. Stevens, 'Baudelaire lecteur de Laclos', *Etudes françaises*, v, i (February 1969), 3–30.

1 The Early Criticism

   Chennevières

1 See A. M. Vial, 'Quand la Normandie nous était contée', *RHLF*, LXXI, iv (July–August 1971), 615–37; E. Poulain, 'Charles Baudelaire et l'Ecole normande', *MF*, 15 October 1933, 214–26, and E. Raynaud, *Charles Baudelaire* (Garnier Frères, 1922), 144–6. Chennevières's name is now associated mainly with catalogues and studies of pictorial art, written when he was curator at the Louvre. In particular, his *Souvenirs d'un directeur des beaux-arts*, with their recollections of the 'bohème écriveuse' of his youth, illuminate Baudelaire's relationship with the *Ecole normande*. For Chennevières's view of Baudelaire see *Juvenilia*, I (Louis Conard, 1939), 560, but also his assessment of *Les Fleurs du mal* quoted in Raynaud, 144. For their later relationships see *C1*, 132, 152.
2 Not *Histoires baguenaudières* as *AR* and the new Pléiade edition have it.
3 E. Prarond, *De quelques écrivains nouveaux* (Michel Lévy Frères, 1852).
4 Barbey d'Aurevilly, *Lettres à Trébutien*, I (A. Blaizot, 1908), 172.
5 P. de Chennevières, *Historiettes baguenaudières* (Caen: Chez les librairies de Normandie, 1845), 58: the slight inexactness in quoting the title suggests that Baudelaire is relying on memory.

6 See H. Peyre, *Louis Ménard* (New Haven: Yale University Press, 1932); F. Calmettes, *Leconte de Lisle et ses amis* (Librairies-Imprimeries réunies, 1902); A. Ferran, *L'Esthétique de Baudelaire* (Hachette, 1933); J. Pommier, *Dans les chemins de Baudelaire* (Librairie José Corti, 1945); and P. Arnold, *Esotérisme de Baudelaire* (J. Vrin, 1972).

7 Ménard's interest in art is revealed, for example, in his article on Delacroix, *DP*, 3 April 1847. Their early friendship had been strengthened by a shared enthusiasm for art and an interest in reformers such as Fourier, Leroux and Cabet: see Peyre, *Louis Ménard*.

8 On Weill see G. Blin, 'Baudelaire et Alexandre Weill', *RHLF*, LXIII, i (January–April 1963), 28–45 and R. Dreyfus, 'Alexandre Weill', *Cahiers de la quinzaine*, IX, 9th series (1908).

9 F. W. Leakey, *Baudelaire and Nature* (Manchester: Manchester University Press, 1969), 364.

10 Weill's review quotes Ménard's assertion that 'la vertu c'est la force'.

11 The painter under fire here is Ary Scheffer, accused in the review of *Prométhée délivré* of seeking to create 'une peinture crânement poétique' (11, 9): a poem, Baudelaire insists, must be 'involontairement philosophique' just as poetry must enter into a painting only 'à l'insu de l'artiste' (11, 474).

12 L. Ménard, *Prométhée délivré* (Au Comptoir des Imprimeurs, 1844), 9, 10, 11.

Champfleury

13 See *C*I, 123 and *C*II, 991 as well as 11, 1088 and Champfleury's *Souvenirs et Portraits de jeunesse* (Geneva: Slatkine Reprints, 1970).

14 See E. Bouvier, *La Bataille réaliste* (Fontemoing, 1914); T. J. Clark, *The Absolute Bourgeois* (Thames and Hudson, 1973) and *Image of the People* (Thames and Hudson, 1973); and Linda Nochlin, *Realism* (Harmondsworth: Penguin, 1971).

15 *AF*, 31 May 1856, 463; *A*, 1 June 1851.

16 *JD*, 5 October 1851; *RE*, VI (1859), 321.

17 For details of what Champfleury had published by this time see Baudelaire, *Juvenilia*, 1, 565.

18 Bouvier, *La Bataille réaliste*, 131.

19 For the interest Baudelaire and Champfleury shared in Hoffmann see R. Lloyd, *Baudelaire et Hoffmann* (Cambridge: Cambridge University Press, 1979).

20 *DP*, 24 June 1847.

21 See C. Pichois, *L'Image de Jean-Paul Richter* (Librairie José Corti, 1963).

22 Champfleury, *Pauvre Trompette* (Martinon, 1847); 'Simple histoire' is in *Feu Miette* (Martinon, 1847).

23 First published in *Contes d'été* (Victor Lacou, 1853).

24 Champfleury, *Pauvre Trompette*, 107.

Dupont

25 J. Prévost, *Baudelaire* (Mercure de France, 1968), 68. See also *AR*, 504 and L. B. and F. E. Hyslop, *Baudelaire as a Literary Critic*, 49–51.

26 Gilman, *Baudelaire the Critic*, 68.

27 Who at times plays fast and loose with his quotations from Baudelaire: see for instance *Image of the People*, 10 and 20.

28 *Ibid.*, 68.

29 L. B. Hyslop, 'Baudelaire, Proudhon et "Le Reniement de Saint Pierre"', *French Studies*, xxx, 3 (July 1976), 273. The political implications of Baudelaire's article are too complex to be examined here in detail. Among critics who have explored them are I. Bugliani, 'Baudelaire tra Fourier e Proudhon', *Critica storica*, x (December 1973), 39–127; M. Ruff, 'La Pensée politique et sociale de Baudelaire', *Littérature et Société* (Desclée de Brouwier, 1973), 65–75; and Peter Hambly, 'Idéologie et Poésie', *Australian Journal of French Studies*, xvi, i–ii (1979), 198–213.

30 See W. T. Bandy and C. Pichois, *Baudelaire devant ses contemporains* (Monaco: Editions du Rocher, 1957), 147, 150–1 and D. Higgins, 'Pierre Dupont', *French Studies*, iii, 3 (April 1949), 122–36: I feel Higgins exaggerates the collapse of Dupont's character and talent after the *coup d'état*.

31 P. Dupont, *Chants et Chansons*, iii (Lecrivain et Toubon, 1858), iv.

32 *La Semaine*, 1 April 1849.

33 *The Morning Chronicle*, 5 May 1851.

34 Baudelaire's preface was completed in July: see *C1*, 173 and 175. Léon Lemonnier, in 'Edgar Poe et les poètes français' (*Nouvelle Revue critique*, 1932) asserts that the preface was written 'certainement plus tôt' (38), but the parallels with other studies published in 1851 make this unlikely.

35 *The Morning Chronicle*, 5 May 1851.

36 *RDM*, 15 June 1851.

37 This is not to deny that poets like Béranger and Reboul, the worker poet, always had a following: it is the change of emphasis that concerns us here.

38 *Corr*, April–June 1843, 276, 274.

39 Nisard, *Portraits et Etudes* (Michel Lévy Frères, 1858), 67: first published 1836.

40 *U*, February 1842.

41 *Individualité*, in that sense, only entered the language in 1830: according to the *Robert*, 'cet emploi, illustré par Fourier [. . .] et critiqué par Hugo [. . .] est signalé comme "néologisme" par Littré'. Note also the word 'humanité', mocked in the review of *Prométhée délivré* (ii, 11).

42 Nerval, *Œuvres*, i (Pléiade, 1974) 242ff. and Flaubert, *L'Education sentimentale* (Louis Conard, 1923), who mentions, like Baudelaire, the *Maison d'or* (249) and quotes 'Les Bœufs' (381).

43 *Const*, 21–2 April 1851 and *RDM*, 15 June 1851.

44 Several commentators stress this connection; see *AR*, 506 and ii, 1092.

45 See P. Bénichou, *Nerval et la chanson folklorique* (Librairie José Corti, 1970).

46 See Clark, *Image of the People*, 96ff.

47 Written between September 1851 and January 1852: published 1 February 1852, but see i, 1043–4.

48 Dupont, *La Muse populaire* (Garnier Frères, 1851), vi.

49 *RDM*, 15 June 1851.

50 Dupont, *Chants et Chansons*, i (Alexandre Houssiaux, 1851), 33.

51 *La Semaine*, 1 April 1849, 411.

52 Dupont, *La Muse populaire*, vi.

53 Dupont, *Chants et Chansons*, i, 35.

54 *RDM*, 15 June 1851.

55 *Ibid.*

56 Champfleury, *A*, 24 May 1846; Sainte-Beuve, *Const*, 21–2 April 1851; Hayward, *Morning Chronicle*, 5 May 1851.

'Les Drames et les romans honnêtes' and 'L'Ecole païenne'

57 The word *milieu* in that sense first came into the language in 1842, one of its first users being Balzac, in the 'Avant-propos' to *La Comédie humaine.*
58 *La Silhouette*, 7 December 1845.
59 *P*, 17 December 1849.
60 See E. Pich, *Leconte de Lisle: Articles* (Les Belles Lettres, 1971), 116.
61 See K. Heitmann, *Der Immoralismus-Prozess gegen die französische Literatur im 19. Jahrhundert* (Bad Homburg: Ars Poetica, Studien-Band 9, 1970).
62 See Gabriel-Robinet, *La Censure* (Hachette, 1965).
63 Gautier, *Mademoiselle de Maupin* (Garnier-Flammarion, 1966), 25: see also Lois Hamrick, 'The Role of Gautier in the Art Criticism of Baudelaire' (Unpublished thesis, Vanderbilt University, 1975), 27.
64 Cf. Gautier, *Mademoiselle de Maupin*, 25: 'la vertu est assurément quelque chose de fort respectable, et nous n'avons pas envie de lui manquer, Dieu nous en préserve! La bonne et digne femme!'
65 See H. Gaillard de Champris, *Emile Augier* (Grasset, 1910), 3.
66 Augier, *Théâtre complet*, 1 (C. Lévy, 1876), 68.
67 Flaubert's character Léon in *Madame Bovary* reveals a similar morality.
68 Augier, *Théâtre complet*, 1, 68.
69 *Le Pays*, 24 December 1849.
70 *DP*, 17 December 1849.
71 *L'Evénement*, 17 December 1849.
72 For an indication of its popularity see A. Méray, *Echo*, 1845, 67–8.
73 Louis Reybaud, *Jérôme Paturot à la recherche d'une position sociale* (Paulin, 1845), 16: the Pléiade edition does not locate the allusions.
74 Reybaud, *Jérôme Paturot à la recherche de la meilleure des républiques* (Michel Lévy Frères, 1849), 45.
75 Reybaud, *Jérôme Paturot à la recherche d'une position sociale*, 5: cf. 9: 'l'alliance du grotesque et du sublime ne me semblait pas le dernier mot de la composition littéraire'.
76 *Ibid.*, 224.
77 *Ibid.*, 334.
78 Gautier, *Mademoiselle de Maupin*, 121: cf. 1, 204 and 350, and 11, 68: to my knowledge this link has not been pointed out before.
79 E. Pich observes that toasts at contemporary banquets often misused religious terminology in this way: he quotes as examples 'au Christ, père du socialisme', 'à Saint-Just, martyr du Thermidor' etc. (see 'Littérature et Codes sociaux', in *Romantisme*, October 1976, 167–82).
80 *S*, 6 August 1845.
81 *AN*, 27 January 1851.
82 Balzac's letter does end by saying: 'vous serez, monsieur, le second exemple d'un critique à qui j'aurai soumis de semblables observations' (*Œuvres diverses*, III (Louis Conard, 1940), 652).
83 Balzac, *Œuvres diverses* (III, 651): cf. II, 184.
84 *Ibid.*, 651.

85 Berquin, *L'Ami de l'adolescence* (Pissot et Barrois, 1786), 40, 91.
86 Reybaud was awarded the Prix Montyon in 1841, Augier in 1850.
87 H. Castille, *Les Hommes et les mœurs* (Paul Henneton, 1853), 356: Montyon died in 1820.
88 Gautier, *Mademoiselle de Maupin*, 46.
89 *P*, 21 August 1858.
90 *RC*, February–March 1853, 300.
91 Gautier, *Mademoiselle de Maupin*, 43.
92 See *AR*, 533–4 and Lemaitre, *Curiosités*, 575.
93 Banville, *Les Stalactites* (Didier, 1942).
94 H. Peyre, *Bibliographie critique* (New Haven: Yale University Press, 1932), 132: the Hyslops suggest Banville, Ménard, Gautier, Leconte de Lisle and Laprade (*Baudelaire as a Literary Critic*, 71).
95 The word *symptôme* becomes very important in Baudelaire's vocabulary as he searches for initial causes: see 11, 145, 154, 167, 169, 172, 220.
96 Rabelais, *Le Quart Livre* (Geneva: Droz, 1947), 137; see 11, 1100.
97 *RP*, xvii, 1840, 309.
98 *A*, 3rd series, v, 1844, 112.
99 Leconte de Lisle, *Poésies*, IV (Geneva: Slatkine Reprints, 1974), 323.
100 *L'Evénement*, 8 August 1848.
101 See for example *A*, January–April 1845, 171.
102 Nerval, *Œuvres complètes*, I (Pléiade, 1974), 311.
103 *RDM*, 15 July 1848, 225.
104 Gautier, *Emaux et Camées* (Geneva: Droz, 1947), 3.
105 Gautier, *Mademoiselle de Maupin*, 43.
106 *RP*, December 1851, 68.
107 Champfleury, *Les Aventures de Mademoiselle Mariette* (Hachette, 1856), 139.
108 Peyre, *Bibliographie critique*, 7.
109 Gautier, *Mademoiselle de Maupin*, 252: cf. 11, 51.
110 Gautier, *Mademoiselle de Maupin*, 252.
111 See M. Desbordes-Valmore, *Œuvres poétiques*, I (Grenoble: Presses universitaires de Grenoble, 1973), 417.
112 Gautier, *Mademoiselle de Maupin*, 151: cf. *ibid.*, 150.

2 The Life and Works of Edgar Allan Poe

1 See Enid Starkie, *Baudelaire* (Harmondsworth: Penguin, 1971), 245–59; and W. T. Bandy's introduction to *Edgar Allan Poe* (Toronto: University of Toronto Press, 1973): henceforth 'Bandy'.
2 Bandy, xx.
3 Gilman, *Baudelaire the Critic*, 67; P. Quinn, *The French Face of Edgar Allan Poe* (Carbondale: Southern Illinois University Press, 1957), 91.
4 *JD*, 16 April 1853; *IB*, 12 February 1857; *MU*, 7 April 1857.
5 See Pichois, *L'Image de Jean-Paul Richter*.
6 The only article entirely devoted to Laclos that I found in contemporary journals was R. de Beauvoir's 'Duels et Duellistes', *GP*, 25 January 1857, which, as the title suggests, is concerned with Laclos as historical figure rather than novelist.
7 D. Kelley, *Le Salon de 1846* (Oxford: Clarendon Press, 1975), 19.

8 Bandy, 56.

9 Compare Balzac, *La Comédie humaine*, I (Louis Conard, 1926), xxv–xxvi.

10 Bandy, xxix–xxxvi.

11 See Bandy, xxxix–xlii and Starkie, *Baudelaire*, 248–51.

12 See P. Arbelet, *L'Histoire de la peinture en Italie* (Calmann-Lévy, 1913).

13 *Histoires extraordinaires* (Louis Conard, 1932), 374–85 gives a summary of the critical reception.

14 C. Richard, *Poe: journaliste et critique* (Klincksieck, 1978), 889–95.

15 Bandy, 59–60.

16 Bandy, 71.

17 According to Littré, *probabilisme* is a 'doctrine suivant laquelle, dans le concours de deux opinions, dont l'une est plus probable et favorable à la morale et à la loi, l'autre moins probable et favorable à la cupidité et à la passion, il est permis de suivre celle-ci dans la pratique, pourvu qu'elle soit approuvée par un auteur considérable'. Baudelaire seems to mean simply the exploration of what is probable as compared with what exists in reality.

18 *RDM*, xvi, 1846, 351.

19 See Baudelaire, *Petits Poèmes en prose*, edited R. Kopp (Librairie José Corti, 1969), 225.

20 Bandy, 77–8.

21 See above, pp. 69–70.

22 Compare Daniel in Bandy, 78: a parallel missed by Bandy.

23 Bandy, 85: H. P. Lovecraft has woven a terrifying tale, 'Tekeleli', around the novel, fully exploiting Poe's theme of the unearthly strangeness of the Polar regions.

24 Bandy, 87.

25 On fate see II, 1206–7. For the link with Borel, see *AR*, 567–8.
    The lines from Barbier are:

    'J'entends de mon cœur la voix mâle et profonde,
    Qui me dit que tout homme est apôtre en ce monde,
    Tout mortel porte au front, comme un bélier mutin,
    Un signe blanc ou noir frappé par le destin.'

    Il Pianto (Geneva: Slatkine Reprints, 1973), 2: I do not think this link has been made before.

26 Leconte de Lisle, *Œuvres*, IV (Alphonse Lemerre, 1899), 200: first published 1864: see also II, 1207.

27 *RDM*, xvi, 1846, 360: it is interesting to find Forgues using the noun 'pourchasseur' in reference to Poe, since this unusual word also appears in Baudelaire's 'Comment on paie ses dettes' (II, 6).

28 *F*, 27 March 1856; *MU*, 12 August 1856.

29 *RC*, 15 July 1857.

30 Alfred Assollant, *Scènes de la vie des Etats-Unis* (Hachette, 1859), 67. Similarly, a Swedenborgian versed in Hindustani and Arabic discovers that 'ces choses-là sont mille fois mieux payées en Europe. Tout le monde ici connaît Washington, Jefferson, le prix du coton, du blé, du cochon salé, le prix et le produit d'un acre de terre. Voilà qui est utile, qui repose l'esprit, qui élève l'âme' (11).

31 Bandy, xxxvi–xxxix.

32 Poe, *The Complete Works*, xvi (New York: A.M.S. Press, 1965), 18.

33 *Ibid.*, 193.

34 See e.g. H. Haswell, 'Baudelaire's self-portrait of Poe', *Romance Notes*, x, ii (Spring 1969), 253–60.

35 He is, for example, very precise in listing the stimuli that can activate memory, the sound of a bell, a musical note, a forgotten perfume: there are, moreover, echoes with *Les Fleurs du mal*, notably 'La Cloche fêlée' in which the poet listens to 'les souvenirs lointains lentement s'élever / Au bruit des carillons qui chantent dans la brume' (I, 71) and 'Le Parfum', with its reference to 'ce grain d'encens qui remplit une église' provoking the 'charme profond, magique, dont nous grise / Dans le présent le passé restauré' (I, 39).

36 C. Maturin, *Melmoth the Wanderer* (Harmondsworth: Penguin, 1977), 388–91: cf. II, 247 and 275. On Melmoth and Baudelaire, see my article in the L. J. Austin *Festschrift*.

37 *Le Pays*, 27 July 1853.

38 See Bandy, 45.

39 *AF*, 10 September 1853, 857.

40 *F*, 27 March 1856.

41 In *Nouvelles Histoires extraordinaires* (Louis Conard, 1933), 282, J. Crépet points out the parallel between 'Ciel brouillé' and 'Shadow', but does not extend the comparison to the preface.

42 See D. Kelley, 'Delacroix, Ingres et Poe', *RHLF*, LXXI (July–August 1971), 606–14.

43 *F*, 27 March 1856: cf. Pontmartin, *Le Spectateur*, 19 September 1857.

44 *RFr*, May 1856.

45 But see Rousseau, *GP*, 27 July 1856: 'Vingt ans avant M. Baudelaire, un romantique forcené, Champavert, donnait à ses héros la passion du suicide.'

46 Lemonnier, *Edgar Poe et la critique française*, 259: the monograph is disappointing, with no discussion of the way in which a critic's assessments of Poe may have been affected by the paper for which he wrote, by his political beliefs or by his own literary persuasions. He also fails to show the importance of Baudelaire's study in shaping contemporary opinion about Poe.

47 A. de Belloy, *RFr*, March 1856; compare Anon., *RDM*, 1 April 1856 and Cartier, *F*, 27 March 1856.

48 Pontmartin, *JD*, 12 November 1856.

49 D. Nisard, *Histoire de la littérature française*, 4 vols (Firmin-Didot, 1844–61).

50 Gautier, *Mademoiselle de Maupin* (Garnier-Flammarion, 1966), 25.

51 Poe, *The Complete Works*, XVI, 77.

52 Poe, *The Complete Works*, XIV, 187.

53 *Ibid.*, 266.

54 *Ibid.*, 267.

55 Poe, *The Complete Works*, XVI, 171.

56 Flaubert, *Correspondance* (Louis Conard, 1927), IV, 289.

57 J. Crépet (ed.), *Nouvelles Histoires extraordinaires* (Louis Conard, 1933), 328.

58 Baudelaire was particularly interested in Diderot's theatrical works: see II, 43.

59 Poe, *The Complete Works*, XIV, 194.

60 *Ibid.*, 204, 199.

61 *Ibid.*, 198.

62 Poe, *The Complete Works*, XVI, 86.

63 See also *C*I, 451, 454; *C*II, 353, 448; II, 248, 306, 578, 636.

64 Poe, *The Complete Works*, XIV, 271.

65 *Ibid.*, 272.
66 Possibly a pastiche, but see 'Conseils aux jeunes littérateurs'.

3 Self-Defence and Self-Analysis

    Madame Bovary

1 Flaubert, *Correspondance*, IV, 205–6: see also *AR*, 563–4; E. Crépet, *Baudelaire* (Messein, 1906), 291–9 and L. G. Miller, 'Gustave Flaubert and Charles Baudelaire', *PMLA*, June 1934.
2 Flaubert, *Correspondance*, IV, 139; see also Bellanger, *Histoire*, II, 285.
3 Hemmings, *Culture and Society in France* (Batsford, 1971), 60.
4 Flaubert, *Madame Bovary* (Garnier Frères, 1955), 197.
5 *JD*, 26 May 1857.
6 *Corr*, XLI, 25 June 1857.
7 *Le Pays*, 6 October 1857: cf. R. Bolster, 'Le Roman de "Madame Bovary"', *Les Amis de Flaubert*, XLVIII (May 1976), 17–28.
8 Flaubert, *Correspondance*, III, 397.
9 *MU*, 4 May 1857: see M. Gilman, in *Madame Bovary and the Critics*, ed. B. F. Bart (New York: New York University Press, 1966), 40–54 and J. Gale, 'Sainte-Beuve and Baudelaire on "Madame Bovary"', *French Review*, XLI (1967), 30–7.
10 On the expression *sans imbroglio* see Flaubert, *Correspondance*, II, 345.
11 See R. Kanters, *Baudelaire* (New York: Barnes and Noble, 1961), 198–9.
12 *MU*, 4 May 1857: since he wrote for a government paper, Sainte-Beuve may not have been entirely free in the expression of his opinions.
13 See T. E. Du Val, *The Subject of Realism* (Philadelphia: University of Philadelphia Press, 1936) and Bouvier, *La Bataille réaliste* as well as G. Robert, 'Le Réalisme devant la critique', *RSH*, 1953, 5–26.
14 *RDM*, 1 May 1857, 218.
15 *MU*, 4 May 1857; *JD*, 26 May 1857.
16 *Le Pays*, 6 October 1857.
17 *L'Illustration*, 9 May 1857.
18 *RDM*, 1 May 1857; *JD*, 26 May 1857.
19 Flaubert, *Correspondance*, III, 344: compare Hugo: 'tout est sujet; tout relève de l'art; tout a droit de cité en poésie', *Œuvres poétiques*, I (Pléiade, 1964), 577.
20 J. Gale, 'Sainte-Beuve and Baudelaire', *French Review*, XLI (1967), 31.
21 *MU*, 4 May 1857.
22 *Corr*, XLI, 25 June 1857.
23 Flaubert, *Correspondance*, IV, 136.
24 Balzac, *La Comédie humaine*, X (Pléiade, 1950), 677: I would like to thank Dr M. Tilby for drawing my attention to this passage.
25 *Chronique artistique et littéraire*, 3 May 1857.
26 *Le Pays*, 6 October 1857.
27 *MU*, 4 May 1857.
28 Leconte de Lisle, *Poésies complètes* (Geneva: Slatkine Reprints, 1974), IV, 219.
29 See Gilman, *Baudelaire the Critic*, 99 and L. B. Hyslop, 'Baudelaire: "Madame Bovary c'est moi"?', *Kentucky Romance Quarterly*, 1973, 343–58.
30 Compare Flaubert's statements in *Correspondance*, II, 461.

31 *Le Pays*, 6 October 1857: to my knowledge this point has not previously been made.

32 L. B. Hyslop, *art. cit.*, 345 sees 'le cœur' as an ironic euphemism for sensuality, but it is more likely that Baudelaire was using the word to mean over-passionate in a romantic sense.

33 *MU*, 4 May 1857.

34 *Corr*, XLI, 25 June 1857, 299.

35 *JD*, 26 May 1857.

36 Cf. Gautier, *Mademoiselle de Maupin*, 121.

37 Flaubert, *Madame Bovary*, 257.

38 *Ibid.*, 85.

39 *Ibid.*, 53.

40 *Ibid.*, 286–7.

41 G. Wajeman, 'Psychologie de la femme', *Romantisme*, XIII–XIV (1976), 57.

42 *L'Illustration*, 9 May 1857.

43 *RDM*, 1 May 1857, 217.

44 *Le Pays*, 6 October 1857.

45 Cf. Balzac's analysis of his *curé* at Tours.

46 Compare Flaubert, *Correspondance*, III, 322: and *Correspondance*, I, 322: 'cette foule [. . .] la faire rêver'.

47 Flaubert, *Correspondance*, IV, 229.

48 *MU*, 4 May 1857; *Le Pays*, 6 October 1857.

49 Flaubert, *Correspondance*, II, 432.

50 Gilman, *Baudelaire the Critic*, 99.

51 *MU*, 4 April 1857.

52 *Le Présent*, I, ii, 9 July 1857.

53 *Le Pays*, 6 October 1857.

54 Thibaudet, *Gustave Flaubert* (Librairie Plon, 1922), 108.

55 A. Green, '"Salammbô" and the Myth of Pasiphaë', *French Studies*, XXXII, 2 (April 1978), 170.

La Double Vie

56 'Le Coucher de soleil romantique' was written for Asselineau's *Mélanges tirés d'une petite bibliographie romantique* (Geneva: Slatkine Reprints, 1967). For their relationship see Asselineau, 'Charles Baudelaire', in *Baudelaire et Asselineau*, ed. J. Crépet and C. Pichois (Nizet, 1964) and J. Richer and M. A. Ruff, *Les Derniers Mois de Baudelaire* (Nizet, 1976).

57 Furetière, *Le Roman bourgeois* (Poulet-Malassis et de Broise, 1859), 11.

58 *RFr*, August–October 1858: this precedes Baudelaire's article and is not a response to it as J. Crépet suggests, *AR*, 567. On Babou and Baudelaire see *C*II, 985.

59 *RCLN*, December 1858, 574.

60 *Ibid.*, 575.

61 *RDM*, 15 October 1858, 967; *RFr*, August–October 1858, 570.

62 *JD*, 14 November 1858.

63 Compare *MO*, 104.

64 Gautier, *Poésies complètes*, ed. R. Jasinski, II (Nizet, 1970), 146.

65 *RFr*, August–October 1858, 568.

66 Asselineau, *La Double Vie* (Poulet-Malassis et de Broise, 1858), 29. Henceforth referred to as *DV*.

67 *DV*, 30.

68 *Ibid.*

69 *DV*, 44: see also F. W. Leakey, 'The Poet as Moralist', in *Studies in Modern French Literature*, ed. L. J. Austin and others (Manchester: Manchester University Press, 1961), 196–219.

70 *DV*, 130.

71 *DV*, 133.

72 *DV*, 149.

73 *CI*, 338–41 and Butor, *Histoire extraordinaire* (Gallimard, 1969).

74 *DV*, 90.

4 The Magician and the Meteor

Gautier

1 See Gide, *Œuvres complètes*, VII (La Nouvelle Revue Française, 1934), 494. Compare L. Cellier, 'Présentation', *RHLF*, LXXII (July–August 1972), 577–82 and Gilman, *Baudelaire the Critic*, 102–8.

2 One recognizes the 'loi fatale' which refuses to allow perfection in man (II, 287–8).

3 Compare Gautier, *Poésies complètes*, ed. R. Jasinski, II (Nizet, 1970), 127 (henceforth *PCG*): 'Ma Poésie, enfant à la grâce ingénue / [...] Avec son collier fait de perles de rosée'.

4 To distinguish between the two Gautier studies, I call this one 'the essay' and the one written for the anthology 'the notice'.

5 *AR*, 480–1 and Gilman, *Baudelaire the Critic*, 102–3.

6 Kane, 'Théophile Gautier' (Unpublished doctoral thesis, Colorado University, 1969), 35.

7 See T. Zeldin, 'Biographie', *Revue d'histoire moderne et contemporaine*, January–March 1974, 58–74.

8 Compare Balzac, *Œuvres complètes*, XVIII, 8.

9 Gautier, *Les Jeunes-France* (Charpentier, 1883), vii; *Portraits contemporains* (Charpentier, 1874), 2.

10 *GP*, 16 January 1859; Pelloquet's article may perhaps have influenced Baudelaire's prose poem 'Les Tentations': 'Maintenant la Renommée est une divinité à la réforme. Sa trompette passerait pour un mirliton en comparaison des ophicléides et des trombones de la déesse Réclame.' Balzac comments on the expression 'l'homme politique' that it is 'un nouveau mot pris pour désigner un ambitieux à la première étape de son chemin', *Œuvres complètes*, XVII, 258.

11 *GP*, 23 January 1859.

12 *RDM*, 1 November 1844, 505.

13 *Les Contemporains: Gautier* (1855), 80: cf. *ibid.*, 32–3.

14 Gautier, *Les Jeunes-France*, 24.

15 Gautier, *Portraits contemporains*, 71–2.

16 Gautier, *Mademoiselle de Maupin*, 48.

17 Gautier, *Voyage en Espagne* (Charpentier, 1856), 105: none of the editors I have consulted gives this reference.

18 See E. Woestyn: 'il est généralement accrédité que la conversation française est la reine des causeries', 'Les Clichés de la conversation', F, 30 April 1854. For Baudelaire and Woestyn see I, 1580.

19 For Baudelaire, Gautier, like Balzac and Barbier, belongs to a second phase of Romanticism. Similarly, Clément de Ris placed him in 'cette seconde division du romantisme, plus jeune, plus ardente, moins circonspecte que la première' (*Portraits*, 145), while Pontmartin described him as 'l'homme qui a servi de trait-d'union entre le romantisme pur, tel qu'on le pratiquait en 1829, et ce réalisme moderne' (*RC*, October–November 1857, 653).

20 Mirecourt, *Gautier*, 53.

21 Clément de Ris, *Portraits à la plume* (Eugène Didier, 1853), 172, 160.

22 Gautier, *Nouvelles* (Charpentier, 1882), 6.

23 Gautier, *Souvenirs de théâtre, d'art et de critique* (Charpentier, 1903), 201; see also I, 661; II, 621.

24 For other discussions on beauty, truth and goodness see I, 194: II, 41, 81, 82, 142: CII, 143, 325: on harmony see *Romantisme*, V (1973) and especially D. Kelley, 'L'art: l'harmonie du beau et de l'utile'. Although stated clearly in the Gautier essay, Baudelaire's ideas on this complex subject do seem to waver. See my conclusion, pp. 282–3.

25 Gautier, *Les Paradis artificiels*, ed. C. Pichois (Club du meilleur livre, 1961), 17 and 8.

26 Flaubert, *Madame Bovary*, 178.

27 See, for example, Labitte: 'que la muse de la *Comédie de la mort* dorme à plaisir sur l'édredon de la rime, ou qu'elle se prélasse dans un palanquin doré en se servant de métaphores comme d'éventails', *RDM*, 1 November 1844.

28 *La Semaine*, 7 February 1851, 95; *JD*, 19 September 1852.

29 *RC*, October–November 1852, 654.

30 Gautier's gifts as art reviewer were admired by most contemporary critics, notably Lucas, Méry, Saglio, Vacquerie and Clément de Ris.

31 *PCG*, II, 304.

32 *PCG*, II, 310.

33 Valéry, *Œuvres*, I (Pléiade, 1959), 1503.

34 *JD*, 19 September 1852; *AF*, 9 April 1853.

35 *P*, 3 October 1852.

36 Toussenel, *L'Esprit des bêtes* (Librairie phalanstérienne, 1853–5), 20.

37 *RDM*, 1 November 1844, 507; *P*, 3 October 1852.

38 Pontmartin, *Causeries littéraires* (Michel Lévy Frères, 1854), 328.

39 *A*, 8 June 1856.

40 On this question see A. Cassagne, *La Théorie de l'art pour l'art* (Lucien Dorbon, 1959) and R. Giraud, 'Gautier's Dehumanization of Art', *L'Esprit créateur*, III, i (Spring 1973), 3–9.

41 *P*, 31 January 1844; *P*, 11 August 1851; *L'Evénement*, 8 August 1848.

42 See M. Spencer, *The Art Criticism of Gautier* (Geneva: Librairie Droz, 1969); Peter Hambly, 'Théophile Gautier et le fouriérisme', *Australian Journal of French Studies*, XI, iii (September–December 1974), 237–52; C. Pichois, *Littérature et Progrès* (Neuchâtel; A la Baconnière, 1973); C. M. Book, 'Théophile Gautier et la notion du progrès', *RSH*, October–December 1967, 545–57 and E. Hartman, 'Théophile Gautier on Progress in the Arts', *Studies in Romanticism*, XII, ii (Spring 1973), 530–50.

Balzac

43 D. Bellos, *Balzac Criticism* (Oxford: Clarendon Press, 1976), 59.
44 R. Hughes, 'Baudelaire et Balzac', *MF*, 1 November 1937, 476–518.
45 E. Prarond, 'Lettres à Eugène Crépet', *MF*, 1 September 1955, 5–31.
46 Proust, *Contre Sainte-Beuve* (Pléiade, 1971), 8.
47 Balzac, *Œuvres complètes*, XIII, 284.
48 Cf. 11, 29, 161, 167, 185, 234, 566.
49 Starkie, *Baudelaire*, 174–5: of course Baudelaire was in no position, financially, to commission hacks!
50 Compare Castille, *Les Hommes et les mœurs* (Paul Henneton, 1853), 314: 'de tous les personnages qui défilent sur cette vaste scène [. . .] il n'en existe aucun aussi merveilleux que l'auteur lui-même'.
51 *RFr*, 10 June 1856, 302.
52 *GP*, 13 April 1856.
53 See the introduction to Baudelaire, *La Fanfarlo*, ed. C. Pichois (Monaco: Editions du Rocher, 1957).
54 *P*, 3 November 1846.
55 *JD*, 24 August 1850.
56 Pontmartin, *Causeries littéraires*, 301.
57 *RDM*, 1 November 1842, 402; *La Semaine*, 1 September 1850, 554.
58 *P*, 18 August 1839: the letter is reprinted in Balzac, *Le Curé de village* (Folio, 1975), 338–42. To my knowledge, the source of this quotation has not been located before.
59 *RDM*, 1 September 1850, 915.
60 Balzac, *Œuvres diverses*, III (Louis Conard, 1940), 650.
61 Chaudes-Aigues, *Les Ecrivains modernes* (Geneva: Slatkine Reprints, 1973), 226.
62 *DP*, 5 January 1847.
63 *JD*, 25 August 1851.
64 *RDM*, XVIII, 1847, 202.
65 See Bellos, *Balzac Criticism*, 23–7 and 63–7.
66 *P*, 26 August 1850.
67 *P*, 1 September 1851.
68 *RDM*, XVIII, 1847, 214.
69 *P*, 15 January 1849: cf. *NE*, 97.
70 Balzac, *Œuvres diverses*, II (Louis Conard, 1938), 677.
71 *Ibid.*, 678.
72 Clément de Ris, *Portraits*, 296.
73 Gilman, *Baudelaire the Critic*, 118–33.
74 *P*, 1 September 1851.
75 Clément de Ris, *Portraits*, 297.

5 The Colossus: Victor Hugo

1 See his preface to *L'Art romantique*.
2 L. Cellier, *Baudelaire et Hugo* (Librairie José Corti, 1970); henceforth *BH*.
3 *BH*, 23.
4 *BH*, 49.
5 *BH*, 52.

6 *BH*, 60.

7 See for example L. Jourdan: 'ô maître! maître cher et vénéré! poète qui fûtes l'enthousiasme de notre jeunesse, qui êtes l'orgueil de notre âge mûr, soyez béni' (*S*, 23 April 1856): Jourdan had several brushes with the censors – see Bellanger, 236 and 250.

8 See for example Gilman, *Baudelaire the Critic*, 186–91 and A. Ubersfeld, 'Hugo et Baudelaire', *RHLF*, LXVIII, vi (November–December 1968), 1047–57.

9 According to Bellanger the organ of 'la gauche dynastique': *Histoire générale de la presse française*, II, 118.

10 *S*, 27 April 1856.

11 *RC*, 15 October 1861, 444: the *Revue contemporaine* was usually pro-government.

12 *Le Pays*, 29 November 1859.

13 Hugo, *Œuvres poétiques*, II, 590.

14 G. Planche, *Portraits littéraires* (Charpentier, 1853; article dated 1838), 133.

15 Hugo, *Œuvres poétiques*, I, 580.

16 *RE*, v, 1859, 786.

17 *RDM*, 15 October 1859, 974.

18 *RP*, 15 May 1856; *RC*, September–October 1859, 524.

19 *JD*, 26 June 1856.

20 *GP*, 4 May 1856; *RCLN*, 1860, 126.

21 *F*, 27 April 1856: on the antipathy of *Le Figaro* towards Hugo see P. Angrand, *Victor Hugo* (Gallimard, 1961).

22 *F*, 18 May 1856.

23 Hugo, *Œuvres poétiques*, I, 773.

24 Hugo, *La Légende des siècles* (Pléiade, 1950), 4.

25 Hugo, *Œuvres poétiques*, I, 773.

26 H. Tuzet, *Le Cosmos et l'imagination* (Librairie José Corti, 1965), 9.

27 *La Légende des siècles*, 4.

28 Cf. Poe: 'Great intellects *guess* well. The laws of Kepler were, professedly, guesses' (*Works*, XIV, 187).

29 Hugo, *La Légende des siècles*, 5.

30 On this vast contemporary debate see H. J. Hunt, *The Epic in Nineteenth-Century France* (Oxford: Basil Blackwell, 1941).

31 *RP*, 15 May 1856, 483; *RE*, v, 1859.

32 Hugo, *La Légende des siècles*, 8.

33 *S*, 27 April 1856.

34 Hugo, *Œuvres complètes*, XIII, 75.

35 Gilman, *Baudelaire the Critic*, 192–3.

36 J. Pommier, 'Baudelaire et Hugo', *RSH*, CXXVII (1967), 345.

37 L. B. Hyslop, 'Baudelaire on "Les Misérables"', *French Review*, XLI (1967), 29.

38 *JD*, 29 April 1862.

39 Desmarest, *La Critique française*, January–June 1862, 366.

40 *P*, 1 October 1862.

41 Mirecourt, *Les Vrais Misérables* (Humbert, 1862), 179.

42 *P*, 1 October 1862.

43 *JD*, 6 May 1862.

44 *P*, 1 October 1862.

45 *RFr*, 1 April 1862, 648; *JD*, 6 May 1862.

46 *BH*, 211.

47 *BH*, 259–63.
48 *BH*, 261.

6 *The Demands of an Editor*

    Desbordes-Valmore

1 See I, 686, 687; II, 19, 282–3, 476. In listing the poems included in the anthology the Pléiade edition adopts a confusing punctuation: 'Romance: S'il avait su' is one poem, not two.
2 E. Jasenas, *Marceline Desbordes-Valmore* (Minard, 1962), 92–3.
3 The Pléiade notes suggest Baudelaire could have read this poem in a review, but M. Bertrand's edition of Desbordes-Valmore's complete poetry states that it was not published before the appearance of *Poésies inédites*: see *Œuvres poétiques* (Grenoble: Presses universitaires de Grenoble, 1973), 752: henceforth *MOP*.
4 Gilman, *Baudelaire the Critic*, 194, 195.
5 Jasenas, *Marceline Desbordes-Valmore*, 93.
6 Barbey d'Aurevilly, *Le Pays*, 21 August 1860; for Desbordes-Valmore and Sainte-Beuve see J. Moulin, *Marceline Desbordes-Valmore* (Seghers, 1955); for Desbordes-Valmore and Balzac see M. Fargeaud, 'Autour de Balzac et de Marceline', *RSH*, LXXXII (April–June 1956), 153–74; tributes to her are printed in *MOP*, 809–26; Mallarmé's judgement appears in his *Œuvres complètes* (Pléiade, 1974), 875.
7 *RDM*, 15 December 1860, 1000.
8 See chapter 2, p. 62.
9 *MOP*, 51.
10 Sainte-Beuve, *Portraits contemporains*, II (Calmann-Lévy, 1888–9), 91.
11 *Le Pays*, 21 August 1860.
12 Several critics saw her as such. Raspail spoke of her as an 'organisation exceptionnelle, j'oserais dire angélique' (*Revue complémentaire des sciences*, 1 September 1859, 56) and Blot described her poems as 'l'incarnation d'une âme supérieure' (*Revue du Lyonnais*, September 1859, 297).
13 *MOP*, 693.
14 A characteristic shared by Desbordes-Valmore herself: see *MOP*, 452.
15 Gilman, *Baudelaire the Critic*, 195.
16 *RDM*, 1 July 1842, 75: Desbordes-Valmore's gentle reply, 'Jeune homme irrité', is in *MOP*, 482–3.
17 *Le Pays*, 21 August 1860.
18 Mallarmé, *Œuvres complètes* (Pléiade, 1974), 875.
19 Jeannine Moulin, *Marceline Desbordes-Valmore*, 98.
20 H. J. Hunt has discovered that Desbordes-Valmore herself wrote for the Fourierist *Démocratie pacifique*: see *Le Socialisme et le Romantisme* (Oxford: Clarendon Press, 1935), 218.
21 Vinet, *Etudes*, II (Les Editeurs, 1851), 578.
22 Compare Lacaussade: 'elle n'était point femme de lettres, elle était femme et poète simplement' (*RE*, XI, 1860).
23 See, e.g., Cladel, *Les Martyrs ridicules* (Poulet-Malassis, 1862), 223, 292; and Leconte de Lisle, *Poèmes et Poésies* (*Poésies complètes*, IV, 219).
24 *MO*, 226: cf. *MO*, 130.

25 Reprinted *MOP*, 826.
26 *MOP*, 66–7; 50.
27 *MOP*, 62, 376.
28 See Pléiade notes and compare Montégut: 'Madame Desbordes-Valmore est morte presque oubliée; elle n'était guère plus qu'un souvenir, que cette chose légère que le poète latin appelle si mélancoliquement l'ombre d'un nom' (*RDM*, 15 December 1860, 998).
29 Sainte-Beuve, *Portraits*, II, 103.
30 See *MOP*, 444.
31 'Tristesse', *MOP*, 540.
32 See *MOP*, 444.
33 *MOP*, 540: I do not think this suggestion has been made before.
34 Jasenas, *Marceline Desbordes-Valmore*, 93.
35 Sainte-Beuve, *Portraits*, II, 104: see also II, 1147–8.
36 Vinet, *Etudes*, II, 581.
37 *RE*, XI, 1860, 328–46.
38 Sainte-Beuve, *Portraits*, II, 95.
39 *MOP*, 412.
40 Sainte-Beuve, *Portraits*, II, 105.

Barbier

41 *RFr*, 15 March 1862.
42 *RDM*, 1 March 1840, 705.
43 *RP*, XXV, 1840; *RDM*, 1 July 1843, 116.
44 *Le Courrier du dimanche*, 15 June 1862.
45 See Y.-G. Le Dantec, 'Baudelaire et Barbier', *La Bouteille à la mer,* 1st quarter, 1953, 13–25.
46 See also II, 1154, 1185: the note at the top of II, 1144 represents a misreading of the text: it is not *Gautier* who recited the *Iambes* while failing 'verse[r] son *pianto* sur l'Italie désolée', but the French *public*, whom Baudelaire is not complimenting, but on the contrary condemning: see II, 106.
47 See chapter 1, pp. 22–23.
48 Planche, *Portraits littéraires*, II, 64.
49 Nettement, *Histoire de la littérature sous le gouvernement de juillet* (Lecoffre, 1859), II, 41.
50 In E. Crépet, ed., *Les Poètes français*, IV (Gide, 1862), 386.
51 *RP*, XXV, 1840.
52 H. Castille, *Les Hommes et les mœurs*, 285: compare Du Camp, *Les Chants modernes* (Michel Lévy Frères, 1855), 2.
53 *RDM*, 15 June 1841, 908.
54 *Ibid.*, 913.
55 *Ibid.*, 908, 909: on indignation in art see Baudelaire's review of Cladel (II, 186).
56 Du Camp, *Les Chants modernes*, 3.
57 See Barbier, *Iambes*, 5ff.
58 The poems included were 'La Curée', 'Dante' and 'Michel-Ange', all from the early volumes. The comment in Baudelaire's letter suggests very strongly that it was Baudelaire himself who chose the anthology poems for the other writers he discussed.

59 *RDM*, 1 March 1840; *RDM*, 1 July 1843, 118; *Echo*, 1840, 17.
60 See for example Barbier, *Iambes*, 287.
61 *RDM*, 15 January 1855, 392.
62 Baudelaire frequently attacks such poetry: see the reviews of *Prométhée délivré* and of 'l'école païenne' as well as the comments on Poe's 'To Helen' (II, 259).
63 Barbier, *Rimes héroïques*, 2.
64 Du Camp, *Les Chants modernes*, 8.
65 Gilman, *Baudelaire the Critic*, 203.
66 Du Camp, *Les Chants modernes*, 39.

Borel

67 Gilman, *Baudelaire the Critic*, 197.
68 See Baudelaire, *Les Fleurs du mal*, ed. J. Crépet (Louis Conard, 1930), xvi.
69 See Gautier, *Histoire du romantisme* (Charpentier, 1874), 19–22; Asselineau, *Bibliographie romantique*, 89–95; E. Starkie, *Pétrus Borel* (Faber and Faber, 1954), 92ff.; and P. Bénichou, 'Jeune-France et Bousingots', *RHLF*, LXXI, iii (May–June 1971), 439–62.
70 *RA*, 20 April 1857, 177–8: Baudelaire is thought to have collaborated on this review.
71 Monselet, *La Lorgnette littéraire*, 26.
72 Where Borel has 'des trompes, des timbales' Baudelaire has remembered 'ces trompes, ces cymbales': see *Madame Putiphar* (Bibliothèque noire, 1972), 3 (henceforth *MP*). The Pléiade edition does not point out this slight error.
73 'Je ne sais s'il y a un fatal destin, mais il y a certainement des destinées fatales; mais il est des hommes qui sont donnés au malheur' (*MP*, 11).
74 *MP*, 11–12.
75 Maturin, *Melmoth*, 121–330: compare Poe's tale 'The Pit and the Pendulum'.
76 Cf. II, 676.
77 See variant II, 1150, note to p. 154, c.
78 Poe, *The Complete Works*, xv, 178.
79 See, for example, 'touts' (*MP*, 29 and passim), 'dixme' (*MP*, 166), 'phrénétique' (*MP*, 120) and 'faulx' (*MP*, 4). 'Gens' is always spelt 'gents'.
80 Asselineau, *Bibliographie romantique*, 46.
81 Borel, *Champavert* (Renduel, 1833), 13.
82 Compare Gautier, *Mademoiselle de Maupin*, 41.
83 Compare Baudelaire's remarks on Asselineau's tales: see chapter 3: *La Double Vie*.

Banville

84 See *AR*, 552 and E. Souffrin, ed., *Les Stalactites* (Didier, 1942), 203–6. The Pléiade edition's list of the poems in the anthology (II, 1155) omits: 'Oh! quand la mort que rien ne saurait apaiser'. See *Les Stalactites*, 143–6.
85 *Les Cariatides* was published in 1842, not 1841 as Baudelaire states: no doubt the emphasis on Banville's precocity reflects his own astonishment at the time, since Banville is two years his junior.

86 *RDM*, 1 July 1843; *CS*, 14 March 1846; Prarond, *De quelques écrivains nouveaux* (Michel Lévy Frères, 1852), 82.
87 See I, 182, 698 and II, 79, 106, 124, 156.
88 *Capharnaüm* is a word of which Baudelaire was fond: see II, 86, 151, 162, 549, 631, 637. Balzac also used it on many occasions.
89 *RFr*, XI (November 1857–January 1858), 397.
90 See II, 30, 48, 179–80, 711.
91 *MU*, 28 April 1856.
92 *Le Présent*, I, 8 September 1857, 417: for Baudelaire's collaboration with this review see *C*I, 943. Certainly this sentence suggests that his influence was strong.
93 *F*, 10 December 1858; *JD*, 22 October 1857.
94 Banville, *Choix de poésies* (Charpentier, 1912), 50.
95 Prarond, *De quelques écrivains nouveaux*, 94.
96 *IB*, 27 July 1856.
97 Sainte-Beuve, *Portraits contemporains*, I, 116–17: see II, 1157.
98 Mallarmé, *Œuvres complètes*, 520.
99 *F*, 27 September 1857. See also Babou's reference to the 'fougue savante de lyrisme excessif' (*RFr*, February–April 1857, 426). For Baudelaire's earlier uses of the word see *C*I, 507, and II, 126 and 142.
100 *Lyre* appears no less than twelve times in *Les Cariatides*, at least six times in *Les Stalactites*, not including the many uses of the word in 'L'Ame de la lyre'.
101 Banville, *Choix de poésies*, 49; 50; 51.
102 Compare Champfleury, *CS*, 14 March 1846 and Chasles, *AF*, 27 February 1856, 85.
103 Banville, *Choix de poésies*, 52.
104 On the meanings of these terms in this context, see my *Baudelaire et Hoffmann*, chapter 5.
105 Banville, *Odes funambulesques* (Michel Lévy Frères, 1857), 20.
106 Compare Des Essarts: 'la réelle originalité de [. . .] Banville ne consiste pas tant dans cette heureuse rivalité avec le peintre de la fantaisie que dans la précieuse découverte de la poésie parisienne. Plus que tout autre il a pris la société moderne pour sujet de ses poétiques études' (*A*, 15 February 1860, 52): Des Essarts was soon to publish his own *Poésies parisiennes*.
107 M. M. Robert's thesis 'Théodore de Banville' (University of Toronto, 1971), which accuses Baudelaire of ignoring Banville's poems of despair and melancholy, is not convincing, because it is based principally on Banville's later poetry.
108 Compare the earlier reference to 'l'Eden perdu' (II, 165), where the emphasis is on a predetermined, rather than voluntary, return.
109 Compare for example Nettement, *Poètes et Artistes contemporains* (Lecoffre, 1862), 508.
110 *MU*, 12 October 1857.

Leconte de Lisle

111 See also Flaubert, *Correspondance* III, 141, 148, 153, 159, 201, 230, 231, 293, 349 and 381 for warm references to Leconte de Lisle. For Leconte de Lisle's relationship with Baudelaire and other contemporaries see Calmettes, *Leconte de Lisle et ses amis* and I. Putter, *Leconte de Lisle and his contemporaries* (Berkeley: University of Los Angeles Press, 1951).

112 See Leconte de Lisle, *Poésies complètes*, IV, notes (henceforth *PCL*).
113 Compare Flaubert, *Dictionnaire des idées reçues* (Naples: Liguori and Paris: Nizet, 1966), 120: 'Créole: vit dans un hamac'; Sainte-Beuve, *Const*, 9 February 1852: 'cette race de créoles semble née pour le rêve et pour le chant'; Melvil-Bloncourt, *B*, 20 April 1862: 'la société créole – remarquable par son esprit anti-philosophique, son tempérament anti-poétique'; and Balzac, *Œuvres complètes*, XVII, 130: 'en vraie Créole de Paris, Madame Marneffe abhorrait la peine'.
114 *RC*, April–May 1857, 267–8.
115 *AF*, 12 March 1853, 234; *RCLN*, December 1858, 574.
116 *MU*, 19 September 1859.
117 *Le Réalisme*, 15 December 1856; *RDM*, 15 September 1853, 1201.
118 *JD*, 6 March 1853.
119 See also *C*I, 679–80 and II, 104, 105, 119, 130, 134, 154, 157, 173, 176, 177, 187, 222.
120 Flaubert, *Correspondance*, IV, 33.
121 *AN*, 25 June 1853.
122 *Const*, 9 February 1852; *B*, 20 April 1862.
123 Cf. Gautier, *Mademoiselle de Maupin*, 33 and II, 30.
124 E. Perrin, *RE*, III, 1859, 191–9.
125 Gilman, *Baudelaire the Critic*, 201.
126 *MU*, 20 September 1859.
127 *PCL*, I, 210–11.
128 *PCL*, I, 135.
129 *PCL*, I, 24; 292; 191.
130 *PCL*, IV, 216.
131 Chadbourne, 'The Generation of 1848', *Essays in French Literature*, VI (November 1968), 1–21.
132 A point also made by Pontmartin (*AN*, 25 June 1853), Levallois (*MU*, 19 September 1859), E. Chasles (*AF*, 2 February 1856), Lafenestre (*RC*, 15 October 1861), and Melvil-Bloncourt (*B*, 20 April 1862).
133 II, 232, 234, 236: compare the more ambiguous I, 351: most of the quotations from Horace identified as such in the Pléiade notes are contemporary clichés, one at least coming directly from Poe: 'genus irritabile vatum' (II, 330): see Poe, *The Complete Works*, XIV, 175.
134 *PCL*, I, 50.
135 *PCL*, II, 85–6.
136 *PCL*, II, 171.
137 For other analogies see I, 183 and II, 111, 126, 136, 231.
138 Among contemporary critics who described his style, Goudall admired his 'langue puissante, imagée, d'une correction grandiose et d'un incomparable éclat' (*A*, 3 February 1856) and Lafenestre referred to 'cette voix large et sonore sans hésitation et sans éclats' (*RC*, 15 October 1861, 448).
139 'Les Jungles', 'Midi', 'Le Manchy', 'Le Sommeil du condor'.

Moreau

140 George Sand, *RDM*, 15 May 1840, 570.
141 *A*, 2nd series, VI, 1840.

142 *S*, 9 November 1845, 46.
143 *U*, 26 July 1851.
144 Moreau, *Myosotis* (Brussels: Mme Laurent, 1840), 59.
145 *Ibid.*
146 Dessalles-Régis (*RDM*, 1 February 1840, 319–38) also quotes these lines.
147 See C. Pichois, 'Baudelaire en 1847', *Baudelaire: Etudes et Témoignages* (Neuchâtel: A la Baconnière, 1976), 95–121.
148 I should like to thank Professor Alison Fairlie for pointing out that 'un poncif dramatique' (11, 159), must represent a misreading of the manuscript.
149 See, for example, Sainte-Beuve's article in *Causeries du lundi*, IV (Garnier Frères, 1868–70), 51–75.

7 Master and Disciple: Léon Cladel

1 Starkie, *Baudelaire*, 629.
2 L. Cladel, *Bonshommes* (Charpentier, 1879), 274 and 283.
3 J. Cladel, *Maître et Disciple* (Corrêa, 1951).
4 J. Cladel, *Maître et Disciple*, 26.
5 First published 27 August 1862.
6 *RA*, IV, 2nd semester 1861, 218–19: also reproduced in *AR*, 571.
7 See Hatin, *Bibliographie historique et critique* (Firmin-Didot Frères, 1866), and Bellanger, *Histoire générale*, IV, 118.
8 *S*, 4 December 1849.
9 It was in 1861 that Pasteur published his monograph proving that microbes are not produced by spontaneous generation.
10 *B*, 5 January 1862.
11 *RFt*, 1, 1 December 1861, 33.
12 Cf. Gautier, *Mademoiselle de Maupin*, 41.
13 *JD*, 16 December 1861.
14 *B*, 5 January 1862.
15 Cladel, *Les Martyrs ridicules*, 67: henceforth *Mr*.
16 *Mr*, 29.
17 *Mr*, 56.
18 *Mr*, 29; 45.
19 J. Crépet in *AR*, 572; Lemaitre in *Curiosités esthétiques*, 792; and Pichois, 11, 1168.
20 *RFt*, 1, 1 December 1861, 33.
21 *B*, 5 January 1862.
22 *Mr*, 148.
23 *RFt*, 1, 1 December 1861, 33.
24 Signed G.I., *RE*, 1 December 1861.
25 *JD*, 16 December 1861.
26 *RFt*, 1, 1 December 1861, 34.
27 *RE*, 1 December 1861.
28 *Mr*, 53.
29 *Mr*, 161.
30 See L. Cellier, 'Baudelaire et George Sand', *RHLF*, LXVII (April–June 1967), 239–59.
31 *Mr*, 252.

32 For this episode see *Mr*, 276ff.
33 *RE*, 1 December 1861.
34 *Mr*, 316.
35 *Mr*, 256.

Conclusion

1 See also 11, 79, 151: not all such quotations have been identified: two that are particularly elusive are in 11, 103 and 148.
2 Austin, *L'Art romantique*, 29; see also Poulet, 'Baudelaire précurseur de la critique moderne', *Journées baudelairiennes* (Brussels, 1968).
3 Gilman, *Baudelaire the Critic*, 221.

❧ Bibliography of Contemporary Articles

Although every effort has been made to offer as detailed a bibliography of contemporary articles as possible, certain limitations have had to be imposed. Firstly, only articles written or published between 1840 and 1863 have, in general, been included, except in the case of such writers as Barbier and Borel, whose main works date from before this period. Secondly, only journals or periodicals published in Paris have been consulted, except for *L'Indépendance belge*, which was widely read in Paris; and in particular instances, such as the articles on Dupont published in the provinces, since Baudelaire's friendship with Dupont makes it not impossible that he saw them. In the case of Balzac and Hugo, both of whom inspired an immense number of reviews, only a selective bibliography has been given, excluding, for example, articles which consider Hugo as politician rather than poet, and emphasizing areas in which Baudelaire took particular interest, such as Balzac's experiments with the theatre. Although particular importance has been placed on those papers for which Baudelaire wrote or which he mentions in his letters, I have tried to include papers of all persuasions: my aim was not so much to study any direct influence on Baudelaire's thought or technique as to provide a background against which his criticism can be assessed more justly.

In this bibliography, titles of articles printed in the contemporary press are given in their simplest form. All works in English are published in London, and all those in French are published in Paris, unless otherwise stated. For abbreviations, see above, p. x and p. 285. I have not had space to include a general bibliography, nor one of contemporary studies on Baudelaire: for this the reader is referred to the many excellent works which already exist and for up-to-date information to the *Bulletin baudelairien*. Full details on all works referred to can be found in the first note relevant to each work: the index contains an italicized entry for such notes.

Asselineau

1857
Du Camp, M., 'Odelettes, préface de C. Asselineau', *RP*, 1 April, 473

1858
Babou, H., 'La Double Vie', *RFr*, August–October, 560–73: reprinted in *Lettres satiriques et critiques* (Poulet-Malassis et de Broise, 1860), 338–51
Cherbuliez, J., 'La Double Vie', *RCLN*, December, 574–5
Cuvillier-Fleury, A. A., 'De quelques femmes du roman français', *JD*, 14 November: reprinted in *Historiens, poëtes et romanciers*, II (Michel Lévy Frères, 1863), 12–13
Lataye, E., 'La Double Vie', *RDM*, 15 October, 967ff.

1859
Wey, F., 'Réimpression des Factums de Furetière', *Bulletin du bibliophile*, 468–77

1860
Anon., 'L'Enfer du bibliophile', *RA*, 15–31 August, 96

1862
Anon., 'Bio-bibliographie', *RA*, 1st semester, 251–4

Balzac

1840
Arago, E., 'Vautrin', *Revue du progrès*, 1 April
Gautier, T., 'Vautrin', *P*, 18 March

1841
Barthélemy-Lanta, A. de, 'Le Curé de village', *Echo*, 25 November
Chaudes-Aigues, J., *Les Ecrivains modernes*, 199–232

1842
Cherbuliez, J., 'Quinola', *RCLN*, May
Laverdant, D., 'Quinola', *Ph*, 27 March
Molènes, G. de, 'Mémoires de deux jeunes mariés', *RDM*, 15 March, 979–86
   'Quinola', *RDM*, 1 April, 136–50
   'Simples essais', *RDM*, 1 November, 390–411

1843
Belenet, E. de, 'Rosalie', *Echo*, November, 323–7
Molènes, G. de, 'Revue littéraire', *RDM*, 15 June, 990–8
   'Derniers Romans', *RDM*, 1 December, 810–29

1844
Anon., 'Un début dans la vie', *RP*, 25 July, 430–1
Asseline, A., 'Modeste Mignon', *RP*, 4 May, 11–12

1845
Gautier, T., 'En-tête pour les "Petites Misères de la vie conjugale"', *P*, 25 December
Gobineau, J. A., 'Balzac', *Le Commerce*, 31 December
Nettement, A., *Etudes critiques*, 1 (Dentu, 1845), 36ff.

1846
Anon., 'Petits Profils', *La Silhouette*, 18 January
Achard, A., 'Balzac', *L'Epoque*, 9 May
Castille, H., 'Romanciers contemporains', *La Semaine*, 4 October, 725–7
Pelletan, E., 'La Comédie humaine', *P*, 3 November: reprinted in *Heures de travail*
   (Pagnerre, 1854)
Sainte-Beuve, C. A., 'Balzac', *Portraits contemporains*, 1, 443–65
Weill, A., 'Les Parents pauvres', *DP*, 12 and 27 December

1847
Babou, H., 'Petites lettres', *Revue nouvelle*, 1 February: reprinted in *Lettres satiriques* (1860), 75–117
Hennequin, V., 'Balzac', *DP*, 19 April
Lerminier, L., 'De la peinture des mœurs contemporaines', *RDM*, XVIII, 193–216
Weill, A., 'Balzac', *DP*, 5 and 9 January
  'Politique et littérature', *DP*, 9 May

1848
Anon., 'La Marâtre', *La Silhouette*, 11–15 June
Elmel, C., 'La Marâtre', *L'Opinion publique*, 29 May
Fleury, J., 'La Marâtre', *DP*, 29 May
Gautier, T., 'La Marâtre', *P*, 29 May
Janin, J., 'Théâtre', *JD*, 29 May
Matharel, C. de, 'La Marâtre', *S*, 29 May

1849
Gautier, T., 'Mme Marneffe', *P*, 15 January
Vacquerie, A., 'Balzac', *L'Evénement*, 9 January

1850
Aubryet, X., 'Quelques Mots', *A*, 1 September, 110
Barbey d'Aurevilly, J., 'Nécrologie', *La Mode*, 24 August
Chasles, P., 'Balzac', *JD*, 24 August
Cohen, J., 'Balzac', *La Semaine*, 1 September
Desnoiresterres, G., 'Balzac', *L'Ordre*, 11, 12 and 13 September: reprinted in *Honoré de Balzac* (1851)
Du Camp, J., 'Balzac', *A*, 1 September, 107–9
Forgues, E. D., 'Balzac', *N*, 27 August
Lecomte, J., 'Courrier de Paris', *IB*, 23 and 25 August: see also 1, 8, 16, 22 and 29 September
Matharel, C., 'Vautrin', *S*, 22 and 29 April
Mazade, C. de., 'De la démocratie en littérature', *RDM*, 28 February, 916
  'Balzac', *RDM*, 1 September, 912–16
Méray, A., 'Mort de Balzac', *DP*, 25 August
  'Vautrin', *DP*, 7 May
Meurice, P., 'Vautrin', *L'Evénement*, 6 May
Nerval, G. de, 'Théâtre de Balzac', *P*, 26 August
  'Balzac', *P*, 7 and 28 October
Sainte-Beuve, 'M. de Balzac', *Const*, 2 September: reprinted *Causeries du lundi*, 11 (1851), 346–62
Thierry, E., 'Vautrin', *AN*, 29 April

1851
Baschet, A., *Variétés littéraires: Honoré de Balzac*
Champfleury, 'M. de Balzac, père de la critique future', *Messager de l'Assemblée*, 14 June
Fillias, A., 'Mercadet', *La Semaine*, 5 September, 570–1
Gautier, T., 'Mercadet', *P*, 1 September
  'La Peau de chagrin, drame', *P*, 8 September

Janin, J., 'Mercadet', *JD*, 25 August
Lemer, J., 'Mercadet', *La Sylphide*, 30 August, 95
Méray, A., 'Mercadet', *DP*, 14 September
Musset, P. de, 'Mercadet', *N*, 25 August
Planche, G., 'Mercadet', *RDM*, 15 September, 1135–8
Saint-Victor, P. de, 'Mercadet', *Le Pays*, 25 August
Thierry, E., 'Mercadet', *AN*, 25 August

1852
Anon., 'Causeries', *AF*, 22 January, 87
Cherbuliez, J., 'Théâtre', *RCLN*, December
Lemer, J., 'Revue critique', *AF*, 18 December, 394
Menche de Loisne, C., *L'Influence de la littérature française* [. . .] *sur l'esprit public* [. . .]
    (Garnier Frères, 1852), 35–259 and 360–87
Mirecourt, E. de, *Les Contemporains: Balzac* (Humbert, 1852)
Molènes, P. de, 'Les Pensées de Balzac', *JD*, 15 April
Nerval, 'Balzac', *La Sylphide*, 20 February

1853
Barbey d'Aurevilly, J., 'Stendhal et Balzac', *Le Pays*, 13 July: reprinted *Romanciers
    d'hier et d'avant-hier* (1904)
Baschet, A., 'Esquisses littéraires', *La Semaine théâtrale*, 22 January
Bernard, T., 'Balzac', *AF*, 1115
Clément de Ris, L., 'Balzac', *Portraits*, 293–333
Delessart, E., 'Traité de la vie élégante', *AF*, 11 June, 549–50
Dufaï, A., 'Maximes et Pensées', *AF*, 5 February, 113–15
Gautier, T., 'Le Lys dans la vallée, drame', *La Presse littéraire*, 26 June, 143
Limayrac, P., 'Du roman moderne', *P*, 14 August
Texier, E., *Critiques* (Michel Lévy Frères, 1853), 107–12
Ulbach, L., 'La Liquidation littéraire', *RP*, March, 377–401: reprinted in *Ecrivains
    et Hommes de lettres* (Delahaye, 1857)

1854
Pontmartin, F. de, 'Balzac', *Causeries littéraires*, 292–303

1855
George Sand, 'Histoire de ma vie', *P*, 14 June

1856
Banville, T. de, 'Echos de Paris', *F*, 27 January
Barbey d'Aurevilly, J., 'Contes drolatiques', *Le Pays*, 12 and 26 February: reprinted
    in *Romanciers d'hier et d'avant-hier* (1904)
Bell, G., 'Contes drolatiques', *GP*, 13 April
Belloy, A. de, 'Balzac', *RFr*, 10 and 17 June
Gozlan, L., *Balzac en pantoufles*
Lurine, L., 'Balzac', *Le Pays*, 3 and 5 May
Monselet, C., 'Contes drolatiques', *CF*, 13 April
Poitou, E., 'Balzac', *RDM*, 15 December, 713–67
Pontmartin, F. de, 'Balzac', *Corr*, 25 November and 25 December: reprinted in
    Causeries du samedi (Michel Lévy Frères, 1857), 32–103
Thierry, E., 'Contes drolatiques', *MU*, 11 March

1857

Audebrand, P., 'Balzac journaliste', *GP*, 8 and 15 November
Barbey d'Aurevilly, J., 'Balzac', *Le Pays*, 1 January
Champfleury, 'Balzac', *Le Réalisme* 1–14, 101–2, 201–2, 228
Monselet, C., *La Lorgnette littéraire*
Poitou, E., *Du roman* [. . .], especially 19 and 69ff.
Watripon, A., 'De la moralité', *Le Présent*, 16 August, 242–9

1858

Babou, H., 'Le Noviciat de Balzac', *RFr*, 1 September, 236–44: reprinted *Lettres satiriques* (1860), 55–74
Gautier, T., 'Balzac', *A*, 21 March, 189–93, 28 March, 205–8, 4 April, 226–30, 18 April, 257–61, 25 April, 273–5, 2 May, 285–90: reprinted as *Honoré de Balzac*
Taine, H., 'Balzac', *JD*, 3, 4, 5, 23 and 25 February and 3 March: reprinted in *Essais*, 102–7, 195–201

1859

Caro, E., 'Balzac', *RE*, v, 5–36, 225–67: reprinted in *Poètes et Romanciers* (Hachette, 1888)
Gautier, T., 'La Marâtre', *MU*, 5 September
'Œuvres complètes', *MU*, 10 December
Jouvin, B., 'Balzac dramaturge', *F*, 17 September
Nefftzer, A., 'Balzac et le théâtre', *RG*, July–October, 701–2.
Nettement, A., 'Balzac', *Histoire de la littérature française sous le gouvernement de juillet*, 11, 263–75
Plée, L., 'Contes drolatiques', *S*, 3 May
Sarcey de Suttières, F., 'La Marâtre', *ON*, 12 September

1861

Anon., 'Balzac', *Le Courrier artistique*, 15–28 February

1862

Clément de Ris, L., *Critiques d'art et de littérature* (Eugène Didier, 1862), 306–8 and 322–4
Proth, M., 'Mouvement littéraire', *Le Courrier du dimanche*, 16 November

Banville

1842

Pernet, E., 'Banville', *RI*, 10 December

1843

Labitte, C., 'Poetae minores', *RDM*, 1 July, 127–8

1846

Champfleury, 'Les Stalactites', *CS*, 14 March
Mazade, C. de, 'Des œuvres littéraires de ce temps', *RDM*, 15 June, 1032ff.
Prudhomme, Léonidas [J. Lovy], 'Banville', *Le Tintamarre*, 12, 22 and 28 March
Stab, N., 'Les Stalactites', *L'Esprit publique*, 21 April

1851
Desnoiresterres, G., 'Ode', *La Semaine*, 31 January, 78

1852
Prarond, E., *De quelques écrivains nouveaux*, 81–102

1856
Asselineau, C., 'Odelettes', *RFr*, 10 August, 107–14
Barbey d'Aurevilly, J., 'Odelettes', *Le Pays*, 22 November: reprinted in *Les Œuvres*,
    XXIII (Geneva: Slatkine Reprints, 1968), 63–82
Chasles, P., *AF*, 27 February, 85
Laurent-Pichat, 'Odelettes', *RP*, 15 July, 630–1
Lecomte, J., 'Courrier de Paris', *IB*, 27 July
Rovigo, R. de, 'Chronique parisienne', *CF*, 2 and 16 March
Saint-Victor, P. de, 'Le Beau Léandre', *P*, 5 October
Terraus, H., 'Les Préfaces littéraires', *Le Réalisme*, 15 December
Thierry, E., 'Odelettes', *MU*, 28 April
Vaucelle, A. de, 'Odelettes', *A*, 15 June, 233–5

1857
Anon., 'Banville', *RP*, 15 July
    'Odes funambulesques', *RA*, 16 February, 90–2
Babou, H., 'Lettre', *RFr*, February–April, 425–31: reprinted in *Lettres satiriques*
    (1860)
Barbey d'Aurevilly, J., 'Odes funambulesques', *Le Pays*, 21 March: reprinted *Les*
    Œuvres, III, 215–26
    'Poésies complètes', *Le Pays*, 1 November: reprinted *Les Œuvres*, XI, 229–44
Bernard, J., 'Œuvres complètes', *Le Présent*, I, 8 September
Desnoyers, F., 'Odes funambulesques', *Polichinelle*, 29 March, 3
Du Camp, M., 'Odelettes', *RP*, 1 April, 472–3
    'Odes funambulesques', *RP*, 1 May, 137–8
Duranty, E., 'Banville', *Le Réalisme*, 15 January
Habans, J., 'Poésies complètes', *F*, 27 September
Janin, J., 'Poésies complètes', *JD*, 22 October
Jouvin, B., 'Odes funambulesques', *F*, 15 March
Monselet, C., *La Lorgnette littéraire*
Sainte-Beuve, C. A., 'Poésies complètes', *MU*, 12 October: reprinted in *Causeries du*
    lundi, XIV (Garnier Frères, 1870), 69–85
Thierry, E., 'Odes funambulesques', *MU*, 10 June

1858
Bell, G., 'Poésies complètes', *P*, 16 June
Mantz, P. de, 'Poètes lyriques contemporains', *RFr*, November 1857–January 1858,
    394–405
Sarcey, F., 'Les Petits Poètes', *F*, 10 December

1859
Cherbuliez, J., 'Esquisses parisiennes', *RCLN*, February, 60–1
    'Odes funambulesques', *RCLN*, March, 115–17
Habans, J., 'Odes funambulesques', *RE*, 11, 897–900

1860
Des Essarts, E., 'Banville', *A*, 15 February, 49–53

1862
Nettement, A., *Poètes et Artistes contemporains*, 503–8

1863
Montégut, E., 'Le Théâtre contemporain', *RDM*, 1 December: reprinted in
    Dramaturges et Romanciers (Hachette, 1890)

Barbier

Articles before 1840 (select list)
Planche, G., 'Poètes et Romanciers modernes', *RDM*, 1 July 1837, 54–78: reprinted
    in *Portraits littéraires*, II (1848), 59–103
Reynaud, J., 'De la poésie politique', *REnc*, November 1831
Sainte-Beuve, C. A., 'Iambes', *RDM*, 1831, 524–34: reprinted in *Portraits con-
    temporains*, II, 222–34
    'Il Pianto', *N*, 21 January 1833: reprinted in *Portraits contemporains*, II, 235–41

1840
Barthélemy-Lanta, A., 'Nouvelles Satires', *Echo*, 16–17
D. M., 'Nouvelles Satires', *RP*, xxv, 362–7
Planche, G., 'Nouvelles Satires', *RDM*, 1 March, 703–11

1841
Gautier, T., 'Chants civils et religieux', *RDM*, 15 June, 908–14

1843
Anon., 'Rimes héroïques', *L'Illustration*, 15 April
Asseline, C., 'Rimes héroïques', *RP*, xviii, 47–56: for Barbier's response see *RI*,
    1 August
Labitte, C., 'Poetae minores', *RDM*, 1 July, 115–20

1846
Anon., 'Œuvres de M. A. Barbier', *REnc*, May, 74–82

1847
Desplaces, A., 'Galerie des poètes vivants', *A*, 7 March, 5–7: reprinted in *Galerie
    des poètes vivants* (Didier, 1847)

1853
Castille, H., *Les Hommes et les Mœurs*, 285ff.

1859
Nettement, A., *Histoire de la littérature française sous le gouvernement de juillet*, II, 141–4

1862
Anon., 'Barbier', *RA*, xiv, 103–4
Manet, H., 'Barbier', *Courrier du dimanche*, 15 June

Rollin, M., 'Chansons et Odelettes', *RFr*, 15 March
Wailly, L. de, 'Barbier', in E. Crépet, ed., *Les Poètes français*, IV, 377–92

1864
Barbey d'Aurevilly, J., 'Silves', *Le Pays*, 3 April: reprinted *Les Œuvres*, XI, 125–40

Borel

1831
Reynaud, J., 'De la poésie politique', *REnc*, November, 427–31

1833
Bureau, A., 'Champavert', *Ph*, 8 March
Lacroix, P., 'Champavert', *RP*, XLVIII, 144
G. L. [Nerval], 'Contes immoraux', *A*, February, 67–8: for attribution see *Œuvres complémentaires*, I (Minard, 1959), 102–6
Sainte-Beuve, C. A., 'Champavert', *RDM*, 1 March, 567–71: reprinted in *Premiers Lundis*, II (Michel Lévy Frères, 1874–5), 170–84

1839
Janin, J., 'Madame Putiphar', *JD*, 3 June: reprinted in Borel, *Madame Putiphar*, 424–35

1846
Louandre, C. and F. Bourguelot, *La Littérature contemporaine* (F. Dagern, 1846), 355

1857
Anon., 'Les Fleurs du mal', *RA*, 20 April, 177–8
Monselet, C., *La Lorgnette littéraire*

1859
Anon., 'Pétrus Borel', *RA*, 16–30 December, 265–6
Lataye, E., 'Daniel', *RDM*, 1 July, 243

1869
Des Essarts, E., 'Pétrus Borel', *Voyages de l'Esprit* (Maillet, 1869), 125–32

Champfleury and 'Realism'

1846
Fleury, J. 'Pierrot valet de la mort', *CS*, 27 September
Gautier, T., 'Pierrot', *P*, 28 September: attribution doubtful: see Spoelberch de Lovenjoul, *Histoire des œuvres de Théophile Gautier* (Geneva: Slatkine Reprints, 1968)
Nerval, G., 'Pierrot', *A*, 27 September
Vacquerie, A., 'Mouvement dramatique et littéraire', *L'Epoque*, 5 and 12 October

1847
Fleury, J., 'Chien-Caillou', *DP*, 13 February
'Fantaisies du printemps', *DP*, 24 June
'Pierrot marquis', *DP*, 19 October

Gautier, T., 'Pierrot pendu', *P*, 25 January
  'Pierrot marquis', *P*, 15 October

1848
Fleury, J., 'Feu Miette', *DP*, 31 January and 1 February

1849
Gautier, T., 'La Cruche cassée', *P*, 28–9 May
  'Henri Monnier', *P*, 8 July

1851
D'Ambly, Paul, 'Contes d'automne', *A*, 1 June, 136–7
Cuvillier-Fleury, A. A., 'Le Roman français en 1851', *JD*, 5 October: reprinted
  Etudes historiques et littéraires, 1 (Michel Lévy Frères, 1854), 291–3
Vitu, A., 'Champfleury', *Le Messager de l'Assemblée*, 8 July

1852
Busquet, A., 'Tablettes contemporaines', *La Semaine*, 16 January, 33–5
Pontmartin, F. de, 'Les Excentriques', *RC*, 1, April–May, 159
Prarond, E., *De quelques écrivains nouveaux*, 131–51
Vinet, A., 'Contes domestiques', *AF*, 19 November, 228–9

1853
Chasles, E., 'Contes du printemps', *AF*, 19 November, 1097–8
Pontmartin, F. de, 'Les Jeunes Conteurs', *AN*, 26 March

1854
Barbey d'Aurevilly, J., 'Contes d'été', *Le Pays*, 14 January
Ulbach, L., 'Contes d'automne', *RP*, 15 June, 953–4
Verdun, J., 'Contes de printemps', *RP*, 1 January, 158–9
Watripon, A., 'Les Réalistes', *Le Moustiquaire*, 14 March

1855
Anon., 'Les Excentriques', *RA*, 1, 180
Goudall, L., 'L'Ecole réaliste', *F*, 7 October
Mirecourt, *Les Contemporains: Champfleury*

1856
Aubryet, X., 'Champfleury', *A*, 9 November, 281–3
Barbey d'Aurevilly, 'Hoffmann', *Le Pays*, 2 July
Chasles, E., 'Les Excentriques', *AF*, 31 May, 463–4
Deschanel, 'Contes choisis', *IB*, 9 August
Fournel, V., 'Hoffmann', *AF*, 12 July, 597
Quevilly, V. de, 'Lettres d'un bon jeune homme', *F*, 7 December
Rousseau, J., 'Une charge de M. Champfleury', *GP*, 26 October

1857
Anon., 'Mariette', *RA*, 16 April
Babou, H., 'La Vérité sur le cas de M. Champfleury', *RFr*, VII, November 1856–
  January 1857, 421–31: reprinted in *Lettres satiriques* (1860)

Laurent-Pichat, A., 'Le Réalisme', *RP*, 15 September, 330–1
Monselet, C., *La Lorgnette littéraire*
Thulié, H., 'Champfleury', *Le Réalisme*, 15 February

1858
Anon., 'Contemporary French Literature', *North American Review*, LXXXVI, 230–2
Cuvillier-Fleury, A. A., 'De quelques femmes du roman français', *JD*, 14 November:
    reprinted in *Historiens, Poètes, Romanciers* (1863), 9–10

1859
Arnould, A., 'Souvenirs des funambules', *RE*, III, 900–2
Bersot, E., 'Les Amoureux de Sainte-Pérène', *JD*, 20 February
Garsonvet, E., 'Le Réalisme', *RE*, III, 779–807
Habans, J., 'Christian', *RE*, III, 661
Merlet, G., 'Le Roman contemporain', *RE*, VI, 298–325: reprinted in *Le Réalisme*
    (Didier, 1861)
Sarcey de Suttières, F., 'Réalisme et Champfleurisme', *F*, 6 February

1860
Anon., 'M. de Bois d'Hyver', *RA*, 16–30 April, 192
    'La Succession Lecamus', *RA*, 16–31 July, 47
Aubryet, X., 'Les Idéalistes sans le savoir', *Les Jugements nouveaux* (A. Bourdilliat),
    331–43
Chavesne, H., 'Chansons populaires', *RE*, VIII, 425–30
    'Les Romans nouveaux', *RE*, XI, 635–43
Merlet, G., 'Le Réaliste imaginaire', *RE*, VIII, 34–63
    'Le Réalisme byronien', *RE*, X, 669–703: reprinted in *Le Réalisme* (1861)
Reymon, W., 'Sur le réalisme', *A*, 15 January, 14–15

1861
Anon., 'Grandes Figures', *RA*, new series III, 70–1

1862
Anon., 'Champfleury', *RA*, new series XIV, 155–9

1863
Merlet, G., *Portraits d'hier et d'aujourd'hui*, IX
Sainte-Beuve, C. A., 'Chansons populaires', *Const*, 5 January: reprinted *Nouveaux*
    lundis (1863), IV, 116–39

1864
Nettement, A., 'Champfleury', *Le Roman contemporain* (J. Lecoffre, 1864), 151–9

Chennevières

1852
Prarond, E., *De quelques écrivains nouveaux*, 51–80
See also Barbey d'Aurevilly, *Lettres à Trébutien*, I (A. Blaizot, 1908), 172–3: letter
    dated 24 April 1850

Cladel

1861
Anon., *RA*, IV, 2nd semester, 218–19
G. I., *RE,* 1 December (Bulletin bibliographique)
Janin, J., *JD*, 16 December
Mendès, C., *RFt*, 1, 1 December, 32–4

1862
Glatigny, A., *B*, 5 January
Goudall, L., *F*, 9 January

Desbordes-Valmore

1839
Sainte-Beuve, C. A., 'Pauvres Fleurs', *RDM*, 1 January, 128–32: reprinted *Portraits
    contemporains*, I, 372–9

1842
Molènes, P. de, 'Simples Essais', *RDM*, 1 July, 48–76
Sainte-Beuve, C. A., 'Marceline Desbordes-Valmore', *RP*, 12 June, 105–15:
    reprinted *Portraits contemporains*, I (1888), 380–90

1843
Asseline, A., 'Bouquets et Prières', *RP*, XVI, 131–8

1847
Desplaces, A., 'Galerie des poètes vivants', *A*, 11 April, 82

1851
Vinet, A., *Etudes*, II, 575–84

1857
Monselet, C., *La Lorgnette littéraire*

1859
Blot, S., 'Quelques Mots', *La Revue du Lyonnais*, September, 296–8
Janin, J., 'Desbordes-Valmore', *JD*, 1 August: reprinted in *Critique, Portraits et
    Caractères*, 330
Nettement, A., *Histoire de la littérature française sous le gouvernement de juillet*, 150
Raspail, F., 'Desbordes-Valmore', *Revue complémentaire des sciences*, 1 September, 56–8

1860
Barbey d'Aurevilly, J., 'Poésies inédites', *Le Pays*, 21 August: reprinted in *Les
    Œuvres et les hommes*, III, 145–58
Cherbuliez, J., 'Poésies inédites', *RCLN*, September, 385–7
Lacaussade, A., 'Mme Desbordes-Valmore', *RE*, XI, 328–46
Levallois, J., 'Poésies inédites', *ON*, 21 October
Montégut, E., 'Mme Desbordes-Valmore', *RDM*, 15 December, 997–1016:
    reprinted in *Esquisses littéraires* (Hachette, 1893)

Olivier, J., 'Poésies inédites', *Revue suisse*, August
Sainte-Beuve, C. A., 'Marceline Desbordes-Valmore', *MU*, 13 August, 979–80: reprinted in *Causeries du lundi*, XIV, 405–16
Vapereau, A., 'Poésies inédites', *L'Année littéraire*, 64–5

Dupont

1846
Champfleury, J., 'Les Paysans', *A*, 24 May, 192–3
Chavigny, A., 'Les Deux Anges', *Echo*, VII, 30 July, 213–16

1849
Anon., 'Chansons et Poésies', *La Semaine*, 1 April, 410–12
Dameth, H., 'La Musique populaire', *DP*, 30 October
Vitu, A., 'Petits Profils contemporains', *La Silhouette*, 2 and 9 September

1851
Cuvillier-Fleury, A. A., 'Le Chant de 1852', *JD*, 23 March
Hayward, G., 'Dupont', *Morning Chronicle*, 5 May
Montégut, E., 'La Poésie et les poètes populaires', *RDM*, 15 June, 1136–52
Sainte-Beuve, C. A., 'Chants et Poésies', *Const*, 21–2 April: reprinted in *Causeries du lundi*, IV, 51–75
Tisseur, C., 'Béranger et Pierre Dupont', *Revue du Lyonnais*, new series, III, 58–84

1852
Adam, A., 'Revue musicale', *AN*, 3 August
Busquet, A., 'Tablettes contemporaines', *La Semaine*, 16 January, 33–5
Reyer, E., 'Pierre Dupont', *AF*, 21 August, 123–4: reprinted as preface to Dupont, *Chants et Chansons* (Lecrivain et Toubon, 1858–9), II

1853
Rouquette, J., 'Chants et Chansons', *Le Monde artistique et littéraire*, 11 June, 130

1854
Mirecourt, E., *Les Contemporains: Dupont*

1855
Gautier, T., 'L'Album', *P*, 9 January
Tavoni, L., 'Les Dernières Œuvres', *La Fronde*, 18 February

1856
Babou, H., 'La Légende du Juif errant', *AF*, 15 March
Gautier, T., 'La Légende', *MU*, 15 August

1857
Monselet, C., *La Lorgnette littéraire*

1858
Mirecourt, E., 'Pierre Dupont', *Les Contemporains*, XII
Proudhon, P., *De la justice* (Garnier Frères, 1858), 399

1860

Barbey d'Aurevilly, J., 'Etudes littéraires', *Le Pays*, 10 January: reprinted in *Les Œuvres*, III, 239–51
Cherbuliez, J., 'La Muse juvénile', *RCLN*, May, 204–5

1862

Nettement, A., *Poètes et Artistes contemporains*, 472–87

1870

Asselineau, C., 'Pierre Dupont', *Bulletin du bibliophile*, 371–80
Banville, T. de, 'Dupont', *N*, 1 August: reprinted in *Critiques*, ed. V. Barrucand, (Charpentier, 1917), 129–56
Janin, J., 'Pierre Dupont', *JD*, 1 August

Flaubert

1857

Anon., 'Madame Bovary', *North American Review*, LXXXV, 529–33
Aubineau, L., 'Du roman nouveau', *U*, 26 June
Aubryet, X., 'Les Niaiseries de la critique', *A*, 20 September
Barbey d'Aurevilly, J., 'Madame Bovary', *Le Pays*, 6 October: reprinted in *Les Œuvres*, IV, 152–5
Castelnau, A., 'Le Roman réaliste', *Revue philosophique et religieuse*, August, 152–5
Cuvillier-Fleury, A. A., 'Madame Bovary', *JD*, 26 May: reprinted in *Dernières Etudes* (1859), 362–6
Darcel, A., 'Madame Bovary', *Journal de Rouen*, 21 April: reprinted in *Les Amis de Flaubert*, XLVI, May 1975, 41–8
Denys, H., 'Madame Bovary', *Le Présent*, I, ii, 9 July, 34–9
Desdemaines, E., 'Les Jeunes', *Le Rabelais*, 23 May
Dumesnil, R., 'Madame Bovary', *Chronique artistique et littéraire*, 3 May
Duranty, E., 'Echos', *Le Réalisme*, 15 January, 15 March
Donis, J. B., 'Le Roman moderne', *La Revue moderne*, 1–10 July, 73–86
Habans, J., 'Madame Bovary', *F*, 28 June
Limayrac, P., 'Des causes et des effets', *Const*, 10 May
Mazade, C. de, 'Chronique', *RDM*, 1 May, 217–20
Pontmartin, F. de, 'Le Roman bourgeois', *Corr*, XLI, 25 June, 289–306; reprinted in *Nouvelles causeries* (Michel Lévy Frères, 1859), 299–326
Réveillon, T., 'Flaubert', *GP*, 18 October
Roqueplan, N., 'Courrier de Paris', *P*, 16 May
Sainte-Beuve, C. A., 'Madame Bovary', *MU*, 4 May: reprinted *Causeries du lundi*, XIII, 346–63
Texier, E., 'Chronique littéraire', *L'Illustration*, 9 May
Villemot, A., 'Courrier de Paris', *IB*, 3 January, 7 and 14 February

1858

Escudier, 'Ut pictura poesis', *Le Réveil*, 13 February
Granier de Cassagnac, A., 'La Bohème dans le roman', *Le Réveil*, 16 January
Vapereau, A., 'Succès du roman psychologique', *L'Année littéraire*, 47–59
Weiss, J. J., 'De la littérature brutale', *RC*, January–February, 144–85: reprinted *Essais* (Calmann Lévy, 1891), 113–86

1859
Legrelle, A., 'Le Réalisme', *Revue de l'instruction publique*, 18 August
Monpont, F., *Les Chantres de l'adultère* (Ledoyen, 1859), 27–38

1860
Merlet, G., 'Le Roman physiologique', *RE*, VIII, 15 June, 707–40: reprinted in
  Réalisme et Fantaisie, 91–141

1861
Blot, A., 'Les Livres', *La Critique française*, I, 492
T. C., 'Les Livres', *La Critique française*, I, 225

1862
Banville, T. de, 'Salammbô', *B*, December
Claveau, A., 'Salammbô', *RC*, 15 December, 643–52
Clément de Ris, L., 'Les Notabilités littéraires', *Critiques d'art et de littérature*, 310–12
Caro, E., 'L'Auteur de "Madame Bovary" à Carthage', *La France*, 9 December:
  reprinted in *Poètes et Romanciers*, 260–70
Cuvillier-Fleury, A. A., 'Variétés', *JD*, 9 and 13 December: reprinted in *Etudes et
  Portraits* (Michel Lévy Frères, 1865), 294–314
Froehner, G., 'Le Roman archéologique', *RC*, 30 December, 853–70
Gautier, T., 'Salammbô', *MU*, 22 December: reprinted in *L'Orient*, II, 281–322
Levallois, J., 'Salammbô', *ON*, 14 December
Luciennes, V., 'Salammbô', *RC*, 15 December, 266–8
Proth, M., 'Salammbô', *Courrier du dimanche*, 7 December
Sainte-Beuve, C. A., 'Salammbô', *Const*, 8, 15 and 22 December: reprinted *Nouveaux
  lundis*, IV, 31–95

1863
Dusolier, A., 'Salammbô', *RFr*, new series, IV, 1 January, 115–22: reprinted in *Nos
  gens de lettres* (A. Faure, 1864), 55–71
Pontmartin, F. de, 'Flaubert', *Nouvelles Semaines littéraires* (Michel Lévy Frères,
  1863), 93–106: article dated December 1862
Taillandier, R., 'Le Réalisme épique', *RDM*, 15 February, 840–61

1864
Nettement, A., 'Flaubert', *Le Roman contemporain*, 118–29

Gautier

1838
Sainte-Beuve, C. A., 'Fortunio', *RP*, 15 September, 856–70: reprinted in *Premiers
  lundis*, II, 322–49

1840
Anon., 'Le Fruit défendu', *Echo*, September, 583–4

1841
Laverdant, D., 'Feuilleton', *Ph*, 18 July

1842
Anon., 'Falstaff', *A*, July–December, 248–9
Asseline, A., 'La Coupe amère', *Echo*, 297

1843
Anon., 'La Péri', *A*, July–December, 94–5
Aubert, 'La Péri', *RI*, 25 July
G. B., 'Tra los montes', *Echo*, February, 33–4

1844
Babou, H., 'Le Goût antique', *RP*, 19 October, 249–52
Cherbuliez, J., 'Les Grotesques', *RCLN*, October
Labitte, C., 'Le Grotesque en littérature', *RDM*, 1 November, 495–516: reprinted
    in *Etudes*, II, 313–39
Laverdant, D., 'Salon', *DP*, 25 April
Sainte-Beuve, C. A., 'Les Grotesques', *RP*, 31 October, 307–11: reprinted *Portraits
    contemporains*, III, 251–70

1845
Anon., 'Petits Profils', *La Silhouette*, 13 July
Lucas, H., 'Le Tricorne enchanté', *S*, 21 April
Méry, J., 'Le Tricorne enchanté', *P*, 14 April

1846
Belenet, E. de, 'Zigzags', *Echo*, VIII, 71–3
Fournier, M., 'La Semaine littéraire', *A*, 15 March, 32
Hennequin, V., 'La Juive', *DP*, 16–17 November
Janin, J., 'La Juive', *JD*, 16 November
Matharel, C. de, 'La Juive', *S*, 16 November
Vacquerie, A., 'Mouvement littéraire', *L'Epoque*, 22 June
    'Mouvement dramatique', *L'Epoque*, 16 November

1847
Desplaces, A., 'Galerie des poètes vivants', *A*, 14 February, 227–9
Hennequin, V., 'Regardez mais ne touchez pas', *DP*, 25–6 October
Séraphin, 'Regardez mais ne touchez pas', *La Silhouette*, 31 October

1851
Desnoiresterres, G., 'Pâquerette', *La Semaine*, 7 February, 95

1852
Anon., 'Romans et nouvelles', *AF*, 18 December
Cuvillier-Fleury, A. A., 'Revue littéraire', *JD*, 19 September: reprinted in *Etudes
    historiques et littéraires*, II (1854), 190–6
Cyrano, 'Le Monde et le Théâtre', *RP*, August, 155–6
Limayrac, P., 'Emaux et Camées', *P*, 3 October
Pontmartin, F. de, 'Revue littéraire', *RC*, October–November, 653–4
Saint-Victor, P. de, 'Emaux et Camées', *Le Pays*, 26 July
Wailly, L. de, 'Italia', *AF*, 10–17 July
    'Caprices et Zigzags', *AF*, 24 July

1853
Anon., 'Romans et Nouvelles', *AF*, 19 February
　'Les Roués innocents', *AF*, 20 August
　'Les Grotesques', *AF*, 1 October
Castille, H., *Les Hommes et les mœurs*, 306–8
Clément de Ris, L., 'Gautier', *Portraits*, 143–72
Dufaï, A., 'Emaux et Camées', *AF*, 9 April, 331–3
Pontmartin, F. de, 'Un salmis de romans', *RC*, April–May, 299–300

1854
Anon., 'Constantinople', *AF*, 28 June
Pontmartin, F. de, 'Constantinople', *AN*, 4 February
　'Gautier', *Causeries littéraires*, 327–38

1855
Mirecourt, E., *Les Contemporains: Gautier*

1856
Eggis, E., 'Gautier', *A*, 8 June, 219–20
Laurent-Pichat, L., 'L'Art moderne', *RP*, 15 July, 634–5
Saglio, E., 'Les Beaux-Arts en Europe', *AF*, 5 July, 568–70
Thierry, E., 'Les Beaux-Arts', *MU*, 4 March

1857
Du Camp, M., 'Avatar', *RP*, 1 October, 500–1
Dupont, P., 'Gautier', *Polichinelle*, 22 February, 2, 3 and 8 March
Laurent-Pichat, L., 'Militona', *RP*, 15 December, 636
Monselet, C., *La Lorgnette littéraire*, 103–8

1859
Barbey d'Aurevilly, J., 'Emaux et Camées', *Le Pays*, 26 January
Cherbuliez, J., 'Emaux et Camées', *RCLN*, March, 118
Jouvin, B., 'Histoire de l'art dramatique', *F*, 10 February
Pelloquet, T., 'Les Réputations surfaites', *GP*, 16 and 23 January

1862
Froehner, G., 'Le Roman archéologique', *RC*, 30 December, 853–70

1863
Lavoix, H., 'Capitaine Fracasse', *MU*, 29 October
Sainte-Beuve, C. A., 'Poésies', *Const*, 16, 23 and 30 November: reprinted in
　Nouveaux lundis, VI, 265–339

1864
Barbey d'Aurevilly, J., 'Capitaine Fracasse', *Le Pays*, 17 January: reprinted *Les
　Œuvres*, IV, 295–308

Hugo

1840
Berthoud, S. H., 'Les Rayons et les ombres', *Le Musée des familles*, 1839–40, 286

Cantagrel, H., 'Hernani', *Ph*, 15 June and 1 July
Chaudes-Aigues, J., 'Les Rayons et les ombres', *RP*, XVII, 287–95
Lamartine, A. de, 'Les Rayons et les ombres', *Echo*, May, 131–4
Magnin, C., 'Les Rayons et les ombres', *RDM*, 1 June, 729–48
[Pelletan], E., 'Les Rayons et les ombres', *P*, 28 June

1841
Gautier, T., 'Hernani', *P*, 22 June

1842
Cantagrel, H., 'Victor Hugo et les journaux', *Ph*, 16 January
Meurice, P., 'Le Rhin', *A*, 3rd series, 1, 106–9
Venedzy, F., 'Lettres sur l'Allemagne', *P*, 18 February
Veuillot, L., 'Le Rhin', *U*, 2, 5, 6 February: reprinted in *Œuvres: Mélanges*, 1, 297–323
    'Ce que le poète a découvert', *U*, 24 December: reprinted in *Œuvres: Mélanges*, 1 (P. Lethielleux, 1933), 434–40

1843
Anon., 'Les Burgraves', *U*, 8 October
    'Les Burgraves', *L'Illustration*, 11 March
Arago, E., 'Les Auteurs dramatiques', *RI*, 21 June
Aubert, F., 'Les Burgraves', *RI*, 10 March
Binault, L., 'Du drame romantique et de sa décadence', *Corr*, 11, April–June
Gautier, T., 'Burgraves', *P*, 13 and 14 March
Génin, E., 'Notes et nouvelles', *RI*, 10 April
Laverdant, D., 'Les Burgraves', *Ph*, 15 March
Magnin, C., 'Les Burgraves', *RDM*, 15 March

1844
Anon., 'Lettres de voyage', *A*, 3rd series, v, 104–5
Laverdant, D., 'Lucrèce Borgia', *DP*, 24 May
    'Revue', *DP*, 11 September
Pelletan, E., 'Caractère social de la littérature française', *DP*, 1 April

1845
Gautier, T., 'Hernani', *P*, 10 March
Lerminier, L., 'Le Rhin', *RDM*, 1 June, 821–40
Lucas, H., 'Hernani', *S*, 17 March
    'Le Rhin', *S*, 16 June

1846
Matharel, C., 'Ruy Blas', *S*, 23 February

1847
Desplaces, A., 'Hugo', *A*, 4 April, 67–70
Fleury, J., 'Marion Delorme', *DP*, 22 May
Gautier, T., 'Marion Delorme', *P*, 10 May
Lucas, H., 'Marion Delorme', *S*, 18 May
Matharel, C., 'Lucrèce Borgia', *S*, 23 June

1848
Planche, G., 'Hugo', *RDM*, 15 March: reprinted in *Portraits littéraires*, 114–79
Vacquerie, A., 'Mouvement dramatique', *L'Evénement*, 15 August

1850
Anon., 'Annonce des Misérables', *DP*, 11 January
Cuvillier-Fleury, A. A., 'Romantisme et démagogie', *JD*, 16 June

1851
Veuillot, L., 'M. Hugo et la peine de mort', *U*, 12 June: reprinted in *Œuvres: Mélanges*, IV, 429–32

1852
Planche, G., 'La Poésie et la critique', *RDM*, 1 December, 913–40
Robin, C., 'L'Enfance', *Le Magasin des familles*, II, 1851–2, 644–58

1853
Limayrac, P., 'L'Edition populaire', *P*, 3 July
Mirecourt, E., 'Hugo', *La Presse littéraire*, 11 December
Raymond, A., 'La Fantaisie', *Le Monde artistique et littéraire*, 28 May
Veuillot, L., 'La Vengeance du poète', *U*, 2 and 6 December: reprinted in *Œuvres: Mélanges*, V, 534–9

1854
Mirecourt, E., *Les Contemporains: Hugo*
Nourrisson, F., '"Julien", par Félix Bungener', *AN*, 18 June

1856
Barbey d'Aurevilly, J., 'Les Contemplations', *Le Pays*, 19 and 25 June
Busquet, A., 'Les Contemplations', *GP*, 4 May
Deschanel, E., 'Les Contemplations', *IB*, 3 and 21 May
Fauvety, C., 'Les Contemplations', *Revue philosophique et religieuse*, April, 435–67
Janin, J., 'Les Contemplations', *JD*, 26 June
Jourdain, L., 'Les Contemplations', *S*, 23 April
Jouvin, B., 'Les Poètes du siècle', *F*, 18 May
Laurent-Pichat, L., 'Les Contemplations', *RP*, 15 May, 481–97
Lecomte, J., 'Courrier', *IB*, 27 April
Legendre, A., 'Les Contemplations', *F*, 27 April
Lemonnier, C., 'Système philosophique et religieux de M. Hugo', *Revue philosophique et religieuse*, July, 468–75
Lucas, H., 'Les Contemplations', *S*, 19 May
Mantz, P., 'Les Contemplations', *RFr*, V, May–July
Pelletan, E., 'Les Contemplations', *P*, 13 May
Planche, G., 'Les Contemplations', *RDM*, 15 May, 413–33
Talbot, E., 'Les Contemplations', *Revue de l'instruction publique*, 24 July
Texier, E., 'Chronique hebdomadaire', *S*, 27 April
Veuillot, L., 'Les Contemplations', *U*, May: reprinted *Œuvres: Mélanges*, VI, 497–534

1857
Béraud, P., 'Etude phrénologique', *La Presse littéraire*, VII, 1 March, 278–81

Duranty, F., 'Les Contemplations', *Le Réalisme*, 15 January and 15 February
Pontmartin, F. de, 'Les Fétiches littéraires', *Causeries du samedi*, 104–35

1858

Nettement, A., 'Hugo', *Histoire de la littérature française sous la Restauration*, I
      (J. Lecoffre, 1858), 292–310 and II, 445–69
Nisard, D., 'Hugo', *Portraits et Etudes*, 57–105

1859

Barbey d'Aurevilly, J., 'La Légende des siècles', *Le Pays*, 29 November: reprinted
      in *Les Œuvres*, III, 35–48
Charnal, S. de, 'Le Théâtre', *Le Réveil*, 16 April, 181–5
Chasles, E., 'La Légende des siècles', *RE*, V, 771–97
Claveau, A., 'La Légende des siècles', *RC*, September–October, 519–27
Gautier, T., 'Critique', *P*, 28 December
Leymarie, C., 'La Légende', *Courrier du dimanche*, 2 October
Montégut, E., 'La Légende des siècles', *RDM*, 15 October, 970–96: reprinted in
      Mélanges critiques (Hachette, 1887)
Nefftzer, A., 'La Légende des siècles', *RE*, VIII, October–December, 237–8
Nettement, A., *Histoire de la littérature française sous le gouvernement de juillet*, II, 116–29
      and 188–204
Pelletan, E., 'La Légende des siècles', *P*, 14 October
Vapereau, G., 'La Légende des siècles', *L'Année littéraire*, 1–29
Vaucelle, A. de, 'La Légende des siècles', *A*, new series VIII, 15 December,
      181–4

1860

Cherbuliez, J., 'Œuvres complètes', *RCLN*, March, 125–8
   'La Légende', *RCLN*, February, 49–53

1861

Lafenestre, G., 'La Légende des siècles', *RC*, 15 October, 437–46

1862

Asselineau, C., 'Bibliographie', *RA*, 2nd semester, 43–9
Banville, T. de, 'Les Misérables', *L'Illustration*, 12 April
Barbey d'Aurevilly, J., 'Les Misérables', *Le Pays*, 19 April, 28 May, 9 June, 13, 22
      and 30 July: reprinted in *Les Misérables*
Bénoît-Champy, R., 'Une question pénale', *JD*, 24 July
Billiant, N., 'Les Misérables', *F*, 10 July
Cherbuliez, J., 'Les Misérables', *RCLN*, May, 197–200 and August, 301–3
Cuvillier-Fleury, A. A., 'Les Misérables', *JD*, 29 April and 6 May: reprinted in *Etudes
      et Portraits*, I, 281–311
Daudet, E., 'Les Misérables', *RFr*, new series I, 1 April, 643–52
Desbordes, H., 'Chronique', *RFr*, new series II, 1 August, 260–1
Desmarest, E., 'Les Misérables', *La Critique française*, January–June, 291–302,
      366–77, 457–73 and July–December, 43–56, 173–84
Ernouff, J., 'Les Misérables', *RC*, XXVI, 15 April, 563–87; and XXVII, 31 May,
      355–87; and 15 July, 104–37
Fournier, E., 'Les Misérables', *La Patrie*, 26 May and 15 September

Gautier, T., 'Préface', *Album*: reprinted in Hugo, *Œuvres complètes* (Le Club français du livre, 1967–70), XVIII, 1–11

Grenier, A., 'Les Misérables', *Const*, 29 May

Jouvin, B., 'Les Misérables', *F*, 24 April

Lamartine, A. de, 'Considérations', *Cours familier*, 83rd, 84th and 85th 'entretien', November and December 1862 and January 1863

Laurent-Pichat, L., 'Hugo', *La Réforme littéraire*, 20 July, 2–3

Lefort, H., 'Les Misérables', *La Réforme littéraire*, 20 April, 1
    'Les Misérables', *La Réforme littéraire*, 1 June, 2–5

Malot, H., 'Les Enfants', *ON*, 6 February
    'Les Misérables', *ON*, 5 April, 8 April

Mirecourt, E., 'Confessions', *F*, 7 September
    'Les Vrais Misérables', *F*, 28 September
    Les Vrais Misérables (Humbert)

Montégut, E., 'Les Misérables', *RDM*, 1 May: reprinted in *Mélanges critiques*

Nettement, A., *Poètes et Artistes*, 184–250

Noriac, J., 'Les Misérables', *Le Monde illustré*, 10 May and 9 August

Pontmartin, F. de, 'Les Misérables', *Corr*, July, 540–1

Sainte-Beuve, C. A., 'Les Misérables', *Const*, 25 August

Saint-Victor, P. de, 'Les Misérables', *P*, 1 October

Ulbach, L., 'Les Misérables', *Courrier du dimanche*, 6 and 13 April, 27 April

Vapereau, G., 'L'Evénement littéraire de l'année', *L'Année littéraire et dramatique*, 41

Veuillot, L., 'Les Misérables', *Revue du monde catholique*, 25 August: reprinted *Œuvres: Mélanges*, VIII, 529–40

1864
Nettement, A., 'Les Misérables', *Le Roman contemporain*, 193–374

Leconte de Lisle

1852
Sainte-Beuve, C. A., 'De la poésie', *Const*, 9 February: reprinted *Causeries du lundi*, V, 380–400

1853
Chasles, E., 'Poèmes antiques', *AF*, 12 March, 233–5

Cuvillier-Fleury, A., 'Poèmes antiques', *JD*, 6 March: reprinted in *Etudes historiques et littéraires*, 11, 208–16

Limayrac, P., 'La Poésie et les Poètes', *P*, 13 and 20 March

Planche, G., 'La Poésie', *RDM*, 15 September, 1193–204 and 1213–15
    'Le Théâtre', *RDM*, 1 October, 5–26

Pontmartin, F. de, 'Les Jeunes Poètes', *AN*, 25 June: reprinted *Causeries littéraires*, 89–99

Tiengou, J. M., 'Poèmes antiques', *Gazette de France*, 15 January

Ulbach, L., 'La Liquidation littéraire', *RP*, March, 377–401

Verdun, F., 'Leconte de Lisle', *RP*, 15 August, 626–30

1855
Du Camp, M., *Les Chants modernes*, preface

1856
Chasles, E., 'Poèmes et Poésies', *AF*, 2 February, 85–6
Goudall, L., 'Mouvement des lettres', *A*, 3 February, 319–20
Laurent-Pichat, L., 'Poèmes et Poésies', *RP*, 1 January, 456–8
Terraus, H., 'Les Préfaces littéraires', *Le Réalisme*, 15 December

1857
Lacaussade, A., 'La Passion', *RC*, April–May, 267–8

1858
Barbey d'Aurevilly, J., 'Poésies complètes', *Le Pays*, 19 August
Cherbuliez, J., 'Poésies complètes', *RCLN*, December, 572–4
Lataye, E., 'La Poésie nouvelle', *RDM*, 1 August, 729–36

1859
Laprade, A., 'Octave Lacroix', *RE*, 1, 420–5
Levallois, J., 'Etudes sur les œuvres de MM. Victor Laprade, Auguste Lacaussade et
    Leconte de Lisle', *MU*, 19 and 20 September

1860
Mazade, C. de, 'L'Arrière-saison de la poésie', *RDM*, 15 June, 873–80

1861
Anon., 'Leconte de Lisle', *RA*, new series IV, 2nd semester, 199
Joubert, L., 'Les Idylles', *RE*, xv, 383–9
Lafenestre, G., 'La Poésie contemporaine', *RC*, 15 October, 446–50
Maron, E., 'Idylles', *RG*, 505–6

1862
Anon., 'Leconte de Lisle', *RA*, xiv, 1st semester, 205
Chauvin, V., 'Idylles', *Revue de l'instruction publique*, 30 October, 483–5
Dollfus, J., 'Chronique littéraire', *Le Temps*, 30 March
Lavoix, H., 'Poésies barbares', *MU*, 3 December
Lefèvre, A., 'Poésies barbares', *Revue de l'instruction publique*, 21 May, 120–2
Mauron, E., 'Poésies barbares', *RG*, 16 August, 605–7
Melvil-Bloncourt, A., 'Leconte de Lisle', *B*, 20 April

1863
Cournau, A. de, 'La Poésie et les poètes', *RFr*, IV, January–April, 22–3
Vapereau, G., 'Leconte de Lisle', *L'Année littéraire et dramatique*

Ménard

1845
Weill, A., 'Prométhée délivré', *DP*, 27 December

1855
Fauvety, C., 'Poèmes', *La Revue philosophique et religieuse*, September, 241–4
Laurent, E., 'Poèmes', *RP*, 1 October, 135–8

Moreau

1838
Pyat, F., *N*, 21 June

1839
N., 'Moreau', *Gazette de France*, 15 July
Pyat, F., 'Moreau', *Revue du progrès*, 15 January

1840
Anon., 'Myosotis', *A*, 2nd series, VI
Dessalles-Régis, L., 'Poètes et Romanciers', *RDM*, 1 February, 319–38
Houssaye, A., 'Moreau', *P*, 4 August
George Sand, *RDM*, 15 May, 570–1

1841
Michaud, J. F., *Biographie*

1842
Magu, P., *Poésies nouvelles* (Delloye, 1842), 59

1845
Anon., 'Les Poètes Nouveaux', 9 November, 46

1847
Chavigny, C., 'Myosotis', *Echo*, 8, 233–5
Pérennès, F., *Les Noviciats littéraires* (Imprimeurs réunis)

1851
Esquiros, A., *Histoire des martyrs de la liberté* (J. Bry aîné, 1851), chapter XXIV
Giraud, A., 'Moreau', *U*, 26 July
Sainte-Beuve, C. A., 'Moreau', *Const*, 21–2 April: reprinted in *Causeries du lundi*, IV,
    51–75

1853
Audebrand, P., 'Moreau', *La Presse littéraire*, 13 March, 732–4

1854
Dumas, A., père, 'Moreau', *La Presse littéraire*, 5 January: reprinted in *Les Morts
    vont vite*, 1 (Michel Lévy Frères, 1861), 155–82

1856
Houssaye, A., *Le 41e Fauteuil de l'Académie française* (Hachette, 1856), 294–6

1857
Denys, H., 'Moreau', *Le Présent*, 8 August, 168–75
Dupont, P., 'Moreau', *Polichinelle*, 22 March, 2–3 and 5 April 3–4: reprinted in
    Etudes littéraires (Garnier Frères, 1859), 329–35

1859
Wailly, L. de, 'Moreau', *L'Illustration*, 19 September

1861
Ratisbonne, L., 'Moreau', *Biographie universelle*

1862
Anon., *Dictionnaire de la conversation*, XIII, 341
Banville, T. de, 'Moreau', *Les Poètes français* (ed. E. Crépet), IV, 421–32
Laurent-Pichat, L., *Les Poètes du combat* (E. Jung-Treuttel, 1862), 187–222

1863
Feyrnet, X., 'Le Collaborateur', *L'Illustration*, 2 May
Lebailly, F., *Hégésippe Moreau* (Bachelin Delorenne, 1863)
Second, A., 'Moreau', *L'Univers illustré*, 7 May
Texier, E., 'Moreau', *S*, 27 April
Ulbach, L., 'Moreau', *Le Temps*, 27 April

1865
Moüy, C. de, *Les Jeunes Ombres* (Hachette, 1865), 216–56

Poe

1846
Forgues, E. D., 'Etudes sur le roman anglais', *RDM*, XVI, 341–66

1852
Chasles, P., 'Cornelius Mathews', *RC*, 15 May, 420
Forgues, E. D., 'Nathaniel Hawthorne', *RDM*, 15 April, 339
Prarond, E., *De quelques écrivains nouveaux*, 191

1853
Bachelier, F., 'Le Scarabée d'or', *MU*, 7 September
Barbey d'Aurevilly, J., 'Le Scarabée d'or', *Le Pays*, 27 July: reprinted in *Les
    Œuvres et les hommes*, XII, 345–60
  'Poe', *Le Pays*, 19 April
Bernard, T., '"The Poetical Works"', *AF*, 10 September, 857–9
Chasles, P., 'Catherine Crowe et Poe', *JD*, 16 April
Poulet-Malassis, A., 'Le Corbeau', *Journal d'Alençon*, 9 January

1854
Fizelière, A. de la, 'Lettre', *Le Mousquetaire*, 23 May
Héduin, H., '"The Poets and the Poetry of America"', *AF*, 1 July
Hughes, W. L., 'Lettre', *Le Mousquetaire*, 2, 3, 9 and 18 November
Le Roy, A., 'D'une littérature nationale', *RP*, 1 July
Wailly, L. de, 'Hawthorne', *AF*, 18 February

1855
Pontmartin, F. de, 'Le Roman en 1855', *RC*, 30 June

1856
Anon., 'Bulletin bibliographique', *RDM*, 1 April

Barbey d'Aurevilly, J., 'Histoires extraordinaires', *Le Pays*, 10 June: reprinted in
    Les Œuvres et les hommes, XII, 360–76
Belloy, A. de, 'Revue', *RFr*, IV, March, 460
Bernard, F., 'Histoires extraordinaires', *AF*, 10 May, 386–7
    'Griswold', RC, December–January 1857, 383–8
Cartier, L., 'Edgar Poe', F, 27 March
Chasles, P., 'Histoires extraordinaires', *JD*, 20 April
Cuvillier-Fleury, A. A., 'Histoires extraordinaires', *JD*, 12 November
Du Camp, M., 'Bibliographie', *RP*, 1 April, 155–6
Duranty, F., 'Les Jeunes', F, 13 November
Fournel, V., 'Edgar Allan Poe', *RFr*, May
Gaston de Saint-Valéry, P., 'Histoires extraordinaires', *GP*, 28 September
Hughes, 'Poe', *Le Mousquetaire*, 11 November
Legendre, A., 'Poe', F, 10 April
Pontmartin, F. de, 'Causeries', *AN*, 12 April
    'Le Roman terrible', *JD*, 12 November
Rousseau, J., 'Madame Bovary et Edgar Poe', *GP*, 27 July
Thierry, E., 'Histoires extraordinaires', *MU*, 12 August

1857
Anon., 'Nouvelles histoires extraordinaires', *Corr*, August
Deschanel, E., 'Histoires extraordinaires', *IB*, 12 February
    'Nouvelles histoires extraordinaires', *IB*, 20 August
Duranty, F., 'Histoires extraordinaires', *Le Réalisme*, 15 March
Etienne, L., 'Les Conteurs américains', *RC*, 15 July
Monselet, C., *La Lorgnette littéraire*
Pontmartin, F. de, 'Nouvelles histoires extraordinaires', *Le Spectateur*, 19 September
Thierry, E., 'Nouvelles histoires extraordinaires', *MU*, 7 April

1858
Asselineau, C., 'Arthur Gordon Pym', *RFr*, XIII, May, 381–2
Barbey d'Aurevilly, J., 'Le Roi des bohèmes', *Le Réveil*, 10 May: reprinted *Les
    Œuvres*, XII, 376–88
Gautier, T., 'Balzac', *A*, 21 March: reprinted in *Honoré de Balzac*, 52
Hello, E., 'Du génie fantastique', *RFr*, October, 39
Vapereau, S., 'Poe', *L'Année littéraire*

1859
Platel, F., 'Jeunes Paroles', *RI*, 1 August

1860
Forgues, E. D., 'La Fantaisie', *RDM*, 15 July, 410–36
Masson, G., 'Poe', *La Correspondance littéraire*, 10 May, 301

1861
Taillandier, R., *Littérature Etrangère* (Michel Lévy Frères, 1861)

1862
Banville, T. de, 'Isis', *B*, 31 August
Troismonts, P. de, 'Le Genre fantastique', *Const*, 28 January

1863
Moüy, C. de, 'Edgar Poe'. *RFr,* 1 October, 145–58

1864
Renaud, A., 'Poe', *RP,* 1 August
Walter, J. H. [Judith Gautier], 'Euréka', *MU,* 29 March

1865
Arnould, A., 'Edgar Poe', *Revue moderne,* 1 April, 1 June, 1 July

✤ Index

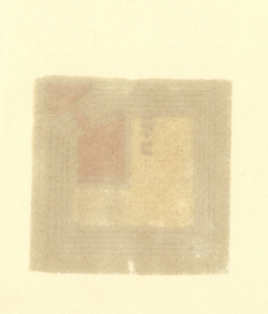